Rhetoric and Kairos

Rhetoric and Kairos

Essays in History, Theory, and Praxis

PHILLIP SIPIORA

and

JAMES S. BAUMLIN

editors

STATE UNIVERSITY OF NEW YORK PRESS

Published by
State University of New York Press, Albany

For information, address State University of New York Press,
90 State Street, Suite 700, Albany, NY 12207

Production by Michael Haggett
Marketing by Patrick Durocher

Library of Congress Cataloging-in-Publication Data

Rhetoric and kairos : essays in history, theory, and praxis / Phillip Sipiora and James
S. Baumlin, editors.
        p.   cm.
    Includes bibliographical references.
    ISBN 0-7914-5233-6 (alk. paper)—ISBN 0-7914-5234-4 (pbk. : alk. paper)
        1. Rhetoric. 2. Rhetoric, Ancient. 3. Kairo (The Greek word) I. Sipiora, Phillip.
II. Baumlin, James S.
PN218.R49 2002
808'.00938—dc21   2001049284

10 9 8 7 6 5 4 3 2 1

To our mentors in rhetoric,
James L. Kinneavy and Jim W. Corder

Contents

Acknowledgments

Several works collected in our volume have appeared previously in some form. Phillip Sipiora's "Introduction: The Ancient Concept of *Kairos* in Isocrates" draws upon his earlier work, "*Kairos* in the Discourse of Isocrates," first published as a chapter (119–35) in *Realms of Rhetoric: Phonic, Graphic, Electronic*, ed. Victor J. Vitanza and Michelle Ballif (Arlington, TX: Rhetoric Society of America, 1991). James L. Kinneavy's essay, "*Kairos* in Classical and Modern Rhetorical Theory," combines materials from two earlier publications, his "*Kairos*: A Neglected Concept in Classical Rhetoric," appearing originally as a chapter (79–105) in *Rhetoric and Praxis: The Contribution of Classical Rhetoric to Practical Reasoning*, ed. Jean Dietz Moss (Washington, DC: The Catholic University of America Press, 1986), and his "*Kairos* in Aristotle's Rhetoric," an article coauthored with Catherine R. Eskin (*Written Communication* 11 [1994]: 131–42). Eskin has graciously given permission to include this work in the present essay. In "*Logos* and *Kairos*: the Pythagorean Origins of Sophistic Rhetoric," Sipiora has translated major sections of Augusto Rostagni's "Un Nuovo Capitolo nella Storia della Retorica e della Sofistica," an article first appearing in *Studi Italiani de Filologica Classica* (n.s. 2 [1922]: 148–201). We thank Francesco Tarelli, Assistant Professor of Languages at Quincy University, for his help translating the Italian, and Joseph J. Hughes for translating the Greek. Gregory Mason's essay, "In Praise of *Kairos* in the Arts: Critical Time, East and West," expands upon work previously published in *The Journal of Intercultural Studies* (25 [1998]: 202–17) under the title, "*Kairos*: A Neglected Concept in Time Criticism." And John E. Smith's "Time and Qualitative Time" is reprinted from *The Review of Metaphysics* (40 [1986]: 3–16). We thank the above journals and presses for permission to reissue these materials.

The editors have their personal debts as well. James S. Baumlin thanks his colleague, Mark Trevor Smith, for serving as a critical, supportive reader. A special nod of gratitude from the editors goes to Priscilla Ross, Director of SUNY Press, for her leadership, encouragement, and inspiration in nurturing the development of this book. Michael Haggett, Production Editor, has earned our deep gratitude for his thorough professionalism in guiding this project from raw manuscript to final text Phillip Sipiora thanks Susan Friedman for her superb research assistance and Maureen D. Ivusic for her exemplary proofreading and indexing. Both of these developing scholars have fine careers in front of them. Any errors remain those of the editors.

Foreword

In a provocative challenge to the current renaissance of rhetorical studies, Dilip Gaonkar has reminded us that rhetoric is rooted in a particular historical period, a particular language, a particular set of cultural purposes (Gaonkar 1997). He questions how satisfactorily that particular framework can be "globalized" to become the universal hermeneutic it is often claimed to be in recent theory and criticism. He points specifically to several key problems with the classical conceptions of rhetoric when applied to contemporary discourse and conceptual problems: the ancient emphasis on practical production rather than theory and interpretation; the accompanying "ideology of human agency" that characterizes ancient rhetoric; and the "thinness" or abstract quality of the ancient productionist vocabulary that can easily be applied to anything and thus conveys little of real critical interest.

This book responds to Gaonkar's challenge to contemporary rhetoric, in several ways. It is at least a partial refutation of the characterization of the classical vocabulary as "thin." Its essays demonstrate the depth, complexity and untranslatability of the Greek concept of *kairos*, which is central to at least some versions of the rhetorical tradition and arguably necessary to all. We learn, for example, that *kairos* is central to both Plato's and Aristotle's conceptions of rhetoric (Kinneavy), central to the rhetoric of Isocrates (Sipiora) and to that of Gorgias (Poulakos), central to Renaissance Humanist rhetoric (Baumlin). A concept central to such diverse conceptions of rhetoric cannot be a "thin" or simple one. Further, many of these essays illustrate the globalization of rhetoric. We learn from them that *kairos* is central to other discourses and disciplines: to Hippocratic medicine (Eskin), to Pythagorean philosophy (Hill), to the New Testament (Sipiora), to American literature (Thompson), to "all major genres of Western literature" (Mason), and to psychoanalysis and psychological ethics (Benedikt).

And as though to prove the conceptual complexity of the rhetorical vocabulary, we encounter in these essays two different, and not fully compatible,

Fig. 1. *Kairos.* Classical (Turin Museum)

'Kairos'; that is, the brief, decisive moment which marks a turning-point in the life of human beings or in the development of the universe. This concept was illustrated by the figure vulgarly known as Opportunity . . . a man (originally nude) in fleeting movement, usually young . . . equipped with wings both at the shoulder and at the heels. His attributes were a pair of scales, originally balanced on the edge of a shaving knife, and, in a somewhat later period, one or two wheels. Moreover his head often showed the proverbial forelock by which bald-headed Opportunity can be seized. . . .

—Erwin Panofsky, *Studies in Iconology* (71–72)

understandings of *kairos.* In one view, most prominent in Cicero, the Stoics, and later Ciceronians, *kairos* is closely associated with propriety or decorum. It becomes a principle of adaptation and accommodation to convention, expectation, predictability. Cicero says, in a much-quoted passage in *Orator:* "The universal rule, in oratory as in life, is to consider propriety" (21.71). In this view, knowing the *kairos* means understanding an order that guides and shapes rhetorical action, whether that order is given and absolute or socially constructed. Violation of that order, failure to know the *kairos* and observe its propriety, will result in rhetorical, aesthetic, and even moral failure. This view of *kairos* is suited to philosophies of order, of realism, of Platonic Being.

In the other view, *kairos* is understood to represent not the expected but its opposite: the uniquely timely, the spontaneous, the radically particular. If decorum counsels us to be accommodative, this sense of *kairos* encourages us to be creative in responding to the unforeseen, to the lack of order in human life. The challenge is to invent, within a set of unfolding and unprecedented circumstances, an action (rhetorical or otherwise) that will be understood as uniquely meaningful within those circumstances. The timely action will be understood as adaptive, as appropriate, *only in retrospect;* it cannot be discovered within the decorum of past actions. As such, it resists method, making rhetoric unteachable. This second view of *kairos* is attributed primarily to Gorgias and to latter-day postmodern sophists. It is a conception indigenous to relativist or process philosophies, to a philosophy of Becoming.

One might conclude that any concept that can be this flexible, that can be central to both Gorgias and Plato, for example, must be thin indeed. And any version of *kairos* that includes only one of these views is an impoverished one. However, the most complex and interesting rhetorics, both ancient and contemporary, include both dimensions of *kairos* in some way, keeping them in productive tension, avoiding what each view by itself can yield: on the one hand, slavish propriety, and on the other, solipsistic novelty. Cicero's dictum that decorum is both a universal requirement and at the same time an ever-changing contingency gets it right (*Orator* 22.74). These two versions of *kairos,* in varying proportions and combinations, pervade the essays in this volume. We would do well to thicken and complicate other concepts in the rhetorical vocabulary in this manner.

Although scholars of rhetoric should certainly find the publication of this work timely, we should also note a way in which its appearance is *akairic:* James L. Kinneavy did not live to see its publication. Professor Kinneavy did more than anyone to revive *kairos* as a term of rhetorical art and inspired, either directly or indirectly, many of the essays this book includes. His life presented for us a model of decorum, and his death reminds us again of the profound contingencies of our existence.

Works Cited

Gaon Kar, Dilip Parameshwar. 1997. "The Idea of Rhetoric in the Rhetoric of Science." In *Rhetorical Hermeneutics: Invention and Interpretation in the Age of Science,* edited by A. G. Gross and W. M. Keith. Albany, NY: State University of New York Press.

Introduction

The Ancient Concept of Kairos

PHILLIP SIPIORA

In ancient Greece, in the city of Olympia, a sanctuary to Zeus was erected at a site where the first Olympiad was held in 776 B.C.E. According to Pausanias, this site housed two shrines: "Quite close to the entrance to the stadium are two altars: one they call Hermes of the Games, the other is the altar of Opportunity. I know that a hymn to Opportunity is one of the poems of Ion of Chios; in the hymn, Opportunity is made out to be the youngest child of Zeus" (1935, 463). Opportunity is, of course, the god Kairos, who personifies a seminal concept in ancient Greek culture that was strategic to classical rhetoric, literature, aesthetics, and ethics.[1]

Kairos is typically thought of as "timing," or the "right time," although its use went far beyond temporal reference,[2] as the essays in this volume demonstrate. A fundamental notion in ancient Greece, *kairos* carried a number of meanings in classical rhetorical theory and history,[3] including "symmetry," "propriety," "occasion," "due measure," "fitness," "tact," "decorum," "convenience," "proportion," "fruit," "profit," and "wise moderation,"[4] to mention some of the more common uses.[5] In some critical ways, *kairos* is similar to another master term, *logos,* in that both concepts generated many significant definitions and interpretations and carried strategic implications for historical interpretation. Although many ancient writers from various arts have capitalized on the richness of *kairos,* one ancient Greek in particular stands out for having built an entire educational system on the concept—and that is Isocrates, whose rhetorical *paideia* is structured upon the principle of *kairos.* Further, Isocrates' personal code of living is based on *kairos,* as articulated in his many treatises suggests. I shall return to Isocrates later, in discussing how he articulates the importance of *kairos* to rhetoric, as well as a *modus vivendi.* Isocrates' respect for the importance of *kairos* complements theories of *Kairos* outlined by Plato and Aristotle—both of which are explored in James L.

Kinneavy's essay; indeed, Isocrates' systematic treatment of *kairos* provides an important historical backdrop against which other theories in this volume may be contrasted.

Before turning to the importance of *kairos* in Isocrates' life and work, I would first like to sketch out its importance in the pre-Socratic traditions that influenced the development of ancient Greek thought. These influences, from literature, philosophy, and rhetoric as well as the medical arts and numerology, reveal how dominant and pervasive was the concept of *kairos* in antiquity. Let me begin by defining, tentatively, the concept of *kairos*.

Defining *Kairos*

As far as it has been determined, *kairos* first appeared in the *Iliad,* where it denotes a *vital* or *lethal* place in the body, one that is particularly susceptible to injury and therefore necessitates special protection; *kairos* thus, initially, carries a spatial meaning. In Hesiod's *Works and Days, kairos* takes on the sense of "due measure" or "proper proportion"; for example, Hesiod cites the overloading of a wagon, which can cause the axle to break. And Hesiod is probably the source of the maxim, "Observe due measure, and proportion *[kairos]* is best in all things" (Liddell and Scott). In time, *kairos* began to be distinguished from *chronos,* or linear time.[6] John E. Smith differentiates these concepts as follows:

> [W]e know that all the English expressions "a time to" are translations of the term *"kairos"*—the right or opportune time to do something often called "right timing." This aspect of time is to be distinguished from *chronos* which means the uniform time of the cosmic system, the time which, in Newton's phrase, *aequabiliter fluit.* In *chronos* we have the fundamental conception of time as measure, the *quantity* of duration, the length of periodicity, the age of an object or artifact and the rate of acceleration of bodies whether on the surface of the earth or in the firmament above. (1986, 4)

Chronos, then, might be distinguished from the "right time" or good time *(eukairos)* and the "wrong time" to do something *(kakakairos).* Frank Kermode characterizes the difference between *chronos* and *kairos* as that between chaos and orderliness (1970, 64); *kairos* is that point of time between a fictional beginning and an end, "a point in time filled with significance, charged with a meaning derived from its relation to the end" (47). And in some cases there is time that is without opportunity *(akairos),* a concept that to my knowledge has been little explored.[7] Prominent ancients such as Pindar, Theognis,

Solon, the Seven Sages ("Seal your word with silence and your silence with the *right time*," "Nothing in excess"), Aeschylus, Euripides, Sophocles, Menander, the pre-Socratics, Pythagoras, some of the Sophists, Pericles, and many others use *kairos* to signify various meanings. *Kairos* is also a significant concept in the Bible, appearing hundreds of times in both the Old and New Testaments. The first words of Christ call attention to the importance of timing: "The time *[kairos]* is fulfilled, and the kingdom of God is at hand" (Mark 1:14). And who is not familiar with this passage from Ecclesiastes (popularized two millennia later by the Birds, a 1960s vocal group): "For everything there is a season, and a time for every purpose under the sun: a time to be born and a time to die . . . a time to kill and a time to heal . . . a time to weep and a time to laugh." *Kairos* was, and is, a seminal concept in numerous arts and discourses.

The concept of *kairos* became a normative principle in Greek poets and playwrights such as Hesiod, Theognis, Pindar, Aeschylus, Meletus, Euripides, and Menander. The history of *kairos* in the development of philosophy is equally important, particularly in the works of such pre-Socratics as Empedocles and Pythagoras as well as in the later philosophies of Plato and Aristotle, where it becomes a foundational term in the determination of ethics and aesthetics.[8] It is in classical Greek rhetoric, however, that *kairos* became a truly dominant concept, particularly in its pre-Isocratean and pre-Aristotelian influences. *Kairos* plays a major role in the First Sophistic movement, especially in the works of Protagoras and Gorgias. The legacy of *kairos* continues in Aristotle's taxonomy of rhetorical principles (as Kinneavy's essay in this volume demonstrates), particularly with regard to proof and style; it also assumes major importance in Plato's concept of a philosophic rhetoric and in Isocrates' rhetorical *paideia*. In short, *kairos* was the cornerstone of rhetoric in the Golden Age of Greece.

We owe much of our understanding of *kairos* in the ancient world to twentieth-century Italian scholarship, much of which remains untranslated.[9] Three scholars are particularly important for their examinations of pre-Socratic thought: Augusto Rostagni, Doro Levi, and Mario Untersteiner. In 1922, Rostagni published the most systematic and comprehensive treatment of the role of *kairos* in sophistic rhetoric, focusing on the influences of Pythagoras and, especially, Gorgias—whose early rhetoric drew upon the musician Damon's claims that harmony and rhythm are linked to psychological moods and are capable of bewitching and persuading. The rhetor and musician, according to Rostagni, are exponents of a single, fully developed doctrine that grows out of the concept of *kairos*. Rostagni details the historical importance of Antisthenes, a disciple of Gorgias, whose *Peri lexeos e peri charakteron* outlines the rhetorical doctrines of that period, particularly the influence of Pythagoras on the work of Gorgias.[10] Pythagoras' abilities as a rhetor are characterized as *polutropos*—a key point of identification—because he demonstrates the special rhetorical ability to invent language appropriate to specific classes of listeners, the *logoi paidikoi*. This rhetorical ability demonstrates the art of *kairos* (and, significantly, predates Plato's assertion that philosophic rhetors must seek to know the "souls of the audience"). According to Rostagni, the various styles and manners of expression *(polutropia loguo)* aim at accommodating different audiences. If the discourse remains unchanged and unsuitable for a specific audience, it becomes *polutropon*, is rejected by the audience, and reveals *kakakairos*. Rostagni recounts Gorgias' *Peri Kairou*, which articulated the principle that the mutability of discourse is justified and required by the necessity of adapting to rhetorical circumstances and exigencies, which include the orientations of both speaker and listeners, the moment, the place, and so forth.[11] The "grasping of concepts" means to think in a particular way at a particular time, a function of epistemology. It is necessary, according to sophistic rhetoric, that a rhetor "scientifically" know the various forms of the discourse *(eide ton logon)*, in order to avoid violating the rules of appropriateness *(ton kairon me diamartein)*; to alter the discourse for convenience *(prepontos holon ton logon katapoikilai)*; and to choose forms that are harmonious with each other. All of these issues demonstrate the magnitude of *kairos*.

Rhetoric then, as an expression of *kairos*, became the center of education for many of the Sophists.[12] Rostagni outlines how Gorgias and Iamblicus both drew upon Pythagorean teaching, which is based upon the combined principles of *kairos* and *dikaion*. For Pythagoras, as well as for Gorgias, *kairos* touches upon the problematic issue of knowledge.[13] To frail human perception, things exist in an uncertain, ultimately unknowable way; a veil of sense separates them, indeed, hides them from us. In accordance with *kairos*, therefore, we are compelled to maintain contrary perceptions, interpretations, and arguments: opposing arguments—the *dissoi logoi* of sophistic rhetoric—remain equally probable, and yet the mystery of *kairos* enables rhetors to choose one *logos* over another, making one and the same thing seem great or small, beautiful or ugly, new or old. Drawing upon ancient sources, Rostagni concludes that the cause and action of eloquence are part of a general theory of art, the intellectual center of which would lie in the greater part of Greece and in the school of Pythagoras:

> Gorgias . . . glorifies the *magical* effects *(goeteia, psychagogia)* of *logos* and teaches and explains that the rhetor must know, scientifically, the ways to the soul, from which the speeches capable of *spellbinding* and *persuading* descend. He is a close friend of Damone from Oa who, during the same years, in a fictitious oration ad-

dressed to the Aeropagites, defends music, showing the secret affinities that link harmony and rhythm to various psychic moods, so that harmonies and rhythms are actually capable of molding human character. The rhetor and the musician are exponents of a single, already fully-developed doctrine which includes two different subjects. (1922, 149)

Along with Pythagoras, Gorgias (as a teacher of rhetoric) was an instrumental early figure in the theoretical development of *kairos;* yet it was Isocrates (considered by some, including Werner Jaeger, to be a Sophist) who offered the first systematic treatment of the theoretical and pragmatic importance of *kairos* to rhetoric and to social responsibility—the ultimate goal of Isocratean *paideia*.

In his 1923 treatment of *kairos* in classical Greek literature, "Kairos in Greek Literature," Doro Levi points out the term's etymological connections to "death," "ruin," "breast," "the seat of spiritual life," "to worry," "to care for," "to cut," "to kill," "to destroy." In Homer, according to Levi, *kairos* usually means "mortal," whereas in Theognis its meaning as "opportunity" begins to emerge, appearing later in the tragedies of Aeschylus. Passages from Euripides reveal the transition in meaning from Homer's "mortal" to the sense of "decisive" or "opportune," changes that occur in both verb and noun forms. From death or "truncation of life," the meaning shifts to decision or "truncation of doubt." Levi also examines instances of *kairos* in the Seven Sages, Thucydides, Democritus, and Pythagoras. In fifth-century literature, *kairos* evolves to represent the "best opportunity," which is the essential opportunity to arrive at the "just measure" in conforming to whatever is necessary. It is this evolution of the term that so influenced Plato, who found in the literary uses of *kairos* a means to link together his concepts of ethics and aesthetics.

Levi's groundbreaking 1924 essay, "The Concept of *Kairos* and the Philosophy of Plato," examines *kairos* as an ethical and aesthetic concept in Plato, one that plays a significant role in shaping Plato's notion of a "philosophic rhetoric." Platonic aesthetics, according to Levi, is based upon principles of harmony, symmetry, and measure, while his ethics is based upon aesthetics, justice, and truth. Justice requires that citizens establish, within themselves, a harmony mirroring (and supporting) just relations within the state; thus, individuals must connect together the many conflicting elements of which they are made into a state of health or inner harmony. Central to Plato's philosophy (and, arguably, one of Greek philosophy's greatest insights), this conception of unity-in-plurality provides the connecting link between ethics and aesthetics; and it is a link provided by *kairos*. *Kairos* is thus the fusion of ethical and aesthetic elements. Concepts such as the "divine *logos*" can be understood only if one knows that conceptions of goodness and evil, life and death, and the cosmos can be known *exclusively* by the principle of proportion. Plato's *Protagoras*, according to Levi, reveals that *kairos* establishes the moral value of human actions. And in the *Philebus,* an indisputable premium is given to proper measure as the first quality of the One, which is the beautiful and the harmonious. Therefore, the first ethical principle in the Platonic system is the principle of proper measure, or *kairos.* The principle of proper measure is also integral to the emotions, especially love.

Love, according to Levi, is yet another Platonic theme delineated by the principle of *kairos.* In the *Phaedrus,* Lysias' oration prompts Socrates to articulate a doctrine of pure love, exemplified by his myth of the charioteer and the two horses. The charioteer, in an anterior life, had experienced the contemplation of the divine. Having fallen into the inferior world of the senses, he is attracted toward the celestial sphere. In this world, one may perceive only the beautiful. But after the reluctant horse is tamed, the bashful, timid lover follows the loved one as a god, allowing the supreme experience to take place: in the lovers' eyes is reflected the beauty which shines in the loved one. This experience leads one to perceive the essence of beauty (and its conjunction with the true and the good). Again, physical beauty alone is transmitted through the senses, and ideas (or ideals) of the good and the true cannot reveal themselves in appearances; only beauty remains in this domain. It is the memory of beauty, however, that inspires conceptions of the divine, thereby transporting the individual to a superior existence. The beautiful, therefore, provides a means of transcendence to the good. The identification of the beautiful with the good is a major issue in the *Phaedrus,* but what is significant is Levi's conclusion that *kairos* provides the connecting link between these concepts.

Kairos is clearly a complex, multidimensional concept and, as Eric Charles White points out in his seminal book, *Kaironomia,* there is much to learn from the ancients' treatment of the concept:

> For Gorgias, *kairos* stands for a radical principle of occasionality which implies a conception of the production of meaning in language as a process of continuous adjustment to and creation of the present occasion, or a process of continuous interpretation in which the speaker seeks to inflect the given "text" to his or her own ends at the same time that the speaker's "text" is "interpreted" in turn by the context surrounding it. (1987, 14)

White thus emphasizes the uniqueness and unpredictability of each occasion, making it impossible for speakers to control discourse by planning or by previous theory. Since each discourse must be shaped in immediate response to the present occasion, instruction in *kairos* becomes virtually impossible. While theory, grounded in successful past discourse, provides models of right and wrong strategies, rhetorical theory cannot cast its net over the unforseen, unpredictable, and uncontrollable moments. In a sense, then, every rhetorical act becomes a reinvention of theory as well as of the discourse itself. Another way of describing the shaping influence of the ever-emerging present occasion is to treat effective, kairic discourse as a mode of "improvisation" (White, 14).

Kairos was clearly a strategic concept in the intellectual arts of the ancient world, yet it is not until the time of Isocrates that we find its detailed expression in a full-scale program of rhetorical *paideia*. It was, indeed, the school of Isocrates that taught the importance of socially responsible living—that is, civic virtue—based upon rhetorical principles articulated in his *Antidosis,* yet echoed in Isocrates' many other discourses.

Kairos and the Rhetorical *Paideia* of Isocrates

Despite his general neglect by historians of rhetoric in English studies, Isocrates (436–338 B.C.E.) was a rhetorician/philosopher of such significance that he has been referred to as the "father of the humanities" by scholars in classics, speech, and philosophy. As Werner Jaeger remarks, "historically, it is perfectly correct to describe him . . . as the father of 'humanistic culture'" (1971, 46). Henri Marrou echoes these sentiments, describing Isocrates as the most important teacher in Greece's Golden Age: "On the whole it was Isocrates, not Plato, who educated fourth-century Greece and subsequently the Hellenistic and Roman worlds" (1982, 79).[14] What may be Isocrates' most important historical contribution, however, is his articulation of the critical importance of *kairos* in rhetorical theory and practice.

Plato's most detailed discussion of "philosophic rhetoric," the *Phaedrus,* concludes with Socrates' observation that Isocrates "has a nature above the speeches of Lysias and possesses a nobler nature; . . . something of philosophy is inborn in his mind" (279a–b).[15] This reference hints at the connection between Isocrates' "philosophy" (he does refer to himself as a cultural philosopher in *Against the Sophists*) and *kairos.* James L. Kinneavy has argued that Isocrates' oration, *On the Peace* (355 B.C.E.), was a strategic discourse because of its timing and that it significantly affected the work of both Plato and Aristotle:

> Plato, after this time, recognized two separate types of wisdom, one theoretical and one practical, and permitted Aristotle to teach rhetoric for the first time in the academy. More important, the speech, the situation, and the practical success of Isocrates' school of rhetoric critically influenced the young Aristotle. It was at this time that Aristotle rejected the scientific ideal of Plato. (*Greek Rhetorical Origins,* 38)

Isocrates' influence and reputation extended into the Roman world and beyond.[16] Much of Isocrates' success over nearly two millennia may be attributed to his formal system of rhetorical *paideia,* structured on the principle of *kairos.* Isocrates' school was arguably one of the most influential schools in

Greek Antiquity, if not the predominant institution in the Golden Age of Greece. One of Isocrates' important contributions to rhetorical history is his conjoining of *phronesis* or "practical wisdom" and pragmatic ethics within the "situation" and "time" of discourse, an emphasis upon contexts that gives primacy to the kairic dimensions of any rhetorical act.

In spite of the attention given to *kairos* by twentieth-century historians, no one, to my knowledge, has offered a systematic articulation of the importance of *kairos* in the rhetorical/cultural system of Isocrates.[17] The general neglect of *kairos* in Isocrates is surprising, given his importance in the rhetorical development of the Golden Age and the fact that *kairos*, in its terminological and conceptual forms, is ubiquitous in the Isocratean corpus. As a term, *kairos* appears nearly one hundred times in substantive, adverbial, and adjectival forms. In order to explore the importance of *kairos* in Isocrates' discourse, let me first summarize Isocrates' system of *phronesis* and pragmatic ethics, and then explore how *kairos* informs this code.[18]

Isocrates is quite explicit in several of his treatises about the goal of his rhetorical *paideia*, which is to serve the public good in multiple arenas of public and private discourse. Isocrates' program stresses a pragmatic "ethics." His system proceeds from the belief that, once students became familiar with certain rhetorical strategies—a weaving together of subject matter, invention, context, and "style"—they would be able to join the ranks of "philosophers" and become effective, socially responsible citizens. This conflation of rhetoric and philosophy prepared students for "community service." As Jacqueline de Romilly puts it,

> For Isocrates . . . learning to speak well is learning to arrive at ideas and advocate values that will be endorsed and prove effective. This ability, moreover, will win for those who acquire it the esteem of their fellows; for the opinion of the community, which is the sole criterion of truth and goodness, is also the finest recognition for one who had proved worthy of it. (1985, 129)

This shift in emphasis is a remarkable rupture with earlier rhetorical schools and traditions, many of which limited their "art" to a concern for mechanical functions of speech. In contrast, Isocrates' theory of rhetorical philosophy is a process of seeking social "justice." It is a *modus vivendi*, an ontology that conjoins private and public activities.

Isocrates' notion of social justice was situated within the personal ethics of the rhetor, and Isocrates' system emphasizes a pragmatic personal ethics by which a rhetor's credibility is determined by the reputation he or she brings to the rhetorical situation. As he says in *Antidosis*: "[W]ho does not know that words carry greater conviction when spoken by men of good repute than when spoken by men who live under a cloud, and that the argument which is made by a man's life is of more weight than that which is furnished by words?" (1968, 278). Further, Isocrates postulates a symbiotic relationship between *phronesis* and effective discourse. Rhetoric cannot be successful without their conjunction and Isocrates' entire educational program is predicated upon the notion that rhetoric and practical wisdom are interdependent.

Although Isocrates' school was in direct competition with both Plato's Academy and Aristotle's Lyceum, it is with Plato and his "divine" epistemology that Isocrates stands in sharpest contrast. The Academy attempted to train students to be dialecticians, the best of whom would be capable of leading the city-state. Isocrates' *paideia*, on the other hand, promoted the education of leaders in many areas—civic, military, and so forth—who would be, above all else, *pragmatic* thinkers and speakers capable of understanding the principle of *phronesis*, with a special emphasis on what is practical and expedient under *any* given set of circumstance—the principle of *kairos*. *Phronesis*, coupled with *kairos*, is integral to effective rhetoric and it must be part of a speaker's value system as it translates into social action:

> [W]hile we call eloquent those who are able to speak before a crowd, we regard as sage those who most skillfully debate their problems in their own minds. And if there is need to speak in brief summary of this power, we shall find that none of the things which are done with intelligence *[phronesis]* takes place without the help of speech, but that in all our actions as well in all our thoughts speech is our guide, and is most employed by those who have the most wisdom. (*Antidosis*, 1968, 257)

Practical wisdom, then, serves at least two functions: *phronesis* is necessary for the activation of a preliminary, "internal" dialectic which, in turn, gives rise to an "intelligence" that expresses itself in words *and* actions. This derived intelligence is based upon a rhetor's understanding of *kairos*. As Michael Cahn points out, "Isocrates underlines what the concept of *kairos* in itself already indicates: in rhetoric, a reliable correlation between rhetorical strategies and desired effects cannot be prescribed because the situational factor is paramount" (1989, 133). And it is precisely because a rhetor cannot anticipate every important situational circumstance that he or she *must* carry a flexible attitude into any given rhetorical situation.

In *Against the Sophists*, his earliest known discussion of rhetoric, Isocrates identifies attention to *kairos* as one of the most important characteristics of effective rhetorical discourse. One of the reasons for the general ineffectiveness of the Sophists, according to Isocrates, is their inability to recognize the kairic exigencies of particular discourses. They fail to consider *the right time* or make the *appropriate* adjustments in any given rhetorical situation. According to Daniel Gillis:

The opportune moment must be chosen for a particular treatment of a theme, the appropriate arguments for each of the historical events must be marshaled, and the actual arrangement of the words must be skillful. The object of all these elements forming good oratory is not the facile deception of the audience. (1969, 335–36)

In *Helen* Isocrates makes multiple references to the Sophists' lack of understanding of *kairos,* going so far as to accuse them of failing to measure intellectual distinctions:

[M]en have grown old, some asserting that it is impossible to say, or to gainsay, what is false, or to speak on both sides of the same questions, others maintaining that courage and wisdom and justice are identical . . . and still others waste their time in captious disputations. (1)

Thus, *kairos,* like all preeminent terms in Greek rhetoric, encompasses practical as well as theoretical dimensions.

Isocrates exhorted other teachers of rhetoric to encourage their students to be mindful of the *kairos* of rhetorical situations. As de Romilly points out, "Isocrates had no faith in 'instant' formulas: after a discussion of the 'general themes used in speeches,' he moved on to exercises, which were always related to practical situations. The pupil had to learn to choose arguments befitting the occasion and arrange them in a complete speech" (1968, 130). An understanding of the importance of *kairos* as a *dynamic* principle rather than a static, codified rhetorical technique is integral to rhetorical success, as Isocrates argues in *Antidosis:* "[T]hose who most apply their minds to [discourse situations] and are able to discern the consequences which for the most part grow out of them, will most often meet these occasions in the right way" (1968, 184). One important step in meeting these occasions "in the right way" is to practice moderation in speech: "[W]hile we prize due measure [*eukairian*] and affirm that there is nothing so precious, yet when we think we have something of importance to say, we throw moderation to the winds" (*Antidosis,* 311). The rhetor must anticipate all exigencies, since he or she can never know the particulars of a discourse situation until actually situated within it.

For Isocrates, an understanding of the principle of *kairos* means that the rhetor remains accommodative—unlike some other philosophers and Sophists, who are bound by rigid laws and systems. As he says in *Against the Sophists:*

I marvel when I observe these men setting themselves up as instructors of youth who cannot see that they are applying the analogy of an art with hard and fast rules to a creative process. For, excepting these teachers, who does not know that the art of using letters remains fixed and unchanged, so that we continually and invariably use the same letters for the same purposes, while exactly the reverse is true of the art of discourse. . . . But the greatest proof of the difference between these two arts [philosophy and rhetoric] is that oratory is good only if it has the qualities of fitness for the occasion *[kairos]*, propriety of style, and originality of treatment. (1968, 12–13)

The properly trained rhetor, unlike corrupt Sophists or facile philosophers, is able to modify his or her discourse according to circumstances and to meet the specific exigencies of each rhetorical situation, since each one involves a unique set of circumstances.

Isocratean rhetoric, like Gorgian rhetoric, stresses the importance of the particular moment or issue, rather than universals or ideals. In *Antidosis* Isocrates explains why he grounds his theory in practical situations. Teachers in his school are instructed to "set [students] at exercises, habituate them to work, and require them to combine in practice the particular things which they have learned in order that they may grasp them more firmly and bring their theories into closer touch with the occasions *[kairon]* for applying them" (1968, 184). These occasions often involve personal encounters. For example, Isocrates advises Demonicus (a wealthy young Cypriot) that he will best serve his friends if he is able to discern the *right time* to assist them: "You will best serve your friends if you do not wait for them to ask your help, but go of your own accord at the crucial moment *[kairois]* to lend them aid" (*To Demonicus*, 25). This emphasis on kairic thought and action in public and private activities is characteristic of Isocratean rhetoric.

In *Panathenaicus*, Isocrates outlines the importance of *kairos* to political diplomacy. In speaking of effective statesmen, Isocrates remarks: "[I]t behooves a man of taste not to indulge his resourcefulness when he has more to say on a given subject than the other speakers, but to preserve always the element of timeliness no matter on what subject he may have occasion to speak" (*Panathenaicus*, 34). In *Panegyricus* (7–9), similarly, Isocrates "adds that it is important in oratory to be able to make proper use of the events of the past, and *at the appropriate time* or *Kairos*" (Kerferd, 82). A significant number of references elsewhere stress the importance of *kairos* (as appropriate time) in rhetoric.

In his advice to Nicocles, Isocrates advises the King of Cyprus to measure his emotions and behavior against the exigencies of the situation: "Do nothing in anger, but simulate anger when the occasion *[kairos]* demands it. Show yourself stern by overlooking nothing which men do, but kind by making the punishment less than the offence" (*To Nicocles*, 23). A successful monarch, according to Isocrates, must exercise caution in speech and behavior and always be ready to capitalize on any given situation at the *right time:* "Keep watch always on your words and actions, that you may fall into as few mistakes as possible. For . . . it is best to grasp your opportunities at exactly the right moment *[kairon]*" (*To Nicocles*, 33). In *Nicocles*, writing in the persona of King Nicocles, Isocrates offers advice on how a king's subjects should conduct themselves. In this discourse, *kairos* plays a major role in justifying monarchical rule. Nicocles argues that those who live in monarchies are superior to appointed leaders because they "apply themselves to the state's business both day and night, do not let opportunities pass them by, but act in each case at the right moment *[kairon]*" (19). Nicocles emphasizes the importance of virtuous behavior, claiming to have demonstrated his virtue to the populace:

> [W]e ought not to test all the virtues in the same set of conditions, but should test justice when a man is in want, temperance when he is in power, continence when he is in the prime of youth. Now in these situations *[kairois]* no one will deny that I have given proof of my nature. (44)

Further, near the end of his address, Nicocles cautions his audience to observe prudence in economy, which is itself dependent upon the principle of appropriateness: "Do not think that getting is gain or spending is less; for neither the one nor the other has the same significance at all times, but either, when done in season *[en kairo]* and with honor, benefits the doer" (50). Such injunctions to pay heed to the principle of *kairos* are pervasive throughout Isocrates' treatises of advice to monarchs and aspiring leaders.

Archidamus is yet another of Isocrates' discourses in which a political conflict illustrates the importance of *kairos*. In this case, the Spartan assembly debates whether or not to wage war against Thebes over a land dispute. Archidamus III, son of ruling King Agesilaus, exhorts his fellow Spartans to battle. His speech is noteworthy for several reasons: it reflects Isocrates' sympathy for Spartan policy (which is curious, considering Isocrates' anti-Spartan sentiment in other of his discourses); it is a lively and forceful polemic, in spite of the fact that it was composed in Isocrates' ninetieth year; and it relies heavily upon a sensitivity to *kairos*, both the speaker's and audience's. As other Spartans consider going to war over contested territory, Archidamus argues that the exigencies of the (rhetorical) situation permit him to ignore Theban legal claims: "I have not, it is true, recounted in detail our original titles to this land (for the present occasion *[kairos]* does not permit me to go into legendary history)" (24). In other words, the principle of *kairos* permits Archidamus to embrace the most advantageous of several competing *logoi;* in so doing he de-emphasizes the legal issues involved in other counterclaims while inflaming the passions of the Spartan council. Later in his address, Archidamus argues that *kairos* is a principle that guides men to do, not what they are entitled to do but, rather, what they should do:

Those who advise us to make peace declare that prudent men ought not to take the same view of things in fortunate as in unfortunate circumstances, but rather that they should always consult their immediate situation and accommodate themselves to their fortunes, and should never entertain ambitions beyond their power, but should at such times *[kairois]* seek, not their just rights but their best interests. (*Archidamus*, 34)

The decision to make war or negotiate peace with Thebes depends upon the expedient exploitation of particular political circumstances. Neither war nor peace is necessarily the "correct" choice; rather, the proper course of action is determined by taking advantage of time and opportunity. As Isocrates avers,

I know of many who through war have acquired great prosperity, and many who have been robbed of all they possessed through keeping the peace; for nothing of this kind is in itself either good or bad, but rather it is the use we make of circumstances and opportunities *[kairois]* which in either case must determine the result. (49–50)

An individual or group that best understands the kairic dimensions of any particular issue has a distinct advantage over an adversary. This message reverberates through many Isocratean discourses, particularly the *Antidosis*.

The "wise" or phronetic individual, according to Isocrates, must always be aware that he or she lives in a contingent universe: "[P]eople of intelligence . . . ought not to think that they have exact knowledge of what the result will be, but to be minded towards these contingencies as men who exercise their best judgment" (*On the Peace*, 8). In outlining a sequence of events necessary for peace between Athens and her enemies, Isocrates emphasizes that each step has a particular *kairos:* "I have already discussed most of the points which bear upon this question, not in sequence, but as each fell into its opportune place *[kairois]*" (*On the Peace*, 132). Isocrates considers the ability to act pragmatically the mark of educated persons—that is, of individuals "who manage well the circumstances which they encounter day by day, and who possess a judgment which is accurate in meeting occasions as they arise and rarely miss the expedient course of action" (*Panathenaicus*, 30–31). Isocrates' central educational goal was the creation of just such a "citizen-orator," a liberally educated person who could serve himself and others through intelligent speech in private discourse, in the assembly, and (if need be) in the law court. If these "public citizens" are of sufficient number and take it upon themselves to dedicate themselves to deliberative activity within the *polis*, the state has the potential to rescue itself from present evils and head off future dangers. In order for these citizens to govern effectively, however, they must be able to make decisions according to the exigencies of particular intra- and international situations. In *Panathenaicus*, Isocrates recounts the "opportunity" of earlier invasions of Athens and the Athenians' successful "occasions" of resistance: "All these whom I have instanced, having invaded our country,—not together nor at the same time, but as opportunity *[kairoi]* and self-interest and desire concurred in each course—our ancestors conquered in battle and put an end to their insolence" (196). Such examples show how important the concept of *kairos* was to the military and cultural imperialism rampant throughout many of the Greek city-states.

Isocrates not only articulated the theory of *kairos;* he also practiced the *kairos* he found so lacking in others. In spite of the fact that Alcidamas attacked Isocrates for failing to practice *kairos,* the oration, *On the Peace,* distributed to members of the Athenian Assembly, successfully argued the futility of Athens and her allies pursuing a policy of hegemony. Also, *Antidosis* was a timely response to the charges made against Isocrates and his educational system. In spite of the fact that the discourse appears years after the actual lawsuit, *Antidosis* was disseminated as a rebuttal to the accusation that he, like Socrates, was a corrupting influence on the youth of Athens—a charge that could result in exile or death. And even in this discourse of self-defense, Isocrates notes that the principle of *kairos* determines which of his previous orations he is going to quote: "I am not going to quote from *[Against the Sophists]* my criticisms of others; for they are too long for the present occasion *[kairou]*" (194). In his many treatises and letters, Isocrates consistently emphasizes the importance of a rhetor understanding his or her audience and the varying circumstances of the occasion.

Perhaps Isocrates' emphasis on *kairos* is best summarized in *Panathenaicus*—one of his most ambitious discourses, since undertaken and published when Isocrates was ninety-seven. In this treatise, Isocrates sums up the goals of his rhetorical *paideia:*

> Whom, then, do I call educated? . . . First, those who manage well the *circumstances* which they encounter day by day, and who possess a judgement which is accurate in meeting occasions as they arise and rarely misses the expedient course of action; next, those who are decent and honourable in their intercourse with all with whom they associate, tolerating easily and good-naturedly what is unpleasant or offensive in others and being themselves as agreeable and reasonable to their associates as it is possible to be; furthermore, those who hold their pleasures always under control and are not unduly overcome by their misfortunes; . . . fourthly, and most important of all, those who are not spoiled by success . . . but hold their ground steadfastly as intelligent individuals. (30–32)

This pragmatic, personal, and socially conscious recapitulation of what it means to be "educated" encapsulates the principle of *kairos* in all its nuances: the importance of living by *phronesis* or "practical wisdom" (which is itself based on an epistemology of probability) with, always, an intense awareness of occasion, audience, and situational context. Such is a life based on *kairos*.

In this volume, we have brought together essays that reveal the various historical meanings, developments, complications, nuances, and implications of *kairos*. Clearly one of the master concepts in the ancient world, *kairos* has critical resonance for today's world as well; indeed, the following far-reaching essays demonstrate how strategic and dominant this concept has been and continues to be. Excerpted here, Rostagni's seminal essay explores the importance of Pythagoras' treatment of *kairos* and its subsequent role in sophistic rhetorical theory. As an expression of *kairos*, rhetoric becomes the foundation of sophistic education. Further, for Pythagoras as well as for Gorgias, *kairos* touches upon the problem of human knowledge. Kinneavy analyzes and evaluates the critical functions of *kairos* in the rhetorical theories of Plato and Aristotle, pointing out the significance of *kairos* in Plato's analysis of the rhetorical addressee and in Aristotle's exposition of extrinsic appeals (particularly the *topoi*), as well as the significance of *kairos* to rhetorical *ethos*. Carolyn Eriksen Hill, applying Pythagorean and Gorgian theories of *kairos*, reconsiders the conflicts between product- and process-orientations in composition.

In his germinal essay comparing *chronos*-time with kairic time, John E. Smith examines the ways *chronos* and *kairos* differ in apprehending metaphysical and historical dimensions of reality. Yet *chronos* and *kairos* are not unrelated: *kairos* requires *chronos*, which becomes a necessary precondition underlying qualitative uses of time; when taken by itself, conversely, *chronos* fails to explain the crisis points of human experience—those moments, for example, when junctures of opportunity arise, calling for ingenuity in apprehending when the time is "right." Reconceived as a unity of *kairos* and *chronos*, time thus furnishes an invaluable grid upon which the processes of nature and historical order can be plotted and, by such means, interpreted and understood. Amélie Frost Benedikt draws upon Smith's essay in her outline of an ethical system grounded in *kairos;* in addition, she examines various uses of *kairos* from sophistic sources to contemporary culture. My essay on the various meanings of *kairos* in the New Testament attempts to demonstrate how strategic the Greek concept was to the formation of Christian thought and narrative.

Richard Leo Enos investigates the role of *kairos* in the situational constraints of civic composition, particularly as writing in Greek society initially served as a technological aid to the more primary and pervasive functions of oral discourse. More specifically, Enos explores ancient Athenian archaeological and textual evidence that reveals inventional constraints placed upon writing used in the service of preserving oral discourse. John Poulakos examines the importance of *kairos* in Gorgias' rhetorical compositions, particularly in the way *kairos* functions *within* rhetorical texts. In *Palamedes* and *Helen* especially, Gorgias offers a glimpse of his practical principle of *kairos*, exemplifying ways in which texts can be composed so as to give the impression of sensitivity to timeliness. Catherine R. Eskin explores the importance of *kairos* in the medical treatises of Hippocrates, examining the most well-known Hippocratic passages in terms of their technical emphasis on *kairos*. Hippocrates is especially interested in aligning *kairos* with experimentation, experience, incident, and phenomena, and he is opposed to any theorizing that is separated from these contacts. Thus, the situational dimension of *kairos* becomes critical to Hippocrates' scientific method. Joseph J. Hughes examines *kairos* in the Roman world, principally through the concept of *decorum*, which approximates *kairos* (but does carry quite the same panoply of meanings). Noting that Cicero is the primary exponent of *kairos/decorum* in Roman rhetorical culture, Hughes analyzes the movement of the concept in Crassus Orator's speech, *De Lege Servilia*.

James S. Baumlin explores the relationship between Ciceronian *kairos/decorum* and Renaissance rhetorical and ethical theory; in addition, he examines the various competing representations of time, as recorded in the age's popular emblem books. In a subsequent essay, he collaborates with Tita French Baumlin in analyzing the strategic function of *kairos* in Elizabethan revenge tragedy, particularly as it informs Hamlet's attempted revenge. As Baumlin and Baumlin argue, *kairos* plays a pivotal role in the age's crisis regarding the powers of human reason and the Humanist aspiration to master worldly fortune.

Gregory H. Mason, like Baumlin and Baumlin, finds *kairos* to be a strategic issue in the interpretation of literature. According to Mason, the neglect of *kairos*, of the qualitative dimension of time, has often skewed our culture's appreciation of the arts. In Japanese poetry, in contrast, the "haiku moment" denotes a *kairos* when a seemingly commonplace event inspires poetry. Like most lyric forms, the haiku is radically kairic, urging a sensitivity to experience that enhances the quality of each passing moment. Indeed, an aesthetic based in *kairos* demands that our culture reconsider its received notions of artistic form; otherwise, we remain haunted by Neoplatonic, anti-kairic, and static or "Ideal" criteria of evaluation. By means of such reassessment, Mason suggests we might learn to bring a more strongly temporal perspective to the entire spectrum of art (and of contemporary art in particular).

Roger Thompson argues for a theory of *kairos* that embraces both James L. Kinneavy's "right timing and due measure" and Paul Tillich's "eternal breaking into the temporal." Indeed, aligning Tillich's understanding of *kairos* with Kinneavy's opens up several new avenues of interpretation. Framing a theory of *kairos* in spiritual terms allows one to reinterpret the rhetorical theories of both Plato and Augustine. It also provides a critical new means to interpret early and mid-nineteenth-century American literary and rhetorical texts—texts that often self-consciously assert their spiritual and/or theological import. Because American literary, rhetorical, and cultural history is permeated by a sense of divine urgency or mission, a theory of *kairos* that accounts for this divine mission offers a more sensitive means of exploration. In particular, Thompson examines Ralph Waldo Emerson's invocation of the "heroic" moment as prerequisite to "true" rhetoric, and places Emerson's conception alongside that of Plato and Augustine as embracing a *kairos* at once historical and transcendent.

The essays in this collection thus range beyond Gorgias to explore notions of *kairos* in Pythagoras, Hippocrates, Isocrates, Plato, Aristotle, Cicero, the New Testament, Renaissance iconography, Elizabethan drama, American Transcendentalism, and the Japanese haiku and tea ceremony. Beyond rhetorical theory (and praxis), the fields examined include theology, philosophy, ethics, the history of medicine, psychology, aesthetics, literary theory, and composition pedagogy. *Kairos* is considered in dynamic relation with other philosophical and rhetorical concepts—for example, with the competing temporalities of *chronos* and *aion* and the formal constraints of *prepon* or *decorum*. Though ancient Greek in origin, the concept's subsequent history is charted through Roman, Judeo-Christian, Renaissance Humanist, nineteenth-century American, and contemporary discourse; also duly noted is its vital presence in Eastern literary-aesthetic culture. As the essays in this collection thus attest, *kairos* remains a master concept cutting across ages, cultures, and disciplines. It is time now to turn to the essays themselves.

Notes

1. Limitations of space preclude discussion of all of these disciplines, but let me stress the importance of *kairos* for ethics. As Aristotle advises, "Know the critical situation in your life, know that it demands a decision, and what decision, train yourself to recognize as such the decisive point in your life, and to act accordingly" (*Nichomachean Ethics* 1.4.1096a32).

2. Eric Charles White explores antecedents of *kairos* that bring together two distinct notions of the concept: "*Kairos* is an ancient Greek word that means 'the right moment' or 'the opportune.' The two meanings of the word apparently come from two different sources. In archery, it refers to an opening or 'opportunity' or, more precisely, a long tunnel-like aperture through which the archer's arrow has to pass. Successful passage of a *kairos* requires, therefore, that the archer's arrow be fired not only accurately but with enough power for penetration. The second meaning of *kairos* traces to the art of

weaving. There it is the 'critical time' when the weaver must draw the yarn through a gap that momentarily opens in the warp of the cloth being woven. Putting the two meanings together, one might understand *kairos* to refer to a passing instant when an opening appears which must be driven through with force if success is to be achieved" (1987, 13). Significant here is the conflation of spatial and temporal metaphors.

3. I have found nearly one hundred scholarly articles and monographs examining *kairos* in classical rhetoric, literature, and philosophy. *Kairos* also plays a very important role in the work of the noted twentieth-century theologian Paul Tillich, who has written several books and nearly a dozen articles on this concept. Tillich's general understanding of *kairos* emphasizes its role in the contextualization of codified systems. What Tillich has done is to take Greek notions of *kairos* and distinguish them from *logos* which, for him, denotes timelessness, particularly *stasis* in customs and laws. *Kairos*, on the other hand, involves a qualitative, dynamic state of time. Tillich argues that it is *kairos* that brings general theory, law, or custom into an individuated *praxis* (in particular, see his "*Kairos* and *Logos*," "*Kairos* and *Kairoi*," and "*Kairos* I"). Tillich's approach to *kairos* would seem to have relevance to contemporary writing theory, particularly composition practice that is concerned with social and ideological contexts.

4. Gerhard Delling notes that in the period after Hesiod, *kairos* took on positive tones. For poets and philosophers, *kairos* meant *sophrosyne* in the sense of "norm." *Kairos* also came to mean "wise moderation" and that which is "decisive." Gerhard Delling writes, "*Kairos* takes on the sense of fateful. Basic to this concept is that *Moira* forces man to a decision by putting him in a specific situation" (1986, 455). Thus, he quotes Aristotle: " . . . Know the critical situation in your life, know that it demands a decision, and what decision, train yourself to recognize as such the decisive point in your life, and to act accordingly" (455).

5. There are more definitions of *kairos* than could reasonably be addressed in an essay of this length. William H. Race, for example, discusses nearly a dozen different meanings of *kairos* in Greek drama alone.

6. Chronos, as a Greek god, has an interesting lineage in regard to his grandson, Kairos. Zeus was the youngest son of Chronos, who was the youngest son of Heaven (Ouranos) and Earth (Gaea), who emerged from chaos, the Void that existed before there was anything (Kelman, 59). For an extensive discussion of the gods Chronos and Kairos, see Cook, "Appendix A: *Kairos*."

7. In *To Demonicus*, Isocrates advises his addressee to avoid behavior that is inappropriate or *akairic:* "[Y]ou must avoid being serious when the occasion is one for mirth, or taking pleasure in mirth when the occasion is serious (for what is unseasonable *[akairon]* is always offensive)" (31).

8. Ethical implications of *kairos* can be found much earlier, as in Hesiod's description of a man who violates his brother's wife as "acting against what is proper" *(parakairos redzon)* (*Works and Days*, 329).

9. There is, for example, a wealth of untranslated Italian scholarship related to many areas of antiquity housed in La Biblioteca Nazionale in Florence, Italy.

10. Dale L. Sullivan, in a penetrating analysis of *kairos* in early Greek rhetoric, suggests that Gorgias departs significantly from Pythagoras in his views on *kairos*: "In [Gorgias'] *Encomium of Helen*, three meanings of *kairos* are apparent: poetic timing that produces connections and thus a special *logos*, a point of indecision encountered when competing opinions are presented, and a sort of irrational power that makes decision possible. We might call these respectively the *kairos* of inspiration, of *stasis*, and of *duna-*

mis, or power. The first *kairos* is located in the mind of the speaker, who forms a *logos* but does not yet express it; the second is in the audience who have not yet heard the *logos;* and the third is in the dynamic situation occasioned by the release of the *logos*" (1992, 318 – 19). This insightful semiotic explanation is reminiscent of Aristotle's configuration of the *pisteis*.

11. Alcidamus, a student of Gorgias, contends that a speech given from a prepared text ignores the context in which it is given: "For those who work hard on a written text before a contest sometimes miss the right response *[ton kairon amartanousin]:* they either become hateful to their audience by speaking longer than is desired or they stop prematurely when the audience wants to hear more" (qtd. in Wilson, "Due Measure," 199).

12. The most detailed examinations of *kairos* in Gorgias are Augusto Rostagni, Mario Untersteiner, and C. J. De Vogel. For a discussion of *kairos* in Alcidamas, see Vallozza, "*Kairos* nella retorica."

13. Pythagoras and his followers believed that numbers are mystical in nature and of cosmic significance, reflecting the natural order of things and the basic rhythms of life. Aristotle notes in his *Metaphysics* that Pythagoras equates *kairos* to the number 7; all human and cosmic events (birth, gestation, maturity, the orbit of the sun, and so forth) are governed by rhythms of seven and, therefore, of *kairos*. According to Paul Kucharski, Pythagoras taught that "*kairos* indicates the durations, or terms, or the times of fulfillment which clearly mark the generations, the growth, and the development of human beings" (143). In his analysis of the Pythagoreans, Wilhelm Roscher argues that Pythagoras and his followers identified *kairos* and health with the number 7: "it is the seventh day (of illness) that is decisive *[kairos]* because it marks the turning point *[krisis]* through which one passes, whether through amelioration or worsening of the condition *[thanatos]*" (qtd. in Kucharski, 147). According to De Vogel, *kairos* for Pythagoras involved appropriateness in the entire cosmic-ontological order (1966, 118). There is no question that *kairos* is a fundamental principle in Pythagoras' numerological explanations of human, natural, and supernatural events.

14. There has been some recent attention to the importance of Isocrates. Edward P. J. Corbett, for example, lauds Isocrates as "the most influential Greek rhetorician among his contemporaries" (596), while Kathleen Welch argues that Isocrates was a pivotal figure in the revitalization of Greek rhetorical culture: "The influence of Isocrates on the classical world was immense. His concept of Greek unity and his system of education based on rhetoric affected ancient Greek history and subsequently Roman culture" (362). Further, Tony Lentz contends that Isocrates was the earliest significant writer in ancient Greece: "Isocrates was the first individual who could be termed a 'writer' in the modern sense of the term" (123). And Brian Vickers identifies Isocrates as the first Greek to establish a permanent school for the teaching of deliberative and forensic discourse: "The pioneer who took the logical step of developing a school to train the Greeks for political and legal speaking, with a fixed school . . . was Isocrates" (1988, 9).

15. There has been much discussion over whether this praise is sincere or ironic. George A. Kennedy believes that this tribute "is probably an allusion to Isocrates' early association with and respect for Socrates compared to what Plato must have regarded as an un-Socratic and even un-philosophic philosophy subsequently pursued" (188). For other views, see Coulter, "*Phaedrus*"; Erbse, "Platons Urteil"; De Vries, "Isocrates in the *Phaedrus*"; Howland, "The Attack on Isocrtes"; and Voliotis, "Isocrates and Plato."

16. In *Institutio Oratoria*, Quintilian names Isocrates "the prince of instructors, whose works proclaim his eloquence no less than his pupils testify to his excellence as a

teacher" (2.8.14). Cicero praises him as "master of all rhetoricians" (*De Oratore* 2.2.94) and cites him as an exemplary teacher: "He was a great orator and an ideal teacher . . . and within the walls of his school brought to fulness a renown such as no one after him has in my judgement attained" (*Brutus*, 32). Seventeen centuries later, no less a classicist than John Milton would call him (in Sonnet X) "Old Man Eloquent."

17. H. Wersdörfer, in his untranslated dissertation, examines the technical dimensions of *kairos* in Isocrates by contrasting the rhetorician's uses of ethical and aesthetic *kairoi*.

18. See Wilhelm Süss, *Ethos*, 18–24 for a discussion of the influence of Gorgias on Isocrates' treatment of *kairos*.

Works Cited

Aristotle. *On Rhetoric: A Theory of Civic Discourse*. Trans. and Ed. George A. Kennedy. New York: Oxford Univrsity Press, 1991.

Burger, Ronna. *Plato's Phaedrus: A Defense of a Philosophic Art of Writing*. University, AL: University of Alabama Press, 1980.

Cahn, Michael. "Reading Rhetoric Rhetorically: Isocrates and the Marketing of Insight." *Rhetorica* 7 (1989): 121–44.

Cicero. *Cicero on Oratory and Orators*. Trans. and Ed. J. S. Watson. 1878. Reprint, Carbondale: Southern Illinois University Press, 1970.

Cook, Arthur Bernard. "Appendix A: *Kairos*." *Zeus: A Study in Ancient Religion*. Vol. 2. part 2: 859–68. Cambridge: Cambridge University Press, 1925.

Corbett, Edward P. J. *Classical Rhetoric for the Modern Student*. 2d ed. New York: Oxford University Press, 1971.

Coulter, J. A. "*Phaedrus* 279e: The Praise of Isocrates." *Greek, Roman, and Byzantine Studies* 8 (1967): 225–36.

Delling, Gerhard. "*Kairos*." *Theological Dictionary of the New Testament*. Ed. Gerhard Kittel. Trans. Geoffrey W. Bramley. 833–39. Grand Rapids, MI: Eerdman, 1986.

De Romilly, Jacqueline. *A Short History of Greek Literature*. Trans. Lillian Doherty. 1980. Chicago: University of Chicago Press, 1985.

De Vogel, C. J. *Pythagoreans and Early Pythagoreanism*. Assen: Van Gorcum, 1966.

De Vries. "Isocrates Reaction to the *Phaedrus*." *Mnemosyne* 6 (1953): 39–45.

———. "Isocrates in the *Phaedrus*: A Reply." *Mnemosyne* 24 (1971): 387–390.

Erbse, H. "Platons Urteil über Isokrates." *Hermes* 91 (1971): 183–97.

Gillis, Daniel. "The Ethical Basis of Isocrates' Rhetoric." *La Parola del Passato* 14 (1969): 321–48.

Howland, R. L. "The Attack on Isocrates in the *Phaedrus*." *Classical Quarterly* 31 (1937): 151–59.

Isocrates. *Isocrates*. Trans. George Norlin. 3 Vols. Loeb Classical Library. 1929. Cambridge, MA: Harvard University Press, 1968.

Jaeger, Werner. *Paideia: The Ideals of Greek Culture*. Trans. Gilbert Highet. Vol. 3. 1944. Reprint, New York: Oxford University Press, 1971.

Kelman, Harold. "*Kairos*: The Auspicious Moment." *The American Journal of Psychoanalysis* 29 (1969): 59–83.

Kennedy, George A. "The Evolution of a Theory of Artistic Prose." In *The Cambridge*

History of Literary Criticism. Ed. George Kennedy. Vol. 1: 184–199. Cambridge: Cambridge University Press, 1989.

Kerferd, G. B. *The Sophistic Movement.* London: Cambridge Universisty Press, 1981.

Kermode, Frank. *The Sense of an Ending: Studies in the Theory of Fiction.* New York: Oxford University Press, 1970.

Kinneavy, James L. *Greek Rhetorical Origins of Christian Faith: An Inquiry.* New York: Oxford University Press, 1987.

———. "*Kairos*: A Neglected Concept in Classical Rhetoric." In *Rhetoric and Praxis: The Contribution of Classical Rhetoric to Practical Reasoning.* Ed. Jean Dietz Moss, 79–105. Washington, DC: The Catholic University of America Press, 1985.

Kucharski, Paul. "Sur la notion pythagoricienne du *kairos.*" *Revue Philosophique* 153 (1963): 141–169.

Lentz, Tony M. *Orality and Literacy In Hellenic Greece.* Carbondale: Southern Illinois University Press, 1989.

Levi, Doro. "*Kairos* in Greek Literature." *Rendiconti della Reale Accademia Nazionale dei Lincei Classe di scienze moralia* RV 32 (1923): 260–81.

———. "The Concept of *Kairos* and the Philosophy of Plato." *Rendiconti della Reale Accademia Nazionale dei Lincei Classe di scienze moralia* RV 33 (1924): 93–118.

Liddell, Henry George and Robert Scott. *A Greek-English Lexicon.* 1889. Reprint, Oxford: Clarendon, 1968.

Marrou, H. I. *A History of Education in Antiquity.* Trans. George Lamb. Madison, WI: University of Wisconsin Press, 1982.

Onians, Richard Broxton. "*Kairos.*" *The Origins of European Thought: About the Body, the Mind, the Soul, the World, Time, and Fate.* 2d ed, 343–48. Cambridge: Cambridge University Press, 1954.

Pausanias. *Description of Greece.* Trans. W. H. Jones. Cambridge, MA: Harvard University Press, 1935.

Plato. *Phaedrus.* Trans. Harold North Fowler. Loeb Classical Library. 1914. Cambridge, MA: Harvard University Press, 1977.

Quintilian. *The Institutio Oratoria of Quintilian.* Trans. H. E. Butler. 4 Vols. Loeb Classical Library. Cambridge, MA: Harvard University Press, 1958.

Race, William H. "The Word *Kairos* in Greek Drama." *Transactions of the American Philological Association* 111 (1981): 197–213.

Rostagni, Augusto. "Un Nuovo capitolo nella storia della retorica e della sofistica." *Studi italiani de filologica classica,* n.s. 2 (1922): 148–201.

Shorey, Paul. "Introduction." *Republic.* By Plato. Ed. G. P. Gould. Trans. Paul Shorey. 2 Vols. 2: ix–lxxiii. Loeb Classical Library. 1935. Reprint, Cambridge, MA: Harvard University Press, 1987.

Smith, John E. "Time and Qualitative Time." *The Review of Metaphysics* 40 (1986): 3–16.

Sullivan, Dale L. "*Kairos* and the Rhetoric of Belief." *Quarterly Journal of Speech* 78 (1992): 317–32.

Süss, Wilhelm. *Ethos.* Leipzig: n.p., 1910.

Tillich, Paul. "Kairos and Logos." In *The Interpretation of History.* Trans. N. A. Rasetzki and Elsa Talmey. New York: Scribner's, 1936.

———. "Kairos and Kairoi." *Systematic Theology.* Vol. 3: 369–72. Chicago: University of Chicago Press, 1963.

———. "Kairos." *Der Widerstreit von Raum und Zeit: Schriften zur Geschichtsphilosophie, Gesammelte Werke* Vol. 1: 10–28.

Untersteiner, Mario. *The Sophists.* Trans. Kathleen Freeman. London: Basil Blackwell, 1954.

Vallozza, Maddelena. *"Kairos* nella retorica di Alcidamante e di Isocrate." *Quaderni urbinati di cultura classica* 50 (1985): 119–23.

Vickers, Brian. *In Defence of Rhetoric.* Oxford: Clarendon, 1988.

Voliotis, N. "Isocrates and Plato: An Effort to Interpret the *Phaedrus* 278e–279b." *Platon* 29 (1977): 145–51.

Welch, Kathleen E. "Isocrates." *Encyclopedia of Rhetoric and Composition: Communication from Ancient Times to the Information Age.* Ed. Theresa Enos. New York: Garland, 1996.

Wersdörfer, H. "Die *Philosophia* des Isocrates im Spiegel ihrer Terminologie." Ph.D. diss., Bonn, 1940.

White, Eric Charles. *Kaironomia: On the Will to Invent.* Ithaca: Cornell University Press, 1987.

Wilson, John R. "Kairos As 'Profit.'" *Classical Quarterly* 31 (1981): 418–420.

———. "Kairos as 'Due Measure.'" *Glotta* 58 (1980): 177–20.

A New Chapter in the History of Rhetoric and Sophistry

AUGUSTO ROSTAGNI

translated by PHILLIP SIPIORA

Premises

The issue concerning the nature of "the word" *(logos)* and the means it uses to influence the soul has a greater importance in Greek thought than is usually acknowledged in histories of ancient rhetoric (which, for the most part, lack an understanding of philosophy). Suffice it to consider that it not only applies to the field of eloquence—that is, to rhetoric in the strict sense of "the word"—but also includes all forms of *expression*. Moreover, it arises in connection with the greatest problems that were discussed in Greek philosophy just when the Greek spirit started to examine itself for the first time and, therefore, permeates with its complicated debates that initial magnificent movement of scientific investigation that is the Age of Sophistry.

Recent studies by Wilhelm Süss and Max Pohlenz have pointed out the major role played by Gorgias of Leontini—one of the most remarkable Sophists—in the scientific definition of *logos,* and many concepts of literary criticism and rhetoric formerly attributed to Plato and Aristotle are now ascribed to Gorgias. Nevertheless, these studies have only discovered an isolated, sudden, and fragmentary manifestation, whereas there is a broad movement of ideas whose origins and connections must be examined in the light of history.

In investigating Aristotles' *Poetics,* I have already observed how Gorgias' concepts of the nature and action of eloquence have a peculiar relationship with Pythagorean concepts regarding the action of music and poetry; therefore, I have assumed that they derived from a general theory of art, whose center of propagation was in the Magna Graecia and, exactly, in the Pythagorean school:

Gorgias, the Sicilian (as I was saying), glorifies the *magic* effects of the *word (goeteia, psychagogia),* and teaches and explains that the rhetor must know, scientifically, the ways to the soul, from which the speeches capable of *spellbinding* and *persuading* descend. He is a close friend of Damone from Oa who, during the same years, in a fictitious oration addressed to the Aeropagites, defends music, showing the secret affinities that link harmony and rhythm to various psychic moods, so that harmonies and rhythms are actually capable of molding human character. The rhetor and the musician are exponents of a single, already fully-developed doctrine which includes two different subjects. It is hardly necessary to recall the ways connecting Gorgias to the Pythagorean milieu and how the former had shaped his education under the influence of Empedocles, witnessing personally not only the operations of mystic *therapeusis* and spellbinding that this philosopher performed, but also the control that he exercised over crowds by means of the studied and fascinating word. It is very useful to consider, instead, that the tradition (accepted by Aristotle and the Alexandrian critics) ascribed to Empedocles, and even to Pythagoras himself, the invention of the rhetorical art. This tradition—which until now has been regarded as vacuous—has a real foundation, in the sense that the experiments and precepts concerning the *psychagogic* value of the word (which later formed the basis of Gorgias' *techne*) must date back to Empedocles and the Pythagoreans. And probably Gorgias himself brought about such rumors, linking, by means of explicit statements, his method to the methods of those predecessors.

Now the time has come to expand the field of investigation, since there are unexplored regions of ancient rhetoric behind those uncertain traditions.

Anthisthenes and Gorgias

I begin with a fragment of Antisthenes, a disciple of Gorgias who, even after his contacts with Socrates, continued to practice his profession of rhetor, maintaining (generally speaking) the habits of mind and methods of his first master. He wrote a treatise, "On Speech, or On Characters" *(Peri lexeos e peri charakteron),* of which nothing is explicitly handed down and, for the time being, I cannot say anything but that it seems to be the most ancient work with this title; and that is important, because it substantiates the development of rhetorical doctrine with implications that had already been arrived at by that time. The fragment which I intend to use does not specifically analyze aesthetic matters and, for this reason, it was completely neglected. It includes one of the many sophistic discussions of Homeric questions in which Antisthenes took great delight. He wrote "On the Cyclops of Odysseus, or On Odysseus" *(Peri Odysseias Kyklops e peri Odysseos)* and many other similar short works, and his fragment is preserved in the *scholium* of the first book of the *Odyssey,* drawn (as we might suppose, but this is also explicitly stated in the

marginal notes of a manuscript) from the compilation of "Homeric Ques-tions" *(Homerika zetemata)* that Porphyry had written in the third century A.D.
What is the meaning of the epithet *polutropos*, which Homer gives to Ulysses? And does the epithet not have a pejorative meaning *(shrewd, deceiv-ing)* that opposes the aim of the poet who is, of course, concerned about cele-brating his own hero? That question was not really unusual at all; on the con-trary, it was prevalent in the circles of the Sophists—to such an extent that, because of that word, someone had decided to settle the uncertainties by cor-recting the Homeric text. Plato's dialogue, *Hippias Minor*, also begins with Ulysses' *polutropos*, comparing him to the sincere and simple Achilles *(alethes kai haplous)* and to the wise Nestor *(sophotatos)*; wondering who would be the best among the characters played by these heroes, it comes to the following paradoxical conclusion: the shrewd man is the wisest and, therefore, the best. There is probably some kind of connection between Plato's dialogue and Antisthenes' fragment, since Antisthenes' aim—even though with very dif-ferent arguments—is also to justify Ulysses; nevertheless, I do not think it possible to establish the priority of one author over the other, all the more so because both works are derived from commonplaces. (I do not agree with Wilamowitz, who speaks with certainty of Antisthenes' dependence upon Plato.)

Antisthenes' thesis, which appears at the beginning of the *scholium*, may be summarized as follows: "Antisthenes says that Homer neither praises nor blames Ulysses by calling him *polutropos*." However, it is necessary to consider how this thesis is developed. At first, the author expounds the difficulties that gave rise to that question. "Homer has not made Achilles and Ajax *polutropoi*, but simple *(haploi)* and generous. And he has not even made Nestor, the "in-ventor of tests," fraudulent or changeable by nature *(dolios kai palimbolos)*, but simple in his conversation with the others, ready to manifest and not hide his good counsel from the army. And Achilles was so far from accepting such a quality of *polutropos* in himself that he estimated ". . . as great an enemy as the gates of Hell the man who holds one thing in his heart and speaks another" *(Iliad* 9.312–313). There follows the reading on which my demonstration is based and which I transcribe entirely, reserving myself the right to extract the salient points later. Resolving the problem, Antisthenes says:

> And what then? Are we perhaps to believe that Odysseus is wicked because he is called *polutropos*? Nevertheless, the poet has called him that at a point where he is thought wise *(sophos)*. Perhaps, in fact, the word *tropos* is not applied to moral character *(ethos)*, as much as to his skill in speaking *(logou khresis)*? One is called *eutropos* if one has a moral character that is "turned" *(tetrammenon)* toward the good, and in discourse *tro-poi* are called diverse styles *(hai poiai plaseis)*. Homer has also adopted the word *tropos* with regard to the voice and variety of melodies, as in the case of the nightingale: ". . .

changing *(troposa)* it over and over again, she pours forth her many-toned voice" *(Odyssey* 19.521). Therefore, if wise men are skilled in speaking and know how to express the same thought in many ways *(kata pollous tropous),* those who know many ways of expression concerning the same thing can rightly be called *polutropoi.* The wise men are therefore also excellent men *(hoi sophoi kai agathoi eisin).* For this reason Homer bestows upon Odysseus, as a wise man, the epithet *polutropos:* because he can speak with men in many ways. So it is also said that Pythagoras, having been invited to speak with children, used the language of children; in speaking with women, the language appropriate to women, in speaking with rulers, the language of rulers; in speaking with youths, the language of youths. For it is a mark of wisdom to discover a form of wisdom appropriate to each person, and a mark of ignorance to use only one form *(mono- tropo)* of speech with dissimilar people. This is a specialty which also belongs to medicine, in a case that is well treated. For the care of the ill ought to be *polutropos,* because of the various predispositions of the cured. *Tropos* is therefore that which changes, that which is variable in the human spirit. The multiplicity of the ways of speaking *(polutropia logou)* and the use of varied speech for various ears becomes a single type *(monotropia)* of speech. For one thing is appropriate for each person. Thus, that which is adapted to each person reduces variety of speech to one thing—that which is suitable for each person. But that which is uniform and unadapted to different ears renders a speech (which is rejected by many) *polutropos,* because it has been rejected by them.

The reading ends here, which Porphyry seems to have faithfully transcribed, to such an extent that it bears the signs of the dialogic form in which Antisthenes' work was obviously composed (note the queries and exclamations: "what, then? indeed? not at all," "no, by Zeus" *(ti oun; ara ge; mepote, ou ma Dia . . .),* limiting himself almost entirely to substitute occasionally infinitive clauses for direct speech. If, on the one hand, this warrants an authenticity greater than critics are inclined to accept, on the other hand it explains and justifies the artful and calculated aspect of the excerpt.

In this passage it is better to distinguish between two parts, one contingent and the other substantive. The contingent section concerns the interpretation of Homer, with which I am not concerned, even though it is the only one that has so far attracted scholars' attention. I only want to observe that Ulysses' very peculiar disguise—clad as a master and a founder, not only of wisdom, but also of the art of speech—has become current since Antisthenes' times onward in the schools of classical antiquity, and the Emperor Julian *(Oration* 2.75c) still considered Ulysses to be the *polutropos* orator from Ithaca *(ho ek tes Ithakes rhetor polutropos).* Furthermore, the interesting relationship established in Antisthenes' fragment between Ulysses and the *poikilia tou logou* (that well-known *poikilia* that constitutes the ideal of Gorgias and Isocrates, with regard to the rhetor's style) makes me suppose that Antisthenes himself defined or, at least, promoted in his work (whose purpose seems to be indicated by the title "On Speech, or On Characters") the well-known classification of the three styles linked with examples of Homeric heroes and found in the Stoic treatises that precede Varro. Thus, Ulysses is representative of the *high* or *majestic* style, called *poikilon (amplum, copiosum, varium);* Menelaus represents the *lower* style, and Nestor the *middle* style.

The substantive part of the discussion consists of concepts of a general nature; that is, the theoretical concepts that support Antisthenes' exegesis, even though he does not explicitly deal with them. And these principles are neither so dull nor negligible that it is impossible to reconstruct them thoroughly. Let us begin with Antisthenes' thesis itself, which Porphyry uses almost as the title of the passage: "Antisthenes says that Homer neither praises nor blames Ulysses by calling him *polutropos.*" In comparison to the following resolution of the issue, these words are truly enlightening. In fact, once we have established that the epithet *polutropos* refers to Ulysses' eloquence, it follows (in the author's line of thought) that the term does not constitute in itself either praise or blame for the hero.

Antisthenes' position is, therefore, one of neutrality and moral indifference, which is all the more clear because it prevents the author from lapsing into the Socratic conception that wisdom is identified with virtue. At a certain point Antisthenes adds that wise men *(sophoi)* are also good men *(agathoi),* and he is very careful not to emphasize this concept and explain (as it would be necessary) the moral sense of the ambiguous term *agathos.* Anthisthenes aims primarily at remaining within the domain of rhetoric and aesthetics, and the remainder of the text appears to him to be unrelated to his aim. Within the domain of rhetoric and aesthetics, Antisthenes is dominated by Gorgias' conceptions (of rhetoric and aesthetics). The following example has the most universal and profound value. Compared with those who either glorified it as ethically useful or censured it as morally harmful, Gorgias' idea of his own art is related, ironically, to Plato, whose characterization of Gorgias represents rhetoric as a wonderful art of *seduction* and *fascination (psychagogia),* one that has the magical power to direct the human soul at its will and to persuade regarding good and evil, the just and the unjust, the beautiful and the ugly, and so forth. Thus, it is up to the rhetor to put to good use this weapon assigned to him, which is, by itself, irresponsible.

The truthfulness of Plato's representation is confirmed by Gorgias' *Helen,* where the power of the word *(logos),* of "this great lord who, although very small and slight, creates works that are truly divine and shapes the human soul as much as he pleases" *(Helen* 8. 13), is compared to the power of medicine, which is capable of killing or saving the body: "For just as different drugs dispel different secretions from the body, and some bring an end to disease and others an end to life, so also in the case of speeches: some distress, others delight, some cause fear, others embolden their hearers, and some drug and bewitch the soul with a kind of evil persuasion *(epharmakeusan kai exegoeteusan)."* This is not just the *logos* of the orator, but also (in a universal sense) of the poet who writes epic or tragedy—indeed, the very poetry that Gorgias (*Helen* 9) confesses to be a deception.

Now that I have clarified the philosopher's moral position, I shall attempt to trace the actual principles of the teaching of rhetoric. What does that wonderful tool—*logos*—mean for Antisthenes? It is a concept infinitely variable and varied, whose nature can be translated into the terms *tropos* and *polutropia;* it is an ability to express the same thought in many ways. This concept, too, is derived from the ideal trends of sophistry, according to which thought, content, and argument are separate and abstract, and the word wraps around them one of its multicolored cloaks; or, rather, thought, content, and argument cannot be grasped so much in their reality as in the opinion—*doxa*—that we have of them, and in the ways we have of presenting and describing them. Indeed, it is entirely drawn from the doctrine of Gorgias (if we follow the descriptions that we find in Isocrates and Plato, always with corresponding terms). Isocrates dislikes to present things in the same manner as others (*Panegyricus,* 7–8): "but since oratory possesses such a nature that it is possible to relate the same subject matter in many different ways—to represent great matters as lowly or to invest small matters with grandeur, to recount the things of old in a new manner or set forth recent events with an air of antiquity." This view was the teaching of Gorgias, as Plato points out, who quotes the same definition in his *Phaedrus* (267a.): "to make small matters appear great, and great matters appear small through the power of speech, and new things old, and old things new."

This teaching of Gorgias, however, relied (due to a logical relationship) on another fundamental concept that can be considered as the heart of his system: the well-known concept of *kairos.* It seems that Gorgias wrote a special treatise on *kairos,* although his *techne* did not follow such a pattern as to deserve the subtitle, "On Kairos" *(Peri kairou).* In any event, let me briefly explain the concept: the changeability of discourse is justified and required by the necessity of adapting to *circumstances* that, in a general sense, include the states of mind of both speaker and audience, the moment, the place, and so forth. It is necessary that one scientifically know the various forms of the discourse in order to avoid violating the rules of opportunity *(ton kairon me diamartein);* to alter the discourse in a suitable *(prepontos)* manner; and to choose each form so that it harmonizes *(prosarmottein)* with every other form. Rhetoric, then, conceived as such, becomes for Gorgias and his disciples the art of living well, the center of education.

Antisthenes' entire discussion revolves around the rhetorical concept of *kairos;* indeed, it presents such precise and insightful interpretations as to make us infer immediately that Antisthenes has preserved a much more immediate and complete image of the Gorgianic treatment than that traditionally held by scholars to date. In fact, the writer dwells on certain specific arguments, in order to demonstrate that those principles, since adapted to various circumstances, form an *authentic* unity (whereas an absolute, limited, and monotonous unity turns into discordance and confusion); his are not arguments that come about randomly, but belong to the main body of a philosophical system. I shall be able to uncover their origin gradually but, first, I must proceed in a certain order.

Antisthenes begins by establishing that Ulysses' art consisted in his knowing "to associate with men in many different ways" *(tois anthropois pollois tropois suneinai):* these words remind us of Gorgias' well-known definition that we find in Plato (*Gorgias* 463a), where rhetoric is "natural cleverness at speaking to men" *(phusei deine prosomilein tois anthropois).* The philosophical disquisitions are presented a little later. In the first place: "to find the way to wisdom in conformity with everyone else is a sign of wisdom, while it is a sign of ignorance to use only one form of discourse with others." This position generally agrees with the way Gorgias and his disciples used to praise their art as the true art of good living. The following argument, based on the comparison between rhetoric and medicine, falls within Gorgias' ideas in an even more symptomatic way. In fact, the antithesis between body and soul, the attribution of rhetoric to the soul and medicine to the body—and, lastly, the analogy of the technical methods that are necessary to both arts with regard to their respective objects—are themes much loved by the Sicilian orator, and we have already seen the most authentic evidence of this in that passage from *Helen,* where the influence of the word on the soul is compared to the effects of drugs on the body (*Helen* 14).

Prior to these arguments, there appears in the fragment of Antisthenes an historical example of Pythagoras, who is considered representative of the use of *kairos* in eloquence: "Pythagoras is also said, having been invited to speak with children, to have used the language of children; in speaking with women, the language appropriate to women; in speaking with rulers, the language of rulers; in speaking with youths, the language of youths."

Even though I do not take into consideration the most important implications of this testimony, anyone can see that it is very important by itself, because it offers an unexpected argument in support of my hypothesis about the Pythagorean origin of Gorgias' rhetoric. If, however, one wants effectively to advance this argument, it is first necessary to dispel a suspicion that might immediately be raised. In fact, one might think that the example of Pythagoras is not part of Antisthenes' original text, but has been inserted into the text by the editor, namely, Porphyry.

I respond to this suspicion as exhaustively as I can by means of two kinds of proofs, the first of which is philosophical and examines the inner link between that information and the concepts that follow, the second of which is historical and demonstrates that the information in Pythagoras' categories of language—"for children, for women, for rulers, for youths" *(paidikoi, gynaikeioi, archontikoi, ephebikoi)*—is not vacuous at all; on the contrary, it expresses a precise and deep-rooted tradition dating back to such an ancient age that Antisthenes (or, better yet, Gorgias) might have been familiar with it.

These two kinds of proofs, of course, are useful not only for the dialectical purpose of eliminating any doubts about the authenticity of Antisthenes' testimony; but they also serve a more general purpose of furnishing the elements necessary to reconstruct (as I have anticipated) the forgotten part of rhetoric and sophistry of the original age. Therefore, I will treat the subject (of Pythagoras) separately.

The Rhetorical and Sophistic Movement of the Pythagoreans

Scholars who have examined only superficially the Homeric *scholium* have drawn the impression that they would find in it Antisthenes' interpretation of the word *polutropos,* as well as ideas and commentaries of the Neoplatonist Porphyry. In my opinion the matter has a completely different complexion, since I have observed the traces of the dialogic form into which Antisthenes' work was woven and, in the ideas presented, I have found not a Neoplatonic hodgepodge but, instead, an authentic reproduction of Gorgias' doctrines. I now assert that these ideas, as they are expressed, cannot be separated from Pythagoras' quotation.

After mentioning Pythagoras, the text adds the following quotation, "It is a mark of wisdom to discover a form of wisdom appropriate to each person, and a mark of ignorance to use only one form of speech with dissimilar people," which appears to be only a general remark and does not suggest a particular circumstance. Instead, both with regard to the form *(gar)* and the concept, it follows that these words apply, first, to the particular case of Pythagoras, who imparts (and teaches how to impart) a level of *sophia* suited to everyone; in fact, the antithesis of *sophia* and *amathia* is Pythagorean. For the Pythagoreans, *sophia* is nothing but harmony, which is equivalent, etymologically, to *harmonia,* the faculty employed by Pythagoras to determine the appropriate language *(logous harmodious)* and appropriate form for each person *(prosarmottein hekaston hekasto):* that is, children's speeches for children, women's speeches for women, archons' speeches for archons, and ephebes' speeches for ephebes. This faculty is called *"kairos,"* a term that has assumed a technical and rather restricted meaning in the field of eloquence, but which had originally a profound meaning in philosophy. Aristotle (*Metaph.* 12.4.1078b) rightly informs us that the Pythagoreans were the first to take *kairos* into significant account and considered it as an expression of *numbers,* namely, as a manifestation of harmony *(arithmon pathos).* All these things, then, are dependent upon *sophia. Amathia* is the opposite manifestation, which the Pythagoreans considered a plague of the soul—a lack of order and harmony in a universal sense and, in a particular sense, an unsuitability in relation to the range of human temperaments.

In the text of the *scholium,* the comparison that follows between the art of the word and the art of medicine—a comparison dear to Gorgias—is also of Pythagorean origin. In fact (as Antisthenes and other sources inform us), the Pythagoreans were the first to establish in theory and cultivate in practice the famous parallel between the care of the body through medicine and the care of the soul through music. Although I say music, "music" had a very broad meaning for the disciples of Pythagoras; aesthetically, it was not different from poetry and eloquence, which depended solely on the principle of harmony or *kairos* and made use of the same spellbinding and persuasive influence *(psychagogia)* on the soul. Gorgias, too, begins with music and identifies, in substance, the "word without measure" *(logos aneu metrou* [*Eth. Nic.* 2.2.1104a: 8–9]). To appeal to medicine in order to show the Pythagorean or Gorgianic rhetorical methods was truly appropriate, because (as Aristotle attests) medicine was deemed to be the most practical and common field of activity for the use of *kairos.*

However, the most exact confirmation of the interpretation that I am developing about Antisthenes' passage can be found in the following argument, the philosophical depth of which I have already pointed out:

> The multiplicity of the ways of speaking *(polutropia logou)* and the use of varied speech for various ears becomes a single type *(monotropia)* of speech. For one thing is appropriate for each person. Thus, that which is adapted to each person reduces variety of speech to one thing—that which is suitable for each person. But that which is uniform and unadapted to different ears renders a speech (which is rejected by many) *polutropos,* because it has been rejected by them.

I do not see how this subtle disquisition can be explained without referring to a seminal philosophical principle. And I do not see how the latter can be other than the Pythagorean principle concerning the nature of the *one* and the *many.* For the Pythagoreans, true unity is *harmony;* therefore, it is not simple, but manifold and derives from the reconciliation of opposites, of which all things, accordingly, consist: "for harmony is a oneness of much-mixed things and an agreement on things thought of in different ways"

(Nicomachus, *Arithmetica Introductio*, 2.19). In other words, variety, tied by the supreme bond of harmony, becomes unity which, in fact, is not symbolically expressed by either *even* or *uneven*, but by the *even-uneven* (*artioperitton* [Philolaus, Fragment, 5.8]). Antisthenes says, specifically, that when the multiple elements of discourse are attuned to each subject, they become unified, whereas the absolute, limited, and immutable unity that uses the same tone with everybody brings about the inverse effect; that is, with regard to the many (with which it cannot coincide because of its rigidity), it is as if it were multiple—it is not *one* but, rather, it is *different*.

In substance, this reasoning reminds us of another Pythagorean argument, which concerns the problem of justice and equality and is derived from the same conception. Justice is a kind of *kairos* and *kairos* is a kind of justice. Justice is based on equality, which does not consist in giving everyone the same thing—which would turn out to be real inequality—but, rather, in giving to each person what is due according to his merits and qualities. Those currently debating the issue of equality and inequality among men should remember this fundamental principle.

At this point the invaluableness of Anthisthenes' fragment becomes apparent. On the one hand, the concepts in the text turn out to be a reproduction of the teachings of Gorgias, more complete and systematic than those available to contemporary scholars; on the other hand, these ideas demonstrate, both for the attribution of Pythagoras and the nature of the issues, that they (that is, Gorgias' teachings) are rooted in Pythagorism.

The unavoidable conclusion is that Gorgias is nothing but an intermediary, an interpreter of a doctrine prior to him that was widespread in Magna Graecia and Sicily. Perhaps he was the first to make the transition from the fields of philosophy, music, and (in a wider sense) aesthetics to the specific field of rhetoric; or, as is more likely, such a transition had already taken place amidst the fiery political and cultural struggles that were stirring in Sicilian and Italian cities. Nevertheless, this conclusion is worth examining thoroughly by resorting to other issues which, after interpreting Antisthenes' passage, now appear in a new light.

The fact that Gorgias based his *techne* on the principles of *kairos* and dealt with it, not only in the narrow sense of formal rhetoric but also philosophically, ensues from a statement by Dionysius of Halicarnassus (*De compositione verborum* [Usener, 45]). As is sometimes the custom of scholars, Dionysius—in preparing to develop the theme of *kairos*, with regard to the synthesis of words—defames his predecessors from whom, nevertheless, he draws his most salient observations. To Dionysius, it seems that no one—neither rhetor nor philosopher—has ever been able to define *kairos*, "not even Gorgias of Leontini, who was the first to examine it." Evidently, this is because the latter had limited himself to studying the essence of the topic and, therefore, did not provide the pedantic, formal classifications in which Dionysius takes delight. However, the little that Dionysius does say about the essence of *kairos* is taken exactly from Gorgias: "the nature of *kairos* is such that it does not fall within a scientific concept of universal value, and is not based so much on science as on opinion." These, in succinct form, are the same arguments that Plato has Gorgias develop in the dialogue by that name (463a): "It seems to me . . . that it is not an artistic pursuit, but a characteristic of a sagacious and manly spirit which is naturally clever at speaking to men." They are the same arguments that Isocrates also uses (reflecting the legacy of the Master, Pythagoras) in the doctrinal allusions of his orations: "these things require much study, and are the work of a manly and original spirit" (*Against the Sophists*, 17). These arguments have a deeper and more complex meaning than appears at first reading. Their direct origin (without going into major details now) lies in the profound distinction that Parmenides—on whom Gorgias relies in many respects—had made between the world of *truth* and the world of *opinion*. The first (which can or cannot be grasped by the human mind, since some who are dogmatic affirm it, while others who are skeptical doubt until they deny the existence of truth itself) is the object of science and philosophy. What remains is the world of phenomena, the world of deceptive appearances, which finds its expression in poetry and rhetoric—both of which are sensory and deceitful, and whose expressions are suited to phenomenological changes. It is important to see how Parmenides himself theorizes the relationship between the alluring, changeable power of the word and the world of *doxa,* a connection that may be considered a cross-fertilization between the well-known aesthetic concepts of the Pythagoreans and the gnostic speculations of Parmenides. In fact, after articulating the rigorous notion of truth, when he is about to describe the *fallacious* world of men's opinions he appeals to the *deceptive* ornamentation of words: "Here I stop my trustworthy speech to you and my thought about truth. From here on, learn from the opinions *(doxai)* of mortals; listen to the guileful ordering of my words" (*Peri physeos* [Diels, Fragment 8.50–53]).

Having established that Gorgias dealt with the issue of *kairos,* not only in the narrow sense of formal rhetoric, but also in a philosophical sense, it is unavoidable that he drew his concepts from those in whose doctrine *kairos* holds a significant place, if not in a specifically rhetorical sense, then surely in a universal sense: namely, the Pythagoreans. It is difficult to understand why no one has anticipated this derivation, since there is testimony, some of which I have previously discussed. Aristotle says that the Pythagoreans were the first to define the nature of *kairos,* regarding it as a manifestation of harmony and numbers, in the same way as justice; that is, for them *kairos* was one of the laws of the universe that was valid for great matters as well as insignificant matters, in general instances as well as in particular cases (*Metaphysics,* 12.4.1078b). The following saying was attributed to Pythagoras: "the best thing in every action is *kairos.*"

However, the most complete and instructive description of this concept is found in a passage in Iamblichus' *Life of Pythagoras.* This description is all the more complete and instructive, because it passes from the high regions of philosophy to the precepts of formal rhetoric (exactly as I had expected). At first, *kairos* appears in alliance with the concept of justice, and this corresponds to the testimony, cited above, in which *kairos* and *dikaion* are allied concepts. Also, both of them find application in relationships and speech *(kata tas homilias)* among men, speech that must vary according to one's age, station, kinship, mood, and relationship to others. And this position is very close to the definitions of Gorgias and Antisthenes, where rhetoric is the art of "speaking to men" or, as in Odysseus' *polutropoia,* of "speaking to men in many ways." Let us see:

> A certain kind of *justice* exists in relationships between men and that is the form of justice that Pythagoras speaks of. He says that there are essentially two manners of conversation—one which is suitable *(eukairon)* and one which is unsuitable *(akairon)*—and they are to be distinguished by differences in age, social position, intimacy of relationship, the advantage of one over the other, or whatever other difference exists between two individuals. For example, a conversation between an old man and a young man that is unsuitable would be suitable if it were between two old men. All forms of ire, threat, or insolence are unsuitable, and one must avoid them in relationships between the young and the old. The same is true with regard to the station one holds in life. A person who has achieved a certain degree of prominence in life does not really have freedom of speech (for certain things said would be unsuitable to his station), and the same holds true for the other things said above. (Iamblichus, *Life of Pythagoras*)

The Pythagoreans' teachings, so far, have a fundamental moral component. In fact, they consist of principles more common and fundamental than the tradition generally ascribed to the speeches of the Master—respect for the old, deference to superiors, reverence to parents, and so forth. But these teachings constitute, in turn, the framework of another theory: I mean the theory of those famous speeches that Antisthenes related (and that Pythagoras himself might have delivered) with an exemplary compliance with *kairos:* children's speeches for children, women's speeches for women, archons' speeches for archons, and ephebes' speeches for ephebes. In short, in the ambiguous meaning of the word *kairos,* one can clearly see the conditions to which the rhetorical arts linked their performance.

There are also other important remarks in the passage of Iamblichus:

> They have said that to be various and multiform *(poikilon kai polyeide)*, use *kairos*. It is also true that ire and anger are suitable for some and unsuitable for others and, similarly, among those who covet or long for something, some employ suitable techniques and others employ unsuitable techniques. The same argument holds true for emotions, actions, dispositions, conversations, and relationships.

Here we are dealing with the topic of *ethos* and *pathos* in orations. However, the most important part comes at the end:

> They say that until a certain point, *kairos* can be taught and is not irrational, but rather fit for a technical explanation *(didakton te kai aparalogon kai technologian epidechomenon)*; however, in a universal and absolute sense, not one of these properties can rival it *(katholou de kai hapos ouden auto touton huparchein)*. They say that they are similar concepts and such that they generally go together with the nature of *kairos*, the so-called *ora* and the *prepon* and the *armotton* and other concepts similar to these.

Therefore, little by little, the passage from Iamblichus has come to coincide with that statement in which Gorgias has summarized the nature of *kairos* (as it follows from Plato, Isocrates, and, especially, Dionysius of Halicarnassus). However, this is not *entechnos* in the absolute sense of the word: "the nature of *kairos* is such that it does not fall within a scientific concept of universal value, and is not based so much on science as on opinion."

Here there are two possibilities. Either we go back to a common source, purely Pythagorean, from which both Iamblichus and Gorgias have drawn (and by Iamblichus I mean the ancient historiographer of whom he is the editor); or we think that the ancient historiographer, edited by Iamblichus, was influenced by Gorgias' treatment of *peri kairou*. In both cases, Gorgias' treatment had to contain facts, experiences, and precepts attributed to the school of Pythagoras, which Gorgias did not invent and, perhaps, was not the first to interpret rhetorically. We are dealing with facts, experiences, and precepts permeating all of Pythagoras' life and the history of the Pythagorean school, teeming with many great or little manifestations of the biography and the system, and penetrating into the simplest and most primitive parts. Not only does Pythagoras give those particular speeches (according to legend), but all of his teachings, as well as his actions as founder of the school and as a man who knew and took care of souls, rests upon the combined principles of *kairos* and *dikaion*. First, when disciples come to him eager for initiation into his school, he, like one who has a good memory for faces, holds a sort of examination and studies the dispositions of each person and chooses, among thousands, the teachings and the cures suitable to those inclinations (Iamblichus, *Life of Pythagoras*, 71 ff.). Then he divides his disciples into various categories, giving to each one the rank and duties that are appropriate according to justice. He also makes distinctions in human life among certain fixed ages *(helikias endedasmenas)*, "for this is how he says they speak," and teaches the duties and functions that are appropriate to each age. With regard to music, which was practiced as a kind of medicine and as a cure for the soul *(katharsis)*, he sets certain songs appropriately composed *(idiotropa asmata)*, which vary according to the afflictions that must be cured.

Therefore, already in the ancient philosophical and legendary Pythagorean heritage, we find elements that, under certain circumstances, would have produced the rhetorical and aesthetic doctrine that we attribute to Gorgias. This doctrine probably preceded Gorgias (as I have indicated earlier), or did not come down due to his work only; it represented an evolution that occurred within the Pythagorean school itself, owing to the natural development of Greek science and spirit. We have scarce information about the development of the Sicilian and Italian cultures around the middle of the fifth century B.C. However, there are various indications that the intellectual currents of sophistry originated largely from these regions, which were sacred to the teachings of Pythagoras and his disciples.

Let us see where Gorgias, who is considered the major representative of the new trend, nourished his ideas. Where, if not at Empedocles' school (as reported in ancient testimonies and confirmed by modern research) and, in general, in the area of his homeland, which was permeated with Pythagorean influence? There is in fact a tradition, usually forgotten, that places Gorgias in a peculiar relationship with these Pythagorean circles, turning him into a kind of intermediary between the friends scattered around the Hellenic continent and his original school. Plutarch recounts that, after the massacre of Pythagoreans in Metaponto, there was no news of Lysias (who had escaped the massacre together with Philalous) until the arrival of Gorgias, who had returned to Sicily from Greece; this probably meant that he was returning from the well-known mission charged to him by his countrymen for the people of Athens (where his eloquence caused a memorable impression in the year 427), at which time he announced to "those who are with Arkesos" (probably the leader of a sect) that he had found Lysias safe and sound in Thebes. Nonetheless, it will be more useful to examine ideas rather than facts.

Up to this point, I have identified the rhetoric of Gorgias with the rhetoric of Pythagoras, disregarding the unusual attitude that the former takes toward the issue of ethics. And yet, we do know (because this appears in Antisthenes' fragment) that Gorgias was relatively indifferent to the faculty with which *logos* is endowed; that is, to persuade toward the good in the same way as toward evil, to be healthy or deadly for the soul as drugs are for the body. On the contrary, drawing from this position, Gorgias found reasons to delight in the power of *logos* and to extol it as a great lord (*dynastes megas* [Diogenes Laertius 8.32]). Now who would have imagined that Gorgias' position—and I do not refer to the spirit of amorality, which is totally individual, but to the facts, observations, and terms themselves—is derived from Pythagoras? Here is an ancient Pythagorean *akousma*, handed down, it seems, from Aristotle: "the greatest power among humans is to persuade either toward good or toward evil" (Diogenes Laertius 8.32).

We must follow the same reasoning to identify more precisely the doctrine of *kairos*. So far I have offered a rather limited explanation of it, relating *kairos* to *harmonia*, by which the speaker becomes attuned to the condition and disposition of the listener. However, it is well-known that in Gorgias it had another meaning, derived from the skeptical foundations of his thought; namely, it wholly concerned the troublesome issue of knowledge. For Gorgias, as for Pythagoras, things either do not exist or cannot be grasped in their naked truth; the veil of the senses hides them from us. Two contrary theses, therefore, and both equally probable, can be defended with regard to all things. According to the maxim introduced by Pythagoras, "there are two things to say about every matter" (Diogenes Laertius 9.51), and it is this mysterious and magnificent quality of *kairos* that allows us, as he would say, to make the same thing seem big or small, beautiful or ugly, new or old.

Well, it may seem risky (to say) but, permeated with skepticism, this conception, too—as it is inseparable from the previous ones—also brings with it its Pythagorean origins. In fact, let us bear in mind the Pythagorean concept *ab antico* with regard to the nature of the universe. All things consist of opposite qualities, as indicated by the categories of finite and infinite, even and odd, one and the many, and so forth. And yet there is a connecting link—*harmonia*—that turns these opposite qualities into unity, creating the universe. It is easy to understand how this notion lent itself to skepticism as soon the advanced Greek mind, embodied by Parmenides, discerned the difference between the world of truth and the world of opinion. It seems to me that two trends emerged within the (Pythagorean) school: one faithful to the tradition and almost willing *not* to see the difficulties and, therefore, limited to the dogmatic interpretation of the system; the other, to which Gorgias adheres, ready to reap the bold results created by the new opportunities in the ancient world.

It is important to determine whether there is clear documentation of this second trend, otherwise unnoticed, in Iamblichus' *Life of Pythagoras;* and this trend must be compared with the other passage in the *Life* itself, in which, as I have already indicated, the first and limited aspect of *kairos* is perfectly expressed. Here the idea of reconciling opposites is connected to civil education *(politike paideia),* a connection of which we may not be immediately aware but which, one senses, corresponds to the intentions of Sophists and rhetoricians. That is, it indicates the field in which Sophists and rhetoricians worked:

> They say that he was the real inventor of civil education, having taught that nothing is simple and pure *(meden eilikrines einai ton onton pragmaton)*, but that the earth partakes of fire, and fire partakes of water, and wind . . . and so also the beautiful partakes of the ugly, and the just of the unjust *(kalon aischrou kai dikaion adikou)* and, analogically, other things also. (Iamblichus, *Life of Pythagoras*)

It is not pure chance that this example culminates in the categories of beautiful and ugly, justice and injustice. These were the categories most often used by the Sophists when they wanted to illustrate the wonderful properties of *kairos*, which allow (they said) one to assert two opposite *logoi* when speaking of the same thing; namely, to demonstrate the same thing *according to circumstances* such as beautiful and ugly, just and unjust. However, almost to assure us that this remark (as well as the historical interpretation) is true, the author adds the following: "this is the reason why the speech takes one direction or another."

Here, then, is a scientific explanation of the rhetorical doctrine of *duo logoi* and *kairos*, both of which have roots in the theory of contraries (as I had presumed before). Yet this explanation is not presented to us as a more modern process of rhetors unrelated to the school but, rather, as a part of the Pythagorean doctrine itself. This indicates, at the very least, that rhetorical-sophistical development took place within the school; it was the fructification of seeds, planted *ab antico,* that matured at the right time.

To conclude that the passage of Iamblichus is a late fabrication would be arbitrary, even if only considering the preceding positions and the certain attribution of the entire system to the age and milieu of Gorgias. Yet this is not necessary, since there is another document that is quite relevant. In fact, the statements that it contains and even the words themselves are confirmed precisely by a fragment from a tragic poet (who seems to be Euripides or someone not later than he): "For, in discerning, you will see that there is another law for mortals, to wit: nothing is good or evil in every respect, but Kairos took them and made them the same, exchanging the evil and the good."

These verses of the unknown tragedian evidently alluded to a certain theory that included not so much the common (at that time) rhetorical concept of *kairos* as much as its philosophical cause, which can be found in the nature and structure of the universe: no being can be completely beautiful or ugly, and so forth. It is surprising that the many critics who studied this interesting fragment have failed to notice its true meaning, in addition to the allusion to the Pythagorean theory contained in the text of Iamblichus; therefore, they have repeatedly accepted corrections and variations that change its original meaning. With regard to the source that the tragedian had used, I am not concerned with whether it was Gorgias' treatment (in which, especially through Antisthenes, we have seen that *kairos* is explicitly derived from Pythagorism) or an authentic part of Pythagorean philosophy. A gospel, so to speak, of Pythagorean philosophy was familiar to Euripides, as the following fragment demonstrates: "but I, learning this from some wise man . . ." Here a precept is quoted that we find in Iamblichus' text itself.

Nevertheless, the verses of the unknown tragedian are for us something more than a fragment. Since they are uprooted from their original context (as are all fragments), they happen to be adopted and set within the framework of certain sophistic discussions that serve my purposes no less than the verses themselves—they belong to that order of ideas and even to the historical milieu that I am reconstructing. These discussions are known by the title, *Dialexeis* (or *Dissoi Logoi*), and are considered as some of the main documents of Greek Sophistry; anonymous and composed in the Doric language, they include four major chapters ("On Good and Evil," "On the Beautiful and the Ugly," "On the Just and the Unjust," "On Truth and Falsehood"), followed by some passages dealing with various topics, such as wisdom and virtue (as to whether they are teachable), the choosing of magistrates by lot (which is knowledge a rhetor must have), and the importance and exercise of memory.

The history of the *Dialexeis* is a curious issue in modern criticism. First published by Henricus Stephanus (who perhaps drew them from a manuscript by Sextus Empiricus, similar to those in which we find them today) as part of the linguistic and philosophical heritage of the Pythagorean school, they were considered Pythagorean until the last century. Stephanus probably attributed them to such a school, because general opinion—rooted in antiquity—held that such writings could not have been preserved through the Middle Ages, had they not been associated with Pythagorism. However, observing that the content of *Dialexis* bears the genuine stamp of sophistry and reflects the ideas of Protagoras, Gorgias, or Hippias of Elaea, Valckenaer and Bergk in particular removed them completely from the Pythagorean domain, firmly believing that, because of their character, they abhorred Pythagorism. Today this judgment is considered one of the most secure in modern philology; and Stephanus' original attribution is rejected so often that the country of the unknown Sophist is sought (based on very weak clues) in Argolide, Cyprus, or Rhodes, but never in Magna Graecia or Sicily, even though its dialect is identical to that in which the other fragments of Pythagorean literature are written, and there is no other extant example of the literary use of such a dialect outside of Southern Italy. Nevertheless, Bergk and other scholars following him could not assume that the sophistic content was perfectly consistent with its Pythagorean origin. In my opinion, these writings quite suitably form part of a sophistic movement, whose presence within the Pythagorean school (and within the surrounding areas) I have discovered from other documents.

The *Dialexeis*, which (by historical allusions) turn out to be written around 400 B.C., do not, of course, belong to the first and most interesting period of this movement, as do other documents that I have cited; however, they indicate an emphasis on certain issues within the context and culture of the times, which grants them almost a claim of citizenship. The author appears to be a teacher interacting with his disciples, and there are some determinations that we can make with a certain degree of certainty—like the degree of anonymity that surrounded him, which corresponds exactly to my interpretation. First of all, the author is an initiate into the mysteries—*mystas eimi*—who speaks to the uninitiated. It is understood that the issues he discussed did not form part, nor had they ever formed part, of the secret doctrine, which contributed to their rapid diffusion. Another more significant and completely neglected indication is provided by the political ideas of the author who, in a small, special chapter, declares himself an opponent of the democratic system *(ton damagorounton)* of appointing magistrates by means of lots. It seemed to him that one must take into consideration the attitudes and merits of everyone, in order to nominate one individual or another to an office, and that the system of lots, considered by many to be good and in favor of the people *(damotikos)*, is instead quite harmful, because it allows the most incompetent to harm the people by allowing the broad bean to be used in the drawing of lots. Androcides and Anaximandes, both Pythagoreans of the fourth century B.C., interpreted the traditional abstinence from eating beans as a political principle intended to combat democracy. In describing the political struggles in Croton during the fifth century, B.C. against the oligarchical government of the Pythagoreans, Timaeus places the following interpretation of these events into the mouth of a popular leader: "the Pythagoreans resisted the beans as they resisted leaders elected by lot and by the practice of appointing those who chanced into public office." It is also evident that the tendency toward oligarchy and the disapproval of election by lottery are linked together, according to the anonymous text, by the Pythagorean concept of *kairos* and justice, upon which the selection of public officials should depend.

Now it is important to define the position of this author with regard to the issue of contraries—the beautiful and the ugly, good and evil, and so forth. This claim, in fact, is ambiguous and dubious. It seems as if the anonymous author is deeply concerned about reconciling two different positions, which are the same ones whose seed I have found in Pythagorean thought and which, I believe, divided the members and the interpreters of the school. These two trends were completely diffused throughout Hellas, and the anonymous author has nothing to do but to look for a point of equilibrium that is in agreement with the basic principles of Pythagorism. On the one hand, there is the skeptical assertion, according to which good and evil, beautiful and ugly, just and unjust, and so forth, are all the same (and this position is enticing because of its seductive nature, illustrated with the kinds of arguments and illustrations dear to the Sophists); on the other hand, there is the dogmatic thesis, according to which such contraries differ in name as well as in fact, or reality. The conclusion, evoking reservations and clouded by numerous double meanings, is that we cannot say what is good, evil, and so forth; we can only say that they are not identical, and that either one or the other *is*, according to the circumstance of the case (1.17): "I do not say what the good is, but I try to learn this: how the good and the bad are not the same thing, but separate." Although contrasting with the extreme manifestations of Gorgianic skepticism, this conclusion is not really far from the position of one who renounces knowledge of reality, nor does it contradict those principles of reconciliation of contraries (from which Gorgias had begun), of which we find the clearest testimony in this passage from Iamblichus (though attributed to Pythagoras): "having taught that nothing is simple and pure, but that the earth partakes of fire, and fire partakes of water, and wind . . . and so also the beautiful partakes of the ugly, and the just of the unjust and, analogically, other things also . . . this is the reason why the speech takes one direction or another" *(Dialexeis)*.

There was another author with a well-known name, who shared certain Pythagorean beliefs and was close to sharing some of the same principles, namely, Archytas, who (approximately during the same time) also struggles against the theory that "there are two things to say about every matter." It is impossible, due to the fragmented textual evidence, to give a precise account of the intentions and position of this philosopher with regard to the major problem of knowledge and the nature of contraries. Nevertheless I quote him, because, after securing the anonymous *Dialexeis*—which no one believed to be Pythagorean, because of the sophistic content—it is better to consult (on the same theme of *dissoi logoi*) a well-known and rather ancient representative of Pythagorism.

It is indeed true that this fragment (as with most of the manuscripts preserved under the name of Archytas, whose subject is neither music nor mathematics) is now believed to be spurious, though for no reason other than the presumption that a Pythagorean philosopher could not be interested in Sophistic questions. This—it goes without saying—is for me a very convincing reason to believe in its authenticity and to suggest a general reassessment of those judgments of aesthetics which are critical to the legacy of this and other Pythagoreans.

Archytas' work, from which the fragment that interests us is taken, is entitled *Peri tou ontos,* which reminds us of the title of Gorgias' well-known
work, in which he developed the ultimate consequences of his skepticism,
maintaining that things do not exist or, if they do exist, they are unknowable—from which this statement evidently followed: *duo logous einai peri
pantos pragmatos.* Archytas' objection is that the *duo logoi* do not refer to the
same object but, if anything, refer rather to two different sides of the same
object; and he proves this by the example of the Athenians, who can be considered skillful in their use of language and also ungrateful—the two statements being neither equivalent nor contradictory. And so, too, statements regarding the soul and the body of man are not equivalent.

It goes without saying that the rhetorical quality of *kairos* consists precisely in being able to locate, with regard to the same group (Athenians, for
instance), suitable aspects to praise *(auxein)* or blame *(tapeinoun).* Archytas
was in perfect agreement with Gorgias, having been educated in the same
tradition with common technical experiences.

The framework within which I have attempted to reconstruct the rhetoric
and sophistry of Pythagorean origins can now be said to be complete. However, some secondary issues remain to be discussed. One of them is from
Plato, and it seems appropriate to provide a commentary *ab externo* on the
Dialexeis as well as on Archytas' fragment. In the *Euthydemus* there are two
young brothers, Euthedymus and Dionysodorus, who are portrayed as typical representatives of sophistry and, in particular, as arrogant supporters of
duo logoi. Plato reminds us that they come from Thurii, a place from which
they had to escape.

Is it possible to believe that this is a simple coincidence? And, perhaps,
does this not refer to one of those political upheavals, of which Pythagoreans
were often victims and participants—not only in other cities of Magna Graecia, but also in Thurii (which had only recently been founded) during the second half of the fifth century, B.C.? Other evidence is provided by comedy of
the middle and later periods that, when representing on stage the typical Pythagorean perspectives, attributed to Pythagoras the cult of eloquence
(among other qualities). A fragment from *Tarantini* of Cratinus (who may
not be the well-known predecessor of Aristophanes, but someone of the
same name who was much younger) contains a humorous description of the
Pythagoreans from Tarentum and their eagerness for disputation and rhetorical artifices, with which they ensnared poor strangers: "Their custom is,
when they catch somebody coming their way, to utilize the power of words,
to confuse him and mix him up oh so cleverly, with antitheses, definitions,
evenly balanced sentences, fallacies and boasts."

This display of eloquence focused, of course, on ethical issues, for purposes of propaganda in order to attract newcomers to Pythagorean ideas. This reminds us of what happened to a young envoy of Dionysius the Younger, namely, Poliarchus (called *"Hedypathes"*), who held strategic discussions with Archytas. On that occasion, the latter gave a well-known oration on the subject of pleasure, one that was orally transmitted for several centuries within the Pythagorean circles of the city and was known to Cicero. Moreover, he illustrates (following the fragments of Cratinus) that Pythagorean eloquence conformed to the technical methods, of which Gorgias was the most renowned practitioner. By the time that Cratinus (particularly if it was Cratinus the Younger) described these methods, the Pythagoreans may have become associated with them through Gorgias. But, perhaps, were not those methods partially derived from the original school?

. . . .

Epilogue

The results of my investigation raise, of course, a question. Why was the rhetorical-sophistical movement that I have reconstructed unknown or disregarded throughout the ancient historical tradition? Why, when they studied the origins of Rhetoric, did not the ancient writers of treatises emphasize more the work of the Pythagoreans?

First, the ancient writers depended generally upon Aristotle, who had a one-sided view of rhetoric quite different from those of Gorgias and Pythagoras. Certainly, they focused their attention on legal eloquence, which they believed was invented by the Sicilians Corax and Tisias and was based on criteria more rational than esthetic. In contrast, Pythagorean eloquence was exclusively epideictic. From all the documents that I have examined, it seems to me that this was so; and this is explicitly stated in a passage from Iamblichus, which has been unaccounted for until now. According to this passage, the Pythagoreans created and disseminated throughout Greece, along with other techniques, "the arts of rhetoric and of public oratory" *(tas technas tas retorikas kai tous logous epideiktikous)*. This eloquence is not based (as Aristotle desired) on *rational* elements, but rather on the *irrational* principles of spellbinding and hypnotic suggestion *(psychagogia)*. It does not consist so much of syllogisms and proofs as of images and feelings. It is not *eloquence* in a specific sense, but in a general expression—namely, *art*. Its most significant representative is Gorgias, who treats rhetoric not as a science but as the domain of opinion, placing it together with music and poetry.

Pythagorean rhetoric, then, must be relegated to obscurity by anyone interested in a different kind of eloquence. And yet, a tradition survived (that many could not explain) that considered Pythagoras the inventor of this art, instead of Corax and Tisias. One scholar attempted to find a compromise among the varying traditions, turning Pythagoras into the teacher of Tisias. Another scholar, pursuing the same line of thought, ascribed to him the composition of *technai;* moreover, he gave the orations named by him (which I have just examined) the arrangement and title of *Kopides,* as if they were similar to the collection of models that the first Sicilian rhetors gave to their clients (*kopides* being a type of knife or weapon), offering a means to protect themselves or to attack when threatened. The fact is that, in a catalogue of Hellenic sources, a work ascribed to Pythagoras begins, *Me anaideu medeni.* These few words, which do not seem to have been correctly understood by scholars, are most valuable to me, since, in the brief turn of a sentence, they coincide with the fundamental concept in the first oration of Pythagoras to the ephebes, which tells them to banish all forms of insolence from their souls and their actions to everyone, especially older people, and to stand out, not by means of impudence, but by wisdom *(ouk ex anaideias, all' ek paideias).*

Notes

This excerpt features Augusto Rostagni's historical analysis of the contributions to rhetorical thought of Gorgias, Pythagoras, and Antisthenes, which appeared originally in "Un nuovo Capitolo nella Storia della Retorica e della Sofistica," in *Studi Italiani di filologia classica,* N.S., vol. 2 (1922): 1–2. The complete translation is forthcoming in *Kairos in Translation: Twentieth-Century Essays on the Temporal Dimensions of Discourse,* ed. Joseph J. Hughes, James S. Baumlin, and Phillip Sipiora (New York: The Edwin Mellen Press). I would like to thank Dr. Hughes for his translation of the Greek texts and Dr. Tarelli for his review of the Italian text. Rostagni's text poses a particular difficulty, in that he draws his classical citations from nineteenth-century (and earlier) editions; where possible, this current translation follows the standard modern editions of classical texts. Rostagni also makes reference to the classical scholarship of Lodewijk Kasper Valckenaer (1715–1785), Theodor Bergk (1812–1881), Max Pohlenz (1872–1962), and Wilhelm Süss (b. 1882), though typically without titles or page citations. The secondary works that can be identified (including Rostagni's own previous essay, from which he quotes) are listed below.

Works Cited

Primary Texts

Anon. *Dialexeis,* or *Dissoi Logoi.*
Antisthenes. *On Speech.*

Aristotle. *Metaphysics. Nicomachean Ethics. Poetics.*
Dionysius of Halicarnassus. *On the Composition of Words.*
Gorgias. *Helen.*
Iamblichus. *Life of Pythagoras.*
Isocrates. *Against the Sophists.*
Plato. *Gorgias. Phaedrus. Hippias Minor.*
Nicomachus. *Arithmetica.*

Secondary Works

Pohlenz, Max. "*To Prepon:* Ein Beitrag zur Geschichte des griechischen Geistes." *Nachrichten von der Gesellschaft der Wissenschaften zu Goettingen, Philologisch-historische Klasse, Heft* 1 (1933): 53–92. Reprint, *Kleine Schrifen.* Ed. Heinrich Dorrie, 2:100–39. Hildesheim: G. Olms, 1965.

Rostagni, Augusto. "Pythagoras and Pythagoreans in *Timaeus.*" *Atti della Reale Accademia delle Scienze di Torino* 49 (1913–1914): 556–59.

Süss, Wilhelm. *Ethos: Studien zur Älteren griecheschen Rhetorik.* Leipzig: Teubner, 1910.

Time and Qualitative Time

JOHN E. SMITH

In a previous study ("Time, Times and the 'Right Time'"), I explored the distinction between these two aspects of time and their relations to each other. I wish to return to this topic, building on my previous discussion but bringing in some new dimensions that were unknown to me earlier on. I did not know, for example, that *kairos,* although it has metaphysical, historical, ethical, and esthetic applications, is a concept whose original home, so to speak, was in the ancient *rhetorical* traditions. A recent study (Kinnneavy, "*Kairos:* A Neglected Concept") is aimed at recovering this important idea in the present situation. It is not insignificant that, while *kairos* has important philosophical implications, students of rhetoric have not been alone in neglecting it, as can be seen from the fact that it is not listed in the four volume *Dictionary of the History of Ideas* (ed. Philip Wiener), nor is it to be found in *The Great Ideas: A Synopticon* (ed. Mortimer Adler). One reason for the omission is no doubt the absence of any cognate word in English for *kairos,* whereas its partner, *chronos,* appears in a host of forms throughout any English dictionary. The only exception that occurs to me is the quite rare word "kairotic," which is listed only in the most complete dictionaries. The loss of the concept of *kairos* is doubly unfortunate for, on the one hand, the idea has been of enormous significance in the past, figuring essentially, for instance, in the religious traditions of the West; and, on the other hand, it expresses a most important feature of temporal process which, despite exceptions here and there, is not expressed in the concept of *chronos.* It is with these facts in mind that I am attempting to rehabilitate, as it were, the *kairos* aspect of time and to show its philosophical importance.

It is best to begin with a basic statement intended to make clear the essential difference in meaning between *chronos* and *kairos.* Such a statement can be derived from what I presume is a well-known passage in the biblical book of *Ecclesiastes;* it runs as follows:

For everything there is a season, and a time for every purpose under heaven: a time to be born and a time to die; a time to plant and a time to pluck up that which is planted; a time to kill and a time to heal . . . a time to weep and a time to laugh. . . . (3:1 ff.)

Thanks to the translators of the *Septuagint* (the Greek version of the Old Testament or Jewish Bible), we know that all the English expressions "a time to" are translations of the term *kairos,* the right or opportune time to do something often called "right timing." This aspect of time is to be distinguished from *chronos,* which means the uniform time of the cosmic system, the time which, in Newton's phrase, *aequabiliter fluit.* In *chronos* we have the fundamental conception of time as measure, the *quantity* of duration, the length of periodicity, the age of an object or artifact, and the rate of acceleration of bodies, whether on the surface of the earth or in the firmament beyond. The questions relevant to this aspect of time are: "How fast?" "How frequent?" "How old?" and the answers to these questions can be given in cardinal numbers or, as it may be, in terms of limits that approach these numbers. By contrast, the term *kairos* points to a *qualitative* character of time, to the special position an event or action occupies in a series, to a season when something appropriately happens that cannot happen just at "any time," but only at *that* time, to a time that marks an opportunity which may not recur. The question especially relevant to *kairos* is "When?" "At what time?" Hence, *kairos,* or the "right time," as the term is often translated, involves ordinality or the conception of a special temporal position, such that what happens or might happen at "that time" and its significance are wholly dependent on an ordinal place in the sequences and intersections of events. It is for this reason, as we shall see, that *kairos* is peculiarly relevant to the interpretation of historical events, because it points to their significance and purpose and to the idea that there are constellations of events pregnant with a possibility (or possibilities) not to be met with at other times and under different circumstances.

There is a second and coordinate meaning attached to *kairos* that is not expressed in the illustration previously cited, although it is of equal importance. *Kairos* means also the "right measure" or proportion as expressed, in the saying of Hesiod, "Observe due measure, and proportion *(kairos)* is best in all things." The same idea is found in the maxims attributed to the Greek Sages, such as "Nothing in excess." It is important to notice at this point that the understanding of *kairos* within the scope of rhetoric primarily tended toward an emphasis, if not overemphasis, on human action, since rhetoric is an art or skill concerned with communication and persuasion. This emphasis, however, must not be allowed to overshadow the ontological dimension of *kairos* as manifest in various orders of happening, such as constellations of historical events, natural processes, and developments which have their own temporal frames and opportune times quite apart from human action, especially the action of this or that individual. Thus, for example, the vintner will be concerned with the "right time" to harvest the grapes, but, while not meaning to minimize the art and ingenuity of the vintner, the fact remains that this time will be largely a function of conditions—soil, temperature, moisture—ingredient in the growing process itself, to say nothing of the organic structure of the grapes and the time required for their maturation. In short *kairos* is not to be understood solely in the practical terms that are uppermost when the primary concern is rhetorical and the problem is to find the most appropriate discourse for the circumstances of time, place, the speaker, and the audience. It is interesting to note that, while the watchword of pre-Socratic ethics was "Know the opportunity" in the context of human action, the Pythagoreans regarded *kairos* as "one of the laws of the universe." This cosmological dimension of *kairos* must not be lost, as indeed it could be if it were supposed that the *chronos* aspect of time is physical and metaphysical in import, while *kairos* is mainly anthropological or practical. This neat division will not do; both aspects of time are ingredient in the nature of things and both have practical import.

It is, of course, true that there will always be a subject-situation correlation where *kairos* is concerned, since someone will have to know or believe that he knows the right "when," but this insight does not create that "when" out of itself. That time belongs to the ontological structure of the order of happening. Against this background, let us consider more closely the features of time denoted by *chronos* and *kairos* with special attention to the metaphysical and historical dimensions of reality and our experience of the world and ourselves. In addition, we must attempt to relate the two features to each other, so that we shall not find ourselves left with, so to speak, two times—a sort of two-timing—in separate compartments. To deal with this problem I shall suggest that *kairos* presupposes *chronos,* which is thus a necessary condition underlying qualitative times, but that, by itself, the *chronos* aspect does not suffice for understanding either specifically historical interpretations or those processes of nature and human experience where the *chronos* aspect reaches certain *critical points* at which a qualitative character begins to emerge, and when there are junctures of opportunity calling for human ingenuity in apprehending when the time is "right."

As regards *chronos,* we find in Aristotle the classic expression of the concept of time as measure. In *Physics* (4.11.219b) he defined *chronos* as the "number of motion with respect to the before and the after," with, of course, the understanding that "before" and "after" are not to be understood in a *spatial* sense.[1]

This definition combines the three essential features of *chronos—change*, a unit of *measure*, and a *serial order* that is asymmetrical. There is, first, the element of change, motion, process, of something going on which lasts through or requires a stretch of time. Time, it appears, is not identical with the movement, but cannot be thought apart from the movement. Second, an appropriate unit of measure must be given, so that the elapsed time and the quantity of the movement can be measured or numbered. Third, there is the element of serial order or direction expressed in the terms "before" and "after."

Time, so conceived, furnishes an essential grid upon which the processes of nature and of the historical order can be plotted and to that extent understood. Time as *chronos*, however, allows no features of events other than those previously indicated to be taken into account. Nevertheless these features enable us to establish a chronology both for what is sometimes called "natural history" or a reconstruction of geological, zoological, and so forth, ages or eras, and the history we associate with human development involving social, cultural, and political dimensions. This chronology is necessary in both cases, even if it is abstract in the sense that the concreteness of the content thus ordered is subordinated to the basic temporal organization. Still that remains indispensable, as can readily be seen in the case of evolutionary development and also in the case of human history where, despite the complexity and self-conscious character of the content, it is necessary to have a basic chronology, making possible the delineation of distinct persons, events and movements. In the evolutionary process, or perhaps we should say, in charting that development, it is essential that some basic dating pattern be established, such as was provided by the fossil record, astonishingly complete in some cases as, for example, the development of the horse known to us *(equus)* from its diminutive ancestor *(eohippus)* from the dim recesses of the past. There everything depended upon determining the true order of events, the kind of development that took place in each period and the length of time involved.[2] In the case of human history, chronicles are the indispensable storehouse of material for the writing of history proper in providing for the dating of events and the identification of persons, governments, wars, religious movements, migrations, and indeed all the stuff of historical reality. Historical persons live and die, governments rise and fall, religious movements wax and wane, but in each case temporal boundaries must be determined which mark off the life or career of identifiable men and movements, climates of opinion and social customs. We may wonder how accurate it is to say that, for example, the medieval world came to an end abruptly and was thus discontinuous with the modern world that took its place. Was it simply a matter of moving from the nonscientific world of religious authority to the age of science and the mathematico-physical explanations of ourselves and the world? These questions and others similar cannot be answered on the basis of the *chronos* aspect of time alone, but it is necessary to have some accepted chronology in which relevant historical constituents—thinkers, manuscripts, ecclesiastical pronouncements, scientific discoveries—can be dated. The discovery, for example, of the scientific work that was being done in the medical faculty of the University of Padua before the "end" of the Middle Ages has done much to force a change in our interpretation of the transition. Without precise dating of events and some conception of their temporal boundaries, such reinterpretation could not take place.

Although the *chronos* aspect of time is abstract in the sense of being universal, as compared with the here and now concreteness of *kairos*, the elements of *chronos* are essential to the subject matter and are not to be seen as defining a merely empty or external network. Process, the ubiquity of becoming, stretches over the entire physical and organic world. We are by now well aware that nothing happens at an instant. This fact directs attention to the functioning of things which, in turn, involves tendency and directionality. Qualities, objects, phases of a process, states of affairs are correlated with the length or measure of time required for them to take place, so that in a time less than the minimal necessary time the phenomenon in question does not occur. The flower now in the vase as something that has become—a determinate outcome—is a unified whole; in the process of its becoming, however, there was a time when it was not yet, which is to say that the time span chosen was less than the minimal time required. The serial order of before and after constitutes the continuity of becoming, which in turn leads to a definite outcome. It is highly significant that Georg Hegel and Alfred North Whitehead, different as their philosophies may be, are at one in seeing the need for a determinate result—Whitehead with the principle of limitation and Hegel with the idea that, unless something *has become*, we should have nothing more than sheer becoming.

The ingredience of the elements of *chronos* are even more perspicuous in the historical order. One of the legacies of the nineteenth century was the conception of history as a dynamic continuum of events marked by novelty and creativity, in contrast to the understanding of history in the previous century especially, as the succession of "ages," which were largely static in themselves, like a series of tableaux in a museum. As regards the relevance of the length or measure of time both for historical development and for the interpreted record, illustrations abound and the point is almost too obvious to mention. It takes time to found a university, to establish a political party, to develop a religious tradition, to make a reputation. Those who, either through vanity or impatience, forget this fact will prove to be the victims of history and not its makers. From the standpoint of assessment and interpretation, the lastingness of an institution, a movement, a pattern of thought will often be an important index of the value to be assigned to it in the historical record. And, conversely, the transience or evanescence of a phenomenon may be a signal of its insignificance. The date and duration of the persons, events and movements in history, together with the determination of their "before" and "after," underlie all historical interpretation. Since the proper sequence of events is bound up with the problem of historical decision and causation, it is essential to determine what events were contemporaneous with each other, what events partially overlapped in an extended present, and what events were separated by an identifiable lapse of time. It is essential for determining and understanding "what really happened" to be able to ascertain whether, for example, an alleged assassin was or was not informed *before* the meeting of the convention where the intended victim would be seated on the platform. This feature of *chronos* is essential for historical knowledge, even if it is not sufficient.

Before turning to a closer examination of the elements included in the *kairos* aspect of time, it will be helpful to build at least one bridge between the two by going back to the example of the vintner noted earlier on. There is the sort of process which, even considered primarily from the standpoint of *chronos*, approaches the qualitative character expressed by *kairos*. The aging of wine—and I am sure that there are many similar processes of maturation—furnishes an excellent example of an organic process in which time takes on a qualitative character. According to the chemistry of wine making, virtually any wine, once it has been constituted, can be consumed while it is "young" but there is, for great wines, a time of maturity—this may involve decades—when the development reaches its peak. It is at *this* time that the wine will be at its best. There is a critical or "right time" for the vintage and prior to this critical point is "too soon" and after it has passed is "too late." The quality possessed by the wine at its peak is obviously not unrelated to time in the sense of *chronos*, but it is not all that is involved, since the *qualitative* feature of the process itself must be taken into account, that is, what happens to the wine in that time and *when* is the critical time when a certain special quality has been reached. That is the "right time," and it is of a piece with those situations that Hegel described in his concept of the "transition from quantity to quality," where the temporal aspect of the development sets the critical time apart from "any time" or the utter indifference of the temporal units in measurement to the qualitative character of the outcome. A parallel point can be made in connection with history. As J. H. Randall has pointed out, history does not designate the mere occurrence of events in sequence but is concerned with their significance. "Our name," he writes, or the record of such occurrences is a "chronicle." If the New York Times had been published from the first day of creation, we should have a most valuable "chronicle" of human history. But without further appraisal of what had been significant, we should have still no "history." (31)

The important point is that the determination of that significance will involve recourse to all the *kairoi* or turning points in the historical order, the opportunities presented, the opportunities seized upon and the opportunities missed, the qualitative changes and transitions in the lives of individuals and nations and those constellations of events which made possible some outcome that could not have happened at any other time.

Turning now to the features of *kairos* time, it is important to note three distinct but related concepts. There is, first, the idea of the "right time" for something to happen in contrast to "any time," a sense that is captured nicely in the word "timing," as when we say, "The Governor's timing was poor; he released the story to the press *too soon* and thus lost the advantage of surprising his political opponents." Second, *kairos* means a time of tension and conflict, a time of crisis implying that the course of events poses a problem that calls for a decision at that time, which is to say that no generalized solution or response supposedly valid at any or every time will suffice. Third, *kairos* means that the problem or crisis has brought with it a time of opportunity *(kairos* is translated by the Latin *opportunitas)* for accomplishing some purpose which could not be carried out at some other time. Implicit in all three meanings embraced by *kairos* is the concept of an *individual* time having a critical ordinal position set apart from its predecessors and successors.

Earlier on it was said that the natural habitat of the concept of *kairos* was originally in the traditions of classical rhetoric; the best example of its use there can be seen in Plato's *Phaedrus* following Socrates's account of an ideal rhetoric. Since the passage contains most of the ingredients of *kairos,* I shall present it in full, but with the proviso that the main emphasis falls on human action and skill in the practice of an art. In short, the emphasis is more practical than metaphysical, but, nevertheless, the essential notions are there and they can be applied to other dimensions of reality.

Since it is in fact the function of speech to influence souls, a man who is going to be a speaker must know how many kinds of souls there are. Let us, then, state that they are of this or that sort, so that individuals also will be of this or that type. Again, the distinctions that apply here apply as well in the cases of speeches: they are of this or that number in type, and each type of one particular sort. So men of a special sort under the influence of speeches of a particular kind are readily persuaded to take action of a definite sort because of the qualitative correlation that obtains between speech and soul; while men of a different sort are hard to persuade because, in their case, this qualitative correlation does not obtain. Very well. When a student has attained an adequate grasp of these facts intellectually, he must next go on to see with his own eyes that they occur in the world of affairs and are operative in practice; he must acquire the capacity to confirm their existence through the sharp use of his senses. If he does not do this, no part of the theoretical knowledge he acquired as a student is as yet of any help to him. But it is only when he has the capacity to declare to himself with complete perception, in the presence of another, that here is the man and here the nature that was discussed theoretically at school—here, now present to him in actuality—to which he must apply *this* kind of speech in *this* sort of manner in order to obtain persuasion for *this* kind of activity—it is when he can do all this and when he has, in addition, grasped the concept of propriety of time *[kairos]*—when to speak and when to hold his tongue *[eukairos* and *akairos]*, when to use brachylogy, piteous language, hyperbole for horrific effect, and, in a word, each of the specific devices of discourse he may have studied—it is only then, and not until then, that the finishing and perfecting touches have been given to his science. (*Phaedrus,* 271–72b)

The passage, I believe, speaks for itself, but there are two points deserving of special notice. First, there is the confrontation in actuality; the speaker must speak to *that* other person and no other, and he is to apply *this* sort of manner in order to succeed in persuasion for *this* kind of activity. There is an undeniable particularity about the situation, which requires that the person identify in fact and *at the time* the sort of man he had studied theoretically at school. Second, the entire situation is encompassed by *kairos*—here translated as "propriety of time"—which means knowing *when* to speak, *when* to be silent, and *when* to use the specific devices of discourse contained in the science of rhetoric. One is reminded here of William James's comment about the encyclopedia in the book case in his office. Here is all knowledge and truth, he said, but the question is *when* do I utter these truths? No one goes about uttering true propositions stretching from "Aardvark" to "Zygote"; on the contrary, we cite this information only *when* it is needed or relevant. It is this aspect of *kairos* that Paul Tillich emphasized in a number of writings aimed at recovering the basic idea. Consequently, he contrasted *kairos* with *logos* where the latter represents truth that is regarded as universal in import and the former the special occasion in the course of events when such truth must be brought to bear by an individual somewhere and somewhen.

There are two further illustrations of the concept of *kairos* in Plato's writings. One is to be found in the *Seventh Letter* (324b) and the other in the fourth book of the *Laws.* The first of these might be regarded as an application of the theory of rhetoric set forth in *Phaedrus,* while the second is specifically ontological in import. In the *Letter,* Plato is responding to a request from the followers of Dion for his support. These followers claim a loyalty to Dion's principles and argue that on that account Plato should lend his support. He then proposes to tell what Dion's policy was and how it originated. The narrative might indeed be told at *any* time, but Plato regards his telling of it at that particular time—"the present moment"—as a seizing of a time which is "opportune." This moment is "right" because it serves the special purpose of laying down a criterion in terms of which Plato will make his own decision and, at the same time, provide Dion's successors with a touchstone for assessing their own views.

In the fourth book of the *Laws* (709b ff.), Plato discusses the different factors that govern human life in connection with the question whether laws are explicitly and designedly made by man or whether external factors are involved. He declares, "Chance *[tyche]* and occasion *[kairos]* cooperate with God in the control of all human affairs." These two mundane factors are said to condition human action and also to be in harmony with each other. Whatever may be the source of that harmony, it is noteworthy that Plato is here contrasting the time expressed by *kairos* with the notion of chance. What happens by "chance" is said to be opaque to human understanding; chance is a coming together of events that, for all we can understand or determine, could have happened at "any time." Occasion, on the contrary, points to a right or favorable time which makes possible what, under different circumstances, could not come to pass. Occasions are times which must be apprehended as such through historical insight; they are, moreover, times for historical decision and action. What comes by "chance" takes place without our having any sense that the events "conspired" to bring about the result. We often express our failure to grasp any pattern in the chance occurrence by saying that the event "just happened to take place that way." The important point here is that the time of *kairos* is seen as an ontological element in the basic structure of things and, while that time calls for a human response, the occasion itself is not of human devising. I stress the point in order to counteract the idea that, as might appear from the context of rhetoric, *kairos* represents no more than a human standpoint. That interpretation is ruled out because of the clearly metaphysical context of the statements in question.

The concept of *kairos,* as I indicated at the outset, not only has had a prominent place in philosophical thinking across the centuries, a fact to be explained in part by the neglect of the idea itself, but also by the tendency among those thinkers who were concerned for the philosophy of history to place a basic emphasis on the *chronos* features of time and to model their thinking after the patterns of natural process. The ancient paradigm of this way of thinking is found in the *History* of Thucydides, where he claims that his work is a creation "forever": because of the cyclical image of time presupposed throughout the book; the events will recur. This image was clearly drawn from the repetitions and recurrences of natural processes, the procession of the seasons, the phases of the moon, and other cycles in nature. It is important to notice, however, that the idea of history fundamental to the

Western religious traditions runs exactly counter to these cyclical views. For both Judaism and Christianity, history has a decidedly linear character, a scene of dramatic unfolding of events, a medium for the disclosure of the Divine. Time is neither a circle ever returning to itself, nor primarily an order of perishing, but a dynamic continuum of events punctuated by turning points and crises that concern the destinies of men and nations. In this sense, history was regarded as having a being of its own to be grasped and interpreted in terms appropriate to itself and not after the image of nature. Paul Tillich was the one thinker in this century to attempt the recovery of the idea of *kairos* which, for him, is the foundation of historical consciousness aware of itself. "Time," he writes,

> is an empty form only for abstract, objective reflection, a form that can receive any kind of content; but to him who is conscious of an ongoing creative life it is laden with tensions, with possibilities and impossibilities. Not everything is possible at every time, not everything is true at every time, nor is everything demanded at every moment. . . . In this tremendous, most profoundly stirred consciousness of history is rooted the idea of the *kairos*. (33)

Here the time of *kairos* is seen as a summons to the attainment of historical consciousness as such, for, as Tillich points out, outlooks unaware of history have been more the rule than the exception and they have had deep roots of a metaphysical kind. If the primary focus of attention is on what is beyond time—the eternal—there can be no change and no history. Conversely, if all time is bound up with the world of nature and the eternally recurrent, history is once again lost, having been engulfed by something other than itself. Tillich's proposal is that a new awareness of the time of crisis and opportunity is the key to the recovery of history as the meaningful development of what matters most in human life. The underlying religious meaning of *kairos* is found, for the Judaic tradition, in the critical times of religious history, when the mundane temporal order intersected with the sacred order in the form of a disclosure of the divine will. From Moses to the last of the great prophetic figures there was a series of "presents" or special times when the voice of the sacred stood in judgment on secular affairs. These times were opportunities for transformation and reformation, a return from waywardness to truth and righteousness. In Christianity, *kairos* was focused on the central event of Christ, who is said in the biblical writings to have come *en kairo*, sometimes translated as "the fullness of time"—implying a culmination in a temporal development marked by the manifestation of God in an actual historical order. Tillich proposed to generalize this concept to apply to the interpretation of history, in which the dynamic is found in those individuals and movements that seek to identify the opportunity in some crucial juncture of history and to seize it in the form of transformatory action undertaken in the name of an ideal. That this basic idea has applications beyond the dimension of the religious in the proper sense can be seen in Hegel's epoch of perfect self-consciousness, Karl Marx's idea of the classless society, and Auguste Comte's final stage of science or the positive philosophy. Tillich calls these *kairoi* in the absolute sense, since they serve as the ideal or objective goal that is to determine the purposeful response to all the occasions upon which an opportunity to foster the ideal is presented or perceived as existing in some present constellation of events. *Kairos* is thus ingredient not only in the interpretation of history but in, we may say, "history in the making" as well. According to the doctrine of *kairos,* there is no logical, physical, or economic necessity in the historical process, because it is seen as moving through a unity of freedom and fate which distinguishes history from the natural order.

The reach and relevance of the *kairos* features of time can be seen in the many dimensions of experience. The presence of these features in the rhetorical, historical, religious, and ontological orders has already been noted; there are others as well. In the ethical domain *kairos* appears as *justice* or the proper measure according to merit or what is "due" to an individual in an order of equality. In the order of knowing, *kairos* signals the need to bring universal ideas and principles to bear in historical time and situations and, thus, calls for decisions about values, means, and ends that cannot be a matter of law alone but require wisdom and critical judgment. In the domain of art, *kairos* is the right measure or proportion directed by the aim of creating a unified, individual work expressive of esthetic value. And this is not all. *Kairos* manifests itself in the therapeutic crises of Freudian psychology and the determination of the "right time" for certain disclosures and confrontations of patients with themselves; in education, where some sense of timing is required in estimating the progress and maturity of the individual student, how much he or she can profitably deal with at a given stage of development, and, most recently, in current literary theory, where the "near autonomy" of the text is being challenged by insisting on the individuality of the reader's response in interpretation.

The last instance presents an occasion—a *kairos*—for closing with some critical remarks concerning the limitations and liabilities involved in the conception of *kairos.* Too much attention to the singularity of the temporal occasion can have the effect of obscuring enduring principles and truths. Some classical scholars, for instance, have suggested that Plato's emphasis on the timelessness of the forms was an attempt to counteract the incipient relativism of the rhetorician bent on nothing more than the adaptation of discourse to the particular circumstances of time, place, speaker, and audience. Something of this problem is posed by so-called situational ethics, where the particularity of the situation overcomes the generality of principle, so that the gap between the two becomes unbridgeable. Much as I admire the thought of William James, I cannot overlook his near obsession with the problem of what general features a philosophical position must embody in order to get itself believed. There are times when it appears that the question whether a given view is true or defensible is entirely overshadowed by the concern that it be presented in a way that will awaken an interest and enlist the allegiance of the listener. Despite these and other dangers surrounding the engaged response to the particular time and circumstance at hand, the important features of life and experience comprehended by the notion of *kairos* far outweigh the disadvantages; without the reality of qualitative times, life would be dull and drab indeed. We would be left with the tyranny known to us all— that of merely being on time.

Notes

1. I shall not enter into a discussion of the possible circularity in the definition. Suffice it to say that the terms he used—*hysteron* and *proteron*—were generally regarded as *temporal* in connotation.

2. The length of time and the nature of the development that took place are essentially related. For example, an important juncture in the evolutionary pattern of the horse was the transition from *browsing* to *grazing*. Since the bulk of fossil remains is in the form of teeth, the fact that the silicon content of the grasses is far higher than that of shrubs and small trees meant that in grazing teeth would be ground down in a shorter time than in the browsing stage. It was thus possible to date the time of transition.

Works Cited

Kinneavy, James L. "*Kairos:* A Neglected Concept in Classical Rhetoric." In *Rhetoric and Praxis: The Contribution of Classical Rhetoric to Practical Reasoning.* Ed. Jean Dietz Moss, 79–105. Washington, DC: The Catholic University of America Press, 1986.

Plato. *Phaedrus.* Trans. Harold North Fowler. Cambridge, MA: Harvard University Press, 1914.

———. *Laws.* Trans. A. E. Taylor. London: Dent, 1960.

Randall, H. Jr. *Nature and Historical Experience.* New York: 1958.

Smith, John E. "Time, Times and the 'Right Time': *Chronos* and *Kairos*." *The Monist* 53 (1969): 1–13.

Tillich, Paul. *The Protestant Era.* Chicago: University of Chicago Press, 1957.

Kairos *in Classical and Modern Rhetorical Theory*

JAMES L. KINNEAVY

The concept of *kairos* was a dominant issue in classical Greek rhetoric and literature, although the term does not appear in many current reference books. *Kairos* is not listed in the first edition of Richard Lanham's *Handlist of Rhetorical Terms*, nor in the four volumes of the *Dictionary of the History of Ideas*, nor in the two volumes of Mortimer Adler's *Great Ideas: A Syntopicon,* which accompanies the *Great Books of the Western World* series.[1] In spite of this neglect, a strong case can be made for the thesis that *kairos* is a dominating concept in sophistic, Isocratean, Platonic, Aristotelian and, in a sense, even in Ciceronian rhetoric (for a discussion of Isocratean uses, see Sipiora; for Roman uses, see Enos). Later in this essay I will provide an extended definition of *kairos*, but provisionally it might be defined as the right or opportune time to do something, or right measure in doing something. Often the two notions are joined; thus, the righteous anger justified in a war situation would be excessive and improper in a family dispute: the *kairos* would not be right. Before expanding and clarifying this definition, it might be worthwhile to give a brief sketch of the history of the notion and an explanation for its neglect by many rhetoricians, both historical and contemporary.

Although the word does not occur in Homer, it already occurs in Hesiod (seventh century B.C.), whose statement became a proverb, "Observe due measure, and proportion *[kairos]* is best in all things" (Liddell and Scott, 859). It is a critical concept in the poetry of Pindar (fifth century B.C.), where the meaning of due or proper measure is given more emphasis than it had been in either Hesiod or Theognis (see Levi for an extensive treatment of *kairos* in classical Greek literary figures, including Pindar). The notion of *kairos* was embodied in several of the maxims attributed to the Seven Sages of Greece, particularly "Nothing in excess" and "Seal your word with silence and your silence with the right time," both of which were sometimes specifically linked with Solon (Levi, "Kairos," 274). It seems clear that with the influence of He-siod, Pindar, and some of the sayings of the Seven Sages, the concept of *kai-ros* had become a part of the educational ideals of early Greece. As Doro Levi says, "To the Socratic 'Know thyself,' the pre-Socratic ethic juxtaposed its own 'Know the opportunity,' *kairon gnothi*" ("Kairos," 275).

The pre-Socratic prominence of *kairos* in Greek thought can particularly be seen in the Pythagorean school. Rostagni has analyzed this aspect of Py-thagorean thought more than anyone else. He states that to Pythagoreans this maxim was inscribed, "The most important thing in every action is *"kai-ros.*"[2] Mario Untersteiner states this in another way: for the Pythagoreans, *kairos* was "one of the laws of the universe" (110). Pythagoras and his school gave further complexity to the concept of *kairos,* linking it closely with jus-tice, and consequently with civic education. Indeed, several of the Pythagore-ans made the mastery of *kairos* to be the essence of philosophy (Untersteiner, 82). Others considered it a faculty equal in importance with the soul and the intellect (Levi, "Kairos," 275).

The Sophists Prodicus, Antiphon, Hippias, and probably also Protagoras used the concept of *kairos* in their philosophical and rhetorical systems. But, as Untersteiner has thoroughly demonstrated, it was Gorgias who made *kai-ros* the cornerstone of his entire epistemology, ethics, aesthetics, and rhetoric. Gorgias and some of the other Sophists carried the implications of the rela-tivism of different situations to such lengths that Plato countered with the stability and permanence of his world of ideas. Yet even Plato did not dis-pense with *kairos,* particularly in rhetoric. And Plato also used *kairos* as the foundation on which to construct his theory of virtue as a mean between two extremes, a theory developed still further by Aristotle.

Some Stoic philosophers used the notion in discussing the ethics of sui-cide, cannibalism, and other actions under certain circumstances (Long, 206). But in Stoicism, particularly Latin Stoicism, the concept of *kairos* merged with that of *prepon* (propriety or fitness), as Max Pohlenz has shown in his admirable study of this latter concept. In this guise, *kairos* is the domi-nating concept in both Cicero's ethics and his rhetoric. Consequently, it is not inaccurate to say that *kairos,* with the related concept of *prepon,* was a major issue in much of classical rhetoric in antiquity, particularly with the Pythagoreans, the Sophists, Plato, and Cicero.

Three Italian scholars in this century are mainly responsible for the recog-nition that *kairos* played an important role in Greek rhetoric and thought generally.[3] In 1922 Augusto Rostagni traced the history of *kairos* and demon-strated the dominating influence of the Pythagorean school, especially on Gorgias and Plato. In 1922 and 1923, Doro Levi published two articles on *kai-ros,* one specifically on the importance of the concept in Plato's philosophy. In

1948 Mario Untersteiner published his innovative and controversial study, *The Sophists,* which analyzed in great detail the influence of *kairos* in Sophistic thought, especially Gorgias. A more recent voice that has called the attention of the twentieth century to *kairos* has been that of the German theologian Paul Tillich, who made the concept of *kairos,* as it is presented in the New Testament, one of the foundational ideas of his entire theology. His works include at least five major statements on *kairos.*[4]

This brief historical survey has already suggested that *kairos* is a complex concept, not easily reduced to a simple formula. I would like now to analyze the various factors of the concept, considering in sequence the two fundamental elements embodied in five major areas in which the concept was relevant. In this analysis, I am following the findings of Rostagni, Levi, Untersteiner, and Tillich, although I have some qualifications about the last three, qualifications that will become clear in the sequel.

The Basic Concept: Two Components

The two basic elements of the concept are already seen in Hesiod and continue unabated through Cicero. They are the principle of right timing and the principle of a proper measure. Usually they are joined in a single concept, although individual occurrences of the term may focus on one or the other aspect. In the sense of "right" time, *kairos* may be opposed to the more common *chronos,* although this opposition is not consistent in Hellenic, Hellenistic, and New Testament Greek (see Barr). Sometimes *kairos* can be viewed as neutral and a "good time" *(eukairos),* as opposed to a time without *kairos* *(akairos* [see Plato's *Phaedrus,* 272a]). The second element is more elusive. The propriety of the concept of *kairos* is sometimes quite explicit, as in the proverb derived from Hesiod, "Observe good measure, and proportion *[kairos]* is best in all things," but other times it is only implicit. An example of this is the *locus classicus* in the rhetorical use of *kairos* in Plato. This occurs in the *Phaedrus* after Socrates has carefully constructed all of the basic dimensions of an ideal rhetoric. He summarizes his conclusions and then adds another dimension:

> Since it is in fact the function of speech to influence souls, a man who is going to be a speaker must know how many kinds of souls there are. Let us, then, state that they are of this or that sort, so that individuals also will be of this or that type. Again, the distinctions that apply here apply as well in the cases of speeches: they are of this or that number in type, and each type of one particular sort. So men of a special sort under the influence of speeches of a particular kind are readily persuaded to take action of a definite sort because of the qualitative correlation that obtains between

speech and soul; while men of a different sort are hard to persuade because, in their case, this qualitative correlation does not obtain. Very well. When a student has attained an adequate grasp of these facts intellectually, he must next go on to see with his own eyes that they occur in the world of affairs and are operative in practice; he must acquire the capacity to confirm their existence through the sharp use of his senses. If he does not do this, no part of the theoretical knowledge he acquired as a student is as yet of any help to him. But it is only when he has the capacity to declare to himself with complete perception, in the presence of another, that here is the man and here the nature that was discussed theoretically at school—here, now present to him in actuality—to which he must apply *this* kind of speech in *this* sort of manner in order to obtain persuasion for *this* kind of activity—it is when he can do all this and when he has, in addition, grasped the concept of propriety of time *[kairos]*—*when* to speak and when to hold his tongue *[eukairos and akairos]*, when to use brachylogy, piteous language, hyperbole for horrific effect, and, in a word, each of the specific devices of discourse he may have studied—it is only then, and not until then, that the finishing and perfecting touches will have been given to his science. (271d-272b)

I quote at such length because of the strategic importance of this passage, in which Plato indicates the primacy of the notion of *kairos* to his rhetorical system.[5] It is the capstone that gives meaning to the entire substructure of the art. The notion of propriety is only implicit, however, even though the translation uses the words "propriety of time" to refer to *kairos*. Yet the translation is quite accurate since the concept of propriety undergirds the entire passage.

But the component of propriety and measure in rhetoric is much richer than just a sense of the adaptation of the speech to the audience. In order to read into the notion of *kairos* its full connotations, even in rhetoric, it is necessary to establish its rich dimensions. In addition to the rhetorical, they embrace ethical, educational, epistemological, and aesthetic levels, all of which are linked to each other.

The Ethical Dimension of *Kairos*

One of the most significant ethical components of *kairos* had to do with its close relation to justice, particularly among the Pythagoreans. Justice was defined as giving to each *according to merit*, that is, generously to those who had worked hard and parsimoniously to those who had shirked. Justice, therefore, was determined by circumstances: justice was *kairos* (Rostagni, 163). This combination was omnipresent in Pythagoras; according to Rostagni, "All of his [Pythagoras's] teachings, his influence as founder of a school and as expert and custodian of minds—everything is based on the combined principles of *kairos* and *dikaion* [justice]" (168).

This facet of *kairos* is obviously related to the proper measure aspect of *kairos,* which is linked with the word in its earliest historical occurrences in Hesiod, Theognis, and later, especially in Pindar. Gorgias, Antisthenes, and other Sophists continued this ethical facet of *kairos,* although some of them flirted dangerously with the extreme relativism that a notion of situational determinism could carry with it. Isocrates and others, for example, accuse Gorgias of carrying situational ethics to the point of complete relativism (Untersteiner, 198–99), although Untersteiner (155–56) and Rostagni (204) dispute this accusation.

Plato and Socrates were seriously concerned with the relativism implicit in such a situational ethic, and Plato's ethic is an attempt to provide an alternative. Yet, curiously, Plato's ethic is also grounded on the notion of *kairos.* Plato used the concept of proper measure and right time—the two fundamental components of the concept of *kairos*—to construct the doctrine of virtue as the mean between two extremes (excess and deficiency). This doctrine is further developed by Aristotle and emerges as the classic Greek doctrine of virtue (this argument for the *kairos* origin of the doctrine of the mean is drawn from Levi ("Kairos," 277–279; see also Rostagni, 164).

More than any one strand of *kairos,* this aspect is continued in the Latin concept of decorum or propriety, especially in Cicero. It is the basis of *De Officiis,* his ethical treatise on duties—according to A. E. Douglas, possibly the single most influential book, other than the Bible, in Western civilization. Any application of *kairos* to the teaching of composition cannot ignore the ethical dimension.

The Epistemological Dimension of *Kairos*

A common epistemological thread is woven into the meaning *of kairos* from Pindar and Bacchylides, writing poetry in the fifth century B.C., through the Pythagoreans, Gorgias, and Plato, and it is still found in the modern extrapolations of the concept by Paul Tillich. At the risk of simplifying, let me provisionally say that *kairos* brings timeless ideas down into the human situations of historical time. It thus imposes value on ideas and forces humans to make free decisions about these values. Let us flesh these ideas out with a little history.

Pindar and, to a lesser extent, Bacchylides felt that it was the task of the poet to make known the divine revelation to man. Pindar claims that his poems are from the gods, through the Muses.[6] Although the gods provide the message and the stimulus to create, the poet must incorporate his god-given wisdom *(sophia)* in the work of his own crafting (Bowra, 21). And Pindar felt that his contribution to the craft of poetry was his ability to single out the critical moment of a story (the *kairos*) and weave a short poem around it. He tells the story of Orestes in twenty-four lines, whereas his predecessor, Stesichorus, filled two books with the same story (Untersteiner, 111). The divine ideas thus acquire a human value (Untersteiner, 104).

Gorgias takes a more strident view of this process. The transcendent divine ideas take no account of the facts of human existence. To apply to man, the divine ideas must become immanent in human life through *kairos.* This can be achieved when the writer enters into the "psychological situation of whoever has perpetrated the deed [being written about], trying to understand its individual character" (Untersteiner, 104). This, for Gorgias, can come about only through the deceptions of persuasive rhetoric and poetry (Untersteiner, 108 – 114).

It is very clear that in Plato's system, rhetorical thought becomes effective only at the moment of *kairos,* as the lengthy passage from the *Phaedrus* quoted above amply illustrates. And I have already called attention to the significance of the notion of *kairos* in Plato's ethic. In both rhetoric and ethic, Plato's world of ideas is brought down to earth by the notion of *kairos.*

Tillich has taken these Greek ideas and has drawn from them some theological, historical, and philosophical corollaries. Although I seriously disagree with some of his conclusions, his contrast of the two philosophical tendencies in Western thought, *kairos* and *logos,* is a valuable addition to the epistemological sketch here being attempted. Tillich distinguishes *logos*-thinking as characterized by an emphasis on timelessness, on form, on law, on stasis, on method; he finds it the dominant pattern of Western thought, from Plato and Aristotle through most of the church fathers, on to Descartes and Kant. Opposing this trend is *kairos*-thinking, characterized by an emphasis on time, on change, on creation, on conflict, on fate, and on individuality. He cites Jakob Boehme, Duns Scotus, Martin Luther, and the late Romantics as instances of this minority approach to Western thought (Tillich, "Kairos," 127 – 129). He argues for the importance of the *kairos* approach because it brings theory into practice, it asserts the continuing necessity of free decision, it insists on the value and norm aspects of ideas, it champions a vital and concerned interest in knowledge (because knowledge always is relevant to the situational context), and it provides a better solution to the problem of uniting idea and historical reality than the solutions of either George Hegel or Karl Marx (Tillich, "Kairos," 130 – 148). Tillich contends that Hegel sacrificed freedom by making historical reality follow the logical norms of ideality, and he maintains that Marx capitulated to relativism and sacrificed real knowledge by subordinating idea to historical situation (Tillich, "Kairos," 152 – 157). He argues for the union of freedom and fate in *kairos* and for a less rigid notion of unchanging idea, a notion of a dynamic idea (Tillich, "Kairos," 157 – 164).

One critic argues that Tillich's concept of *kairos* is at least partially indebted to the Marxist concern for historical consciousness (Bulman, 240). It certainly is closely allied to Walter Benjamin's notion of the importance of being aware of the "now-time," the revolutionary possibilities inherent in the moment, the "state of emergency" in which we live, and the potentials for change inherent in the historical situation (Benjamin, 257–262).

The Rhetorical Dimension of *Kairos*

I have already established the rhetorical dimension of *kairos* in Plato's *Phaedrus,* cited earlier to illustrate the implicit sense of right measure and *kairos.* Plato was responding to the Sophistic concept of rhetoric, specifically repudiating the sophistic basis of probability and some of the sophistic conceptions of mechanical structure and organization; still, he does not repudiate the thoroughly Gorgian idea of *kairos* as being the cornerstone of rhetoric. Untersteiner has fully outlined this aspect of sophistic rhetoric, particularly in Gorgias (119–120; 194–205). Rostagni sees a heavy Pythagorean influence on Gorgias and Antisthenes in their notions of rhetoric, persuasion, and the close affinity these have to *kairos* (Rostagni, 160–168). Aristotle's *Rhetoric* is also grounded in *kairos,* as following paragraphs demonstrate.

The Aesthetic Dimension of *Kairos*

Doro Levi begins his article on *kairos* in Plato with this statement, "The concept of *kairos,* as we have often observed, is both an ethical and an aesthetic concept" ("Concetto," 93). He goes on to point out that throughout Greek thought the ethical and the aesthetic are consistently intertwined. Indeed, he devotes half of his article to an analysis of the beautiful in Plato and to its relationship to the good. The common basis of Plato's ethics and aesthetics is the concern for "right measure"; this had formed the popular and the philosophic basis for these areas throughout Greek history ("Concetto," 110–114). And "right measure" is intimately connected with *kairos,* as indicated earlier. Plato had summarized the relation of the beautiful to the good and to the proportionate near the end of the *Timaeus:* "Everything that is good is fair, and the fair is not without proportion; and the animal which is to be fair must have due proportion" (87c).

More even than Plato, Gorgias had asserted the necessity of *kairos* for a theory of aesthetics, a topic that has been given considerable attention by Untersteiner (185–194). And, in discussing Pindar's epistemology of *kairos,* we saw that it was difficult to separate it from his theory of poetry. Finally, the residue *of kairos* in Cicero, the notion of propriety, is at the basis of his entire theory of style, particularly in the *Orator.*

The Civic Educational Dimension of *Kairos*

The educational implications of the various dimensions of *kairos* are obvious, and they were not lost on the Greeks. On this issue, three considerations, central to my general thesis, must be made. Throughout the period that we have been considering, *kairos* was closely aligned with education; we have only to remind ourselves of the early maxims of Hesiod and Solon on the topic. In addition, we know that Pythagoras had oriented his training in education to civic education, to training for public affairs, for life in the *polis* (Rostagni, 188). Iamblichus in his *Life of Pythagoras* states, "They say that he would have been the inventor of all civic education *[politike paideia]*" (Rostagni, 71). The constant theme of all of his speeches was virtue, with *kairos* the determining principle in each case (Rostagni, 193). For the Greeks, the importance of the city was the common bond of humanity that it afforded those living together and the strangers who visited them. In fact, the origins of the concept of "humanity" are traced by Fritz Wehrli to this idea, grounded in the existence of the *polis* (12–14). Since freedom and the ability to persuade and be persuaded are the essence of the *polis*, it is not surprising to see the education to the life of the *polis* grounded in persuasion and to see this closely related to the notion of *kairos*. Gorgias, for instance, relates the sense of *philanthropia* to persuasion, which was, as we have noted, for him necessarily grounded in *kairos* (Untersteiner, 115).

Probably the most obvious connection of *kairos* to civic education, however, is a symbolic one. Since the Greeks deified many of their ideals, it is not surprising that *Kairos* was also a god. The usual representation of *Kairos* was as an ephebe, a young man attending the two years of required civic and military education, at the end of which rite of passage he came into manhood (*ephebeia* [Delling, 457]). The young athletic man was characterized by a striking hair style, a lock at the front with short hair behind. The presence of the forelock, says Delling, "confirms the fact that even religiously *Kairos* originally had the character of decision, since the lock of hair is a symbol that one must take the favourable opportunity by the forelock" (457). *Kairos*, the god, was thus symbolically linked to the public education program that prepared the young man for initiation into citizenship—the program, incidentally, dominated by rhetoric.

Kairos in Aristotle's *Rhetoric*

The neglect of the study of the term *kairos* in research on Aristotle's *Rhetoric* can be seen as a manifestation of the more general neglect of the concept, as alluded to above. Yet as more and more scholars are not only discovering the concept but incorporating *kairos* into their work, it is still generally associated with Platonic rhetoric and has remained relatively unexplored in Aristotle's *Rhetoric*. In spite of this lack of study, it should in no way be ruled irrelevant to his work. *Kairos* plays an important role in Aristotle's definition of rhetoric, the kinds of rhetoric, and the different arguments; and it is also included in his view of such related terms as virtue, equity, fitness, and occasion.

Timely advances in computer-aided referencing have helped to facilitate our studies. Traditional underrepresentation in the concordances was abated somewhat with the advent in 1982 of A. Wartelle's *Lexique de la "Rhetorique" d'Aristotle*, which revealed thirteen references. But it is through PERSEUS, a computer program which can find the root of the word as well as the word itself, that scholars are now able to search the *Thesaurus Linguae Graecae* version of the *Rhetoric* and find a total of sixteen references. In addition, the concept stands out in spite of the relative absence of the term. Aristotle's inclusion of *kairos* is not limited to its literal appearances, but is related to some of the main themes of the *Rhetoric*, often bound up with the four concepts mentioned earlier.

Aristotle's Definition of Rhetoric—The *Kairos* Element

Aristotle defines rhetoric fairly systematically twice in the early chapters of the *Rhetoric*. He first clearly delineates its function in Book I, chapter i, 14 (1354b13): "its function is not so much to persuade as to find out in each case *[peri hekáston]* the existing means of persuasion." The Greek and the translation both emphasize the application of the general rules of the art to the individual case or situation. The second definition is the main definition of rhetoric, at the beginning of Book I, chapter ii, 1 (1355b25–26): "Rhetoric then may be defined as "the faculty of discovering the possible means of persuasion in reference to any subject whatever *[peri hekáston]*." The issue of the individual case is here translated "to any subject whatever," a translation that may be justified by the context. This emphasis, however, does neglect the individuality of the situation, an emphasis called for by the Greek, and most translations manage to preserve both concerns. Thus, in W. Rhys Roberts' translation, "Rhetoric may be defined as the faculty of observing in any case the available means of persuasion" (Ross, 595), and the context refers to the subject matter. Mederic Dufour translates the passage, *Admettons donc que la rhétorique est la faculté de découvrir speculativement ce qui, dans chaque cas, peut être propre à persuader* (76). This translation also emphasizes the individuality of the situation. Thus, although the term does not occur in Aristotle's definitions of rhetoric, the concept of a specific act in a concrete case does. As in Plato, Aristotle's art is to be applied at a particular *kairos.*

In several instances, Aristotle is very careful to call attention to the individuality of the rhetorical situation, whether it is political or legal. In the first chapter, before either of his definitions of rhetoric, Aristotle attempts to show the difference between the actions of a legislator and those rhetorical decisions made by an assembly or by a jury. According to Aristotle:

> But what is most important of all is that the judgement of the legislator does not apply to a particular case *[kata meros]*, but is universal and applies to the future, whereas the member of the public assembly and the dicast have to decide *[ede]*, present *[paronton]*, and define *[aphorismenon]* issues, and in their case love, hate, or personal interest is often involved, so that they are no longer capable of discerning the truth adequately, their judgement being obscured by their own pleasure or pain. (1354b3–1354b8)

Much has been made of the fact that the citation deals with the emotional rather than the rational reaction of the voters or the jury. But the passage is just as interesting in terms of the rhetorical act. Four lines in Greek emphasize the individuality of each situation, yet one of them is not translated by John Freese: *ede* means immediately, forthwith, or urgently. Rhetorical decisions in the assembly or the court have to be made on the spot.

Thus, these three important definitions or distinctions emphasize the nature of the rhetorical act: it applies the rules of the art of rhetoric to the particular situation at issue. This concept repeats Plato's notion in the *Phaedrus* of the *theoria-praxis* distinction, which is mediated by *kairos* (272). Thus, the rhetorical act is situationally determined in both Plato and Aristotle. And both distinguish the general rules of the art of rhetoric from their situational application.

On three particular occasions, Aristotle uses the term *kairos* when discussing his own act of writing. When treating deliberative rhetoric, he remarks that "there is no need at present *[kairon]* to endeavor to enumerate with scrupulous exactness" certain subjects of political importance (1359b–6). He puts a similar limitation upon his treatment of the kinds of government, saying that he has discussed enough, "as far as was within the scope of the present occasion *[kairo]*" (1366a26). He then refers the student to his *Politics* for further information. Finally, Aristotle uses this same term to cut off the discussion of virtue and vice: "enough has been said for the moment *[kairon]*"

(1355b29 –30). In each case, he indicates that a more extensive treatment of the issue would be proper at another time.

Legal, Political, and Ceremonial Rhetoric

The third passage cited above (Book I, chapter i, 7 [1354b3–1354b8]), which distinguishes the urgent decisions of the court and the assembly about particular cases involving present and definite issues from the more reflective decisions of legislators, already indicates the kairic nature of legal and political rhetoric. But there are other connections of *kairos* to each of the kinds of rhetoric.

In legal rhetoric, *kairos* has a clear relation to the legal concept of equity *(epieikeia)*. Aristotle defines equity as "justice that goes beyond the written law" (1374a31). Its usage in medical discourse (Hippocrates, *On Fractures*) as well as in judicial writings embodies a kind of *kairic* law. It is law when it is applied in particular circumstances, at specific times, to specific situations not foreseen by the legislators. This usage of situational context reveals the strong base concept of *kairos* in Aristotle's view of law and justice and in his *Rhetoric*. Aristotle's treatment of equity in the *Rhetoric* (Book I, chapter xiii [1373b–1374b]) is one of the most extensive and influential treatments of equity in antiquity, especially when it is joined to the treatment in *Nicomachean Ethics* (Book V, chapter x [1137a–1138a]).

Equity *(epieikeia)*, then, can be viewed as *kairic* law. Aristotle states, "and it is equitable to pardon human weaknesses, and to look, not to the letter of the law but to the *intention* of the legislator; not to the action itself, but to the moral purpose; not to the part, but to the whole" (1374b12–17). The generality and ambiguity of this representation of law is the basis for its entanglement with *kairos*. It is only in a particular case toward a particular individual at a particular time that true legal justice can be found—when *kairos* can truly occur. In Judeo-Christian religious tradition, this concept occurs in Paul, Romans 2:29, where the letter of the law is distinguished from the spirit of the law. Boaz Cohen says that Paul "coined the antithesis between letter and spirit," and derived it from Greek rhetorical theory (1966, 56–57). From Greece, the concept of equity moved into Roman law and, thence, into the major legal systems of Europe and America.

In Aristotle's discussion of political rhetoric, there is an important passage that combines three important concepts, all of which relate closely to the situational concept as applied to individual governments. Aristotle says, "Moreover, with reference to acts of legislation, it is useful *[chresimon]* to understand what form of government is expedient *[sumpherei]* judging in light of the past, but also to become acquainted with those in existence in other nations, and to learn what kinds of government are suitable *[harmottousin]* to what kinds of people" (Book I, chapter iv, 13 [1360a36 – 40]). The notions of usefulness, expediency, and suitability are all situationally determined.

Another passage dealing with expediency also underscores the importance of *kairos*. In assuming "good to be whatever is desirable for its own sake," Aristotle affirms that the orator must argue for "whatever reason does assign to each in individual cases" (Book I, chapter vi, 2 [1362a25 – 26]). This affirmation recalls what was said above about Aristotle's definition of rhetoric. In all arguments, even those which discuss events that have not yet occurred, rhetoric must focus on that which is appropriate to present circumstances. While discussing political rhetoric, Aristotle also considers the notion of honor:

> Honour is a token of a reputation for doing good; and those who have already done good are justly and above all honoured, not but that he who is capable of doing good is also honoured. Doing good relates either to personal security and all the causes of existence; or to wealth; or to any other good things which are not easy to acquire, either in any conditions, or at such a place *[entautha]*, or at such a time *[pote]*; for many obtain honour for things that appear trifling, but this depends on place and time *[karoi]*. (Book I, chapter v, 9 [1361a30 – 39])

It is clear from this passage that honor depends on the particularity of both place and time; that is, on situational context.

This is also true of noble actions, which Aristotle discusses in ceremonial rhetoric in Book I, chapter ix. Aristotle says of a noble action done, "alone, or first, or with a few or [by the one who] has been chiefly responsible for it; all these circumstances render an action noble. Similarly, topics derived from times and seasons *[kairon]*, that is to say, if our expectation is surpassed" (1368a13 – 16). Thus, *kairos* is operative in each of the three kinds of rhetoric: legal, political, and epideictic. It is also relevant to the different kinds of rhetorical proof: pathetic, ethical, and logical.

Kairos and the Pathetic Argument

There is an unnoticed *kairos* element in Aristotle's treatment of the emotions, which is announced in a formula in the chapter that immediately precedes the first chapter on the emotions and is explicitly repeated, as a full formula, fifteen times in the next ten chapters, usually at the beginning and, in half of the chapters, also at the end. The first formulation comes at the end of Book II, chapter i, devoted to the ethical argument. In the transition to the pathetic argument, Aristotle says, speaking about the emotions, "And each of them may be divided under three heads; for instance, in regard to anger, the disposition of mind which makes men angry, the persons with whom they are usually angry, and the *occasions* which give rise to anger" (1378a27–30). This triple formula (mental disposition, persons against whom one is angry, and situations) is repeated in every chapter devoted to the emotions, and in five of the ten chapters it is repeated twice (chapters on anger, on shame, on benevolence, on pity, and on indignation). The repetition of this formula sixteen times, a repetition not paralleled in the entire *Rhetoric,* gives the reader a sense of its importance. Clearly, Aristotle intended to give a situational grounding to the notion of an emotional argument.

This grounding is used in his definition of love. In explaining what occasions move people to this emotion, he uses *kairos* specifically by saying that things done either "cordially rendered, or under certain *circumstances [kairois]*" (1381a) will make the giver appear even more generous and worthy of love. Passages such as this one show that Aristotle saw these concepts as part of his "art"; yet students of rhetoric have not previously seen the extent to which timing controls many of his ideas. In his discussion of benevolence, situational context is again a key element: "and the favour will be great if the recipient is in pressing need, or if the *times and circumstances [kairois]* are important or difficult" (1385a24). When aiding someone, one is regarded with special "favour owing to the *urgency and occasion [kairon]* of the need" (1385a32).

The section on the emotions is inundated with uses of *kairos.* Aristotle repeatedly indicates that the most beneficial way to perform an act is in the "right time." Also, at this juncture, he begins to use *kairos* as a "crisis" situation. The discussion of pity similarly relies upon action at a critical time. It is often cited by critics in discussing pity and fear in connection with tragedy. Aristotle uses it to describe men at the point of death who "show themselves undaunted at such *critical times*" (1386b6). Grace under pressure is an attribute which moves the audience to pity—and is therefore an important element in the pathetic appeal. The discussion of fear involves the causes of fear and what or whom should be feared. Those who fear being wronged or have been wronged in the past should be feared because "they are forever on the lookout for an *opportunity*" (1382b12). Their vigilance and observance of *kairos* is something of which the rhetor should be wary and conscious. This stance might be called "passive *kairos.*"

The discussions of love, benevolence, pity, and fear specifically use the term *kairos.* However, in the sixteen statements of the formula referred to above, Aristotle usually uses the term *poia,* generally translated as reasons or occasions. Thus, having already announced the aims and points of coverage for his argument on anger, Aristotle has used *kairos* in his introduction. Approximately halfway through his discussion, *kairos* in the word form of *poia is* used again: "It is now evident from these considerations what is the disposition of those who are angry, with whom they are angry, and for what *reasons [poia]*" (1379a). His discussion still incomplete, Aristotle takes the time to refer back to his original framework: the three necessary questions to understanding and utilizing an emotion in rhetoric. At the beginning of the next chapter, he makes the transition to mildness by stating that since "becoming angry is the opposite of becoming mild . . . we must determine the state of mind which makes men mild, toward whom they become mild, and the *reasons [poia]* which make them so" (1380a5 – 8). Through the cyclical nature of his discussions of the emotions, his reliance on the concept of *kairos is* evoked continually.

The Ethical Argument

This emphasis on *kairos* is made all the more intriguing when turning to the ethical argument. The importance of *kairos* for the ethical argument can be seen in a passage which is usually discussed for two other reasons. In the second chapter of the first book Aristotle says:

> The orator persuades by moral character when his speech is delivered in such a manner as to render him worthy of confidence. . . . But this confidence must be due to the character; for it is not the case, as some writers of rhetorical treatises lay down in their "Art," that the worth of the orator in no way contributes to his powers of persuasion; on the contrary, moral character, so to say, constitutes the most effective method of proof. (Book I, chapter ii, 4 [1365a5 –15])

Many commentators juxtapose the last clause of this passage with the passage early in the first chapter that emphasizes the importance of the logical argument. And other commentators have disagreed with Aristotle's notion that confidence may not come from any preconceived idea of the speaker's character. Aside from these two issues, however, Aristotle's idea that the confidence must be due to the speech itself is clearly an affirmation of the importance of the individual situation; that is, the *kairos* of the case. Second, two of the three components of the ethical argument, good character *(arete)* and good sense *(phronesis)*, are intimately related to *kairos,* as Levi has shown.

The Logical Argument

The logical argument is not as imbued with a sense of timing as are the ethical and emotional arguments, but Aristotle does advert to the notion of timing and propriety when discussing maxims. He begins the chapter on maxims with this remark: "In regard to the use of maxims, it will most readily be evident on what *subjects [poion]*, and on what *occasions [pote]*, and by whom it is *appropriate [harmottei]* that maxims should be employed in speeches" (1394a25–26). This passage clearly demonstrates the importance of timing in propriety, a conjunction we will see again. In fact, the formula for maxims is almost the same formula as was used for all of the emotions. It is not surprising that, in the chapter on maxims, the phrase "it is appropriate" occurs in five different contexts. Again, in dealing with interrogation, he states that the student must know when "its employment is especially *opportune" [eukairon]* (1418b50). This advice, of course, also applies to the organization of the speech; in fact, it is in discussing organization that Aristotle makes this statement. The final reference deals with enthymemes. Aristotle refers to their usefulness and to a special type:

> As for those to be used in *sudden emergencies [epikairotaton]*, the same method of inquiry should be adopted; we look, not at what is indefinite, but at what is inherent in the subject treated of in the speech, marking off as many facts as possible, particularly those intimately connected with the subject; for the more facts one has, the easier it is to demonstrate, and the more closely connected they are with the subject, the more suitable they are and less common. (1396b5–13)

This passage reiterates several motifs connected with the *kairic* in rhetoric: the relation to the individual case, the necessity of definite issues, and the notion of suitability.

Style and Organization

References to *kairos* abound under the heading of "style," beginning with faults of style, specifically in the use of epithets. Frigidity of style results from four cases, says Aristotle, the third of which "is the use of epithets that are either long or *unseasonable [akairois]* or too crowded; thus, in poetry it is appropriate *[prepei]* to speak of white milk, but in prose it is less so; and if epithets are employed in excess, they reveal the art and make it evident that it is poetry" (1406a14–17). This is an interesting passage, which shows the close connection of right timing to propriety and to the mean. Indeed, *kairos* in style plays its most important role in Aristotle's understanding of propriety. In the use of stylistic tropes, Aristotle insists that "the *seasonal* or *unseasonal* use of these devices applies to all kinds of rhetoric" (1408a45–46). In the Greek these are *kairos and akairos*.

Although Aristotle only spends one full chapter on this "virtue" of style

(Book III, chapter vii), *prepon* is a most important element in all of the chapters on style. The concept of fitness *(prepon)* runs through Aristotle's treatment of all of the virtues and rhetorical devices, such as rhythm, metaphor, epithet, and correctness. It is also included in all three appeals: the logical, ethical, and pathetic, as we have seen. As he says, in a general statement, "Propriety of style will be obtained by the expression of emotion [pathetic] and character [ethical], and by proportion to the subject matter [logical]" (1408a13–15).

Besides style, Aristotle also treats organization in the third book of his *Rhetoric*. And he has an interesting remark about getting the attention of the audience. Clearly, he says, this is important at the beginning of the speech, but it is sometimes necessary to reawaken this attention: "Wherefore, when the right moment [*kairos*] comes, one must say, 'And give me your attention, for it concerns you as much as myself'; and, 'I will tell you such a thing as you have never yet' heard of, so strange and wonderful. This is what Prodicus used to do; whenever his hearers began to nod, he would throw in a dash of his fifty-drachma lecture" (1415b14–20). As we have seen above while discussing the logical argument, Aristotle also remarks upon the opportune [*eukairon*] use of interrogation. But the interrogation had a particular place in the organization of the speech; that is why Aristotle treats it at 1418b50.

What this all points to, inevitably, is the necessity of *kairos* in the *Rhetoric* of Aristotle; indeed, *kairos* is as important to Aristotle as it is to Plato. Every section of the *Rhetoric* utilizes this notion in one form or another. Scholars' failure to address this dependency has been due, in part, to its absence in reference dictionaries. But beyond this, it has sometimes been due to the insistence that Aristotle did not adhere to the Platonic ideal. This notion, as has been illustrated, is simply not true. Aristotle's use of *kairos* in the "act" of rhetoric is illustrated throughout his "art."

Notes

1. Continental references are also relatively rare. For example, *kairos* is mentioned in Heinrich Lausberg's *Handbuch der Literarischen Rhetorik*, but not in Henri Morier's *Dictionnaire de poetique et de rhetorique*.

2. Augusto Rostagni finds this statement in Iamblichus, *Life of Pythagoras* (49). I am using an unpublished translation of Rostagni's article by Phillip Sipiora (29).

3. English translations of the essays by Rostagni and Levi are being prepared for *Kairos in Translation*, ed. James S. Baumlin and Phillip Sipiora (under contract, Edwin Mellen Press).

4. These major scholars have been calling our attention to *kairos* for more than seventy-five years, but few rhetoricians have given them much attention. Yet I am firmly

convinced that rhetoric desperately needs the notion of *kairos*. I have made several pleas for its reincorporation into the systematic study of composition, because I see it as a dominant motif in disciplines related to our own ("Relation"). The concept of situational context, which is a modern term for *kairos*, is in the forefront of research and thought in many areas. The phrase "rhetorical situation" has almost become a slogan in the field of speech communications since Lloyd Bitzer's article on the subject appeared in 1964. All of these voices saying ultimately the same thing ought to convince us that some consideration in any rhetorical theory must be given to the issue raised by the concept of *kairos*—the appropriateness of the discourse to the particular circumstances of the time, place, speaker, and audience involved. If this is so, it may be that modern treatments of situational context can learn something from the handling of the same topic in antiquity. I would argue that they can, particularly in the realms of the ethical and the educational.

5. The critical element in applying *kairos*, or situational context, to any discussion of composition problems was made by Plato in his discussion of the place of *kairos* in rhetorical theory. The theory is only theory until it has been applied to a concrete situation with unique circumstances. For this reason it is desirable, in rhetorical (and scientific and literary) writing, to enable students to find a realistic audience, apart from the teacher, if this is at all possible.

6. C. M. Bowra cites Olympia XI, 10; Olympia IX, 100–104; and Olympia II, 86–88 to support this point.

Works Cited

Adler, Mortimer J., ed. *The Great Ideas: A Syntopicon of Great Books of the Western World.* Chicago: Encyclopaedia Britannica, 1950.

Aristotle. *The "Art" of Rhetoric.* Trans. John Freese. The Loeb Classical Library. Cambridge, MA: Harvard University Press, 1925.

———. *Rhetoric.* Trans. R. Roberts. *Great Books of the Western World.* Ed. R. M. Hutchins. Vol. 9. Chicago: Encyclopaedia Britannica, 1952.

———. *Rhetorique.* Trans. Mederic Dufour. 3 Vols. Paris: Socitètè d'edition "les belles lettres," 1967.

Barr, James. *Biblical Words for Time.* London: S. C. M. Press, 1969.

Benjamin, Walter. *Illuminations.* Trans. Harry Zohn. New York: Harcourt, Brace, 1968.

Bitzer, Lloyd F. "The Rhetorical Situation." *Philosophy and Rhetoric* 1 (1968): 1–14.

Bowra, C. M. *Pindar.* Oxford: Clarendon, 1964.

Bulman, Raymond F. "Theonomy and Technology." In *Kairos and Logos: Studies in the Roots and Implications of Tillich's Theology.* Ed. John J. Carey. Cambridge, MA: North American Paul Tillich Society, 1978.

Cohen, Boaz. *Jewish and Roman Law: A Comparative Study.* New York: Jewish Theological Seminary of America, 1966.

Cook, Arthur Bernard. "Appendix A: Kairos." In *Zeus: A Study in Ancient Religion.* Vol. 2, pt. 2: Cambridge: University Press, 1925. 859–68.

Delling, G. "Kairos." *Theological Dictionary of the New Testament.* Trans. and Ed. Geoffrey W. Bramley. Vol. 3: 833–39. Grand Rapids, MI: Eerdman, 1986.

Douglas, A. E. "Cicero the Philosopher." In *Cicero.* Ed. T. P. Dorey, 149. New York: Basic Books, 1965.

Enos, Richard Leo. *The Literate Mode of Cicero's Legal Rhetoric.* Carbondale: Southern Illinois University Press, 1988.

Hirsch, E. D., Jr. "Culture and Literacy." *Journal of Basic Writing* 3 (1980): 27 – 47.

Kinneavy, James L. "*Kairos:* A Neglected Concept in Classical Rhetoric." In *Rhetoric and Praxis: The Contribution of Classical Rhetoric to Practical Reasoning.* Ed. Jean Dietz Moss, 79 – 105. Washington, DC: The Catholic University of America Press, 1985.

———. "Contemporary Rhetoric." In *The Present State of Scholarship in Historical and Contemporary Rhetoric.* Ed. Winifred Bryan Horner, 167 – 213. Columbia: University of Missouri Press, 1983.

———. "The Relation of the Whole to the Part in Interpretation Theory and in the Composing Process." In *Linguistics, Stylistics, and the Teaching of Composition.* Ed. Donald McQuade, 1 – 23. Akron, OH: Language and Style, 1979.

———. "Freshman English: An American Rite of Passage." *Freshman English News* 7 (1977): 1 – 3.

Kinneavy, James L., and Catherine R. Eskin. "*Kairos* in Aristotle's *Rhetoric.*" *Written Communication* 11 (1994): 131 – 42.

Lanham, Richard A. *A Handlist of Rhetorical Terms: A Guide for Students of English Literature.* Berkeley, CA: University of California Press, 1969.

Lausberg, Heinrich. *Handbüch der literarischen Rhetorik: Eine Grundlegung der Literaturwissenschaft.* Munich: Max Heuber Verlag, 1960.

Levi, Doro. "Il kairos attraverso la letterature greca." *Rendiconti della Reale Academia Nazionale dei Lincei classe di scienzia morali* RV 32 (1923): 260 – 281.

———. "Il concetto di kairos e la filosofia di Platone." *Rendiconti della Reale Academia Nazionale dei Lincei classe di scienzia morali* RV 33 (1924): 93 – 118.

Liddell, Henry George, and Robert Scott. *A Greek-English Lexicon.* Oxford: Clarendon, 1968.

Long, A. A. *Hellenistic Philosophy: Stoics, Epicureans, Sceptics.* London: Gerald Duckworth, 1974.

Morier, Henri. *Dictionnaire de politique et de rhétorique.* Paris: Presses Universitaires de France.

Moutsopoulos, E. "La fonction du *kairos* selon Aristote." *Revue Philosophique de la France et de l'étranger* (1985): 222 – 226.

Norwood, Gilbert. *Pindar.* Berkeley, CA: University of California Press, 1945.

Plato. *Euthyphro, Apology, Crito, Phaedo, Phaedrus.* Trans. H. N. Fowler. The Loeb Classical Library. Cambridge, MA: Harvard University Press, 1927.

———. *Timaeus.* Trans. Benjamin Jowett. Indianapolis: Bobbs-Merrill, 1949.

Pohlenz, Max. "*To Prepon:* Ein Beitrag zur Geschichte des griechischen Geistes," In *Nachrichten von der Gesellschaft der Wissenschafien zu Goettingen, Philologisch-historische Klasse, Heft* 1 (1933): 53 – 92. Reprint *Kleine Schrifen.* Ed. Heinrich Dorrie, 2:100 – 39. Hildesheim: G. Olms, 1965.

Rostagni, Augusto. "Un nuovo capitolo nella storia della retorica e della sofistica," *Studi italiani di filologia classica,* n.s. 2 (1922): 148 – 201.

Ross, W. D., ed. *The Works of Aristotle.* Trans. W. Rhys Roberts. Oxford: Oxford University Press, 1924.

Sipiora, Phillip. "*Kairos* in the Discourse of Isocrates." In *Realms of Rhetoric: Phonic, Graphic, Electronic.* Ed. Victor J. Vitanza and Michelle Ballif, 119 – 35. Arlington, TX: Rhetoric Society of America, 1991.

Smith, J. E. "Time and Qualitative time." *Review of Metaphysics* 40 (1986): 3 – 16.

Tillich, Paul "Kairos and Logos." In *The Interpretation of History.* Trans. N. A. Rasetzki and Elsa Talmey. New York: Scribner's, 1936.

———. "Kairos and Kairoi." In *Systematic Theology.* 369–372. Chicago: The University of Chicago Press, 1963.

———. "Kairos I." In *Der Widerstreit von Raum und Zeit: Schriften zur Geschichtsphilosophie, Gesammelte Werke.* 10–28.

———. "Kairos II, Ideen zur Geisteslage der Gegenwart." 29–41.

———. "Kairos und Utopie." 149–65.

Untersteiner, Mario. *The Sophists.* Trans. Kathleen Freeman. Oxford: Basil Blackwell, 1954.

Wartelle, A. *Lexique de la "Rhétorique" d'Aristote.* Paris: Les belles lettres, 1982.

Wehrli, Fritz R. "Vom antiken Humanitätsbegriff." In *Theoria und Humanitas. Gesammelte Schriften zur antiken Gedankenwelt.* Zurich: Artemis Verlag, 1972.

Wiener, Philip P., ed. *Dictionary of the History of Ideas: Studies of Selected Pivotal Ideas.* New York: Scribner's, 1973.

Inventional Constraints on the Technographers of Ancient Athens
A Study of Kairos

RICHARD LEO ENOS

Introduction: Writing in the Service of Orality

In the opening passages of his *Rhetoric,* Aristotle criticizes "technographers" who taught and practiced only the surface features of their craft and did not understand rhetoric as an "art," that is, an actual *techne* for creating rational proofs (*Rhetoric,* 1354a–1355). At the time that Aristotle wrote his *Rhetoric,* Athens was in the midst of what historians of rhetoric have termed a "literate revolution," where writing was shifting in emphasis from an aid to oratory to an art unto itself. The revolution of literacy, however, was not so much based on the fact that more and more people could read and write—although that appears to be the case. The actual "revolution," as recognized by thinkers such as Aristotle, was that written rhetoric could be a system for enhancing more complex patterns of thought and expression. Yet, in the midst of this intellectual revolution, and in the protoliterate period that preceded it, writing served other civic functions in Athenian life, functions that imposed inventional constraints not evident in our current conception of composition. The various technical functions of writing help to explain not only everyday writing practices in Athens but how they served as a bridge leading to written rhetoric's emergence as an art in its own right.

This essay, in effect, is a study of *kairos,* an examination of the situational constraints of civic composition. Writing in Greek society initially served as a technological aid to the more primary and pervasive functions of oral discourse. For example, during this period the *hupogrammateus* emerged as a secretary charged with the responsibility of recording oral transactions of civic deliberations. Such recordings were, on occasion, subject to time constraints since speakers were limited by the *klepsydra* or water clock and, correspondingly, so were those who had to transcribe their speeches. This example of writing in the service of orality illustrates how composition under such conditions brought with it inventional constraints that are not readily apparent but are important to recognize if we are to understand well the complexities of Athens' literate revolution. This study offers archaeological and textual evidence that reveals the inventional constraints on writing used in the service of preserving oral discourse in ancient Athens and advances the following claim: when civic writing was used in the service of orality the constraint of time must be acknowledged as a factor in Greek rhetoric.

The Unconsidered Constraints of Immediate Time

One of the first concepts we discuss with introductory writing students is time. More specifically, we tell students that their papers must be done "on time" and that it is their responsibility as writers to learn how to manage "their time." Students hardly need to be reminded of this constraint, for they already are sensitive to the importance of time. Often, students will excuse poor writing by claiming that they "ran out of time" or that "you [the teacher] didn't give us enough time." Although these illustrations are mundane, they nonetheless reveal that time is on the minds of both teacher and student when it comes to writing. Surprisingly, however, while being "timely" is inherent in the invention process of every act of rhetoric, time is rarely considered by historians of rhetoric. That is, we often discuss rhetoric, especially classical rhetoric, as situated discourse and stress the importance of *kairos* as necessary for a sensitive understanding of discourse within its context but often neglect to factor in the constraints of immediate time. On occasion, we have been guilty of veering in the opposite direction, by valuing the timelessness of rhetoric.

Our sensitivity to understanding not only *kairos*, but also classical rhetoric itself is diminished when we do not account for time as a factor, particularly when we understand how orality and literacy interact in ancient Athens. Perhaps time is not considered in the historical study of literacy because we tend to think in distinct categories about orality and literacy. That is, we view orality as momentary communication and literacy as stable and enduring communication. Yet, our remarks about momentary factors are frequently vague. In classical Athens, orality and literacy not only interacted but also were endemically tied together in many civic practices. Our efforts to understand classical rhetoric have not included a sensitivity to what is called "immediate time," that is, units of hours and minutes. Our current research in classical rhetoric shows no accounting for, and demonstrates no real awareness of, the momentary in Greek rhetoric. The consequence is that we are tempted to treat the artifacts of rhetoric as we once treated literary texts, placing them in a timeless vacuum removed from the context within which they occurred. Until we again make the notion of time a factor we will limit our understanding of *kairos* and, by default, classical rhetoric itself.

The Concept of Immediate Time in Greek Rhetoric

We regularly ask, "What time is it?" but we never seem to ask, "What is time?" Or, more to the point, "What did time mean to ancient Athenian rhetors?" In order to provide an appropriate perspective, the criticism that historians of rhetoric do not adequately consider the notion of time in classical rhetoric should be specified. Certainly grammar reveals time with respect to tense endings of verbs and, in the case of Greek, these differentiations can be quite specific. While philology reveals sophistication in the sensitivity to time through grammatical expressions of inflected tense, it does not reveal the more immediate, temporal issues that operate in spontaneous composition.

Theorists of rhetoric offer research on issues and topics that relate to time but these notions are often vague and general. For example, time is indirectly considered when we explain rhetorical discourse as contextual and appropriate through such concepts as *kairos* (situation), *peristasis* (circumstances), and *prepon* (appropriateness). These rhetorical terms implicitly acknowledge that rhetoric is constrained by the moment and assume that sensitivity to the timeliness of discourse is a valuable trait. While these concepts remind us of situational constraints, they do not capture well the notions of immediate time in the dynamics of composition. Recent archaeological evidence and on-site field examination presented here make it apparent that the concept of immediate time—the presence of the moment—was not only a part of the mentality of classical Athens, but that it was also a real factor in shaping the relationship between orality and literacy, especially when writing was done in the service of orality.

Ancient Athenians had a range of concepts to express time and some of these are directly applicable to rhetoric. In the most general and macroscopic sense, *Kronos* or *Aios* and *Kairos* represented forces of time. These general and mythical notions, which are evident in the literature of Homer and Hesiod, were refined as later Greeks felt the need to be more precise in time reckoning beyond the cycles of seasons and menstruation. The most important of these precise time reckonings is based on the day. Ancient Greeks viewed the day as beginning and ending with the rising and setting of the sun. The invention of the sundial, which Herodotus (2.109) claims the Greeks imported from Babylonia, but which may have been invented by Anaximander (Diogenes Laertius 2.1), enabled Athenians to time the diurnal parallel of the sun through its four equinox and solstice patterns into three concentric circles that could be divided into twelve equal parts to obtain hours *(horae)*. Constructing a concave hemisphere of stone *(polos)* with a pointed metal stylus *(gnomon)* provided an accurate "hour counter" *(orologion)* or what Romans later called a *"horologium."*

Immediate time became especially important to Athenians when the intensity of civic affairs, such as forensic and deliberative proceedings, increased. The *horologium* was useful to Athenians, and there is some belief that the "hour counter" was in use as early as the fifth century B.C. A "monumental" water clock that functioned as a public timepiece dating back to at least the fourth century B.C. has been excavated at the northwest corner of the north facade of the Heliaia in the Agora (*The Athenian Agora,* 181; see drawings and restorations in Figure 2) near one of the primary entrances. This clock was eventually replaced in the second century B.C. by the water clock in the Tower of the Winds, which remains to this day. A large, civic water clock in the Athenian Agora meant that time reckoning "literacy" was a public activity.

Clocks that could tell time by hourly units were important for rhetorical functions. We know that later in Rome, the Greek *horologium* or sundial (Pliny, *NH* 7.213–15) was used and helpful to rhetors. Pleading, to be "valid," must be presented before the tribunal prior to midday (Carcopino, 145). While we do not have evidence of such time constraints for pleading in Athens as we do in Rome, it is nonetheless apparent that the sun did provide a means for reckoning that made the occasions of rhetoric systematic. That is, the general "hour" for rhetorical presentations could be scheduled. It also should not be forgotten that Athens averages over three hundred sunny days a year, which makes the sundial a regularly functioning tool.

While such tools do provide some degree of temporal reckoning, they only provide gross indices and do not reveal the finely tuned constraints of immediate time that impact rhetorical composition. When Athenians needed to have precise reckoning of immediate time at night, they would use such instruments as the *klepsydra* or water clock. In all, it should be apparent that Athenians and Romans both recognized the need for the precise accounting of time and regularly incorporated inventions for time reckoning into their daily lives and civic affairs. The importance of this point is made even more evident when we further specify immediate time down to smaller units than the hour, especially when composing in the service of orality.

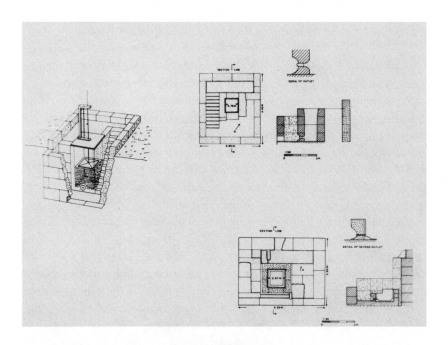

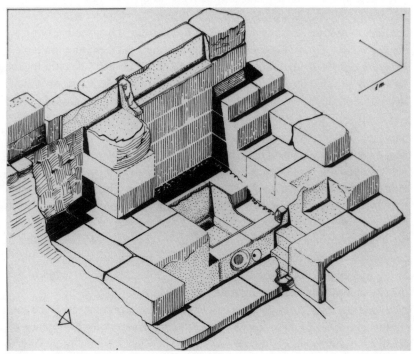

Fig. 2. Drawing and restoration of the water clock, late 4th century B.C. (With permission of the Agora Excavation, The American School of Classical Studies at Athens.)

Timing in Rhetorical Situations

One of the most obvious needs for an accurate reckoning of time in rhetorical situations is during civic functions, especially in legal matters. There is archaeological evidence revealing that Athenians had invented ways of accounting for minute-time as early as the fifth century B.C. In fact, there is a very clear correlation between the development of legal procedures and timing devices to measure pleading. The most important of these instruments was the *klepsydra* or water clock. As revealed by the picture from the Agora excavations at Athens (see Figure 3), the water clock excavated in the Athenian Agora, and now on display at the Agora's Stoa of Attalos (P2084), consists of two jars with a small opening that allows water to escape and be collected in a corresponding lower jar. This particular jar fills in about six minutes. The archaeological report reveals that the lower hole was sealed with a plug until the rhetor began, with the presumption that the speaker could continue until the water ran out. In this example the volume is indicated by the "XX" on the lower pot, two *choes* or about 6.4 liters (*The Athenian Agora*, 224, 244).

Extant speeches reveal that the constraints of the water clock were on the minds of orators. The Attic orator, Aeschines, for example, not only commented on the use of the water clock in the middle of his oration, but even the procedure (*Against Ctesiphon*, 197–198). In this case, Aeschines explained, *klepsydra* time is divided into three parts: the first allotment of water for the accuser, the second for the defendant, and the third for the discussion of penalty and procedure. Aeschines' references also reveal that these procedures for oral deliberation had to be written and publicly posted (200). The extant forensic orations of this period show speeches much longer than six minutes, which could mean that each jug was a unit and not a full allotment of time. Another possibility is that the speeches that we now have were substantially modified and elaborated upon after the actual proceedings were concluded. Evidently, laments about the constraints of the *klepsydra* may have evolved into a commonplace for terminating a speech. Isocrates, in his lengthy *Antidosis*, wryly complains that his water clock is drying up—compelling him to condense his thoughts and conclude (320). This passage is particularly interesting to students of orality and literacy, since Isocrates did not actually give the speech but published it as a written text (Marrou, 81).

In addition to orations, we have other primary sources that reveal the constraints of time in composition. We often think of Aristotle as the primary authority for understanding rhetoric in classical Athens and, naturally, turn to his *Rhetoric* as the best source. Two other Aristotelian sources, the *Politics* and *The Athenian Constitution*, are also valuable sources for understanding how

Fig. 3. Model of water clock in use (With permission of the Agora Excavation, The American School of Classical Studies at Athens.)

writing served orality. The latter work, *The Athenian Constitution,* is especially valuable not only because it details the relationship between orality and literacy during civic functions but because it was only discovered a little more than a century ago (1890), and thus offers information unavailable to earlier historians of rhetoric.

This important document provides a much clearer picture of the use of the *klepsydra* than the anecdotal remarks of Aeschines and Isocrates. *The Athenian Constitution* reveals that the amount of time—correspondingly the amount of water—varied according to the amount of drachmas at issue in the case (67). In short, the greater the costs the more water. To regulate both flow and proceedings, the "water-tender" stood ready to block water and stop time if the clerk had to read documents. In major criminal cases, however, the flow of water was uninterrupted with both sides allotted an equal supply of water (67). The procedures outlined by Aristotle reveal how closely deliberations were timed and how closely reading and writing interact within the oral process.

Writing in the "Process" of Oral Deliberations

Aristotle's *Politics* makes clear his belief that public education is necessary for society (1337a) and that reading and writing are not only useful but also valuable in political affairs (1338a). It hardly needs to be stated that oratory played an essential role in the daily operations of Athenian Democracy. What is not as apparent, but is no less important, is the role that writing played. The first point to clarify is how writing participated in the affairs of civic deliberation that are essentially oral. Writing was important in three respects: the preparation for oral deliberation, the recording of oral transactions, and the determining of judgment by auditors.

Writing in Preparation for Oral Deliberation

Writing was essential in the orchestration of oral deliberation of charges, which were inscribed on whitened tablets (*The Athenian Constitution*, 48). The Clerk of the Prytany, who had general custody for archives and "official" transcripts, was responsible for all such public documents (*The Athenian Constitution*, 54). Inscribed documents were read aloud and voted by a show of hands *(cheirotonei)* or lots (*The Athenian Constitution*, 55).

There is, however, other, more abundant evidence of writing in the service of orality during the Classical Period (fifth and fourth centuries B.C.). The concept of "logography" existed during the Archaic Period (late seventh-early fifth centuries B.C.) as a specialized skill to record accounts of important events. In this respect, early chroniclers and even Herodotus—called the "father of historians"—would be considered "logographers." This form of specialized writing, however, altered during the Classical Period, principally because it was applied to the immediate constraints of oral deliberation (Enos). During the Classical Period logography emerged as a profession in which individuals would compose speeches for others, normally during legal proceedings where each male citizen was compelled to speak for himself. Logographers wrote these speeches for a price and instructed clients in their "readings," that is, in the preparation for their oral performance before courts. Our evidence is that the most successful of logographers, such as Lysias and quite possibly Isocrates, were popular because they composed oral arguments well for others. That is, both rhetoricians were able to capture the nuances of spontaneous speech while benefiting from the stability of text that comes from writing. The success of logographers began to alter the perception of writing, which came to be viewed more and more as part of an intellectual process. Writing speeches helped to refine oral arguments by shaping words that would otherwise be only fleeting notions of oral discourse subject to memory alone. Such texts were, on occasion, subject to time constraints since orators were limited by the *klepsydra* and, correspondingly, so were those who composed their speeches under these restrictions. In short, logographers wrote speeches sensitive to the constraints of the orators who delivered them.

Writing and the Recording of Oral Transactions

Writing was, as an instrument, recognized as serving orality in civic functions governed by time. As was true in the Archaic Period, Athenians of the Classical Period continued to utilize artisan writers, but new, more specialized writing tasks developed and with them more specialized writers. Composition took on a more immediate and pragmatic dimension. As Democracy stabilized political procedures in Athens, the need for writers to record specific events of oral civic functions increased. As mentioned earlier, during this period the *hupogrammateus* emerged as a secretary charged with the responsibility of recording oral transactions of civic deliberation. Plato refers to these individuals as the "letter-makers" who have acquired the technical skill necessary for composing functional literary tasks (*Protagoras*, 326B–D). A similar reference to the *hupogrammateus* as a secretary/recorder is made by Antiphon ("On the Choreutes," 35), while Lysias describes the *hupogrammateus* as a clerk ("Against Nicomachus," 27–29). One extant inscription, housed in Athens' Epigraphical Museum (EM 6667), lists the *hupogrammateus* [Purgion] as a part of the official civic transactions (*IG* i [2].374.110 – iii, 258) of 408/7 – 407/6 B.C. The recording of the *hupogrammateus* reflects another form of writing that is constrained by time.

The new constraints of writing in the service of orality altered the nature of writing, at least of writing for these specialized purposes. The spontaneous and fleeting discourse that is the nature of oral deliberation prompted the *hupogrammateus* to develop shorthand systems of writing, or tachygraphy, as a heuristic to transcribe oral deliberations. Accounts recorded by Diogenes Laertius (*Xenophon* 2.48) claim that Xenophon was the first Athenian to use shorthand symbols. Unfortunately, we have no immediate evidence of Xenophon's work or any direct examples of systematic tachygraphy until the early Christian centuries (Eunapius, 489), and even these artifacts come from Egypt, not Athens. Yet, if we trust the account of Diogenes Laertius, we have a very important piece of evidence about the shifting emphasis of writing among the upper classes. Xenophon was from an old and well-established aristocratic family. The fact that he would "invent" a writing heuristic to aid orality also provides an instance of the diminishing stereotype of writing as a lower-class craft while, correspondingly, illustrating its use by a member of the upper classes of Athenian society.

Writing and the Determining of Judgment by Auditors

When ostracism, the banishment by popular vote of an Athenian who had fallen out of public favor, was introduced by Cleisthenes in 508/507 B.C., citizens were required to record their votes on potsherds or *ostraca* (Plutarch, *Aristeides*, 7). Athenians who voted on ostracism (*Athenian Constitution*, 22) did so by scratching names on potsherds. Some researchers have taken this practice as a sign of widespread literacy. An examination of these *ostraca*, many of which have been unearthed in Athens, with some on display in the Agora Museum (Case 38), shows little more than the ability to scratch out letters of the alphabet in a primitive way. Moreover, there is also some good reason to believe that it was not uncommon for illiterate fellow-citizens to ask fellow literate citizens to scratch down a name for those who could not write (*Athenian Agora*, 256 – 57; Harris, 54 – 114; Broneer). While it is possible that literate voters could have written names for others, it is evident that some general familiarity with writing was apparent (Vanderpool, 229). Other evidence reveals that reading was widespread and important in civic affairs. Bronze voting disks *(psephos demosia)* that were used by jurors (68) are inscribed, as are the bronze "tickets" *(pinakia)* that identify each voter by name. Both of these items are currently on display in the Agora (*Athenian Agora*, 245 – 47). This archaeological evidence reveals that writing was important in the very determination of judgment and often played a role in each phase of civic deliberation.

Conclusion: The Impact of Writing on Timed Rhetoric

As Athens moved from the Archaic and into the Classical Period of the fifth and fourth centuries B.C. the nature of writing instruction, and even its purposes and benefits, altered dramatically. We have seen that writing during the Archaic Period was little more than a recording device learned as a trade in the service of the upper classes. During the Archaic Period, writing served to stabilize texts and thus make them permanent. Hence, the transcriptions of Homeric discourse, the chronicling of historical events, and the recording of laws began to complement and extend the more formal craft skills of artisan writers. The wealthier and more aristocratic classes of Athens did, as discussed earlier, learn to write. During this early period, however, these classes learned writing as an aid in carrying out the routine and mundane tasks of the day. The emphasis on literacy for these upper-class Athenians was primarily reading, and there is some evidence to support the belief that reading knowledge was fairly widespread during the Classical Period.

The Classical Period, however, ushered in significant changes in writing and, accordingly, altered its instruction dramatically. While it is accurate to state that writing-in-order-to-read was still (by degree) the orientation of the upper classes, that emphasis was shifting during the Classical Period. Writing during this period became a feature of civic deliberations. The distinguishing feature of this emerging form of civic writing is its service to orality. That is, writing was used to record events that had a more immediate and pragmatic impact.

It should be clear that Athenians of the Classical Period did have a reckoning of immediate time and a public, temporal literacy that was widespread. Correspondingly, if we wish to better understand classical rhetorical discourse we need to view it not as a timeless, atemporal artifact but rather as situated, contingent and operating (literally) within the *kairos* of the moment. Sensitivity to time is important not only in oral rhetoric but in literate rhetoric as well. During the Classical Period writing and reading is evident in the preparation, recording, and assessment of oral rhetoric. In fact, this study of external evidence allows us to advance the following claim: when civic writing was used in the service of orality the constraint of time must be acknowledged as a factor in the study of Greek rhetoric. Certainly, if we do have a sensitivity to immediate time in classical rhetoric, such notions as *kairos*, *peristasis* and *prepon* will take on greater importance not only in our theoretical understanding of these central concepts, but also in our study of how they played out in the rhetorical situations that brought them into existence.

Works Cited

This project was made possible through the cooperation of the American School of Classical Studies at Athens and the Agora Excavation, who kindly granted permission to reproduce the photograph and illustrations that appear in this essay. This work is dedicated to Fordyce W. Mitchell.

References to all classical sources cited in the text (and listed below) are the standard, authoritative texts found in the Teubner and Oxford University Press editions. Excellent translations of these classical works, with the accompanying primary language, can be found in the Loeb Classical Library series of the Harvard University Press. Readers should note, however, that the Loeb edition of Aristotle's *The Athenian Constitution* does not include selected fragments. Relevant to this study, section 67 is omitted from the Greek and English texts of the Loeb edition. Those who wish to read an English translation of section 67 should consult the edition translated by John Warrington (listed below).

Aeschines. "Against Ctesiphon." Oxonia: Ex theatroux en Oxonia excudebat Johan. Grooke, 1696. Microfilm. Ann Arbor, MI, 1977.

Antiphon. "On the Choreutes." Lipsiae: in aedibus B. G. Teuberni, 1914.

Aristotle. *Politics.* Trans. H. Rackham. Cambridge, MA: Harvard University Press, 1932.

———. *Rhetoric. The "Art" of Rhetoric.* Trans. John Freese. Cambridge, MA: Harvard University Press, 1926.

The Athenian Agora. American School of Classical Studies at Athens. 4th ed. Princeton, NJ: Institute for Advanced Study, 1990.

Broneer, Oscar. "Excavations on the North Slope of the Acropolis, 1937." *Hesperia,* 7 (1938): 161–263.

Carcopino, Jerome. *Daily Life in Ancient Rome.* Ed. Henry T. Rowell. Trans. E. O. Lorimer. New Haven and London: Yale University Press, 1940.

Diogenes Laertius. *Lives of Eminent Philosophers.* Trans. R. D. Hicks. Two Volumes. Loeb Classical Library Series. Cambridge, MA: Harvard University Press, 1970.

Enos, Richard Leo. *Greek Rhetoric Before Aristotle.* Prospect Heights, IL: Waveland, 1993.

Eunapius. *Vitae Sophistarum.* London: R. Bentley, 1696. Microfilm. Ann Arbor, MI: University Microfilms, 1961.

Harris, William V. *Ancient Literacy.* Cambridge, MA: Harvard University Press, 1989.

Herodotus. *The Persian Wars.* Trans. George Rawlinson. New York Modern Library, 1942.

Inscriptiones Graecae. Epigraphical Museum 6667.

Isocrates. *Antidosis.* Trans. George Norlin. Cambridge, MA: Harvard University Press, 1929.

Lysias. "Against Nicomachus." In *Speeches.* Trans. S. C. Dodd. Austin: University of Texas Press, 2000.

Marrou, H. I. *A History of Education in Antiquity.* Trans. George Lamb. Madison, WI: The University of Wisconsin Press, 1956. Reprint, 1982.

Plato. *Gorgias.* Trans. W. C. Helmhold. New York: Liberal Arts Press, 1952.

———. *Protagoras.* Trans. C. C. W. Taylor. Oxford: Clarendon Press, 1976.

Pliny. *Naturalis Historia.* Stuttgart: Teubner, 1985.

Plutarch. *Aristeides.* Ed. and Trans. David Sabsone. Warminster: Aris and Phillips, 1989.

———. *Vitae Parallelae: Cato Minor.*

Robb, Kevin. *Literacy and Paideia in Ancient Greece.* New York and Oxford: Oxford University Press, 1994.

Vanderpool, Eugene. "Ostracism at Athens." In *Lectures in Memory of Louise Taft Semple.* University of Cincinnati Classical Series 2. Ed. C. G. Boulter, D. W. Braden, A. Cameron, J. L. Casey, A. J. Christopher son, G. M. Cohen, and P. Topping. Norman, OK: University of Oklahoma Press for The University of Cincinnati, 1973.

Warrington, John, ed. and trans. *Aristotle: Politics and The Athenian Constitution.* New York: E. P. Dutton, 1959.

Kairos *in Gorgias'*
Rhetorical Compositions

JOHN POULAKOS

Scholars who have discussed the place of *kairos* in classical Greek rhetoric have generally located the meaning of the term outside the actual production of the oration. *Kairos,* they suggest, either precedes or succeeds the speech itself. In the first instance, the orator is said to become aware of an opportune moment and speak spontaneously in response to that awareness; in the second, the audience is said to listen to an oration and immediately (or soon thereafter) realize its timeliness. Both instances are often combined into a third understanding, according to which *kairos* refers to a certain confluence of utterance and time, or to a marking of time with speech. The nuances of the various interpretations of the term (i.e., "opportune moment," "due measure," "right occasion") aside, most commentators agree that *kairos* is an important concept in the theory of Hellenic rhetoric. Its importance lies in the fact that the perception of an oration's timeliness adds to its force and effectiveness. Conversely, an oration is thought to be forceful and effective on account of its timeliness.

Even if we assert the centrality of *kairos* in the early days of rhetorical theory, its teachability still emerges as a practical issue. How did the teachers of the art of persuasion teach this notion to their students? How, for example, did Gorgias, who is said to have "turned his own attention to what was timely" (DK, A24) and to have "trusted to the moment to speak on any subject" (DK, A1a), instruct his pupils to observe the principle of *kairos* while composing orations?[1] If we speculate that he taught primarily by means of a specific theory of *kairos,* a theory he presumably expounded to his students, such a theory would seem to undermine the spontaneity of speaking implied by the very notion of *kairos.* As Eric Charles White points out, "no treatise on the occasional nature of utterance could be itself exempt from occasionality, or the inevitability of its own supersession" (20). White explains further: "If every occasion presents a unique challenge to the situational, context-oriented consciousness of the Sophist, then the Sophist's interpretive ingenuity will nowhere find itself resumed in a definitive statement"(20).[2] If, on the other hand, we speculate that Gorgias taught by example (Guthrie, 192), submitting his own orations as models for imitation, it would seem that they, too, would be hindrances in the observance of *kairos*—the whole idea of a model goes against the view that it is the instant moment, not the finished form, that largely determines the meaning and success of a particular utterance.

The attempt to address the issue of the teachability of *kairos* is further limited by the written nature of the preserved textual evidence. If Gorgias' extant orations *(Palamedes* and *Helen)* are helpful neither as illustrations of a derived theory of *kairos* nor as formal models for imitation, how can these rhetorical compositions help us answer our question? If we do not and can never have access to the moment in which they were delivered (and it is doubtful they were actually delivered in the first place), and if all we have is the written version of these oratorical pieces, how can we begin to understand *kairos* as a notion that can be observed in the composition of an oration? To what extent can *kairos* be said to operate as a formal strategy within a rhetorical text? What kinds of expectations can this strategy raise and satisfy in the presumed audience? In short, how does timeliness work within a text?

Despite the conceptual and material limitations I have identified, I argue in this essay that Gorgias' remaining compositions do provide us with a glimpse of his practical teaching of the principle of *kairos*.[3] Assuming that the *Palamedes* and the *Helen* were used to teach rhetoric, I contend that both orations exemplify ways in which rhetoric can be composed so as to give the impression of sensitivity to timeliness. In effect, I argue that *kairos* can be observed not only intuitively, which does not require instruction, but also technically, which does. Put differently, responding orally (by means of an oration) to the awareness of an opportune moment is one thing; creating and managing self-consciously opportunities within rhetorical composition is quite another. In the first instance, the orator seeks to match words with his perception of timeliness; in the second, to create an impression of timeliness in the audience. And even though the two instances might coincide, there is no guarantee that they will. Because we cannot determine whether Gorgias' rhetorical compositions were indeed timely utterances—that is, acts performed in response to a specific occasion before an actual audience—we are left with the task of exploring how he might have shown his students ways of creating the impression of timeliness in their listeners.

In both compositions, Gorgias creates the impression that his words are largely a function of *kairos* by manufacturing controlled opportunities within his texts. As I show below, the opportunities in the *Palamedes* are afforded by descriptions of a sudden and unexpected event, an unusually decent defendant, and an exceptionally upstanding jury. These opportunities are in turn captured by means of a discourse that relies on the resources of the speaker to respond to that which is surprising, the understanding being that typical or common arguments are not especially helpful in extraordinary cases. In the *Helen*, the opportunities are created by reference to the poets' effort, which Gorgias' new discourse seeks to correct by relying on reasoning. These opportunities are captured by words that focus not on Helen's action itself but its possible causes, the point being that views based on her action alone can be overturned the moment one inquires into the causes of that action. In both orations, Gorgias creates and captures opportunities by demonstrating ways in which the force of unforeseen circumstances determines human words and deeds. A close look at each oration shows how this is so.

In the *Palamedes* the challenge is to depict a typical event uniquely, and put in the mouth of the defendant words that seem to respond to that event kairotically. In effect, Gorgias' task here is to dramatize the occasion and audience of the oration. Occasioned by Odysseus' charges, this speech presumably constitutes a response to a common occurrence (a lawsuit), during which a group of listeners (jurors) is authorized to adjudicate a legal contest between two competing parties. Gorgias knew the obvious: legal trials start with the discourse of the accuser and end with the jury's verdict. He also knew that the defendant, one of the two protagonists in such occasions, is generally obligated to address the jury by providing a defense against the accuser's charges. But because forensic occasions are typical, the range of expected defenses is also typical (i.e., I did not do what the accuser alleges, the charges are groundless, the accuser's logic is flawed, the witnesses are liars, etc.). Gorgias' challenge, then, is to avoid employing what is normatively typical because the typical in the form of the expected is the exact opposite of the unique in the form of the timely. Doing so would enable him to capitalize on the resources of *kairos* over against those of *to prepon* or "the appropriate" (Poulakos, 60–64).

Working against the background of typical forensic situations addressed by means of standard legal arguments *(topoi)*, Gorgias scripts and stages a drama by bringing defendant, jury, and accuser inside the oration. Rather than offer a straightforward *apologia* to a presumed audience of jurors familiar with the accuser and aware of the charges at hand, rather than let the reader of the *Palamedes* infer the charges and imagine the character of the jurors from the defendant's words, Gorgias ushers both jury and accuser into the very discourse meant to address them. In this way, he situates the defendant and his speech in the context of an occasion precipitated by a set of

unusual circumstances. Instead, then, of letting the occasion be supposed, in-
ferred, or imagined by the audience, he creates it and places it before them.
Thus, he has Palamedes insert himself into a particular situation, address his
jury and his accuser explicitly, discuss his relationship to both, recount his
venerable past, and wonder aloud about his own life and fate.

In the hands of Gorgias, then, an ordinary, typical forensic occasion becomes a unique rhetorical event as he makes Odysseus' charges against Palamedes appear sudden and preposterous. The charges are so outrageous, so
unbelievable that they stun and perplex the defendant. Hence, his three rhetorical questions (4): "Where shall I start to speak about these matters?
What shall I say first? To what part of the defense shall I turn my attention?"
In effect, Palamedes is made to admit that he is utterly surprised; so much
so, in fact, that he finds himself at a loss for words and trying to regain his
rhetorical composure. By portraying the charges as preposterous and the defendant as startled and momentarily disoriented, Gorgias attempts to im-
press on the audience that a man in a state of shock cannot but speak extem-
poraneously and without premeditation. Had the charges been plausible, so
the thinking goes, one would have expected an equally plausible *apologia*.
But as things stand, the oration can be neither fully deliberate nor entirely
polished; quite the contrary, it can barely cover the expected ground. The
only hope is that, as Palamedes tries to address the charges against him, he
just might "discover something out of the truth itself and out of the present
necessity" (4).

Another rhetorical gesture meant to address a typical trial kairotically is
the particularization of accusation. Gorgias particularizes the general case
and shows that it loses much of its weight the moment it is applied to a specific individual, in this case Palamedes (see Tordesillas). Accordingly, he has
the defendant dismiss the general charge of betrayal *(prodosia)* by pointing
out how groundless and unlikely it becomes when viewed in the light of
Palamedes' past life, a life that is well-known and "free of all blame" (29). At
the same time, he makes Palamedes adopt the posture that what he is about
to do, offer a positive account of his own past life, is ordinarily considered in-
vidious—praise about our deeds and character should normally come from
others, not ourselves. Even so, the defendant insists that the circumstances in
which he finds himself are extraordinary: the things I am about to say normally fall outside the domain of the appropriate but must nevertheless be
seen as appropriate *(prosekonta)* because my predicament is outside the domain of the normal—I am being accused of something I did not do (28),
something I could not have and would not have done. Once again, extraordinary circumstances and unprecedented conditions compel one to resort to kairotic speech, that is, speech that risks violating established norms of propriety

and decorum. Accordingly, Gorgias has Palamedes apologize to the jury for reminding them that he has been a good man and a good citizen. At the same time, he has him explain that his unusual rhetorical conduct is a function of the urgency of his predicament (32): "but the present situation has forced me to defend myself any which way" *(o de paron kairos enangase . . . pantos apologesasthai)*.

The *Palamedes* illustrates the notion of *kairos* one more time as the defendant points to yet another nontypical feature of his circumstances. The last section of the oration (33–37) lends weight to the idea that words spoken to an exceptional audience must deviate markedly from what one says when addressing a typical one. Here Gorgias has Palamedes acknowledge that he is trying to adapt his speech to an unusually outstanding jury, a distinguished panel of men of good reputation and impeccable integrity. Had the jury been a typical mob of mindless, unwise, and error-prone men, his defense would have had to include "appeals to pity and entreaties and the intercession of friends" (33), strategies all too familiar under normal conditions. But the character of these particular jurors dictates that Palamedes take a different path, the path leading away from attempts to deceive, that is, the path leading to truth and justice. Similarly, had the jurors been, like most, inattentive and forgetful, the speech would have had to conclude by the typical means of recapitulation. But these jurors are so mindful and responsible that recapitulation is unnecessary.

The *Palamedes*, then, can be said to illustrate ways in which the principle of *kairos* can be observed in the making of a rhetorical composition. On the basis of the above discussion, Gorgias' lesson is threefold. First, the orator needs to set the stage by portraying his oration as a unique response to an unusual set of circumstances. The element of uniqueness in this oration is furnished by the surprising and shocking allegations leveled against Palamedes. Second, the orator must particularize the generally accepted case of legal charges by pointing to situational exceptions that it leaves out of account. One exception that the general case of accusation fails to include in this instance is the defendant's character: Palamedes, this particular person, is no ordinary citizen as he lacks both the motivation and the capacity for treason. Third, the orator must construe the audience addressed along the lines of the extraordinary. The jury hearing Palamedes' defense consists of extraordinarily decent men, "the first of the first" (37). When all three of these suggestions are followed, the orator might be able to escape the categories of the typical, the ordinary, and the usual. At the same time, he might succeed in creating the impression that his discourse is timely, spoken on the spur of the moment, the result of nature rather than artifice. For their part, the listeners will be inclined to realize that the established *topoi* of common rhetorical practice are impotent against the force of circumstantial contingency. Accordingly, they will opt for that which *kairos* reveals to them through the orator.

The notion of *kairos* receives yet another illustration in the *Helen*. The challenge in this rhetorical composition is to effect a shift from what is known (Helen's ancestry, her beauty, her voyage to Troy) to what has yet to be considered (why she eloped with Paris). Presumably provoked by the traditional edict of the poets, this speech constitutes a critical response to the universally held view that Helen is blameworthy for having gone to Troy with Paris. Gorgias knew his poetic past and the influence of the poets and rhapsodes in shaping popular belief. He also knew that the rethinking of the old legacies of the Hellenic culture required new and ingenious arguments. But because such rethinking risked resistance or rejection, Gorgias takes care to preface his arguments by references to three apparently undeniable propositions: *(a)* one should praise the praiseworthy and blame the blameworthy; *(b)* it is an error to blame the praiseworthy and praise the blameworthy; *(c)* an orator is duty bound to speak the needful rightly and refute the unrightfully spoken (1-2).

With the above three propositions in place, Gorgias avails himself of the opportunity provided by what he regards as an error of the poets: they have blamed Helen unjustly. In so doing, he promises to move away from the poet's discourse, which is familiar, and, because often spoken, generally accepted. But how reverse their verdict? How oppose their unanimous condemnation of Helen? Gorgias declares that he will execute his task by introducing some reasoning *(logismon tina)* into his speech (2), reasoning being the counterforce to inspiration, the typical basis of poetical discourses. Clearly, his preference here is for words that have yet to be uttered, words that when uttered for the first time will be relying on the chance of the moment to make sense to their audience. But if this is so, Gorgias' stated purpose—"I wish to free the accused of blame" (2)—is an attempt to prepare his audience for something unheard of, something other than what they have believed all along. In effect, Gorgias is employing, although indirectly, the very same technique attributed to Prodicus by Aristotle: "I will tell you such a thing as you have never yet heard of . . ." (*Rhetoric* 3.14, 9).

Unlike the *Palamedes,* which illustrates the use of *kairos* by staging an event unfolding in and through the oration, the *Helen* demonstrates the same principle by attempting to dislodge a generally held view by means of new and surprising arguments. In the *Palamedes* the surprise comes from the accuser's discourse, which the defendant tries to outdo. In the *Helen,* however, the surprise comes from the defender's discourse, which recasts common belief in a new light. Accordingly, Gorgias explains Helen's action by steering away from will, the standard *topos* of explaining the cause of human deeds. The alternative explanation he advances posits that Helen cannot be held responsible for her journey to Troy because her deed was not a result of her own free will. Gorgias' logic resembles the one he employs in the *Palamedes:* circumstances are powerful determinants of human words and actions. Palamedes defends himself the way he does, because he finds himself in the midst of extraordinary circumstances; and Helen did what she did, because her own will was overpowered by forces much stronger than herself.

Following the same technique he employs in the *Palamedes,* Gorgias particularizes his general claim (circumstances often determine human deeds) by grafting Helen's action onto four possible scenaria, each overwhelming in its own right (the gods' predetermined plans for Helen, the physical violence of her abductor, the magical influence of the *logos* that persuaded her, or her love-at-first-sight encounter with Paris). This time, however, particularization is not meant to prove the impossibility of a given action but to reverse a negative judgment. Gorgias' four arguments are well known and there is no need to repeat them here.[4] All we need concern ourselves with is Gorgias' effort to reopen a seemingly closed case, an effort meant to give his audience a new opportunity to reconsider their judgment of Helen.

The *Helen,* then, trusts to make the case for the importance of *kairos* by reopening a seemingly settled account and by introducing new ways of reasoning, ways leading to the formation of new beliefs. Gorgias' lesson here is threefold. First, any established belief, be it scientific, logical, or philosophical, constitutes an opportunity for rhetorical action (13). Depending on the orator's ingenuity, artistry, and swiftness of thought, rhetorical action ought to aim at the production of new arguments. The established belief in the *Helen* is that Helen is blameworthy for what she did. The new argument is that this belief is erroneous because it is predicated on a limited principle: human action is only a function of the will. Second, the orator must create room for new beliefs by reference to additional principles (i.e., human action is also a function of circumstances or forces greater than human will). In this speech, Helen's action is placed in the context of irresistible forces, forces that, if properly understood, offer a more satisfactory explanation why she did what she did. Third, the orator must construe the audience addressed as susceptible to and welcoming of artistic innovation. The *Helen* notes that telling the same old story brings no delight to one's listeners (5), and suggests that if a speech is to persuade it must do so by pleasing the audience (13). When all three of these suggestions are followed, the orator toils to revisit a familiar discursive terrain and resettle it in more attractive ways. By doing so, the orator can be said to subject a fixed belief to the power of *kairos,* which "takes the same things and makes them disgraceful and then alters them and makes them seemly" (*Dissoi Logoi,* 2, 19).

On the assumption that the *Palamedes* and the *Helen* served as models of rhetorical composition, I have shown in this essay two ways in which these models can be said to illustrate the principle of *kairos.* The *Palamedes* illustrates that words can be shown to be determined kairotically if they are made to provide responses to a surprising utterance. For its part, the *Helen* shows that traditional beliefs can be brought under the force of *kairos* in and through the creation of new arguments. In effect, Gorgias can be said to have shown his students that the employment of the principle of *kairos* can achieve at least two ends: it can respond to discursive surprises as well as create them.

Notes

1. I quote the pre-Socratic texts from Rosamond Sprague's edition, *The Older Sophists*. The designation DK refers to Hermann Diels and Walther Kranz, who collected the pre-Socratic fragments. The designation A refers to that section of the fragments entitled "Life and Works." The number following designates the number of the particular fragment.

2. Eric Charles White's comments can be read as an answer to Dionysius of Halicarnassus, who notes in his *On the Arrangement of Words* (12) that no orator or philosopher, not even Gorgias, has written a *techne* on *kairos*.

3. For a review of the *Palamedes* and the *Helen* as kairotic "exemplifications of the rhetorician's art," see A. A. Long's "Methods of Argument."

4. See A. W. H. Adkins, "Form and Content in Gorgias' *Helen* and *Palamedes*."

Works Cited

Adkins, W. H. "Form and Content in Gorgias' *Helen* and *Palamedes*: Rhetoric, Philosophy, Inconsistency and Invalid Argument in Some Greek Thinkers." Anton and Preuss, *Essays in Ancient Greek Philosophy*, 107–28.

Anton, John P. and Anthony Preuss, ed. *Essays in Ancient Greek Philosophy*. Vol. 3. Albany: State University of New York Press, 1983.

Aristotle. *"Art" of Rhetoric*. Trans. John H. Freese. Cambridge, Ma: Harvard University Press, 1982.

Boudouris, Konstantine, Ἡ Ἀρχαία Σοφιστική. Athens: Ἐκδόσεις Καρδαμίτσα, 1984.

Dionysius of Halicarnassus. *Critical Essays*. Trans. Stephen Usher. Vol. 1. Cambridge, MA: Harvard University Press, 1974.

Guthrie, W. K. C. *The Sophists*. Cambridge, England: Cambridge University Press, 1971.

Long, A. A. "Methods of Argument in Gorgias' *Palamedes*." Boudouris, Ἡ Ἀρχαία Σοφιστική, 233–41.

Poulakos, John. *Sophistical Rhetoric in Classical Greece*. Columbia, SC: University of South Carolina Press, 1995.

Sprague, Rosamond Kent. *The Older Sophists*. Columbia, SC: University of South Carolina Press, 1971.

Tordesillas, Alonso. *La Naissance de la Raison en Grece*. Paris: Editions Gallimard, 1987.

White, Eric Charles. *Kaironomia: On the Will-to-Invent*. Ithaca: Cornell University Press, 1987.

Hippocrates, Kairos, and Writing in the Sciences

CATHERINE R. ESKIN

It could be argued that, of the various meanings of *kairos*, the interpretation given to it by Hippocrates (460 –357 B.C.) has exerted the most lasting influence in the field of discourse theory and practice. Two of the three major theoretical treatises by Hippocrates on the nature of medical science and methodology include in the first sentence *kairos* as a main term. Yet even in those texts which lack a literal use of *kairos*, timing and time-related issues are prevalent. *Kairos* represents a significant aspect of Hippocrates' core theories of observational methodology and the term is used in the representation and presentation of significant findings.

Although Hippocrates is generally accepted as the father of medicine, few have recognized, or even realized, the extent to which he is responsible for the discourse of science more generally (and some might even claim, of history as well). Perhaps the reason for this oversight is the lack of agreement about the connection between the historical figure of Hippocrates and what is generally called the *"Corpus Hippocraticum."* There is no doubt that an historical physician named Hippocrates existed, but the ability of scholars to prove (or disprove) his authorship of certain medical texts throws his reliability into doubt (Levine, 19; Prioreschi, 231). For this reason, when I refer to "Hippocrates," I am not referring to the doctor born on Cos in 460 B.C., but rather to the Hippocratic Collection gathered c.300 B.C. by the Alexandrian Medical School. These texts are what has come to represent for us the notion of Hippocrates and Hippocratic medicine. Beyond the issues of textual assignation, however, are the very innovative ideas which Hippocrates left for posterity.

In both the practice of healing and the art of prognosis, Hippocrates relied heavily on the recognition of variables—time, weather, age, sex—and the experienced doctor's usage of judgment in the interpretation of available data.[1] He was also a firm believer in the importance of interdisciplinarity: that the physician needed to study more than medicine to be an effective healer. Hippocrates pushed medicine in the direction of empirically based reasoning at a time when other cultures (including his own) were steadfastly bound to the shaman's rituals for medical relief. According to Hippocrates' methods, the physician must take note of all of the factors affecting the patient: like the naturalist, he saw the subject (patient) within a total environment. The same logical reasoning at work in observation was also used in approaches to treatment. Hippocrates' texts are more often than not practical, giving the reader a sense of what could be (or was) done to help the patient, yet they show a genuine respect for the experience and judgment of the individual practitioner to apply his advice to the particular circumstances of a case.

In order to make room for individuality and case specificity, Hippocrates used the concept of *kairos*. Hippocrates' literal use of the word *kairos* is frequent and telling: among the fifty-six works included in IBYCUS, *kairos* appears in thirty-three; within those thirty-three works, some form of the root *kair-* appears 264 times. *Kairos* required a basis in experimentation with the observed individual, not just speculation. *Kairos* also assumed a certain degree of latitude that took into account the experience and rational judgment of the professional physician. Most often used to mean a "right time" or "proper measure" in doing something, *kairos* has also been associated with the proportionate, the mean, the implicit sense of right measure. By choosing *kairos*, Hippocrates was able to express the variable components of medical practice more accurately. In order to be a successful physician, one must recognize individuals and their changing environments; one must turn theory into practice. As a writer or a speaker, Hippocrates insisted on being able to recognize verbally the often unpredictable nature of the physician's experience.

This essay will look at some of the more famous usages of *kairos* in Hippocrates and then look at how *kairos* is so integral to the scientific method practiced by Hippocrates and those who followed him. From there we will see how a situational determinism, which heavily relied upon the individual practitioner's judgment, went beyond mere description in the practice of medical discourse. This essay will culminate in the claim that Hippocrates' theories, being integrally tied to discourse theory, make him not just the father of medicine, but also the father of scientific writing.

Aphorisms and *Precepts:* Starting with (at) the Right Time

Hippocrates uses timing and time issues continually throughout his medical works. His most famous statement on *kairos* occurs at the beginning of his book called *Precepts*. It has been translated as: "every *kairos* is a *chronos*, but not every *chronos* is a *kairos*." I will quote it more fully:

Time [*chrónos*] is that wherein there is opportunity [*kairós*], and opportunity [*kairós*] is that wherein there is no great time [*chrónos*]. Healing is a matter of time [*chrónos*] but it is sometimes also a matter of opportunity [*kairós*]. However, knowing this, one must attend in medical practice not primarily to plausible theories, but to experience combined with reason. For a theory is a composite memory of things apprehended with the sense- perception. For the sense-perception, coming first in experience and conveying to the intellect the things subjected to it, is clearly imaged, and the intellect, receiving these things many times, noting the occasion, the time and the manner, stores them up in itself and remembers. Now I approve of theorizing also if it lays its foundation in incident, and deduces its conclusions in accordance with phenomena. (Jones I.313–15)[2]

Kairos here is clearly aligned with experimentation, with experience, with incident, with phenomena. It is opposed to theorizing separated from these contacts. This solid declaration placed medical methodology on the path which it has fairly steadfastly pursued in Western civilization since that time. Hippocrates also defines "theory," insisting that it is intimately tied to and reliant upon the particular context of observed experience. The process of theorizing is thus made more complex, but certainly not cut off from the realities of normal experience. The definition's proximity to the statement on time and the theoretical weight of timeliness in the definition further prove the importance of *kairos* in the overall outlook of Hippocrates.

Aphorisms begins with the famous statement: "Life is short, the Art long" (Jones IV.99). But the rest of the sentence is often omitted: "the crisis fleeting; experience perilous, and decisions difficult." The Greek word translated above as "crisis" is *kairos* (which Littré translates as "l'occasion fugitive" [Littré 4.461], a transient or fleeting occasion); that for "experience" is *peíra* (as in empirical); and that for "decisions" is *krísis*. All three terms emphasize the situational context of the medical decision. Like the quote in *Precepts,* this line from *Aphorisms* (which was used as a medical textbook up to and including the nineteenth century [Jones IV.xxiii]) reminds us that Hippocrates' view of scientific discovery was based on the particular and the observable. *Kairos,* as the term denoting a particular context and a time dependent upon situational determinants, was necessarily the best word available to Hippocrates to express his ideas. In fact, Hippocrates' name even appears in the *Greek-English Lexicon* in connection with the term's meaning (Liddell and Scott, 859).

The Scientific Method: Observation and Description

I have already introduced Hippocrates' method through his definition of theory, but the method itself requires more specific discussion in relation to its verbal manifestations. This is especially true because Hippocrates' *Epidemics* are famous for more than just their historical view of medicine during the third century B.C. Instead, they are significant because they document the first time a healer recorded for posterity his experience with diseases that he was unable to cure. Hippocrates does not cover up his failure to save those who were suffering so much as he hopes, by careful recording of physical data, to increase the likelihood of success in the future (Jones II.67–69). Notice the listing of symptoms from Book III of *Epidemics:* "On the fifth day, everything worsened; much mental wandering, then, suddenly, reason promptly came back to her; thirsty at points; insomnia; ill-timed *[akairoidi]* and copious stools up to the end; urine scanty, flimsy and blackish; extremities cold, and a little withered" (Littré 3.63). Far from the vague descriptions of sickness prevalent before him (where available at all), Hippocrates refers specifically to observed details and creates a vocabulary for patient symptomology.[3] Hippocrates often uses *kairos* in the description of symptoms to make his details more precise.[4] G. E. R. Lloyd claims that "there is nothing to equal these case-histories in extant medical literature until the sixteenth century—and one of the chief figures responsible for the revival . . . , Guillaume de Baillou (born c.1538), explicitly took Hippocratic *Epidemics* as his model" (57).

Sometimes Hippocrates will explain the onset of a disease vis-à-vis the season or seasonal change. Changes in the weather have a strong effect on the symptoms and survival of those suffering from a particular disease within a particular climate. He warns that shifts in the weather can have hazardous effects on patients: "In seasons that are normal [fixed, established, regular], and bring seasonable things at seasonable times *[kairoidi]*, diseases prove normal and have an easy crisis; in abnormal seasons diseases are abnormal and have a difficult crisis" (Jones IV.125). Because he is so detailed in his cases, information about weather can be gleaned quite easily.

Issues of season and weather are less important when dealing with *Fractures,* but precise observation is certainly key to recognizing particular problems and their possible solutions. Here, too, *kairos* plays an important role in emphasizing the severity of a break or the critical nature of a particular bone: "The bones, however, cannot be so well settled in their proper place *[kairón],* but become somewhat unduly swollen at the point of fracture" (Withington III.151). Though present-day physicians may now be able to more accurately diagnose the exact location and extent of damage in fracture cases because of technological developments (the X-ray), it is still important that physicians be aware of critical anatomical locations. In *On Joints,* Hippocrates is similarly emphatic about particular key points: "for the head of the femur in these cases lies very close to important *[epikairón]* cords" (Withington III.341). For these observations, the definition of *kairos* is expanded to denote the relative importance of a given point; no longer strictly related to time issues, *kairos* answers the question of degree.

What is particularly illuminating about Hippocrates' insistence upon observation and descriptive techniques is the way his method helped put into doubt the more magico-ritualistic beliefs about certain diseases. Epilepsy, during this period of medical history, was considered (and therefore called) the "sacred disease." Convinced that there was no credible explanation for the fits which accompany the condition, most contemporary physicians resorted to "purifications and magic" for treatment, according to Hippocrates (Jones II.183). In the very first section of *The Sacred Disease,* he expresses his frustration with those charlatans who claim that the disease is sacred and therefore can only be approached through magical "incantations" (Jones II.139). He counters these methods and the accepted view of epilepsy: "it is not, in my opinion, any more divine or more sacred than other diseases, but has a natural cause, and its supposed divine origin is due to men's inexperience, and to their wonder at its peculiar character" (Jones II.139). Hippocrates claims that if epilepsy is divine because it is "wonderful, there will be not one sacred disease but many, for I will show that other diseases are no less wonderful and portentous" (Jones II.139–140). He offers solutions to this categorical dilemma, suggesting that observation will yield the answer:

> Through it [the brain] in particular, we think, see, hear, and distinguish the ugly from the beautiful, the bad from the good, the pleasant from the unpleasant, in some cases using custom as a test, in others perceiving them from their utility. It is the same thing which makes us mad or delirious, inspires us with dread and fear, whether by night or by day, brings sleeplessness, inopportune *[akairói]* mistakes, aimless anxieties, absent-mindedness, and acts that are contrary to habit. (Jones II.175)

Hippocrates connects the symptoms of epilepsy with the brain, recognizing that some irregularity in brain function must be the cause of the fits peculiar to the condition. So after determining the source of the disease, Hippocrates claims that it is possible to treat patients, and even to do so with some success.

As in the case above, the reader can see how Hippocrates uses his texts as an opportunity to demonstrate the value and importance of relying only on demonstrable evidence in the treatment of patients. He warns his audience early in *Precepts* that being a physician is about proper and careful observation and inquiry:

> But conclusions which are merely verbal cannot bear fruit, only those do which are based on demonstrated fact. For affirmation and talk are deceptive and treacherous. Wherefore one must hold fast to facts in generalizations also, and occupy oneself with facts persistently, if one is to acquire that ready and infallible habit which we call "the art of medicine." For so to do will bestow a very great advantage *[kairón]* upon sick folk and medical practitioners. Do not hesitate to inquire of laymen, if thereby there seems likely to result any improvement in treatment. For so I think the

whole art has been set forth, by observing some part of the final end in each of many particulars, and then combining all into a single whole. So one must pay attention to generalities in incidents, with help and quietness rather than with professions and the excuses that accompany ill-success. (Jones I.315)

In the process of insisting upon the importance of "demonstrated fact," Hippocrates finds it necessary to cast doubt upon the "verbal" as "deceptive and treacherous." Yet he does not imply by these statements that silence on the part of the physician is the only answer a physician can or should make to verbal challenges.

In fact, Hippocrates insists that relying only on the facts provided by observation is even dangerous for the health of a patient. He criticizes another author for making a conclusion based on evidence alone in his *Regimen in Acute Diseases:*

The authors of the work entitled *Cnidian Sentences* have correctly described the experiences of patients in individual diseases and the issues of some of them. So much even a layman could correctly describe by carefully inquiring from each patient the nature of his experiences. But much of what the physician should know besides, without the patient's telling him, they have omitted; this knowledge varies in varying circumstances *[epíkaira]*, and in some cases is important for the interpretation of symptoms. (Jones II.63)

The physician should not just be proficient at description, but at the interpretation of the signs and tokens of disease. Once all of the "facts" of the case have been gathered, the doctor must make a recommendation based upon a combination of symptoms, experience, and instinct. It is here where *kairos* becomes even more complex in its usage by Hippocrates—the sheer number of factors involved in human disease and recovery can be daunting. The physician needs to know about more than just medicine.

Situational Determinism: Interdisciplinarity and Individual Health

The current interest in holistic medicine and the academic desire for increased interdisciplinarity makes Hippocrates' suggestions about the integration of different branches of learning—made nearly two thousand years ago—seem both ironic and fitting. He suggests the interdependent relationship that medicine has to other disciplines:

For knowing the changes of the seasons, and the risings and settings of the stars, with the circumstances of each of these phenomena, [the physician] will know beforehand the nature of the year that is coming. Through these considerations and by learning the times *[kairóns]* beforehand, he will have full knowledge of *each particular case [perĕhekáston],* will succeed best in securing health, and will achieve the greatest triumphs in the practice of his art. If it be thought that all this belongs to meteorology, he will find out, on second thoughts, that the contribution of astronomy to medicine is not a very small one but a very great one indeed. For with the seasons men's diseases, like their digestive organs, suffer change. (Jones I.73; emphasis added)

In this passage from *Airs, Waters, Places,* the work that represents the first treatise on human ecology, Hippocrates suggests that the physician must have a wide body of knowledge at his disposal. In order to successfully treat the individual, the physician must study some of the general circumstances within which human beings actually live. Just by skimming through Hippocrates' treatises, the reader will find the author making regular reference to the art of meteorology (see Jones I.153). In order to describe accurately the conditions under which a particular disease took place, the medical writer (or scientific recorder) must be aware of weather patterns (meteorology) for particular places (geography was also of interest to Hippocrates) and the movements of the stars (astronomy).[5]

Yet even more important than knowledge of other relevant disciplines is the physician's ability to apply that knowledge in an accurate and timely manner. What is most crucial about situational context for the physician is the doctor's experience and judgment in particular instances. By far the most occurrences of *kairos* involve recognizing the "right time" to perform a particular procedure or administer a particular medication. The sheer number of examples might render this section tedious, so a few should suffice. In this example from *Diseases,* Book II, he focuses on dietary issues: "When you think it is the right moment *[kairós],* give foods of the most laxative kind" (Potter V.227).[6] *Kairos* applies in surgical procedures as well, as this excerpt from *Ulcers* shows: "It is also beneficial to make blood flow frequently from long standing lesions, whenever it seems opportune *[kairós],* both from the lesions themselves and from the area around them" (Potter VIII.345).[7] *Kairos* also appears frequently in reference to mixing or preparing medications. "Wax, aged and fresh lard, olive oil, verdigris, squill and resin: let there be two parts of the aged lard, and of the other components as much as seems appropriate *[kairós]*" (Potter VIII.367).[8]

Women's Health

Included in issues of judgment, according to Hippocrates, was the common "problem" of women's health.[9] Hippocrates complains that "physicians often make the mistake of . . . treating [women's illnesses] as if they were men's

diseases and I have seen more than one woman die following such affections.
. . . Women's disease and men's disease are very different as far as treatment is
concerned" (Littré, 8.126). Hippocrates was probably the first physician to
record in writing the vital recognition that women's health was different than
men's without implying that women were somehow deficient as a result. Plinio
Prioreschi claims, too, that the Hippocratic "physician relied more on the experience of women than on his [own] knowledge" in treating certain gyneco-
logical and obstetrical problems (359). So the female patient and, in some
cases, the local midwife, were given some degree of respect by Hippocratic
physicians. The reason was clearly allied to both the timely and the practical:
they were there, and they had both personal and professional experience. This
belief did not, of course, prevent him from writing a considerable number of
treatises on the subject of women—*On the Nature of Women, On Women's Diseases, On Sterile Women, On Young Girls* (or *On Virgins*)—nor did it seem to
convince him that women should be included in the "art" of which we see him
as founder. Yet he did make some protofeminist distinctions in his discussions
of gender.

Unlike those who came immediately after him, Hippocrates believed that
conception involved the active participation of both genders (see Dickason):
"For growth belongs, not only to the man's secretion, but also to that of the
woman. . . . Either part alone has not motion enough, owing to the bulk of its
moisture and the weakness of its fire. . . . On one day in each month it can so-
lidify, and master the advancing parts, and that only if it happen that parts are
emitted from *both parents* together in one place" (Jones IV.265 – 67; emphasis
added). Hippocrates' claim of equal participation in reproduction is based on
his theory of the humors. He also insisted on equality from a spiritual standpoint as well: "Male and female have the power to fuse into one solid, both
because both are nourished in both and also because soul is the same thing in
living creatures, although the body of each is different" (Jones IV.267). So it
is important to Hippocratic thought to recognize parity on this spiritual
level, while it is equally important to recognize difference: "Now soul is always alike, in a larger creature as in a smaller, for it changes neither through
nature nor through force. But the body of no creature is ever the same, either
by nature or by force" (Jones IV.267). This recognition of essential difference
made his approach to women's health profoundly more effective for women
than that of many of his male progenitors, or even descendants.

Kairos and the Doctor's Bedside Manner

Part of the reason Hippocrates felt that the physician must be able to accept
difference and analyze its role was that it was important for him to be deci-

sive and self-assured. In *Precepts,* he admonishes his audience to remember the physician's potential power: "For when a diseased condition is stubborn and the evil grows, in the perplexity of the moment most things go wrong. So on such occasions *[kairó]* one must be bold" (Jones I.323). The doctor must recognize the essential power of a patient's fear and use his experience to help alleviate the stress by dealing with situations effectively and efficiently: "while skillfully treating the patient, [a physician should] not refrain from exhortations not to worry in mind in the eagerness to reach the hour *[kairón]* of recovery" (Jones I.325). So situational context relies upon more than just scientific observation, but attention to human emotion as well. This is the birth of "bedside manner," both a rhetorical and a medical circumstance which Hippocrates felt was important enough to discuss in some detail.

In essence, the treatment of patients is a question of decorum (*to prepon* in the Greek), both medical and social.[10] And Hippocrates does not stop short of advising doctors about handling the business-related aspects of the art: "So one must not be anxious about fixing a fee. For I consider such a worry to be harmful to a troubled patient, particularly if the disease be acute *[kairón]*. For the quickness of the disease, offering no opportunity *[kairói]* for turning back, spurs on the good physician not to seek his profit but rather to lay hold on reputation" (Jones I.317). There are times for particular actions that must be chosen with care and experience. In *Precepts,* Hippocrates even dictates gentlemanly behavior in relation to charity: "And if there be an opportunity *[kairós]* of serving one who is a stranger in financial straits, give full assistance to all such. For where there is love of man, there is also love of the art. . . . observe what is seemly" (Jones I.319). The connection with both Aristotle and Plato's claims about the appropriate (decorum) is immediately clear. The physician, like the orator, must recognize the necessity of building a reputation (his *ethos*) by utilizing and appealing to the emotions of his audience *(pathos)*. He must recognize not just the current medical needs of patients and their families or communities, but the long-term effect of his public utterances and actions (see also Jones I.315 above).[11]

So *kairos* is not just about time, and Hippocrates' work on medicine often deals with more than just when something should be done. The corpus is most often practical, talking about how treatment might be given. From *Places in Man:* "In medicine the correct measure *[kairós]* is narrow. . . . Correct measure *[kairós]* is the following: to administer as much food as, being administered, will be mastered by the body. . . . Now if the body gains a mastery over the food, neither will any disease nor anything else contrary to the nature of what is administered result; this is the correct measure *[kairós]* the physician must recognize" (Potter VIII.89). The idea of the mean is not only related to medicine and science specifically, but to rhetoric as well. As in rhetoric, going beyond the mean in either direction can have disastrous results.

Discourse Theory and Writing in the Sciences

Hippocrates was not just interested in the body. As a good ancient Greek, he placed great weight on utterances and rhetorical facility; G. E. R. Lloyd even claims that some of his treatises were "designed for rhetorical performances" (*Early*, 58). At the very beginning of *Diseases* (Book I, section 1), Hippocrates is even more specific about linguistic facility in his advice for physicians:

> Anyone who wishes to ask correctly about healing, and, on being asked, *to reply and rebut* correctly, must consider the following: first, whence all diseases in men arise. . . . What physicians treating patients achieve by luck. What good or bad things patients suffer in diseases. What is *said or done* on conjecture by the physician to the patient, or by the patient to the physician. What is *said and done* with precision in medicine, which things are correct in it, and which not correct. . . . What it is possible to perceive, to say, to see, and to do, and what it is not possible to perceive, to say, to see, or to do. What is dexterity in medicine, and what is awkwardness. What the opportune moment *[kairós]* is, and what inopportunity *[akairín]*. (Potter V.99–101; emphasis added)

Hippocrates realizes that a physician must "reply and rebut" on the subject of medicine (whether to a patient, a family, or another practitioner). Part of the practitioner's responsibility is to be aware of his rhetorical situation and respond to the particular situation accordingly. Hippocrates' comment about "dexterity" or "awkwardness" in medicine may just as easily be about verbal behavior as about the physical care of patients. Notice that Hippocrates repeats "said or done" twice in as many lines, since both words and actions are the bailiwick of the physician. Although the word *kairos* is not used specifically until the end of the section, he refers to a variety of contextual circumstances associated with the concept. What is especially interesting in this passage, too, is the way that *logos* (timelessness, stasis, method) seems to be replaced with the more flexible aspects of *kairos* (time, change, conflict, individual). Words like "luck" and "conjecture" are balanced with others like "precision" and "correct." Flexibility rather than rigidity are the hallmarks of Hippocrates' advice to physicians.

Given the fact that *kairos* helps introduce several of the tenets of *Diseases*, it is not surprising that Hippocrates devotes an entire section to discussing its uses. Because of the many uses of the term and its theoretical importance, I will quote it at length:

> Opportune moments *[kairoĕ]* in medicine, generally speaking, are many and varied, just as are the diseases and affections and their treatments.
> . . . These opportune moments are acute, and a little later does not suffice, for a little later most patients die. The opportune moment *[kairoĕ]* is when a person is suffering . . . : whatever aid anyone gives before the patient's spirit departs he gives at

the opportune moment *[kairó]*. Generally speaking, such opportune moments *[kairós]* exist in other diseases as well, for whenever a person provides help, he is helping at an opportune moment *[kairó]*.

There are also non-mortal diseases and wounds that have opportune moments *[kairía]*; these are diseases that involve suffering and that, if treated properly, can be made to go away. . . .

There are other diseases which have their opportune time *[kairós]* for treatment early in the day, it making no difference whether very early or a little later. Other diseases have their opportune time *[kairós]* for treatment once a day. . . . These are the opportune times *[kairói]* of some diseases, and opportunity has no other kind of precision than this.

Inopportunity *[Akairíe]* is as follows: if diseases that should be treated early in the day are handled at midday, they are treated inopportunely *[akairón]*; inopportunely *[akairós]*, since they have a turn for the worse because their treatment was not opportune *[kairó]*. Those that should be treated immediately are treated inopportunely *[akairós]*, if they are treated at noon, in the evening, or at night, those that should be treated in the spring, if they are treated in winter, those that should be treated in winter, if they are treated in summer; if what should be treated at once is put off, or if what should be put off is treated at once: things of this sort constitute treating inopportunely *[akairós]*. (Potter V.107 – 11)

This chapter is the fullest discussion of *kairos* as it relates to timing in medicine. Hippocrates' statements, though often specifically related to health issues, might as easily be applied to discourse and rhetoric. Even the issue of a patient's life—"a little later does not suffice, for a little later most patients die"—might just as easily be replaced with "prisoner" and refer to a lawyer's pleading of a criminal case. Timing is as important to physicians as it is to men who deal in the art of words. What is key to both is the ability of the speaker to recognize the "right" moment, and, knowing that right moment, to take decisive action. The opposite is equally true, since it follows the same theoretical and methodological rules. The dangers of poor timing in medicine are perhaps even more real and pressing.

From this view of timing also comes certain organizational tendencies in the setting forth of a text. Not just medical writers, but scientific writers are careful to be efficient in their texts, generally choosing a tight organization that allows for little to no deviation. The tendency among writers to insist on keeping to topic often results in verbal deferral. It happens twice in *On Joints,* as in the following discussion of "friction" (massage): "Though called by one name it has not one and the same effect, for friction will make a joint firm when looser than it should be, and relax it when too stiff. But we shall define the rules for friction in another *[kairón]* treatise" (Withington III.221).[12] Here *kairos* is translated as "another," though "appropriate" might be a more fitting word—the *kairos* of the present textual moment is not right, but some other time in the future will presumably be better. Deferral is often justified in Hippocrates' texts as a way to avoid verbosity and wandering: "In the body there are also other very small glands, but I do not want to wander off from my subject; this treatise, after all, pertains to the essentials *[epíkairons]*. So now I shall go on in my argument and discuss the general nature of the glands of the throat" (Potter VIII.113–15). Again, it is *kairos* that helps reveal what is most appropriate. There are particular times when discussion is fitting: "I have in part discussed these things already, and shall do so further when the occasions *[kaíroidi]* arise" (Jones II.119). These are issues of appropriateness, but verbal, rather than social ones. Hippocrates' claim about medicine even sounds like a definition of rhetoric: "Medicine . . . teaches in each instance the particular details and the correct measures *[kairóns]*" (Potter VIII.93). Similarly, Aristotle defined rhetoric as seeking "not so much to persuade as to find out in each case *[perĕ hekáston]* the existing means of persuasion" (*Rhetoric* 1355b14).[13]

Hippocrates' Legacy

Having used Aristotle's definition of rhetoric in my previous example, it seems only appropriate to begin this section on Hippocrates' legacy with that same Greek thinker. Aristotle was the son of a physician and he certainly applied Hippocratic methodology to his various studies. He viewed the use of *kairos* in medicine as exemplary; he even uses it as such when describing his own methodology in the *Nicomachean Ethics:*

> [T]he whole theory of conduct is bound to be an outline only and not an exact system . . . matters of conduct and expediency have nothing fixed or invariable about them, any more than have matters of health. And if this is true of the general theory of ethics, still less is exact precision possible in dealing with particular cases of conduct *[perĕ hekásta]*; for these come under no science or professional tradition, but the agents themselves have to consider what is suited to the circumstances on each occasion *[kairón]*, just as is the case with the art of medicine or of navigation. (1104a, 3–5)

This may sound familiar, having just heard Hippocrates discuss the problem in *On Ancient Medicine,* above. It is not an isolated claim in the corpus, either. Hippocrates mentions the issue again in his *Places in Man:*

> Medicine cannot be learned quickly because it is impossible to create any established principle in it, the way that a person who learns writing according to one system that people teach understands everything; for all who understand writing in the same way do so because the same symbol does not sometimes become opposite, but is always steadfastly the same and not subject to chance. Medicine, on the other hand, does not do the same thing at this moment *[kairón]* and the next, and it does opposite things to the same person, and at that things that are self-contradictory. (Potter VIII.81)

Both agree that no steadfast "laws" of conduct and practice are possible, given the variable nature of experience. It seems ironic that Hippocrates chose to use writing as his example, since we have seen Aristotle use medicine again and again. And Aristotle extended his methodology to all of the physical sciences, as his own practice attests. Beyond the theoretical similarities, Aristotle's biological treatises are replete with material drawn from the Hippocratic corpus (Byl, 374).

We might also hear an echo of Hippocrates' discussion of the importance of observation in Aristotle's *Posterior Analytics* (2.19.100a): "Sense-perception gives rise to memory . . . and repeated memories of the same thing give rise to experience . . . and experience . . . provides the starting-point of . . . science." So, like his forefather, Aristotle put most stock in that which could be ascertained through the senses. In his *Generation of Animals,* after making some hypotheses regarding the generation of bees, Aristotle makes this statement: "But the facts have not been sufficiently ascertained; and if at any future time they are ascertained, then credence must be given to the direct evidence of the senses more than to theories,—and to theories too provided that the results that they show agree with what is observed" (3.10.760b). The theoretical echoes are abundantly clear. The literal is also in evidence. *Kairos* turns up quite frequently in Aristotle's scientific works: In *Generation of Animals,* fourteen times; *History of Animals,* twenty-six times; *Parts of Animals,* four; *De virtutibus et vitiis,* three; and even *Meteorology,* three times. Given the importance of the concepts, the number of uses does not seem strange. Aristotle's theoretical practice of science owes much to the ground-breaking work of Hippocrates.

It makes equal sense that Galen (c. A.D. 130 –c.200), the founder of experimental physiology, is indebted to Hippocrates. Galen's methods were much like those of Hippocrates; he was a dissector who wrote up what he saw with precision and furthered descriptive practice and terminology, in the tradition of Hippocrates. Of the 121 works listed in IBYCUS for Galen, *-kair-* occurs 1,485 times, demonstrating how widespread was Galen's use of the concept.

The Renaissance scientific thinkers also owe something to Hippocrates. Paracelsus was a great admirer of Hippocrates and wrote some commentaries on his work (Smith, 16 – 17, 19). He recognizes Hippocrates' insistence on the importance of interdisciplinarity, fully comprehending and applying Hippocratic theories of situational determinism. Though we no longer hear the Greek word *kairos,* the echo of its concept rings clearly. Francis Bacon felt that Hippocrates' theories were applicable to the new science (Smith, 18), and Bacon quotes Hippocrates directly in both his *Advancement of Learning* and *De Augmentis Scientiarum* (141, 572). He discusses the necessity of proper recording: as a proponent of careful scientific methodology and a voluminous writer himself, Bacon recommends to his contemporaries that they study and emulate the Hippocratic method.

My last subject under Hippocrates' legacy is a fairly controversial one. Beginning with Herodotus, the Hippocratic methodology has much in common with the practice of writing history (Momigliano). Thucydides' exile in Scapte Hyle, very near Abdera, put him in close physical proximity with Hippocrates when he was still a practicing physician (Proctor, 41). É. Littré, the French translator of Hippocrates, was the first to point out a "certain affinity" between the two authors, and others followed. C. N. Cochrane claimed that Thucydides got his "principles of rational empiricism" from Hippocrates (7). Cochrane also believed that Hippocrates was the reason that Thucydides "first laid down the distinction between the 'occasion' and the 'true cause'" of historical events (169). But it was Klaus Weidauer who looked at the similarities between Thucydides' descriptions of the plague in his *Histories* and Hippocrates' *Epidemics* and claimed that the historical work's construction and orientation were a direct result of Hippocrates' influence. Dennis Proctor, among others, believes the relationship between the two thinkers was more like that of kindred spirits, rather than teacher-student (Proctor, 41; see also Hornblower, Holladay, and Poole). James Longrigg maintains that Thucydides' observational technique has the same "rational attitude" as that of Hippocrates (33). Yet he also suggests that, "while there seems no good reason to doubt that he was familiar with contemporary medical literature and influenced by the spirit of Hippocratic medicine, it would be unwise to conclude that his rationality of approach was derived exclusively from contemporary medicine" (Longrigg, 33).

The appearance of *kairos* in his texts, however, leaves little doubt that the concepts used by both Thucydides and Hippocrates were similar in presentation. In the two works by Thucydides available on IBYCUS, *kair-* appears sixty-five times (there are only thirteen uses by Herodotus in his *Histories*).

The connection between Hippocrates and history is a subject of some contention, but there can be little room for doubt that the father of medicine is also the father of scientific discourse. The Hippocratic corpus "deals not merely with strictly medical questions," as Lloyd writes, "but with problems ranging over the whole field of biology, and it contains some of our most valuable evidence for early Greek science" (*Polarity,* 9 – 10).[14] By being one of the first to actually write down his observations and theories, Hippocrates set the tone and even the form for those who would follow him. *Kairos* informs both the tone and the form.

Hippocrates was generally a pragmatist in his approach to problems; he saw *kairos* as the most efficient and useful concept and term available. Even when the term itself is not directly involved, the issues of *kairos* permeate the corpus: we sense its implicit presence in timing and time-related issues, proper measure, and the necessity of the mean. Introducing the idea that the scientist must use accurate and verifiable data as the basis for theoretical conclusions, Hippocrates kept *kairos* as an important element in his practice. In addition, his painstaking and scrupulous attention to detail helped initiate the system of specific nomenclatures for the various disciplines.

The most universally applicable of the *kairos*-related concepts put forward by Hippocrates is undeniably situational context. Hippocrates was the first to see the need for cross-disciplinary study and the integration of information from various sources in the successful treatment of individual patients. In fact, he was the first truly to respect the importance of looking at each particular case (including history) and at each patient as unique and singular, an entity not interchangeable with any other patient. (Situational context is also the heading that might contain certain aspects of decorum: the establishment of professional standards and ethics.) Looking just at the writings of Aristotle we can see the long-term effect that Hippocrates' usage had on Western science and civilization. Even the general disuse of Greek concepts during the Roman ascendancy could not prevent later thinkers like Paracelsus and Bacon from admiring and utilizing Hippocratic concepts.

Notes

1. The work of Hippocrates on the decision-making process is still recognized today. See, for example, Zarin and Pauker, "Decision Analysis as a Basis for Medical Decision Making."

2. All references to Greek texts are taken from the Loeb series, whose editions of Hippocrates (volumes I-VIII) are cited parenthetically by translator, volume, and page number(s). W. H. S. Jones prepared volumes I (1923), II (1923), and IV (1931); E. T. Withington, volume III (1927); Paul Potter, volumes V (1988), VI (1988), and VIII (1995); Wesley D. Smith, volume VII (1994). In addition to the Loeb Hippocrates, I have also relied on the French edition by É. Littré; translations from the French are thanks to the patience and assistance of Abioseh Porter.

3. In his introduction to the Loeb Hippocrates, Jones claims that the ancient Greeks were impatient and unable to exert the discipline necessary for accurate science (IV.xxiii). "All Greeks," of course, except for Hippocrates. (Jones is strangely belittling of the Greek character in this introduction.)

4. Examples of the use of *kairos* in descriptions of symptoms include *Of Breath* (Littré, 6.113); *Epidemics* (Littré, 2.629, 2.657–59, 2.703, 3.75, 3.95, 5.375, 5.385; Jones, I.151, I.163); *On Fractures* (Withington, III.123, III.123, III.171, III.193); *On Humors* (Jones, IV.69–71); *Internal Affections* (Potter, VI.225; Littré, 7.207); *On Joints* (Withington, III.361); *Prorrhetic* (Potter, VIII.265); *Regimen* (Potter, IV.363); *Regimen in Acute Diseases* (Jones, II.109, II.123); *The Sacred Disease* (Jones, II.141, II.177, II.177); *On Women's Diseases* (Littré, 8.65, 8.107, 8.123).

5. For other moments where Hippocrates uses *kairos* to point out the necessity of a physician's education being interdisciplinary, see *Airs, Waters, Places* (Jones, I.99);

Epidemics (Littré, 2.629, 2.677–79, 5.75); *Internal Affections* (Potter, VI.211; Littré, 7.271); *Physician* (Potter, VIII.313–15; Littré 7.271); *On Women's Diseases* (Littré, 8.241).

6. Other examples of dietary-related uses of *kairos* include *Affections* (Potter, V.77, V.91); *Diseases* (Potter, V.281); *Epidemics* (Littré, 2.677–79; 3.91); *On Glands* (Potter, VIII.111); *Internal Affections* (Potter, VI.171, VI.171, VI.211; Littré, 7.241); *Regimen* (Potter, IV.34, IV.227); *Regimen in Acute Diseases* (Jones, II.77, II.79, II.91, II.97, II.119–21); *Sacred Disease* (Jones, II.141–3); *On Women's Diseases* (Littré, 8.69, 8.155, 8.299, 8.255).

7. Other examples of surgical *kairos* occur in *Affections* (Potter, V.75, V.83); *Diseases* (Littré, 3.7); *On Fractures* (Withington, III.153, III.169–71, III.181); *On Humors* (Potter, IV.95); *Internal Affections* (Potter, VI.185); *On Joints* (Withington, III.293, III.373); *On the Nature of Women* (Littré, 7.379); *Prognostic* (Jones, II.49); *Ulcers* (Potter, VIII.351, VIII.373); *On Vision* (Littré, 10.155); *On Women's Diseases* (Littré, 8.133, 8.259, 8.295, 8.423, 8.455, 8.483).

8. Other examples of *kairos* and pharmacology occur in *Affections* (Potter, V.91); *Diseases* (Littré, 6.153); *On Joints* (Withington, III.299–301); *On the Nature of Women* (Littré, 7.343); *Regimen in Acute Diseases* (Jones, II.109, II.113, II.119–21); *Sacred Disease* (Jones, II.183); *On Women's Diseases* (Littré, 8.77, 8.133, 8.135, 8.189, 8.243, 8.247, 8.255, 8.479, 8.505).

9. Helen King explains that "the very autonomy of the study of female diseases reflects the separation of woman from the superior, complete human form, man" (112, n.9).

10. Paul Carrick claims that Hippocrates gave "directives" about "such comparatively mundane matters as the proper deportment, dress, and demeanor of the socially correct doctor" (91). These are all clearly issues of *decorum* and rhetorical presentation.

11. William Arthur Heidel explicitly connects medical discourse and oratory (10–11): "the procedure in medicine is much the same as in public speaking: one must begin by analyzing nature." He continues later, "Furthermore, the orator must recognize the 'appropriate'—and here Plato resorts to a technical term (*kairos*) with interesting connotations in Hippocratic literature, for, besides its usual meaning of 'opportune moment,' the word is sometimes used in the sense of 'proper measure,' neither too little nor too much" (12).

12. Other instances of textual deferral occur in *Regimen in Acute Diseases* (Jones, II.73, II.95, II.119; Withington, III.253).

13. The following quote, very much like Aristotle's definition of rhetoric, comes from Hippocrates' *Airs, Waters, Places*: "by learning the times beforehand, he will have full knowledge of each particular case [*perĕ hekáston*], will succeed best in securing health, and will achieve the greatest triumphs in the practice of his art" (Jones I.73). I should add that Aristotle refers directly to medicine one sentence after his definition of rhetoric: ". . . it is not the function of medicine to restore a patient to health, but only to promote this end as far as possible; for even those whose recovery is impossible may be properly treated" (*Rhetoric*, 1355b14).

14. Examples of more "scientific research" in Hippocrates occur, for example, in *On Diseases* IV, chapter 39. G. E. R. Lloyd discusses several experiments in some detail in his *Methods and Problems*.

Works Cited

Aristotle. *The Art of Rhetoric*. Trans. John Henry Freese. Cambridge: Harvard University Press, 1982.

Bacon, Francis. *The Philosophical Works of Francis Bacon.* Ed. John M. Robertson. London: Routledge and Kegan Paul, 1905.

Byl, S. "Les grands traités biologiques d'Aristote et la Collection hippocratique." In *Corpus Hippocraticum: Actes du Colloque Hippocratique de Mons.* Ed. R. Joly, 313–31. (22–26 Sept. 1975). Mons, France: Université de Mons, 1977.

Carrick, Paul. *Medical Ethics in Antiquity: Philosophical Perspectives on Abortion and Euthanasia.* Boston: D. Reidel, 1985.

Cochrane, C. N. *Thucydides and the Science of History.* London: Oxford University Press, 1929.

Cohen, Morris R. and I. E. Drabkin. *A Source Book in Greek Science.* New York: McGraw-Hill, 1948.

Dickason, Anne. "Anatomy and Destiny: The Role of Biology in Plato's Views of Women." *The Philosophical Forum* 1–2 (1973–74): 45–53.

Heidel, William Arthur. *Hippocratic Medicine.* New York: Arno, 1981.

Holladay, A. J. and J. C. F. Poole. "Thucydides and the Plague of Athens." *Classical Quarterly* 29 (1979): 282–300.

Hornblower, Simon. *Thucydides.* London: Johns Hopkins University Press, 1987.

King, Helen. "Bound to Bleed: Artemis and Greek Women." In *Images of Women in Antiquity.* Ed. Averil Cameron and Amélie Kuhrt, 109–27. London: Croom Helm, 1983.

Levine, Edwin Burton. *Hippocrates.* New York: Twayne, 1971.

Liddell,Henry George and Robert Scott. *A Greek-English Lexicon.* Oxford: Clarendon, 1940.

Littré, É. *Oeuvres Complètes d'Hippocrate.* 10 Vols. Amsterdam: Adolf M. Hakkert, 1962.

Lloyd, G. E. R. *Early Greek Science: Thales to Aristotle.* New York: Norton, 1970.

———. *Methods and Problems in Greek Science.* New York: Cambridge University Press, 1991.

———. *Polarity and Analogy: Two Types of Argumentation in Early Greek Thought.* Cambridge, Cambridge University Press, 1966.

Longrigg, James. *Greek Rational Medicine: Philosophy and Medicine from Alcmaeon to the Alexandrians.* New York: Routledge and Kegan Paul, 1993.

Momigliano, A. "History Between Medicine and Rhetoric." *Annali della Scuola Normale Superiore de Pisa,* Ll. Di Lettere e Filosofia, Pisa V, 15 (1985): 767–780.

Prioreschi, Plinio. *A History of Medicine, Volume 2: Greek Medicine.* Lewiston, New York: Edwin Mellen, 1994.

Proctor, Dennis. *The Experience of Thucydides.* Surrey: Billes, 1980.

Smith, Wesley D. *The Hippocratic Tradition.* Ithaca: Cornell University Press, 1979.

Weidauer, Klaus. *Der Einfluss der Medizin auf Zielsetzung und Darstellungsweise des Geschichte.* Heidelberg: C. Winter, 1954.

Zarin, Deborah A. and Stephen G. Pauker. "Decision Analysis as a Basis for Medical Decision Making: The Tree of Hippocrates." *The Journal of Medicine and Philosophy* 9 (1984): 181–213.

Kairos

The Rhetoric of Time and Timing

in the New Testament

PHILLIP SIPIORA

"The time has been fulfilled and the kingdom of God has drawn near. Repent and believe in the gospel" (Mark 1:15). These words are the first utterance of Christ. The first noun from the mouth of the Son of God is *kairos,* a Greek word for time which carries a number of strategic rhetorical meanings. Conjoined with *kairos* in this sentence is a present-perfect construction of the Greek verb for persuade, *pisteuein.* These master terms, *pisteuein* and *kairos,* along with *pistis* (the noun for belief) constitute, it might be argued, critical elements in a rhetorical template of the New Testament.

As we mark the second millennium after the birth of the Christian era, a plethora of biblical research has focused on rhetorical dimensions of the Testaments, Old and New. Work by scholars such as Hans Dieter Betz, James Muilenberg, Jack Lundbom, Yehoshua Gitay, Vernon Robbins, Thomas Olbricht, Anders Erikkson, James L. Kinneavy, George A. Kennedy, and others have explored the challenge of a rhetorical analysis of the Holy Scripture, as distinct from the more general analyses that have characterized scriptural research over the past two centuries. Hans Dieter Betz, in his extensive analysis of Paul's *Letter to the Galatians,* remarks: "[T]he letter was composed in accordance with the conventions of Greco-Roman rhetoric and epistolography" (xiv). And Werner Jaeger, in *Early Christianity and Greek Paideia,* has argued that early Christian faith represents a continuation of the educational (that is, rhetorical) system of the Greeks: "In calling Christianity the *paideia* of Christ, the imitator senses the intention of the apostle to make Christianity to be a continuation of the classical *paideia,* which it would be logical for those who possessed the older one to accept" (61–62). In the 1980s, two major scholars of rhetoric, George A. Kennedy and James L. Kinneavy, approached the New Testament from rhetorical perspectives.

In his 1987 study of the relationship between Greek rhetoric and Christian faith, Kinneavy argued that the gospel writers were well-trained in Greek rhetoric and their audience was of a culture that had experienced widespread Hellenization and would have anticipated Greek rhetorical concepts and techniques in New Testament discourse, particularly because of pervasive training in local *gymnasia*. Limits of space prevent an extensive summary of Kinneavy's argument. However, for the purpose of my exploration, it is important to bear in mind Kinneavy's hypothesis for the derivation of the concept of Christian faith from Greek rhetoric, namely, from the meanings of the Greek noun *pistis* (faith, appeal) and the verb *pisteuein* (to believe) as they appear in various forms in the New Testament. Kinneavy offers substantive semantic, historical, and lexical evidence in support of his hypothesis, which, to my knowledge, has not been confuted.

My hypothesis, that the Greek word *kairos* is a strategic New Testament rhetorical concept, is an extension of Kinneavy's argument supporting the pervasive influence of Greek rhetoric in Christian theology.[1] I would like to begin by discussing briefly the Greek rhetorical meanings of *kairos*, followed by an illustration of *kairos* in the New Testament. The concept of *kairos*—very generally defined as timing, opportunity, or due measure—is now generally understood to have been a seminal notion in ancient Greek rhetoric, literature, and philosophy.

Kairos is not a term easily defined, as other essays in this volume suggest. John E. Smith, in attempting to explain this complex concept as it was used in antiquity, describes it as carefully and expansively as anyone:

> [K]airos points to a *qualitative* character of time, to the special position an event or action occupies in a series, to a season when something appropriately happens that cannot happen at "any" time, but only at 'that time,' to a time that marks an opportunity which may not recur. The question especially relevant to *kairos* time is "when," "At what time," to a time that marks an opportunity which may not recur. (1)

For purposes of scriptural analysis, let me suggest that *kairos* is a rich concept, with a multiplicity of meanings and a rich legacy of resonance including timing, opportunity, location, season(s), and profit. There are many meanings relevant to the New Testament, including *kairos* as eschatological time. I would also suggest that there is a *kairos* that is "God's time." The primary objective of this essay is to explore various meanings of *kairos* as they appear in the New Testament. There is no presumption of comprehensiveness or taxonomic coverage. Surely there are definitions of *kairos* in the New Testament that are not treated in this analysis. My intention is to be illustrative and sug-gestive rather than comprehensive and definitive (which would be a redoubt-able task).

Greek Roots of New Testament *Kairos*

Kairos, lexically and conceptually, appears first in Homer's *Iliad*, where it de-notes a *vital* or *lethal* place in the body, one that is particularly susceptible to injury and therefore necessitates special protection; *kairos* thus carries a spa-tial meaning. In Hesiod's *Works and Days*, *kairos* takes on the sense of "due measure" or "proper proportion"; for example, Hesiod cites the overloading of a wagon, which can cause the axle to break. And Hesiod is probably the source of the maxim, "Observe due measure, and proportion *[kairos]* is best in all things" (Liddell and Scott). In time, *kairos* began to be distinguished from *chronos*, or linear time (although *chronos* takes on different meanings in differ-ent forms: the verb form *chronzio*, for example, means to take time, linger, delay; *chronotribeo* means to spend, lose or waste time). Smith differentiates *kairos* from *chronos* as follows:

> [W]e know that all the English expressions "a time to" are translations of the term "*kairos*"—the right or opportune time to do something often called "right timing." This aspect of time is to be distinguished from *chronos* which means the uniform time of the cosmic system, the time which, in Newton's phrase, *aequabiliter fluit*. In *chronos* we have the fundamental conception of time as measure, the *quantity* of du-ration, the length of periodicity, the age of an object or artifact and the rate of accel-eration of bodies whether on the surface of the earth or in the firmament above. (4)

Chronos, then, might be distinguished from the "right time" or good time *(eu-kairos)* and the "wrong time" to do something *(kakakairos)*.[2] And in some cases there is time that is without opportunity *(akairos)*, a concept that, to my knowledge, has never been explored to any significant extent (yet *akairos* ap-pears in the New Testament, lexically and conceptually).[3] Prominent ancients such as Pindar, Theognis, Solon, the Seven Sages ("Seal your word with si-lence and your silence with the *right time*," "Nothing in excess"), Aeschylus, Euripides, Sophocles, Menander, the pre-Socratics, Pythagoras, some of the Sophists, Pericles, and many others use *kairos* to signify opportunity, occa-sion, crisis or urgency, measure, proportionality (which carries connotations of justice), convenience, advantage, profit, fruit, fitness, propriety, and deco-rum. And these are only some of the uses of *kairos* in antiquity. There is much yet to be done, for example, on the relationship between *kairos* and ethics and *kairos* and aesthetics. We know from Doro Levi's research, for example, that

Plato saw central connections in these areas. The relationship between *kairos* and *ethos* in the New Testament is fertile ground for exploration.

There is now no question that *kairos* was critical to the rhetorical paradigms of Isocrates, Plato, and Aristotle. Isocrates, major competitor to the schools of Plato and Aristotle, made *kairos* the cornerstone of his rhetorical *paideia,* in which he taught his students to live well by speaking well and honorably. In *Against the Sophists,* his earliest known discussion of rhetoric, Isocrates identifies attention to *kairos* as one of the most important characteristics of effective rhetorical discourse. The opportune moment must be chosen for a particular treatment of a theme, the appropriate arguments for each of the historical events must be marshaled, and the actual arrangement of the words must be skillful. Many passages of the New Testament read as if they were written under the tutelage of Isocrates (and perhaps, indirectly, they were). Isocrates' major treatise on rhetoric, *Antidosis,* is a systematic exposition of the qualities of a rhetorically based education, at the center of which are the principles of *kairos* and *phronesis.*

Although Plato never articulated a systematic theory of rhetoric, we know that he allowed Aristotle to teach rhetoric at the Academy. And from the *Phaedrus,* a late dialogue, we know that Plato considered the central elements of an "honorific rhetoric." Plato considered *kairos* to be a central element in any effective rhetoric, and the leader of the Academy was careful to define *kairos* with great care. Near the end of the *Phaedrus,* Socrates summarizes his assessment of rhetoric and then comments on the importance of *kairos,* which he defines as the measurement of the discourse to the souls of the auditors:

> Since it is in fact the function of speech to influence souls, a man who is going to be a speaker must know how many kinds of souls there are. . . . [H]e must apply *this* kind of speech in *this* kind of manner in order to obtain persuasion for *this* kind of activity—it is when he can do all this and when he has, in addition, grasped the propriety of time *[kairos]*—when to speak and when to hold his tongue *[eukairos* and *akairos],* when to use brachylogy, piteous language, hyperbole for horrific effect, and, in a word, each of the specific devices of discourse . . .—it is only then, and not until then, that the finishing and perfecting touches will have been given to his science. (271d-272b)

This concept of *kairos*—addressing one's discourse measured to one's audience—would seem to be a cornerstone of the New Testament. There is no question that New Testament *kairos,* like pagan uses of *kairos,* is very much concerned with the "strategic moment," yet there was a discernible shift away from the pagan emphasis on fortune and fate.[4] According to Glenn F. Chestnut,

> Pagan Greco-Roman historiography had often been fascinated with the "key event" and the "critical moment"—the time and place where something tiny, like a small decision by a single man, started the giant forces of history grinding and rolling in a completely different direction. The critical moment, the *kairos*, was simply another face of Fortune *[Tyche]*. It was this word *kairos* which Socrates [Scholasticus] seized upon, and gave a novel twist to, by combining it with the concept of cosmic sympathy. (162)

The word *Tyche*, to my knowledge, never appears in the New Testament.

In the case of Aristotle, the importance of *kairos* begins with his definition of rhetoric as "the faculty of discovering the possible means of persuasion in reference to any subject whatever." The operative words are "any subject whatever"; an effective rhetor must invent and adapt his discourse according to a "right measure" or "proportion" of topic and audience. Each *pistis*—*ethos*, *pathos*, and *logos*—is thus analyzed according to its *kairos*. An effective ethical appeal is dependent upon speaker morality, judgment, and ability to bond with members of the audience. A rhetor cannot be successful unless he or she knows the audience's propensities, prejudices, and logical predispositions. There must be an appropriate measure of *ethos* in all three subethical proofs. An effective logical appeal contains persuasive examples and enthymemes, all of which must convey a sense of proportionality to the subject matter. Audiences can make neither inductive generalizations nor deductive conclusions if particulars and propositions are inappropriate to either the subject matter or the logical assumptions and background of the audience. An effective pathetic appeal must evoke certain emotional responses in the audience, which, once again, require that the rhetor know the emotional predispositions of his or her audience and be able to persuasively articulate the "right" emotional arguments. A rhetor who fails to consider the *kairos* of each *pistis* may well prove to be a most ineffective persuader of Christian values.

There are nearly five hundred occurrences of the noun *pistis* (faith, appeal) and the verb *pisteuein* (to believe) in the New Testament, which form the overall macrostructure of the rhetorical argument. There are also at least one hundred occurrences of the word *kairos* in the New Testament, which can be broken down as follows: nominative singular (17 occurrences), nominative plural (3 occurrences), genitive singular (7 occurrences), genitive plural (3 occurrences), dative singular (24 occurrences), dative plural (5 occurrences), accusative singular (22 occurrences), and accusative plural (4 occurrences). There are also two occurrences of *eukairos* (meaning a particularly beneficial or efficacious time) and one occurrence of *akairos*. These examples represent rhetorical dimensions of *kairos*, operating at the level of diction, that shape any grammatical interpretation. (And this raises an important question: is it possible to speak of grammatical interpretation without rhetorical influence, or of rhetorical interpretation without grammatical basis? I think not, as rhetoric and grammar are inextricably intertwined in complex ways.)

Kairos in the New Testament

My analysis of *kairos* in the New Testament is based upon an English translation (the new King James Version), a Greek text, and the Vulgate Latin text. I might add that there are more than fifty occurrences of the word *chronos* in the New Testament, and most of these usages are in sharp contrast to meanings of *kairos.*[5] There are important connections between *chronos* and *kairos,* some of which defy simple explanation.

It would take quite an extensive analysis, far beyond the scope of this essay, to examine all occurrences of *kairos* in the New Testament. There have been, however, some excellent discussions that initiate further analyses of *kairos* in the New Testament. Smith offers a general paradigm when he describes three general meanings of *kairos:*

> It means, first the "right time" for something to happen. . . . Second, *kairos* means a time of tension or conflict, a time of "crisis" implying that the course of events poses a problem which calls for a decision at that time. Third, *kairos* means a time when an opportunity for accomplishing some purpose has opened up as a result of the problem that led to the crisis. (6)

I have selected certain instances of *kairos* as illustrative of the ways in which *kairos* serves to situate and complement the overall rhetorical argument of the New Testament.[6] My analysis is primarily lexical and rhetorical. I would like now to show how *kairos,* as a rhetorical construction, catalyzes or amplifies other primary components of Greek rhetoric. For example, the concept of the "example" is itself a critical dimension of the rhetorical logical appeal, or argument (at least in Aristotle's theory of rhetoric, the most comprehensive extant treatment of classical rhetoric). The New Testament is rife with exemplary subnarratives, and rhetorical examples abound within them. For example, in Mark's parable of the wicked vinedressers, we are told: "And when the time of the harvest of the fruits drew near, he sent his servants to the vinedressers, that they might receive his fruit" (Matthew 21:34). The "timing" of the harvest triggers the dispatch of the servants.

The "right time" or "special time" of *kairos* is sometimes distinguished explicitly from linear or chronological time. Christians must learn to distinguish chronological time from kairic time precisely because the occasion of *kairos* carries strategic imperatives for faith and action. An example of this imperative occurs in Luke 21:8, when Christ implores the faithful to distinguish the right time from the false time: "And He said, 'Take heed that ye not be deceived: for many shall come in My name, saying I am He and the time has drawn near. Therefore, do not go after them.'" Sometimes Christ's time, which is often but not always kairic time,[7] is conjoined with the linear movements of human time, as in Jesus' admonition to always be prepared for His time: "Then Jesus said unto them, 'My time has not yet come but your time is always ready'" (John 7:6). Two verses later, Christ says, "You go up to this feast. I am not yet going to this feast, for my time has not yet fully come" (John 7:8).

Lexicographers have always considered "advantage" or "profit" one of the meanings of *kairos*, according to John R. Wilson.[8] There are several instances of this meaning of *kairos* (which usually appears as *en kairo*) in the New Testament. Christ reminds his followers that a "timely profit" is theirs if they follow Him: "Who shall not receive a hundredfold now in this time *[en kairo touto]*—houses and brothers and sisters and mothers and children and lands, with persecutions—and in the age to come, eternal life" (Mark 10:30). This passage is powerful in its imagery, as Christ asks His followers to abandon temporal "riches" for timeless wealth by taking advantage of the timely opportunity. Kairic overtures are not always so positive, however, and vary significantly in their emphasis, as in Christ's exhortation to His followers in Luke 12:56: "Hypocrites! You can discern the face of the sky and of the earth, but how is it you do not discern this time *[kairon touton]*?" This type of rhetorical question, containing an embedded kairic question, is not uncommon in the New Testament.

Perhaps the most striking semantic use of *kairos* lies in the meaning of urgency or crisis, and this usage constitutes a significant proportion of the occurrences of *kairos*.[9] The concept of *kairos* energizes or catalyzes the rhetorical imperative of many sentences and longer passages, yet in discernibly different ways. *Kairos* always contextualizes or mediates circumstances, usually in making situations conducive for the persuasive act of belief and trust, which lead in turn to changes in conviction, emotion, and action. In his first epistle, for example, Peter speaks of suffering for God's glory: "For the time has come for judgment to begin at the house of God; and if it begins with us first, what will be the end of those who do not obey the gospel of God?" (1 Peter 4:17). Peter is *not* posing a rhetorical question; surely readers are invited to inscribe themselves within this hypothetical rhetorical enthymeme, with accompanying powerful emotional undercurrents. If they (we) accept the premise that judgment will begin with us, then the strategic use of *kairos* intensifies our motive to conform to standards of Christian behavior at this special time. Later time—chronological time—does not necessarily offer the same opportunity for action and commitment. And *kairos* often means special opportunity. A more emotional rhetorical appeal occurs in the second epistle to Timothy, in which the appeal to fear is explicit: "But know this, that in the last days perilous times will come" (2 Timothy 3:1).

New Testament persuasive strategies are advanced in numerous ways through the use of *kairos*. Peter's admonition above takes an aggressive stance in urging the commitment to Christianity, yet there are examples of *kairos* as a more subtle catalyst to change. In Revelation 1:3 we are told: "Blessed is he who reads and those who hear the words of this prophecy, and keep those things which are written in it; for the time is near." The tone of this passage is clearly different from Peter's injunction. Although time here is special (as in impending), there is a diminished crisis atmosphere, because of the shift in emphasis from exclusion (as in Peter's epistle) to one of inclusion.

Kairos is sometimes used in the sense of culmination, as in adjudication. For example, in the first epistle of Peter, Pilgrims are warned that they "are kept by the power of God through faith *[pisteos]* unto salvation ready to be revealed in the last time *[kairo]*" (1 Peter 1:5). This construction is a dative of time, a common occurrence in the New Testament, and it serves to condition faith (that is, belief plus trust) until "final time" or messianic time, at which time belief will be proved to have been justified. In the first epistle of Timothy, in the section containing "instructions to the rich," there is a similar admonition: "Which he will manifest in his own time, He who is the blessed and only Potentate, the King of kings and Lord of Lords" (1 Timothy 6:15). There are theological-legal tones to these constructions.

The kairic dative of time also suggests something like "God's Time," uninfluenced by the rhythms and cycles of chronological, earthly time. According to Warshaw's gloss, this use of *kairos* is the divine arrangement of time adjusted to the economy of salvation (318). The concept of God's time is illustrated in the Acts of the Apostles, when Jesus promises to send the Holy Spirit: "And he said to them, 'It is not for you to know times or seasons which the Father has put in His own authority'" (Acts 1:7). There is no question that there are weighty eschatological implications to *kairos* as "the last time" and the "time of crisis." The sense of *eschatos kairos,* a "final" term of time, is recurrent in the New Testament as well as in later Judaism. In one sense, chronological time must be completed before kairic time or messianic time—end time and final judgment—is catalyzed to fruition. It might be argued that *kairos,* as God's time, reveals *the* most strategic and critical time. According to Gerhard Delling,

> The "fateful and decisive point," with strong, though not always explicit emphasis (except at Acts 24:25) on the fact that it is ordained by God. In accordance with the New Testament concept of God, however, there is now a clearer grasp of the rich and incalculable and gracious goodness of God in the gift of *kairos* and of the judicial severity of its once-for-all demand. (459)

The loss of Jerusalem because of its failure to seize the kairic moment (Luke 19:14) is but one example. The first epistle of Peter reminds pilgrims that they are maintained by faith for final salvation: "who are kept by the power of God through faith for salvation ready to be revealed in the last time *[kairo eschato]*" (1 Peter 1:5).

Kairos often signifies a sobriety of moment, a precarious time of grave solemnity. According to Delling,

> [T]he seriousness of decision, already present in the Greek concept of *kairos,* is given an intensity which we find strange both in the religious proclamation of Jesus and in the moral demands of Paul. The more fully the end is viewed together with present fulfillment, the more urgent is the demand of the *kairos,* which recurs with each moment of the Christian life, and which in its instantaneousness requires of the Christian that he should recognize it and concretely fulfill its demand (Rv. 13:8–10) in the exercise of brotherly love. (460)

This reading suggests that the Christian, always and already, faces eschatological choices in the decisions of daily life. Indeed, it might be argued that the daily life of the Christian is a continuing moment of kairic choice.

Time, as *chronos,* proceeds linearly until He authorizes the coming of the ultimate kairic moment, the time of judgment. There is possibly also an ethical dimension to this movement, in that "final justice" is deferred until the kairic moment. One's ultimate fate becomes sealed forever only when the time is appropriate for judgment. The notion of "God's time" adds an element of mystery and uncertainty into the calculus of human behavior and action, particularly as it refers to God's ultimate judgment of human behavior. In Ephesians 5:15 there is an imperative to walk in wisdom: "Watch therefore that you walk carefully, not as unwise but as wise, redeeming the opportunity, because the days are evil." In the epistle to the Hebrews, there is a call to the heavenly hope of faith: "And truly, if they had called to mind that country from which they had come, they would have had an opportunity to return" (Hebrews 11:15). In Romans 13:11, pilgrims are admonished to reject carnality and accept Christ: "And do this, knowing the time *(kairos),* that it is now high time to awake out of sleep: for now our salvation is nearer than we believed." In this passage, time as "daily" time is translated as "*hora,*" and "high time" or opportune time is "*kairos.*" The two perspectives on time are clearly differentiated. In Romans 13:11, Paul contrasts the immediate, linear moment (hour, *hora*) with the opportunistic, timely moment *(eidotes ton kairon):* "And do this, knowing the time *[kairon],* that now it is high time *[hora]* for us already out of sleep; for now our salvation is nearer than when we first believed." Timely time *(kairos)* intersects with temporal time *(hora),* which creates the opportunity for timeless time (eternal salvation). In his letter to the Galatians, Paul reminds his listeners that in "final time" they will be judged on what they do in "opportunity time": "And let us not grow weary while doing good, for in due season *[kairo]* we shall reap if we do not lose heart. Therefore, as we have opportunity *[kairon]*, let us do good to all, especially to those who are of the household of faith" (6:9–10). Paul echoes this imperative to "spread the opportunity" in his letter to the Colossians: "Walk in wisdom toward those who are outside, redeeming the time *[ton kairon]*" (4:3).

Yet there are other conjunctions of *kairos* in which the term (and concept) are clearly differentiated. In Paul's second letter to the Corinthians, he notes Christ's recollection of the favorable time, or precondition of time, for the reception of his followers: "In an acceptable time *[kairo dekto]* I have heard you. And in the day of salvation I have helped you." Paul follows Christ's words with an injunction of time that carries with it the intensity and solemnity of urgency: "Behold, now is the accepted time *[kairos euprosdektos]*; behold, now is the time of salvation" (2 Corinthians 6:2). The first instance echoes Smith's notation of *kairos* as the right time for something to happen. The second instance recalls *kairos* as a "time of tension or conflict, a time of crisis implying that the course of events poses a problem which calls for a decision at that time." The first instance of *kairos* creates the necessary condition for the second appearance in 2 Corinthians 6:2.

Kairos is sometimes used in the sense of season, or an extension of immediate (or chronological) time into the natural cycle of time: for example, in Mark 12:2: "And at the season he sent to the husbandmen a servant, that he might receive from the husbandmen of the fruit of the vineyard." When Jesus leaves Bethany after having visited Jerusalem, he and His apostles are hungry: "And seeing from afar a fig tree having leaves, He went to see if perhaps He would find something on it. He found nothing but leaves, for it was not the season for figs" (Mark 11:13). Christ condemns the tree by saying, "Let no one eat from you ever again" (Mark 11:14). The following day they again pass by the tree and Peter says to Christ, "Rabbi, look! The fig tree which you cursed has withered away" (Mark 11:21). (The message of the "bad timing" of the tree is lost neither on Peter nor on the reader. Earthly time did not correspond to human needs and the tree was summarily punished.)

The micro-narrative of the fig tree may seem inconsistent unless considered within the context of the rhetorical lesson within which it is embedded, and it is clearly part of an exercise in belief (that is, *pistis*). Christ responds to Peter by saying,

> Have Faith in God. For assuredly, I say to you, whoever says to this mountain, "Be removed and be cast into the sea," and does not doubt in his heart, but believes that those things he says will be done, he will have whatever he says. Therefore I say to you, whatever things you ask when you pray, believe *[pistis]* that you receive them, and you will have them. (Mark 11:22–24)

Christ's condemnation of the fig tree for its failure of *kairos* serves to bolster the rhetorical message of faith. Christ's credibility is clearly enhanced by this demonstration of His power over natural events.

Earlier I referred to *eukairos*, or timing that is particularly significant or efficacious. The first occurrence of *eukairos* appears in Mark 6:21, where John the Baptist is beheaded: "Then an opportune day came when Herod on his birthday gave a feast for his nobles, high officers and the men of Galilee." The second occurrence comes in Hebrews 4:16, where Jesus is referred to as a compassionate high priest and one who has been tempted, just as we are. Readers are encouraged to come forward in the special time of necessity: "Let us therefore come bodily to the throne of grace, that we may obtain mercy and find grace to help in time of need *[eukairos]*." The third occurrence comes in the second epistle of Paul to Timothy, where there is an exhortation to preach the word of God: "Preach the word! Be ready in season and out of season. Convince, rebuke, exhort, with all long suffering and teaching" (2 Timothy 4:2). *Eukairos* is clearly reserved for special occasions.

These instances of *eukairos* point to occasional time that does not obtain under "normal," linear circumstances of temporal time. Herod, for example, appears not to want to kill John the Baptist. Before the dancing exhibition of the daughter of Herodias and the obligations it places upon Herod, we are told that Herod "feared John, knowing that he was a just and holy man" (Mark 6:21). After Herod ordered the beheading of John, we are told that "the king was exceedingly sorry." It is the *eukairos* of the occasion that prompts Herod to behave in a way contrary to his usual dispositions.

In the second occasion of *eukairos*, there are a number of reverberations of special time. Readers, one might suggest, are encouraged to hold their faith in the time of special circumstance, because it calls for extraordinary effort, comparable in a manner to the efforts of Christ, in ways familiar to humans, in which He is particularly sympathetic to our special circumstances because he has experienced the same temptations as we. The *eukairos* of the occasion binds us to Christ as ethical agents. It may not be an exaggeration to suggest that we become analogues of Christ, and there is at least an effort to appositize Christ and his followers. The *eukairos* of the occasion makes Him like us and us like Him, with an implied reciprocity of behavior. The rhetoric of *kairos* in this passage seems to me to be particularly powerful.

In his exhortation to Timothy, Paul differentiates regular time *(akairos)* from *eukairos*, the "season" or special opportunity for preaching (or rhetoric) to take hold. Paul is keenly aware of the fact that conditions lend themselves to persuasion. It is interesting to note that Warshaw's gloss of *eukairos* cites the earliest written source as Plato's *Phaedrus* (272a), where Socrates declares the importance of measuring the quality of the souls of the audience in order to more effectively persuade them. Such knowledge is critical to Paul's rhetoric.

I have explored only terminological instances of *kairos* and have not considered its conceptual uses although, indeed, they are also of strategic importance in the New Testament. There are other rhetorical dimensions of *kairos* that I have not examined, especially its ethical implications. Further, I have deliberately avoided discussing rhetoric as trope, not because it is unimportant, but precisely because it is such a complicated and significant issue in scriptural interpretation. In concluding, let me refer to a passage which, I believe, exemplifies the rich resonance of tropic movements, conjoined with the rhetorical force of *kairos* discussed above. From Revelation 12:14, note this powerful passage: "And to the woman were given two wings of a great eagle, that she might fly into the wilderness, into her place, where she is nourished for a time, and times, and half a time, from the face of the servant." The Greek word for all three references to time is *kairos*. These usages ripple with metaphorical power in which time itself, as a stable or determined construction, would seem to be called into question. I quote this passage not to interpret it, but to suggest that so much of the Bible is rich in such rhetorical flourishes. The classical trope of hyperbole meets the trope of time and, in so doing, reflects a rich tapestry of semantic polysemy. The rhetoric of time and timing becomes timeless in scriptural hermeneutic possibilities.

Notes

1. For Paul Tillich, the moment of *kairos* is that time when timeless values are catalyzed into qualities of human experience within contextualized circumstances. The kairic moment is the meeting of *kairos* and *logos* (timeless values).

2. There are times when *chronos* takes on the significance of *kairos*. In this regard, John E. Smith notes: "[T]here are processes of nature which, though determined in accordance with *chronos*, cannot be exhaustively understood from the standpoint of *chronos* time. For in these processes, *chronos* attains to 'critical points' and thus begins to take on qualitative character" (2). There are such instances in the New Testament, where *chronos* appears approximately half as often as *kairos*.

3. The concept of "no time" or "no opportunity" is also represented in the verb *akaireomai*, as in Paul's letter to the Philippians: "But I rejoiced in the Lord greatly that now at last your care for me has flourished again; though you surely did care, but you lacked opportunity" (4:10).

4. The notion of *kairos* as strategic moment in Christian theology is reflected in contemporary times. *Kairos*, as "the right time," is the basis of "The Kairos Document," a critique of state theology in South Africa that supported racism and a host of other civil ills. This treatise, first published by the Kairos Theologians in 1985, reflected the thinking of dozens of ministers attempting to resolve a national crisis. (The document

was signed by more than 150 theologians, pastors, and lay persons.) The major themes of the document, according to John De Gruchy, are "social analysis, the priority of praxis, and resistance to tyranny and oppression. . . . The final chapter is a call to action. Once again in this respect it differs from other confessional statements because it not only issues the summons but also makes very specific suggestions, including acts of civil disobedience" (8). Gustavo Gutiérrez has articulated the importance of "timing" (as in the crisis facing the poor in Latin America) in bringing about social change. Gutiérrez invokes St. Paul and his understanding of *kairos* as a call to action for Christians in Latin America and elsewhere: "Today on this sub-continent we are living in what St. Paul calls 'the favourable time,' 'the day of salvation' (Cor. 2:6)" (39). The *Kairos* treatise of South Africa and the call for action by Gutiérrez echo the kairic time of the New Testament in calling for Christian action.

5. Jerome apparently chose *tempus* as the Latin equivalent rather than Cicero's *decorum*. There could be a number of reasons for this: it may have been Jerome's personal choice, or it may have been that *decorum* had acquired a different sense by Jerome's time because there is a four hundred year difference between Cicero and Jerome. Or, it may be that Cicero's *decorum* carried explicit forensic connotations, forcing Jerome to use a synonym. (*Decorum* never appears in the New Testament, but does appear three times in the Old Testament. I have not analyzed these occurrences.)

6. The reciprocating interrelationships of rhetoric, as metaphor, and grammar raise interesting issues of movements between the rhetorization of grammar and the grammatization of rhetoric, but this brief analysis is not the appropriate occasion to probe these strategic connections.

7. Thayer suggests that differences between *chronos* and *kairos* may be without significant distinction precisely because *kairos* carries so many nuances of time. Examples of the use of *chronos* and the way(s) they are differentiated from *kairos* are not always clear. Consider the announcement of the birth of John the Baptist: "Now Elizabeth's full time *[chronos]* came for her to be delivered, and she brought forth a son" (Luke 1:57). This notion of the "fulfillment of time" would seem more appropriate to *kairos* than *chronos*. There are many examples in the New Testament of *kairos* as the fruition of God's will, as in the passage that tells of God delivering Israel through Moses (and the operative Greek word for time is *chronos*): "But when the time of the promise drew near which God had sworn to Abraham, the people grew and multiplied in Egypt" (Acts 7:17).

8. John R. Wilson himself argues against many of these meanings, although he does consider certain classical examples of *en kairo* as possibly signifying profit. For further discussion of *kairos* as profit, see Regenbogen, "Kairos," and Wilamowitz-Moellendorff, *Kleine Schriften*.

9. I cannot provide a specific numerical account, because the "crisis" of "urgency" sense of *kairos* is often conjoined with other functional uses, such as due measure, proportion, exigency, and situational context (especially the conditional imperative of "knowing" the minds and souls of listeners and readers).

Works Cited

Aristotle. *On Rhetoric: A Theory of Civic Discourse*. Trans. George A. Kennedy. New York: Oxford University Press, 1991.

Arndt, William F. and F. Wilbur Gingrich. *A Greek-English Lexicon of the New Testament (and other Early Christian Literature)*. Chicago: University of Chicago Press, 1957.

Betz, Hans Dieter. *Galatians: A Commentary of St. Paul's Letter to the Churches in Galatia*. Philadelphia: Fortress, 1979.

Burke, Kenneth. *The Rhetoric of Religion: Studies in Logology*. Boston: Beacon, 1961.

Chestnut, Glenn F. "*Kairos* and Cosmic Sympathy in the Church Historian Socrates Scholasticus." *Church History*, Vol. 44 (June 1975): 161–66.

Gutiérrez, Gustavo. "Drink from your own Well." Trans. Paul Burns. In *Learning to Pray*. Ed. Casiano Floristán and Christian Duquoc. Edinburgh: T. & T. Clark, 1982.

De Gruchy, John W. "Foreward to 'The Kairos Document'." Grand Rapids, MI: Eerdmans, 1986.

Delling, Gerhard. "*Kairos.*" *Theological Dictionary of the New Testament*. Ed. Gerhard Kittel. Trans. Geoffrey W. Bramley. Grand Rapids, MI: Eerdmans, 1965.

Gitay, Yehoshua. *Prophecy and Persuasion: A Study of Isaiah 40–48*. Forum Theologiae Linguisticae, No. 14. Erhardt Güttemans. Bonn: Linguistica Biblica, 1981.

Jaeger, Werner. *Early Christianity and Greek Paideia*. Cambridge, MA: Harvard University Press, 1948.

"The Kairos Document: Challenge to the Church." Grand Rapids, MI: Eerdmans, 1986.

Kennedy, George A. *New Testament Interpretation through Rhetorical Criticism*. Chapel Hill: University of North Carolina Press, 1984.

———. *Classical Rhetoric and Its Christian and Secular Tradition from Ancient to Modern Times*. Chapel Hill: University of North Carolina Press, 1980.

Kinneavy, James L. *Greek Rhetorical Origins of the Christian Concept of Faith*. New York: Oxford University Press, 1987.

Levi, Doro. The Concept of *Kairos* and the Philosophy of Plato. *Rendiconti della Reale Accademia Nazionale dei Lincei Classe di scienze moralia* RV 33 (1924): 93–118.

Liddell, Henry George, and Robert Scott. *A Greek-English Lexicon*. Oxford: Clarendon Press, 1968.

Lundbom, Jack R. *Jeremiah: A Study in Ancient Hebrew Rhetoric*. Society of Biblical Literature and Scholars Press, Dissertation Series, No. 18. Missoula, MT: Society of Biblical Literature, 1975.

The New King James Version Greek-English Interlinear New Testament. Trans. Arthur L. Farstad, Zane C. Hodges, C. Michael Moss, Robert E. Picirilli, and Wilbur N. Pickering. Nashville: Thomas Nelson, 1994.

Plato. *Phaedrus*. Trans. Harold North Fowler. Loeb Classical Library. 1914. Reprint, Cambridge, MA: Harvard University Press, 1977.

Regenbogen, Otto. "Kairos." *Eranos* 48 (1950): 1–24.

Robbins, Vernon K. *The Tapestry of Early Christian Discourse: Rhetoric, Society and Ideology*. London: Routledge and Kegan Paul, 1996.

———. *Jesus the Teacher: a Socio-Rhetorical Interpretation of Mark*. Philadelphia: Fortress, 1984.

Smith, John E. "Time, Times, and the 'Right Time'; *Chronos* and *Kairos*." *The Monist* 53 (1969): 1–13.

Sullivan, Dale L. "*Kairos* and the Rhetoric of Belief." *Quarterly Journal of Speech* 78 (1992): 317–32.

Warshaw, Thayer S. *Glossary of Religious Terms*. Nashville: Abingdon, 1980.

Wilamowitz-Moellendorff, Ulrich von. *Kleine Schriften* I. 42–46.

Wilson, John R. "Kairos As 'Profit'." *Classical Quarterly* 31 (1981): 418–420.

Kairos *and* Decorum

Crassus Orator's Speech de lege Servilia

JOSEPH J. HUGHES

> Observing decorum is the main thing about art, but it is also the one
> thing that cannot be passed on by means of art *[caput esse artis decere, quod
> tamen unum id esse, quod tradi arte non possit].*
> —Cicero, *De Oratore* (1.132)

Although the above epigraph is used of eloquence, its original speaker, the
legendary comedic actor Quintus Roscius Gallus, was actually talking about
the theater. While Roscius was so famous for his seemingly effortless grace
that his name became a synonym for theatrical artistry, he was best known for
his role as Ballio, the pimp in Plautus's *Pseudolus.* Portraying such a reprehen-
sible character rendered it doubly difficult for Roscius to observe *decorum.*
Stylistic *decorum* (perhaps better known by its Aristotelian name of *to prepon*)
demanded that Roscius convince an audience of men and women drawn
from all walks of life—the Roman *populus* in its broadest sense—that he was
a heartless liar who made his living by trading in young women. On the other
hand, the Roman sense of social *decorum* forbade both too exuberant a portrayal and too enthusiastic a response. Throughout their history, upper-class
Romans viewed theater as a mere diversion, and none too honorable a diversion at that. The bias will have been all the more strongly felt when the
drama's protagonist was a pimp. Another name for the dilemma Roscius
faced when he played Ballio is *kairos:* a crucial or otherwise novel situation,
calling for a quick, appropriate, and effective response. Nor were *kairos* and
decorum easily reconciled. Clearly, Roscius's success in the role of Ballio was
in large part predicated on his skill in sizing up the *kairos* presented by each
performance and then addressing it within the bounds of *decorum.*

Cicero's texts are quoted from the standard editions by Teubner and Oxford University Press.
All translations are by the author.

128

Like the actor, the Roman orator relied on voice and movement to produce the desired effect in his auditors. The Romans' appreciation of this similarity is well attested: Cicero, for example, took voice lessons from Roscius in his youth and they later became the closest of friends (Hughes, "*Inter Tribunal*" 182–183). But at the same time, Roman attitudes toward the theater precluded too direct a connection. In the words of Amy Richlin (99), ". . . the handbooks are full of insistent disclaimers explaining how orators, though as talented as actors, though very like actors, are not like actors at all." Approaching the question from a perspective combining traditional philology and modern feminist thought, Richlin identifies the cause for these strictures as well-attested Roman attitudes against effeminacy, homosexuality, and artistic affectation. Correctly so. Coming from a radically different viewpoint, Cicero reaches much the same conclusion. His lengthy discussion of *decorum* in *Orator* is introduced with words that recall the comments of his actor friend Roscius (21.70–71):

> In life as in oratory, there is nothing more difficult than identifying what is appropriate *[quid deceat videre]*. The Greeks refer to appropriateness as *prepon;* let us call it *decorum*. It is the subject of much outstanding teaching, and it is most worthy of understanding. Failure to appreciate it leads to mistakes not only in life, but also quite often in poetry and oratory. Moreover, the orator must observe *decorum* not only in his thoughts but in his language. For he must not use the same language and thoughts for portraying individuals of every condition, status, position, or age, nor in every place, or at every time, or before every audience. In every part of an oration as in life, decorum must be taken into account *[quid deceat est considerandum]*.

Although Cicero sees a clear connection between Aristotelian stylistic *decorum* and Roman social *decorum,* he finds the latter more difficult to describe (21.73–74):

> Since we habitually say "This is appropriate" *[hoc decere]* with regard to all words and deeds, great and small—since, I repeat, we say "This is appropriate" and "That is not appropriate" *[illud non decere]*, and since the importance of appropriateness in every context is apparent, let it be considered a completely different matter whether we should actually say "This is appropriate" or "This is obligatory" *[utrum decere an oportere]*. For the term "obligation" *[oportere]* indicates an ideal state of duty, to be observed at all times by all people, but "appropriateness" *[decere]* covers what is fitting to and consistent with an occasion and a person. . . . If even the actor seeks appropriateness, to what standard shall we hold the orator?

Most simply put, Roman public speakers were held to a far higher standard of *decorum* than was anyone else. As propertied males involved in public life, they were expected to guide and set a moral tone for the *populus*. As orators trained in the Hellenistic tradition, they were expected to express themselves in appropriate language. Although *kairos* requires that the orator assess and address his audience's expectations—and not the other way around—*decorum* came first. How did Roman orators balance these competing demands, especially when addressing the *populus*? Did one tend to be sacrificed to the other, and at what cost?

At first glance, the question would appear moot. Despite its democratic institutions, Republican Rome was in fact far closer to an aristocracy in its last century. Three assemblies (Centuriate, Tribal, and Plebeian) were open to all citizens, elected magistrates annually, and passed binding legislation for the state. A fourth body, the Senate, was made up of former magistrates empowered to advise the current magistrates. In practice, however, citizens attended the Assemblies not to deliberate over legislation, but to vote on legislation placed before them by the current magistrates. The results of the Senate's deliberations had the force of law, but its meetings were not open to the *populus*. The common Roman citizen, along with noncitizens such as women, freedmen, and foreigners, was effectively deprived of a voice in state affairs. Though members of the *populus* might attend public trials, only members of the Senatorial or Equestrian Orders could serve on the jury. A Roman orator of the Republic, therefore, would be far more accustomed to persuading other upper-class Roman males than to persuading the *populus* in all its diversity. Given this smaller and more homogeneous audience, the range of *kairoi* an orator in Republican Rome could expect to encounter would be proportionally limited.

The one anomaly in this system was the *contio*, a meeting held in the Forum by a magistrate to discuss proposed legislation or other state business prior to a formal vote in one of the assemblies. The convening magistrate determined the procedure. He could address the *contio* himself, invite others to address the assembled, and/or engage in deliberation with them. Anyone present in the Forum could attend and could even, with the convening magistrate's permission, participate in the discussion. As opposed to the assemblies, where Romans voted in collective units known as centuries and tribes, the *contio* also provided individual empowerment regardless of social stratum. Regardless of how much the vote of the *populus* was worth, the favor of the Forum crowd was usually vociferously expressed and always eagerly courted. Thus, the *contio* became, in the political heat of the Republic's last hundred years, what Fergus Millar has called "the essential vehicle of persuasion and debate" (219). More importantly for this inquiry, the *contio* was also the only likely venue for a Roman public speaker to discuss public affairs with a truly representative section of the diverse and unpredictable Roman *populus*. A detailed study of *contiones* would yield valuable insights into how Roman orators responded to situational *kairoi*. Unfortunately, the primary sources tell us very little about specific *contiones*. The second and third of Cicero's famous *Catilinarian Orations*, for instance, were delivered *ad populum*. But like Cicero's other published orations, his *contiones* show clear signs of having been edited for the emerging *reading* public, to be circulated as political pamphlets or perused by aficionados in their libraries (Fantham, *Roman*, 8).

A seldom remarked account of an important *contio* occurs at *De Oratore* (2.239–242), in a humorous anecdote cited from Crassus Orator's speech *de lege Servilia* ("On The Servilian Law") of 106 B.C. Examination of Crassus Orator's anecdote will demonstrate that this "popular" form of argumentation, which had more in common with the comedic stage than with the received Hellenistic rhetorical tradition or prevailing Roman standards of *decorum*, can only have been a response to situational *kairos*. Cicero's discussion, however, obscures the kairotic elements of Crassus Orator's speech, instead focusing on the benefits and far more substantial dangers involved in the use of humorous narrative. He thus illustrates the subordination of *kairos* (as response to a specific situation) to appropriateness as embodied in the Aristotelian *prepon* and the Latin *decorum*, as explained in *Orator* (21.70–71).

Lucius Licinius Crassus was already cognominated "the Orator" when he delivered his speech *de lege Servilia*. He had studied Hellenistic school rhetoric in his youth (*De Oratore* 1.137–147) and discussed it critically with prominent rhetoricians, both Greek and Roman (1.154–157). He will already have been aware of what texts such as *De Inventione* and *Rhetorica ad Herennium* would soon afterwards (*ca.* 90–85 B.C.) prescribe for a deliberative oration. Regardless of the assembly he was addressing, the speaker should build good will in the *exordium*, explain the circumstances succinctly in the *narratio*, and make the case for his prescribed course of action in the *confirmatio*. The only mention of specific prescriptions for specific assemblies occurs thirty years later, in *De Oratore:*

> Such matters should be treated with less adornment in the Senate, for it is a wise council and sufficient time must be left for many others to speak. Moreover, even the suspicion of showing off one's talent has to be avoided. But the *contio* encompasses all the force of oratory, and requires both variety and dignity. (2.333–334)

The provenance of such advice—atypical for a Roman rhetorical handbook—is suggested by Eric Charles White's remarks on the "Gorgianic" or "mannerist" approach to rhetorical *kairos:*

> By relying on the inspiration of the moment to insure that speech answers uniquely to its time, mannerism counsels a stylistic pluralism that refuses to privilege one style over all others. The aesthetic effect the mannerist orator seeks would be one of sublimity, a sudden shock of awe, wonder, terror, euphoria. . . . (31)

The Aristotelian branch of rhetorical tradition was of but limited use to Crassus Orator in persuading the Forum crowd to support the *lex Servilia*. It offered no guidelines for gauging the *kairos* and was more likely to proscribe stylistic pluralism than to prescribe it. Instead, Crassus had to rely, like the "manneristic" orator, on his practical knowledge of the Roman political scene and play to his audience's psychological makeup. Although the end result was closer to modern improvisational comedy than to the ponderous appropriateness prescribed for the Roman orator, it proved effective.

A quarter century earlier, the reformer Tiberius Gracchus had granted power over the criminal courts, once the prerogative of the Senatorial Order alone, to the Equestrian Order. The Equestrians, in turn, used the courts as a weapon against those magistrates and Senators who opposed their entrepreneurial interests. Despite Tiberius Gracchus's murder in A.D. 131, and that of his equally reform-minded brother Gaius in 121 (both at the hands of crowds led by Senatorial supporters), the criminal courts remained in the Equestrians' hands. One of the consuls of 106 B.C., the blue-blooded conservative Q. Servilius Caepio, proposed a law to return the criminal courts to Senatorial control, which took the designation *lex Servilia* after its originator. Historically, neither the Senatorial nor the Equestrian Order had ever demonstrated any genuine concern for the lowly *populus*, which undoubtedly reciprocated their lack of esteem. But the *populus* also had an understandable tendency to support underdogs of any sort against the entrenched Senatorial elite. The *populus* was also politically sophisticated. Four centuries of annual elections had rendered electioneering not only a political necessity but also a form of public entertainment. Finally, the *populus* was literarily astute, with a distinct taste for comedy and farce. Dramatic performances had been taking place in the Forum for more than two centuries, sometimes with marked political overtones. Audiences had ways of expressing their displeasure with a show that did not meet their tastes: even the immortal Terence's "Mother in Law" had been hooted off the stage for being insufficiently entertaining. Cicero's famous description of the *populus* (*Ad Atticum* 1.16.11) as "the meeting-going Treasury leeches, the poor starving people" can safely be disregarded. Explaining to them the benefits of the *lex Servilia* was only part of Crassus Orator's job. He would also have to entertain them.

It appears that Crassus Orator succeeded on every count. Thanks in large part to his use of "popular" language, the *lex Servilia* is believed to have passed. The speech he gave on its behalf was considered an artistic masterpiece, studied eagerly by Cicero and other aspiring orators:

> That speech for Caepio's law was like a childhood teacher to me. It enhanced the authority of the Senate, on whose behalf it was delivered; it stirred up ill will against

the jurors and prosecutors' faction, against whom Crassus then had to speak in language the *populus* would appreciate *[populariter tum dicendum fuit]*. He said many weighty things, many trifling things, many harsh things and many funny things. He said more than is in the written version, which can be seen from certain topics mentioned but not explained. (*Brutus,* 164)

The circumstances under which Crassus compiled and disseminated this "written version" can not, of course, be known (Douglas, 124–127). But the juxtaposition of the Latin adverb *populariter* with the gerundive *dicendum fuit* (the Latin language's strongest means of expressing obligation: see Cato the Elder's famous *Karthago delenda est*) suggests why some topics were merely "mentioned but not explained" therein. When publishing his *de lege Servilia,* Crassus sought to avoid any possible breach of *decorum,* either stylistic or social. No doubt much of the stylistic pluralism Cicero hints at was consigned to oblivion by Crassus's own hand. Fortunately, one such "mentioned but not explained" topic is discussed at somewhat greater length in Book 2 of *De Oratore* (2.216–290), Cicero's discursus on oratorical humor. There an anecdote I will call "The Eating of Largus's Limb" is offered as a prime example of humor based on fact:

It is humor based on fact when something like a little tale is related, such as you, Crassus, once told on Memmius and how he "lunched on Largus's limb" when he had wrangled with Largus at Tarracina over a little girlfriend. The narrative was clever, but you yourself made it all up. You added a little epilogue to the effect that the letters L.L.L.M.M. were written on walls all over Tarracina. When you asked what that was, some old townsman replied "Munchin' Memmius Lunched on Largus's Limb." (2.240–241)

"The Eating of Largus's Limb" functions as an example of how Roman orators used comedic characterization, language, and plot structure in their work. The "epilogue" suggests an abbreviation of a formulaic campaign slogan—such as "Vote happily for Memmius, who deserves it" *[Lege Laetus Lubens Merito Memmium]*—which the old townsman misinterpreted to mean "Munchin' Memmius lunched on Largus's limb" *[Lacerat Lacertum Largi Mordax Memmius]*. Aside from this linguistic play, the triangle of Memmius, Largus, and the girl from Tarracina suggests any number of similar love triangles from Roman New Comedy; the old townsman is likewise a comedic type; further, the slapstick aspect of physical abuse, while comparatively absent in Terence, is a staple in Plautus's works (Hughes, *"Inter Tribunal,"* 187–188). More importantly, Cicero's treatment of Crassus Orator's remarks sheds a great deal of light on how he perceived the potentially competing demands of *kairos* and *decorum.* Cicero's analysis of the anecdote (*De Oratore* 2.241) states that, regardless of its truth or falsity, such an anecdote should possess the following characteristics: " . . . you should demonstrate the actions *[facta]* of the man you are talking about and his habits *[mores]*, his speech patterns *[sermo]*, and all of his facial expressions *[voltus omnes]* in such a way that they appear to take place as they are enacted *[geri . . . fierique]* before the audience's eyes." Given the historical context of Crassus's example—a speech to the *populus*, with its craving for entertainment and appreciation of comic theater—Cicero can only be describing how Crassus impersonated Memmius, Largus, and the other characters in his story. The details of the story, as I have sketched them out above, perished with the published version of *de lege Servilia*. But the aspiring orators to whom Cicero addressed his remarks will have had the published version at hand, and will have recognized what to look for.

Though this is Cicero's final word on the speech *de lege Servilia,* he has far more to say about how the aspiring orator must avoid descending to the level of Forum entertainers (Grant, 73–99). The notion that oratorical humor has its own *kairoi* is developed very early in the excursus on humor—first at 2.221 and, more fully, at the following:

> Still, Julius, although you denied that an art of humor exists, you brought to light something that seems well worth teaching. For you stated that a speaker must take account of persons, subject matter, and occasion so that his use of humor does not detract from his dignity. Crassus is known for strictly observing this principle. (2.229)

Dignitas is a primary consideration in Cicero's assessment of the proper use of humor in oratory. Closely related to social *decorum*, this peculiarly Roman concept included not only the esteem a man enjoyed in his lifetime, but also his reputation after death. We have already encountered Cicero's statement on the importance of maintaining *dignitas* when addressing the people at a *contio*. A concern for *dignitas* also explains why the *fabulae palliatae* (comedies performed in Latin with Greek characters and Greek settings) of Plautus and Terence were more popular than those situated in Rome with Roman characters. And *dignitas* was the reason behind every "decent" Roman's aversion to the lowest form of entertainment found in the Forum: the mime. Defining it as "imitation of speech and action without reference, the lascivious imitation of shameful words and deeds," the grammarian Diomedes well expresses the standard derogatory attitude. A more current assessment (Fantham, "Mime" 154) is less judgmental and more helpful: "a narrative entertainment in the media of speech, song, and dance." As the *fabulae palliatae* became moribund in the late second century B.C., the mime rose in popularity. The classics of Plautus, Terence, and others were revived from time to time; literary aficionados studied them and wrote their own comedies. But by the time that Crassus spoke on behalf of the *lex Servilia*, the mime had swept the Roman stage.

Considerations of genre aside, mimes were characterized (Beacham, 46) by "a highly expressive acting style using physical gesticulation and pronounced vocal inflexion to create an exaggerated, caricatured impersonation." This is just the sort of affectation Richlin points out in her remarks on the obvious but indecorous similarities between the orator and the actor. Plautus's comedies, which abounded in such techniques, brought him an enormous popular following. Indeed, it is vain to speculate whether "The Eating of Largus's Limb" was performed in the spirit of Plautine comedy or of mime, since even in its present, skeletal form it so clearly partakes of both. Terence, on the other hand, preferred to return to the psychological subtleties in which Greek New Comedy, particularly that of Menander, excelled. Cicero sympathized wholeheartedly with this tendency toward *dignitas* and *decorum*, as is evident from the scorn he pours upon the mime throughout his excursus. When employing humor, the orator must avoid the sort of banter that characterizes the *scurra* or "buffoon" *[scurrilis dicacitas]* (2.244); instead, he should be guided by a sense of the occasion and by moderation, restraint, and economy of words *[moderatio et temperantia et raritas dictorum]* (2.247). Cicero defines the difference between the buffoon and the orator in no uncertain terms:

> But [a comedic character] is laughed at because of his face *[ore]*, appearance *[vultu]*, mimicry of personal habits *[imitandis moribus]*, voice *[voce]*, and finally his body itself *[corpore ipso]*. I can call such a man funny, but in the fashion of a mime actor, not in the sense I think an orator should be funny. (2.250)

These remarks are entirely in keeping with the idea that a Roman orator should maintain *decorum* above all. At the same time, they directly contradict the praise Cicero lavishes on Crassus (2.240–242) for paying careful attention to precisely these personal characteristics. In matters of characterization, it would seem that both stylistic and social *decorum* posit definite boundaries which ought not to be crossed, regardless of *kairos* . . . unless by an orator of Crassus's standing.

Indeed Cicero—the orator, that is, not the rhetorical theorist—was quite willing to cross this boundary when the *kairos* demanded. In his speech in defense of M. Caelius Rufus (delivered in 56 B.C., one year before the publication of *De Oratore*) Cicero begins by noting that the trial is taking the jurors away from the Megalensian Games, a festival at which dramas were performed. As Katherine Geffcken has noted, the occasion on which Cicero delivered the *pro Caelio* empowers him to compensate the jurors by impersonating a wide range of characters, old and young, male and female, dead and alive, thus turning the speech into somewhat of a comic farce (Geffcken, passim; Dumont, 424–429). Still, Cicero is frustratingly reticent on the subject of dramatic impersonation when he passes from the excursus on humor and takes up the formal *partes orationis*. In his discussion of *narratio*, Cicero cites the speech of the old man Simo (lines 51–171, which set out the background for Terence's comedy, *Andria*) as an ideal example:

> But the *narratio* possesses liveliness when embellished with developed characters *[distincta personis]* and interspersed with dialogues *[interpuncta sermonibus]*, and what you say to have taken place is both more plausible when you set it forth in the manner in which it happened, and much more clearly understandable if it comes to a halt at times, instead of being raced through with that brevity. (*De Oratore* 2.327–328)

Cicero's choice of example reflects his emphasis on a wide literary education. His personal facility with this sort of expository style paid great dividends in the law courts and won him the admiration of successive generations (Hughes, "Dramatic *Ethos*," 216–221). But the reader will look in vain for explicit acknowledgment that Cicero considered impersonation and other, more farcical, comedic techniques to be appropriate on occasions—such as at a *contio* or a trial held during the Megalensian Games—when the *kairos* might demand it.

Cicero—the rhetorical theorist, that is, not the orator—comes down firmly on the side of *dignitas* and *decorum*. Does this mean that Cicero has abandoned the notion that considerations of *kairos* might, on occasion, override the necessity of maintaining *decorum*? Hardly. Returning to his old teacher Roscius's dictum that *decorum* was both essential and incapable of being taught, Cicero relies—here as elsewhere in *De Oratore*—on Crassus Orator as an exemplar of both learning and critical judgment. Equipped with the historical and philosophical learning for which Cicero calls throughout *De Oratore*, any aspiring orator who studied "The Eating of Largus's Limb" would have a better idea of how to identify *kairoi* calling for "popular" argumentation and just how far one's improvisations could be taken without violating *decorum*. "The Eating of Largus's Limb" also provided for the attentive student a context in which he could appreciate and learn from Cicero's forays into this area, just as close study of the speeches *Palamedes* and *Helen* reveals Gorgias's theory and practice of manipulating *kairos* (Poulakos). If the aspiring orator could not learn by example, he would likely never learn at all and, in any case, would be better off not attempting to emulate Crassus's (and Cicero's) mastery.

Nor would subsequent Roman rhetoricians ever press the matter further. The constraints placed upon Roman public address in the Republic's waning days (lamented by Cicero at the beginning of *Brutus*) were strengthened and rendered permanent by Augustus's establishment of the Principate. The Assemblies lapsed into disuse and the Senate became little more than a debating society concerned with preserving such *dignitas* as an individual emperor allowed it. Henceforth, such *kairoi* as can be found in the literature of the Roman Empire tend to occur in the contrived *controversiae* of the declamation schools or as a function of the *letteraturizzazione* (Kennedy, 5) of primary rhetoric.

Works Cited

Beacham, Richard C. *The Roman Theatre and its Audience.* Cambridge: Harvard University Press, 1992.

Cicero. *De Inventione.*

———. *Brutus.*

———. *De Oratore.*

———. *Epistulae ad Atticum.*

———. *Orator.*

Dominik, William J., ed. *Roman Eloquence: Rhetoric in Society and Literature.* New York: Routledge and Kegan Paul, 1997.

Douglas, A. E., ed. *M. Tulli Ciceronis Brutus.* Oxford: Oxford University Press, 1966.

Dumont, J. C. "Ciceron et le theatre." In *Actes du IXe Congres Association Guillaume Bude,* 424–429. Paris: Association Guillaume Bude, 1975.

Fantham, Elaine. "Mime: The Missing Link in Roman Literary History." *Classical World* 82 (1989): 153–163.

———. *Roman Literary Culture.* Baltimore: Johns Hopkins University Press, 1996.

Geffcken, Katherine. *Comedy in the Pro Caelio, with an Appendix on the In Clodium et Curionem.* Leiden: E. J. Brill, 1973.

Grant, Mary A. "The Ancient Rhetorical Theories of the Laughable: The Greek Rhetoricians and Cicero." In *University of Wisconsin Studies In Language and Literature* 21. Madison, WI: University of Wisconsin Press, 1924.

Hughes, Joseph J. "Dramatic *Ethos* in Cicero's Later Rhetorical Works." In *Ethos: New Essays in Rhetorical and Critical Theory.* Ed. James S. Baumlin and Tita F. Baumlin, 211–225. Dallas: Southern Methodist UP, 1994.

———. "*Inter Tribunal et Scaenam*: Comedy and Rhetoric in Rome." In Dominik, *Roman Eloquence,* 182–197.

Kennedy, George A. *Classical Rhetoric and Its Christian and Secular Tradition from Ancient to Modern Times.* Chapel Hill: University of North Carolina Press, 1987.

Millar, Fergus. *The Crowd in Rome in the Late Republic.* Ann Arbor, MI: University of Michigan Press, 1998.

Poulakos, John. "Kairos in Gorgias' Rhetorical Conceptions." In *Rhetoric and* Kairos: *Essays in History, Theory, and Praxis.* Ed. Phillip Sipiora and James S. Baumlin (State University of New York Press, 2002).

Richlin, Amy. "Gender and Rhetoric." In Dominik, *Roman Eloquence,* 90–110.

White, Eric Charles. *Kaironomia: On the Will-to-Invent.* Ithaca: Cornell University Press, 1987.

Ciceronian Decorum and the Temporalities of Renaissance Rhetoric

The Greekes call this good grace of euery thing in his kinde,
to prepon, the Latines *decorum:* we in our vulgar call it
by a scholasticall terme *decencie.*
—George Puttenham, *The Arte of English Poesie* (1589)

There is no greater impediment of action than an over-curious observance of decency, and the guide of decency, which is time and season. . . .
a man must make his opportunity, as oft as find it.
—Sir Francis Bacon, *The Advancement of Learning* (1605)

Any comprehensive survey of *kairos* must turn at some point to the contributions of Renaissance Humanism, which form a significant chapter in the history of rhetoric generally and of *kairos* in particular. In a seminal discussion,
James L. Kinneavy observes the influence of Greek *kairos* upon Ciceronian
practice:

> In Stoicism, particularly Latin Stoicism, the concept of *kairos* merged with that of
> *prepon* (propriety or fitness). . . . In this guise, *kairos* is the dominating concept in
> both Cicero's rhetoric and his ethics. Consequently, it is not inaccurate to say that
> *kairos,* with the related concept of *prepon,* was a major influence in much of classical
> rhetoric in antiquity, particularly with the Pythagoreans, the sophists, Plato, and
> Cicero. (82)

Having made such an observation, Kinneavy proceeds, nonetheless, to dismiss any further influence: "although the Ciceronian notion of propriety persisted throughout the mediaeval and Renaissance periods, the residual influence of *kairos* is almost a negligible chapter in the history of rhetoric since

antiquity, partly because of the overwhelming influence of Aristotelian rhetoric upon that history" (82). This seems overstated. Excepting Cicero's uniquely Roman adaptation of the *pisteis* (Wisse, 9 – 76), Aristotle's *Rhetoric* remained virtually unnoticed (outside of Byzantine circles) until George of Trebizond's fifteenth-century Latin translation. And though Aristotle would be "more widely studied" (Kennedy, 81) throughout the sixteenth century and prove increasingly influential with each generation of scholars, still, as George A. Kennedy notes, his *Rhetoric* "failed to replace the works of Cicero or Quintilian" (81) as major authorities of Renaissance Humanism. Indeed, Cicero remained "the very embodiment of the Renaissance educational ideal" (Major, 141), his *De Oratore* being "one of the half-dozen ancient treatises that created the formative ideal of Renaissance education" (Bush, *Classical Influences*, 21). According to Daniel Javitch:

> The ideal aim of the rhetorical education advocated by humanists remained utilitarian and civic: to make men capable of communicating political and ethical truths so persuasively that they would thereby reform and civilize society. The importance and singularity of Cicero's *De Oratore* lay in offering an authoritative model of the orator performing such a role. Its secular orientation notwithstanding, the ideal of the eloquent man fashioned in Cicero's book came close to representing the exemplary citizen that humanist education sought to produce. (23)

For Continental Humanists, then, as for Cicero, "rhetoric was a coherent body of knowledge of human behavior with a special focus on the relation of discourse to action" (Struever, 116), one placing "a high value on a sense of *opportunità (kairos)*" and "a grasp of the relationship of choice to circumstance" (Struever, 116). A similar case can be made for English Humanists, as the following pages suggest.[1]

And yet, as a zealous servant of republicanism, Cicero's ideal orator would meet with a troubled reception throughout the courts of Europe, whose autocratic governments rendered free speech—the very lifeblood of Ciceronian oratory—a dangerous affair. Indeed in England, as throughout Europe generally, the Humanists' political and educational programs were bound to fail, "largely because their aspirations were incompatible with the exigencies of Tudor despotism" (Javitch, 9; see also Whigham, 1–31). Their ultimate failure did not, however, prevent Humanist educators from shaping the age's rhetoric, ethics, and imaginative literature in accordance with Ciceronian theory—of which a defining feature, as Walter H. Beale suggests, is its "melding of formal, strategic, aesthetic, and indeed moral concerns in the all-embracing concept of decorum"(169). We shall find that, among its many concerns, Ciceronian decorum stresses "right-timing" in all human action, most especially speech. Thus, *kairos*—or *eukairia*, as Cicero terms it (*De*

Officiis 1.142)—remains a significant influence upon Renaissance literary-rhetorical and ethical theory. Which does not surprise, given the age's renewed interest in time.

As Ricardo J. Quinones writes, "time is not an element that one divines in the men of the Renaissance; it is a force of their consciousness by which they themselves indicate the differences that set apart their new awareness of the world and their place in it from an older one. Time itself and temporal response are factors in distinguishing Renaissance from medieval" (3–4). True enough. Though the Renaissance did not "discover" time, as Quinones and other scholars have recently declared, nonetheless it did express an urgency to master worldly time in both its *chronos*- and *kairos*-aspects. Just as technological improvements in clock-making increased the age's awareness (as well as its effective use) of *chronos*-time, so Humanist rhetoric raised an awareness of *kairos*-time—an awareness, that is, of "right-timing" in prudent deliberation, action, and speech. Though fully conceptualized in antiquity, the temporalities of ethics and rhetoric—the two quintessentially human realms of material and symbolic action—were apparently either forgotten or ignored during the Middle Ages. But such neglect is hardly surprising, given the indifference that medieval consciousness showed toward time generally.[2] Indeed, by viewing worldly, human time *sub specie aeternitatis* (that is, "under the aspect of eternity") and binding communal life to the yearly returns of a liturgical calendar, the Christian Middle Ages sought to embrace *aion* or *aeternitas* over "sluttish time," to borrow a Shakespearian phrase. In addition, Humanist rhetoric contradicted Christian doctrine (both medieval and Protestant) in its tendencies toward epistemological skepticism, its implicit presumption of human sufficiency-of-will and its assertion that, through *prudentia*—the ultimate goal of Humanist rhetorical education—one might achieve mastery over fortune. Thoroughly classical, such assumptions remain at odds with Christian notions of human depravity, worldly evil, and the workings of divine Providence. The aim of this essay, then, is twofold: first, to demonstrate the temporal consciousness pervading Tudor Humanist rhetorical and ethical theory (noting that rhetoric and ethics are united in Ciceronian-Humanist thought) and, second, to explore the various competing representations of time, as recorded in the age's popular emblem books.

Emblems relating to time and prudence have often been discussed in the light of English Renaissance literature (Chew, Green, Simonds). Rarely addressed, however, is the extent to which such emblems juxtapose conflicting temporal categories, deliberately intermingling the symbolisms of *chronos, kairos,* and *aion.* This tendency reflects not just on the age's recognition of time's complexities, but also on the habit of controversial thinking that lies at the heart of Humanist rhetorical theory—a habit of acknowledging the multiplicity of things symbolized by the two-headed (and often three-headed)

Janus-figure, by far the most pervasive emblem of prudential rhetoric. The habit of "looking before and after" (4.4.38), as Shakespeare's Hamlet puts it, and of arguing both sides of an issue—in a phrase, the Humanist *argumentum ad utramque partem* (Sloane, Kahn)—is a technique learned from Cicero, though originating in Greek sophistic practice. In subtle ways, the habit of observing both sides of any issue seems to have taught Humanists to treat time itself (and human actions within time) with a similar "double-vision." For the student of *prudentia,* time reveals itself as golden Opportunity rather than as fickle, devastating Fortune. Like the *Prudentia-Fortuna* ensembles popular in emblem tradition, the conjoined figures of *Occasio* and *Fortuna* reflect Humanist aspirations to master worldly time and its effects. In marked contrast, emblems depicting "Father-Time," death, and eternity reflect an older *memento mori* tradition encouraging an ascetic submission to time. Devaluing worldly accomplishments and even worldly time itself, this essentially medieval tradition of *contemptus mundi* teaches that life is to be lived "under the aspect of eternity" and, thus, as a constant meditation upon death. The juxtaposition of these several traditions reflects on the complexities of Renaissance temporal and ethical consciousness, all of which give unique shape to its rhetoric—the subject to which we now turn.

"In an oration, as in life, nothing is harder to determine than what is appropriate" (*Orator* 21.70); thus, Cicero begins his extensive discussion of decorum, the single most important possession of the ideal orator. He continues:

> The Greeks call it πρεπον; let us call it *decorum* or "propriety." . . . From ignorance of this mistakes are made not only in life but very frequently in writing, both in poetry and in prose. . . . For the same style and the same thoughts must not be used in portraying every condition in life, or every rank, position or age, and in fact a similar distinction must be made in respect of place, time and audience. The universal rule, in oratory as in life, is to consider propriety *[quid deceat est considerandum].* (21.70 – 71)

In *Orator,* as throughout his writings, Cicero refuses to separate the intellectual and moral faculties; for indeed, as Victoria Kahn explains, "the faculty of prudence is inseparable from the ideal practice" (35) of the Ciceronian orator:

> Just as the orator is guided by decorum in adapting his speech to the exigencies of the moment, so the prudent man enacts decorum in the moral sphere by responding to the particular and contingent in human affairs (*Orator,* 71). Furthermore, the prudent man and the orator are not only analogous for Cicero; they are ideally the same, since the good man to be effective must be persuasive, and the orator who is not good is not worthy of the name. (Kahn, 35)

Following Isocratean tradition, Cicero distinguishes abstract philosophical wisdom or *sapientia* from *prudentia,* "the practical knowledge of things to be sought for and things to be avoided" (*De Officiis* 1.43). A major issue occupying the speakers in *De Oratore* is thus the problem of requisite knowledge. Whereas Cicero's Crassus argues for wide, nearly universal knowledge (thereby wedding rhetoric and philosophy), Antonius limits the orator's scope (1.48 – 54), emphasizing popular belief, conventional morality, and the techniques of persuasion per se. While Renaissance Humanists continue this debate, their "rhetoric of prudence" typically sought out the more practical knowledge suited to oratory, as Antonius advised, the sort aiding in public deliberation, prudent choice, and civic action. Hence, decorum, at once the capstone of ethics and rhetoric, becomes a "universal rule, in oratory as in life." The philosophers, Cicero adds, "are accustomed to consider this extensive subject under the head of duties *[officia]* ... literary critics consider it in connexion with poetry; orators in dealing with every kind of speech, and in every part thereof" (*Orator* 21.72). The observance of decorum is thus "universal," and yet its specific expression continually changes, since "'propriety' is what is fitting and agreeable to an occasion or person *[decere quasi aptum esse consentaneumque temporis et personae]*" (*Orator* 22.74).

Cicero's reference to the philosophers' *officia* or "duties" calls attention to yet another of his treatises, *De Officiis*—the "most important single text for the study of moral philosophy during the Renaissance" (7), as T. McAlindon terms it—which contains the fullest and most influential classical discussion of "decorum as a comprehensive aesthetic, moral, and political ideal" (Beale, 169). In *De Officiis*, as Beale notes, "one finds the fundamental ethical imperative of human existence construed as the doctrine of decorum writ large: In all things, man should behave in ways appropriate to his nature as a rational creature, made for cooperation and society" (169). Or, as Tully himself says, "to employ reason and speech rationally, to do with careful consideration whatever one does, and in everything to discern the truth and to uphold it— that is proper" (*De Officiis* 1.94). In its social aspect, decorum "is inseparable from moral goodness; for what is proper is morally right *[quod decet, honestum est]*, and what is morally right is proper" (*De Officiis* 1.93). Propriety, indeed, "can be nothing more than uniform consistency in the course of our life as a whole and all its individual actions" (1.111); as such, decorum "shows itself also in every deed, in every word, even in every movement and attitude of the body" (1.126).

In governing one's speech and physical actions, decorum seeks practical answers not only to "what" and "how much," but also to "when." For "orderliness of conduct," Cicero tells us, must be conjoined to the "seasonableness of occasions *[opportunitate temporum]*"—both of which are embraced "in that science which the Greeks call εὐταξία ... by which we understand *orderly conduct*"(*De Officiis* 1.142):

And so, if we may call it also *moderation,* it is defined by the Stoics as follows: "Moderation is the science of disposing aright everything that is done or said." So the essence of orderliness and of right-placing, it seems, will be the same. . . . By "place of action," moreover, they mean *seasonableness of circumstance [opportunitatem temporis];* and the *seasonable circumstance* for an action is called in Greek εὐκαιρία, in Latin *occasio.* (1.142)

By this reference to *eukairia* or "opportune moment," Cicero asserts "the special importance of time in the doctrine of decorum" (McAlindon, 10). In his youthful *De Inventione,* Cicero had already acknowledged the kairotic aspect of rhetoric (Wittkower, 313), distinguishing *occasio* from *tempus* or, as his Greek sources put it, *eukairia* from *chronos,* "an *occasion* [being] a period of time offering a convenient opportunity *[idoneam opportunitatem]* for doing or not doing something. And it is on the matter of opportunity that occasion differs from time" (*De Inventione* 1.27). Thus, as McAlindon notes, Cicero identifies *occasio* or *opportunitas* "with the prudential aspect of decorum; and that is how it always appears in Renaissance literature" (10)—decorum being, in the words of Tudor Humanist Sir Thomas Elyot, "the knowledge of opportunity of things to be done or spoken, in appointing and setting them in time or place to them convenient and proper" (80). Elyot's Ciceronianism should hardly surprise, since his *Boke Named the Gouernour* (1531) is modeled, as John M. Major notes, "upon the *De Officiis*" (143).

Though Latin *decorum* specifically translates the Greek *to prepon,* it would appear that Ciceronian theory combines *to prepon* and *to kairos,* "the fitting" and "the timely," in a complex synthesis, at once observing both the formal and the temporal or situational aspects of discourse. In fact the terms were already linked in Greek sophistic rhetoric, wherein *to prepon,* as Mario Untersteiner notes, "represents the formal aspect of the epistemological content expressed in *kairos*" (198).[3] Decorum, then, is presumed to reign over all human action and expression; indeed, as Beale suggests, "so seamless is the fabric of Ciceronian humanism that it is difficult to say whether . . . decorum is an aesthetic principle applied to life or a moral principle applied to art. In either case decorum is properly associated with harmony, grace, and comeliness as well as timeliness and appropriateness, just as the beauty of nature is associated with its rational design" (169). Concluding his discussion in *De Officiis,* Cicero notes that "such orderliness of conduct is, therefore, to be observed, that everything in the conduct of our life shall balance and harmonize, as in a finished speech" (1.144)—a sentiment echoed throughout English Humanist literature.

For Ciceronian decorum reigns over Elizabethan rhetorical theory as well. In his *Arte of English Poesie* (1589), "one of the most significant arts of conduct of the Elizabethan age," as Javitch describes it, though "ostensibly a treatise on poetry" (69), the courtier-poet George Puttenham observes the changing circumstances of decorum (or "decencie," as he is wont to term it), which "comes to be very much alterable . . . insomuch as our speach asketh one manner of *decencie,* in respect of the person who speakes: another of whom we speake: . . . and in what place and time and to what purpose" (270). In particular, "some things and speaches are decent or indecent in respect of the time" (273),

> as when a great clerk presented king *Antiochus* with a booke treating all of iustice, the king that time lying at the siege of a towne, who lookt vpon the title of the booke, and cast it to him againe: saying, what a diuell tellest thou to me of iustice, now thou seest me vse force and do the best I can to bereeue mine enimie of his towne? Euery thing hath his season which is called Opportunitie, and the unfitnesse or undecency of the time is called Importunitie. (273–74)

More than distinguish *eukairia* from *akairia,* or "Opportunitie" from "Importunitie," Puttenham calls attention to one of the more salient features of Renaissance literary, intellectual, and political culture: the inequality of power separating courtiers from the aristocratic audiences whom they address and seek to serve.

Preceding Puttenham by some decades, Thomas Wilson's *Arte of Rhetorique* (1560) offers similar advice to aspiring lawyers. "It is wisdom," Wilson states, "to consider the time, the place, the man for whom we speak, the man against whom we speak, . . . and always to use whatsoever can be said to win the chief hearer's good wills" (51–52). But above all, speakers must take care "not to hinder or hurt" their cause (52), a point Cicero's Antonius stresses throughout his discussion of legal rhetoric (*De Oratore* 2.72–75). Thus, Wilson writes, "not only is it wisdom to speak so much as is needful, but also it is good reason to leave unspoken so much as is needless. . . . Yea, sometimes a man must not speak all that he knoweth, for if he do, he is like to find small favor" (53). Not even "just cause" (53) overcomes the importunity of a speech addressed to an "easily offended power" (134), as Thomas O. Sloane describes Wilson's courtly audience. For "who will speak that which he knoweth will not be liked, if he purpose to find favor at their hands before whom he speaketh? What man of reason will praise that before the judges (before whom he knoweth the determination of his cause resteth) which the judges self cannot abide to hear spoken at all?" (Wilson, 53). Sensitive to the dangers arising from such inequality of power, Wilson advises readers "to take heed that we touch not those whom we would be most loath to offend" (167). Throughout Wilson's numerous examples, the judge or "chief hearer" holds power literally of life and death over a speaker and his client.[4] Thus, the prudent speaker falls upon a range of defensive strategies, including equivocation and silence.

Cicero makes much of the *genera dicendi,* the "high," "middle," and "low" styles, each accommodated to specific rhetorical functions of teaching, pleasing, or persuading an audience (*Orator*, 21). Renaissance theorists follow his lead, adapting the different styles not only to one's changing rhetorical intentions but also to one's courtly audience.[5] Like Baldassare Castiglione's "handbook of the rhetorical frame of mind" (183), as Thomas O. Sloane terms *Il Cortegiano*, Sir Thomas Elyot's *Boke Named the Gouernour*, Thomas Wilson's *Arte of Rhetorique*, and George Puttenham's *Arte of English Poesie* all teach a Ciceronian "rhetoric of decorum," adapting classical precepts to contemporary cultural conditions of court, aristocratic patronage, and absolute monarchy. One's access to court demands decorous, prudent, "courtly" speech and behavior. Indeed, "courtliness" becomes defined by a range of ritualized behaviors, each regulated by the principle of decorum: one's role, one's status, one's very identity as a courtier is bound to the mastery and expression of such behaviors. Such an education in rhetoric, Stephen Greenblatt observes, offers "the power to shape" one's world, to "calculate the probabilities, and master the contingent" (162); to this extent, Humanist rhetoric offers its practitioners a means to negotiate power. Doubtless, however, the constraints of decorum provide an equally potent means of social control, effectually sustaining the aristocratic status quo. Violations of decorum, after all, implicitly threaten the court's power to regulate its discourse and to assign levels of power and status within that discourse. Hence, the age's near-obsession with "decencie," propriety, and "courtly," genteel behavior.

As we have gathered thus far, considerations of *kairos* (that is, of *opportunitas* or *occasio*) and related temporal concepts are vital to the workings of Humanist prudential rhetoric. And, within such a tradition, to speak of the temporalities of rhetoric is at the same time to articulate an ethics of rhetoric, since all rhetorical action is deliberative (and, hence, governed by prudence), situated in time, and expressive of moral agency. From this it follows, too, that an ethics of decorum is necessarily an ethics of time, since all deliberation unfolds temporally and is judged by its "right-timing," among other effects. Thus, having discussed the age's concern with the proprieties and temporalities of rhetoric, we might now broaden our topic to include the philosophical categories themselves, particularly the distinctions among *aion*, *chronos*, and *kairos*.

"There is a twofold conception of time that is new in the Renaissance: time as duration and time as occasion." So argues Douglas L. Peterson (1973, 1), who cites John Foxe's *Time and the End of Time* (1664): "Time and opportunity differ, time is the duration or succession of so many minutes, hours, days. . . . Opportunity is the time apted and fitted in order to this or that work of business, namely, a meeting of time and means together" (1–2). Somewhat

Though Fortune, *hath a* po*werfull* Name,
Yet, Vertue *overcomes the* same.

ILLVSTR. XLVII.   *Book.* 2

Fig. 4. George Wither, *A Collection of Emblemes, Ancient and Moderne* (1635).

overstated, this "twofold conception" is by no means new, though it does re-
cover categories of temporal consciousness prevalent throughout classical antiquity and yet neglected, as we have suggested, throughout the Middle
Ages. The complexity of Renaissance attitudes toward time may be observed
in the age's numerous emblem books, of which Geffrey Whitney's *Choice of
Emblemes* (1586) and George Wither's *Collection of Emblemes, Ancient and
Moderne* (1635) are representative. Treating the familiar themes of neoclassicizing Humanism (Clements, 223), such books were "a depository for many
earlier literary and artistic traditions, themes, and opinions," as Robert
Clements notes (33). In addition to offering training in the techniques of
symbolic interpretation, an emblem's visual program provided aids to memory, condensing into a single complex image the various *topoi* surrounding

prudence, occasion or opportunity, fortune, and time, among other Humanist themes; for which reason such collections were often "used as textbooks of rhetoric in the seventeenth century" (Clements, 65).

Since *prudentia* and *occasio* are among the emblematists' favorite subjects, it is not surprising that emblem tradition both reinforces and complicates Humanist theory. In one of several related emblems (see figure 4), George Wither invokes the classical commonplaces regarding prudence and its mastery over Fortune. "Afford[ing] instructions fit" (12) to readers "whose *Fortunes* must be mended by their *Wits*" (11), he interprets the emblem thus:

> A *Snake* (which was by wise *Antiquitie*
> Much us'd the type of *Prudencie* to be)
> Hemmes in a *Winged-ball*, which doth imply
> That *Fickle-fortune*, from which, none are free.
> Above this *Ball*, the *Snake* advanceth too,
> The *Laurell*, and the *Sword*; which, *Emblems* are,
> Whereby our *Authour* maketh much adoe,
> A *Conquest* over *Fortune*, to declare. . . .
>
> (1–8)

Apparently Wither echoes Matthew 10:16 in rendering the serpent a "type of *Prudencie*" though, elsewhere in his *Collection*, the uroboros or circled snake represents *aion*-eternity. Declared "*Mistresse* over *Fate*" (15), such prudence seems to reinforce Humanist rhetorical and ethical theory, offering readers the means to choose rightly and, thereby, assert greater control over "*Fickle-fortune*," here represented by a ball with wings, both traditional symbols of the goddess *Occasio* (the ball in particular serving as a variant upon Fortune's wheel). And yet this particular emblem (not to mention Wither's accompanying poem) reduces *prudentia* to an abstraction, a philosophical ideal divorced from the temporalities of human choice and action. When situating human action within time, the age's emblems offer a more complex response.

Wither's poetic "illustration" of *Occasio* (figure 5), for example, reveals the many contradictions inherent in Renaissance attitudes toward time. As M. Christopher Pecheux observes, "Greek *kairos*, Latin *occasio*, English *occasion* or *opportunity* all represented a moment that might change the direction of a man's life as would a sudden turn of Fortune's wheel" (1978, 202). Surely such applies to Wither's emblem, as would Ausonius' poetic dialogue, *In Simulacrum Occasionis et Paenitentiae* (fourth century A.D.); explicating the conventional image the late-classical poet writes, by means of an elaborate *prosopopoeia*, "'I am a goddess seldom found and known to few, Opportunity my name.' 'Why standest thou on a wheel?' 'I cannot stand still.' 'why wearest thou winged sandals?' 'I am ever flying.' . . ." (*Epigrams* 33.3–6).[6] Wither's own

Fig. 5. George Wither, *A Collection of Emblemes, Ancient and Moderne* (1635).

poem plays variations upon the conventional themes, beginning, "Unwise are they that spend their youthful *Prime* / In Vanities; as if they did suppose / That men, at pleasure, might redeeme the *Time*; / For, they a faire advantage fondly lose" (1–4). While thus exhorting readers to seize opportunity—

> The first *Occasions*, therefore, see thou take
> (Which offred are), to bring thy hopes about;
> And, minde thou, still, what *Haste* away they make,
> Before thy swift-pac't houres are quite runne out.
>
> (13–16)

—Wither's poem nonetheless invokes competing temporalities, contrasting *kairos*-opportunity with the "swift-pac't houres" of *chronos*-time. Earlier the poet had railed against those who "depend / On *transitorie things* as if their Powre / Could . . . compasse that, which *Time* will not devoure" (9–12), thereby contrasting the effects of flawed worldly time with eternity. Yet following upon his own exhortation—"The first *Occasions*, therefore, see thou take"—Wither continues, in apparent self-contradiction: "if an *Opportunity* be past, / Despair not thou . . . / Since, *Time* may so revolve again, at last, / That *New-Occasions* may be offred thee" (17–20). While one must strive to seize Opportunity by the forelock, time's cyclical nature (suggested by her ever-turning wheel) ensures "*New-Occasions*," which one may yet succeed in grasping. Granted, the emblem-image is itself optimistic: whereas numerous earlier versions—such as in Theodore de Bry's *Emblemata* (1592)—depict two ships on either side of the goddess, the one sailing, the other sinking, Wither's emblem depicts a single ship in full sail, enjoying fair weather. Yet Wither's poem confuses virtually every temporal category. Time becomes both unique and cyclical in its opportunities; it offers the "hopes" of "fair advantage" and yet "devoure[s]" all, making time both ally and enemy, creator and destroyer; time is at once a precious commodity (though wasted by youth) and an aspect of "transitorie," worldly life, of negligible value compared to that eternity toward which all Christians hasten. What is the reader to make of such apparent contradictions?

Frederick Kiefer has argued that the distinctions between *Fortuna* and *Occasio* were "blurred if not obliterated altogether by the middle of the sixteenth century" (211). As we have seen, the qualities of both figures were already linked in antiquity. Nonetheless, as one charts the subsequent iconographic history of the two figures there appears a relative shift in emphasis, suggesting a corresponding shift in consciousness from the medieval to the Renaissance. Whereas *Fortuna* reigns over the medieval imagination, symbolizing all that is "arbitrary and capricious" (Kiefer, *Fortune,* xv) and subject to the sudden reversals of chance, the qualities of "right-timing" and prudent action associated with *Occasio* gain greater power in the Renaissance. And with reason. By emphasizing the blindness of chance and the fragility of worldly power, fame, and wealth, *Fortuna* teaches a grim sort of Christian sufferance and resignation to time; indeed all men and women, however powerful or prosperous, fall victim to misfortune, failure, loss, sickness, death. In contrast, the mythology surrounding *Occasio* offers prospects of greater control over life, stressing that opportunities arise for prudent action at right moments. For "chiefly," Sir Francis Bacon asserts, "the mould of a man's fortune is in his own hands" (*Philosophical Works,* 784).[7]

As emblem tradition amply demonstrates, the Renaissance placed greater emphasis upon *kairos*-time than did its medieval forebears. This emphasis is only relative, as I have suggested, since *Fortuna* remains very much part of the

Renaissance imagination. Yet I take issue with Kiefer's assertion that the distinctions between *Fortuna* and *Occasio* were "blurred if not obliterated altogether." Their distinguishing qualities were typically conjoined, but in ways that allowed each to comment on the other's symbolisms. In borrowing Fortune's wheel, for example, *Occasio* subtly expands its range of meanings. Such symbolic juxtapositions reflect the age's tendencies, well-established within its literary and visual arts, to pair subjects dialectically, thereby highlighting their oppositional (or often, as here, complementary) forces and effects. Numerous Janus-figures exploit similar effects, though none more strikingly than the ideal courtier depicted in the anonymous *Mirror of Majestie* (1618), whose left side stands clothed in scholar's robes and bearing a book, while the right side stands in full armor, bearing sword, shield, and lance, thereby uniting the *vita contemplativa* and *vita activa,* the scholar's wisdom and the soldier's fortitude. In addition, Renaissance emblem tradition plays variations upon the classical iconography, adding paradox and wit.

Whereas Geffrey Whitney and George A. Wither remain faithful to the classical iconography, the Continental emblematist Achille Bocchi (figure 6) depicts *Occasio* comically "stretched on her own wheel," as Elizabeth See Watson (124) notes, "as though on an instrument of torture" (124). To the Latin inscription, *Occasionem qui sapis ne amiseris,* "You who are wise will not let occasion slip by," Bocchi adds the Greek ΓΝΩΘΙΚΑΙΡΟΝ; or *gnothi kairon*—which Kiefer translates, simply, as "know the time" ("Renaissance Stage," 33) though, in accordance with humanist prudential rhetoric, a more subtle translation might be "know the (right-) time." Echoing the Socratic *gnothi seauton,* "know thyself," Bocchi follows Ciceronian-Humanist tradition in making *kairos* a foundation of *prudentia* or practical wisdom. While Fortune's turning wheel continues to claim its victims—including *Occasio* herself—those who "know the (right-) time" and "do not let Occasion slip by" may still hope to triumph. Richard Taverner's *Proverbs or Adages, Gathered Out of the Chiliades of Erasmus* (1569) points to the similarities between the Latin *nosce teipsum* (19v)—that is, "know thyself"—and *nosce tempus* (23r), Erasmus' Latin translation of *gnothi kairon,* glossing the latter thus:

> Know time. Oportunitie is of such force, that of honest it maketh unhonest, of dammage auauntage, of pleasure, greauance, . . . and briefly to conclude it cleane chaungeth the nature of thinges. This oportunitie or occasion (for so also ye may call it in auenturinge and finishinge a busines) doubtles beareth the chiefe stroke, so that not without good skill the painims of old time counted [it] a diuine thinge.
>
> And in this wise they painted her. They made her a goddess standing with fethered faete upon a whele. . . . (23r)

For further variations upon classical tradition, consider the emblem (figure 7) from Jan David's *Occasio Arrepta, Neglecta* (1605), whose Latin inscription

OCCASIONEM QVI SAPIS NE AMISERIS·

SYMB. LXIX.

Fig. 6. Achille Bocchi, *Symbolicae Questiones* (1555).

Fig. 7. Jan David, *Occasio Arrepta, Neglecta* (1605).

(Dum Tempus labitur, Occasionem fronte capillata remorantur) translates, "While Time passes onward, men keep Occasion back by the hair on her forehead." David's emblem thus personifies two competing temporalities, *Tempus* (that is, "Time flying," replete with sickle and hourglass) and *Occasio*, whose forelock one of the men rather violently has seized. In Otho Van Veen's "Time flying" (figure 8), we again note a juxtaposition of temporal categories. Depicting the four "seasons" or ages of human life, four figures march off in single file, led by a cherub bearing a sun dial (representing the swift

passage of *chronos*-time). As they follow this personification of time, the figures remain oblivious of the uroboros or circled serpent, representing both time's seasonal, cyclical nature and the timelessness of *aion*-eternity, to which they march posthaste. For Van Veen's contemporary readers, then, the coiled serpent casts the entire scene *sub specie aeternitatis:* time marches steadily on, toward death and dissolution. Invoking an older, medieval-Augustinian "dichotomy between the eternal and the temporal" (Peterson, 21), Van Veen's image compares to other of Wither's emblems, particularly of a flower encircled by an uroboros (figure 9)—which is itself encircled by the Greek

Fig. 8. Van Veen, *Emblemata Horatiana* (1612).

Fig. 9. George Wither, *A Collection of Emblemes, Ancient and Moderne* (1635).

ΑΙΩΝΙΟΝ ΚΑΙ ΠΡΟΣ ΚΑΙΡΟΝ; or *aionion kai pros kairon*, "eternally and in time." As Wither glosses the image, "*Time* is a *Fading-flowre*, that's found / Within *Eternities* wide round."

Among the many paradoxes inscribed in Renaissance emblematic tradition is its simultaneous embrace of self-assertion and asceticism, on the one hand seeking to master time, on the other hand repudiating time and its worldly effects. We have already mentioned Wither's apparently optimistic depiction of *Occasio* (figure 5). Curiously, his poetic "illustration" concludes with the commonplaces of *memento mori* tradition: "And see, thou trust not on those fading things, / Which by thine owne *Endeavours* thou acquir'st: / For, *Time* (whiche her own *Births* to ruin brings) / Will spare, nor *thee*, nor ought which thou desir'st" (21–24). Thus, he advises readers to seize that which, ultimately, one should "trust not." In fact Wither's most telling phrase occurs early on, in his declaration that "men . . . might redeeme the *Time*" (3). On its surface, the phrase suggests an economics of time which, conceived as a commodity, can be wasted, saved, spent, and even bought back or, as here, "redeemed." From a Christian perspective, of course, the phrase suggests that fallen worldly time, much like a repentant human creature, stands in need of redemption and spiritual renewal.[8]

More remains to be said regarding the necessity of time's "redemption," though we might pause to observe the various spatial metaphors embedded in the age's iconography. Whereas *Occasio* presents itself as a single point-in-time—that unique moment when Opportunity may be seized "by the fore-lock"—the linearity of *chronos*-time appears in the iconographic symbolism of flight or of marching single-file; in contrast, the circled serpent makes visual reference to the seasonality and circularity of *aion*-time. A spatial-temporal sequence thus arises, proceeding from point, to line, to circle. Other symbolic patterings suggest themselves, based particularly on the distinctions among natural, human, and divine orders. In large part *chronos*-time is nonhuman, its workings belonging to impersonal, objective nature; hence the predominance of such natural symbols as the fading flower. (But to the extent that humankind is part of nature, our bodies, too, remain subject to age, death, and decay. Given our own mixed, "middle" state—we are bodies bound to material nature as well as immortal souls—such emblems as we have studied suggest the various constraints placed upon human life, which remains subject to natural law on the one hand, and divine commandment on the other. Hence, the fading flower is joined by the human skull, both images par excellence of *memento mori* tradition.) Whereas *aion*, too, expresses seasonal (and, thus, natural) effects, its essential workings reflect the fulfillments or completions of worldly time as foreordained by Providence—which, Boethius writes, is "the unfolding of temporal events as this is present to the vision of the divine mind."[9] While Providence thus accords with "the vision of the divine mind," the Ciceronian-Humanist, *kairos* describes the quintessentially human experience of time as an aspect of individual consciousness, deliberation, and action. In asserting the uniqueness of each moment rather than the constant, linear passage of time (again, *chronos*) or the fulfillment of time (that is, *aion*), *kairos* marks that single, fleeting moment when an individual chooses from among all competing alternatives and eventualities, thereby changing one's world-as-lived. In this sense, the relationship between *Occasio* and *Fortuna* can be charted as cause and effect; *Occasio* representing that unique moment when an individual's fortune is "set in motion," like a wheel cycling either up or down, depending on circumstances. If *Occasio* provides the means, *Fortuna* suggests the consequences. Interpreted thus, one's fortune can never remain fixed: cycling through times of health and sickness, prosperity and tragedy, life changes with each new occasion, each moment presenting new causes creating new consequences. In its broadest sense, then, *kairos* immerses speakers in a moral-intellectual crisis when the choice to speak or act (and what and how one speaks or acts) determines an individual's "fate." Hence, the Humanists' habit of weighing alternatives and occasions, of "looking both ways" and speaking (or acting) accordingly—a habit, in short, of *prudentia*.

Douglas Bush notes "the high tension and intensity that Renaissance writers brought to the contemplation of time" ("English Poetry," 1966, 68–69); indeed, had we but world enough and time, we should turn now to apply these many temporal concepts to the age's imaginative literature, its love poetry in particular, in which the spirit of *carpe diem* is deeply inscribed. Exhorting his "coy mistress" to seize the moment, Andrew Marvell writes, "But at my back I always hear / Time's wingèd chariot hurrying near: / And yonder all before us lie / Deserts of vast eternity" (21–24), thus weaving *kairos, chronos,* and *aion* together in a complex unity. Of course, being a comedy of seduction—like so many other poems of the age—Marvell's lyric also grates against the decorum of courtly address, both in its implicit bawdiness and in its explicitly fallacious reasoning. As such a poem demonstrates, Tudor and Stuart literature affirms even as it parodies social strictures of polite, courtly behavior and decorum, calling attention to its own comic violations of the same (there being more deliberate comedy inscribed in the age's love poetry than is often acknowledged). For example, the more libertine of John Donne's *Elegies* and *Songs and Sonets* offer witty violations of decorum in their speaker's youthful (and somewhat indiscriminate) pursuit of *eros*. Alternatively, one can also observe the ways that a speaker's addressee or intended audience—which, in the case of Shakespeare's sonnets, ranges conjecturally from the Earl of Southampton to the "dark lady"—demands continual adjustments in subject, tone, and style. More suggestive still are the ways love poetry enacts implicit dialogues between speakers and their imagined interlocutors, thus highlighting the temporal, indeed kairotic, unfolding of argument. The most telling rhetorical application of *kairos* may be charted in the internal temporalities of discourse itself; for arguments necessarily unfold in time, subtly changing as one line of reasoning extends, completes, or overthrows another, continually adjusting in accordance with an audience's complex response. Occasions, in other words, occur not just within time but within texts. The dramatic monologue—of which Donne's "Flea" offers a stunning comic example—highlights the *kairos* of poetic argument, demonstrating the ways that an implied interlocutor compels changes, even reversals, in a speaker's rhetoric. But all this is by way of suggesting what *cannot* be fully addressed in so brief an essay; suffice it to say that the internal temporalities of discourse remain a subject for further investigation.

We began by observing the ultimate failure of the Ciceronian-Humanist "rhetoric of decorum." Having offered a partial outline of the same, let us end by observing, in greater detail, several of the issues raised that make Renaissance theory both distinctive and problematic. Throughout the above discussion, for example, the reader might well object, "But how does one *know* when an occasion is 'timely' or an argument or style 'fitting'?" The fact is that decorous (or indecorous) speech and behavior is necessarily judged after the fact, based on an audience's immediate, concrete response. And while a speaker may predict an audience's response, one can never guarantee that any behavior will yield its desired effects. For all the concern theorists show in observing decorum, no one articulates rules sufficient to govern its effective use. Rhetoricians from Cicero to Puttenham offer numerous examples, as often of failures as of successes; but such a concept as decorum, clearly, cannot be reduced to a set of precepts.[10] Indeed, when Puttenham writes of the "difficultie" in knowing "what this good grace is, and wherein it consisteth, for peraduenture it be easier to conceaue than to expresse" (268), he suggests the difficulty—perhaps even impossibility—of adequate definition. Like Donne's (or Dryden's) "wit" or Castiglione's *sprezzatura*, such a concept as decorum refuses pinning-down, for which reason Puttenham resorts to a range of synonyms—including "good grace," "seemleyness," "comeleyness," "aptnesse," "proportion," "conformitie," and "conueniencie," as David Hillman (76) observes—each gesturing toward while failing to comprehend decorum *in toto*. Like "wit" or *sprezzatura*, decorum points to that "certain something" pervading successful courtly performance. Then again, the Latin (or, for that matter, English) decorum reveals much the same lexical complexity as the Greek *kairos*, whose subtle shifts in meaning render the term virtually untranslatable, whether into Latin or into English. Thoroughly overdetermined in meaning, *kairos* comprehends a range of rhetorical effects that include "due measure," "harmony," "fitness," "appropriateness," and "proportionality," as well as "timing" and "timeliness." The difficulty in translating such a term is that any English equivalent captures only a fraction of its full range of meanings, whereas any given usage is likely to suggest several senses simultaneously. Specific uses of *kairos* may best be translated as a combination of qualities, such as "that harmony which is proportionate," or "that timing which harmonizes," or "that proportionate measure," or "that measure which is fit and timely." As with other instances of the Greek philosophical vocabulary (*logos* for one, whose meanings include "word," "speech," "discourse," "reckoning," "argument," "oracle," "proof," "proposition," "explanation," "measure," "reason," "ratio," "logic," and "rational principle"), the need for circumlocution renders translation a daunting task indeed.

The age's "rhetoric of decorum" proceeds on the assumption that "truth itself changes according to the circumstances in which one finds oneself" (Kahn, 35), a sophistic notion that many Humanists embraced. Thus, when Donne's youthful, libertine poet writes (in response to an imagined interlocutor's counterargument), ". . . against these 'scapes I could / Dispute, and conquer, if I would, / Which I abstain to do, / For by tomorrow, I may think so too" ("Woman's Constancy" 14–17), he plays the Sophist's part, implying not simply that one's arguments change: with time, even truth changes—as, obviously, do the objects of human desire. The notion that one can change arguments at will, with much the same nonchalance that one changes clothing, is very much in the spirit of the original, Gorgianic *kairos*. Yet it flies in the teeth of Christian morality, for which "Truth is the daughter of Time." Depicted in numerous emblems, *Veritas filia Temporis* personifies time as the great revealer and executrix of divine Providence. During the Renaissance, as Douglas Bush observes, "time was rather a religious than a scientific idea" ("English Poetry," 66). While it would be more accurate to say that an *aspect* of time was religious rather than scientific, the role of providential history in human affairs remained a central tenet of Christian theology.

For a Sophist like Gorgias, truth changes with time; for the Christian, truth is fulfilled and revealed in time. Thus, we note the significant epistemological distinctions separating what are, in fact, competing sophistic and Christian *kairoi*, the former proceeding from a radical skepticism that reduces truth—the very foundation of the latter's divine reality—to a Nietzschean will to power. As practiced by Gorgias and his disciples, *kairos* defines that rhetorical moment when words perform their world-building magic—a moment, that is, of enchantment or persuasion, when the speaker embraces one of several competing *logoi*. Though no more than *apate* or deliberate deception (within Gorgias' radically skeptical world view, the choice of any one *logos* over other *logoi* remains thoroughly arbitrary, an act of will), nonetheless the Sophist's persuasion effects a "joyful deception," freeing its audience from moral/deliberative paralysis. (Whereas subsequent theory conceives of persuasion as compelling an audience's beliefs and actions in accordance with a speaker's will, sophistic practice views persuasion as therapeutic and liberating—a means of overcoming the paralysis of will generated by *dissoi logoi*.) While this describes sophistic practice well enough, what relevance has it to the rhetorical epistemology of Renaissance Humanism?

Again the Gorgianic *kairos* is liberating, if deceptive, enabling the rhetor to create contingent, socially constructed truths. But while Ciceronian *occasio* remains grounded in moderate, "academic" skepticism, it considerably narrowed the field of contingency within which persuasion operates; in addition, Cicero would never assert the same level of confidence regarding the absolute, irresistible powers of Gorgianic rhetoric. And while Renaissance Humanists rediscovered the Sophists' more radical skepticism, nonetheless their field of contingency narrowed further, since no one—not Montaigne, not Machiavelli, not Marlowe's Dr. Faustus—would dare deny divine reality, whatever else they might doubt or place in spiritual danger.[11] In contrast to the Sophists' self-assertions, the Christian *kairos* identifies foreordained moments of divine decision, whose archetypal manifestations include Christ's incarnation, death, and the resurrection—and, forward-looking, Christ's Second Coming and final Judgment, when "time shall be no more." While the individual Christian aims to conform his will to the divine *kairos*, it would be a mistake to assume that fallen humanity ever achieves mastery over its own destiny. "There's a divinity that shapes our ends, / Rough-hew them how we will" (5.2.9 – 11); so Hamlet discovers, English literature's most majestic, most tragic humanist, Elsinore's ideal courtier and strict observer of decorum (though called to murderous revenge). In so many ways, Shakespeare's play records the failure of humanist *prudentia* and the protagonist's need to subordinate human *kairos* to divine Providence; for every attempt on Hamlet's part to seize occasion and enact revenge fails miserably, leading to needless slaughter.

In sum, the cultural restraints placed on discourse, whether in Cicero's Roman *Senatus* or Elizabeth's English Parliament, considerably reduced an individual's powers of persuasion (not to mention one's opportunities for speaking). I have mentioned that Ciceronian decorum represents a synthesis of *kairos* and *prepon*. It would seem that each acts upon the other as an opposing force. When successful, *kairos* undermines *prepon* by changing the status quo; in contrast, *prepon* strives to regulate *kairos*, thereby weakening the latter's capacities for effecting change. In a sense, *kairos* and *prepon* enact a dialectic between freedom and formal restraint; stated rhetorically, *kairos* and *prepon* pit an individual's powers of invention against the formidable constraints of social convention and audience expectations. In the political realm, Humanists sought to resurrect this Gorgianic "will-to-invent," as Eric Charles White (7) puts it; yet the more conservative courts of Europe emphasized conformity and "tradition" over innovation. Hence, the tenor of courtly rhetoric, in Tudor England as elsewhere, shifts from persuasion to flattery, from advising to "pleasing" the monarch. Ultimately, Gorgianic rhetoric demands more than a sensitivity to occasion, an intimate knowledge of one's audience, a healthy skepticism and a strong will; it would seem also to require a rough equality between speaker and audience, the sort that Athenian democracy promoted, though Tudor despotism denied.

Notes

1. I follow Victoria Kahn's definition of Humanism, designating "those writers who were concerned with the recovery and imitation of classical texts and classical notions of rhetoric, the criticism of Scholasticism, and the development of an ethic and rhetoric of decorum which, at least in Italy, would be responsive to a newly developing civic consciousness" (193). This "rhetoric of decorum," as Kahn notes elsewhere, proceeds from the assumption that "truth itself changes according to the circumstances in which one finds oneself" (35); as such, it recapitulates the skeptical epistemology of the Greek Sophists.

2. Significantly, Alfred von Martin explains Renaissance culture's heightened temporal consciousness as an effect of capitalism and its concomitant ideology of the individual. Whereas "time was always short and hence valuable" during the Renaissance, such an attitude "had been unknown to the Middle Ages," for which "time was plentiful and there was no need to look upon it as something precious":

> It became so only when regarded from the point of view of the individual who could think in terms of the time measured out to him. . . . [It] became necessary to build quickly, as the patron was now building for himself. In the Middle Ages it was possible to spend tens and even hundreds of years on the completion of one building . . . for life was the life of the community in which one generation quietly succeeds another. (16)

3. John Poulakos elaborates on this point: "In conjunction with the notion of *kairos*, the Sophists gave impetus to the related concept of *to prepon* (the appropriate), apparently prescribing that what is said must conform to both audience and occasion" (41). Complementary, then, to the notion of *kairos*, *to prepon* "points out that situations have formal characteristics, and demands that speaking as a response to a situation be suitable to those very characteristics. . . . In distinction to *kairos*, which focuses on man's sense of time, *to prepon* emphasizes his sense of propriety" (Poulakos, 41).

4. To such as cannot keep silent, Thomas Wilson offers the following poignant anecdote: "But shall I say of such willful men as a Spaniard spoke of an earnest gospeler that for words spoken against an ecclesiastical law suffereth death in Smithfield: 'Ah miser, *non potuit tacere et vivere?*' (Ah wretch that he was, could he not live and hold his peace?)" (167). Literary examples abound, though none greater than Shakespeare's *Hamlet*. With his father "but two months dead" (1.2.138), Hamlet complains of his mother's "o'er-hasty marriage" to the usurping Claudius. "But break my heart," he avers, "for I must hold my tongue" (159). Though their marriage violates decorum, Hamlet's own prudent nature counsels him to "live and hold his peace."

5. "The adjustment of the classical notion of *Decorum* to English style" is, as G. Gregory Smith notes, "one of the most persistent topics" in Elizabethan literary theory (xli), discussed at length by Roger Ascham, George Gascoigne, and Spenser's "E.K." as well as George Puttenham. Their arguments follow Aristotle (*Rhetoric* 3.7.1–2; 3.7.6), Horace (*Ars Poetica* 91–118), and Cicero (*Orator*, 21), each of whom grounds literary decorum in the distinctive subjects, structures, and styles of the various poetic genres, a consistency of characterization, and careful observance of the "three styles." For further discussion of literary decorum in the English Renaissance, see Kranidas, *The Fierce Equation*, 13–48.

6. Similarly, as Mother M. Christopher Pecheux notes, the pseudo-Ciceronian *Rhetorica ad Herennium* "illustrates the synthesis of attributes: 'The goddess Fortune . . .

stands upon a revolving globe of stone: whither Chance impels this stone, thither, they say, does Fortune fall'"(202). Yet Edward W. Tayler cites Cartari's *Le Imagini* (1556 [fol.96ᵛ]) for its clear awareness of the earlier, Greek iconography, which depicted Kairos as a male youth: "This one, which the Latins called Occasion and Opportunity, and revered as a Goddess, was called Opportune Time by the Greeks. Therefore they worshiped him as a God, not a Goddess. His name for them was caerus, for that word among the Greeks signifies opportunity of time. Thus for the Greeks, the God Caerus was the same as Occasion for the Latins" (257). For more detailed discussion of the iconographic traditions surrounding *Kairos, Occasio,* and *Fortuna,* see Green, *Shakespeare and the Emblem Writers,* 258–63; Kiefer, "Fortune," 193–231; Panofsky, *Studies in Iconology,* 69–94; Pecheux, "Milton and Kairos," 201–09; Wind, *Pagan Mysteries,* 89–99; and Wittkower, "Chance, Time, and Virtue."

7. In his essay, "Of Delays," Sir Francis Bacon gathers up aphorisms relevant to the two figures. "Fortune," he begins, "is like the market; if you can stay a little, the price will fall" (*Philosophical Works* 762), implying some predictability in Life's chances, from which a prudent man might profit. Turning next to *Occasio,* Bacon writes, "there is surely no greater wisdom than well to time the beginnings and onset of things. . . . The ripeness or unripeness of the occasion . . . must ever be well weighed; and generally it is good to commit the beginnings of all great actions to Argus with his hundred eyes, and the ends to Briareus with his hundred hands; first to watch, and then to speed" (762). And as with action, so with speech: "the honourablest part of talk is to give the occasion," Bacon writes in "Of Discourse" (*Philosophical Works,* 775), adding, "discretion of speech is more than eloquence" (*Philosophical Works,* 776).

8. The phrase is a Pauline commonplace repeated in *Ephesians* 5.16 and *Colossians* 4.5: to "redeem the time" Englishes the Greek ἐξαγοραζόμενοι τὸν καιρόν, rendered in the Vulgate as *tempus redimentes.*

9. Boethius adds, "but this same unfolding of events as it is worked out in time is called Fate." I quote *The Consolation of Philosophy* from Kiefer (*Fortune,* 7), who offers a detailed survey of late classical and early Christian attitudes toward time, chance, and divine Providence.

10. Eric Charles White argues similarly with respect to Gorgias, who understood that *kairos* "can never form the basis of a systematic treatise on the management of the opportune" (20). Standing "precisely for the irrational novelty of the moment that escapes formalization," any attempt at a "science of 'kaironomy'" would find itself incoherently promising foreknowledge of chance. To put it another way, no treatise on the occasional nature of utterance could be itself exempt from occasionality, or the inevitability of its own supersession" (20).

11. Early in his *Discours de la Méthode* (1637), Descartes imagines that he can doubt all; he cannot, however, doubt God's existence, which remains (albeit problematically) both a premise and a conclusion of Cartesian proof. In this age, atheism is unthinkable. Yet the acknowledgment of divine reality carries with it further consequences that shape the age's rhetorical epistemology. Truth, for example, becomes stable, singular, and testable against the authority of Scripture; it can never be man-made (as Protagoras imagined, articulating the sophistic doctrine of *metron anthropos*), but remains forever God-made, revealed rather than socially constructed. Accordingly, the moderate skepticism and watered down relativism espoused by Ciceronian-Humanists fall far short of Gorgias' radical skepticism, the intellectual environment in which *kairos,* as a specifically rhetorical concept, is most fully and forcefully articulated.

Works Cited

Ausonius. *Ausonius*. Trans. Hugh G. Evelyn White. Loeb Classical Library. 2 Vols. London: Heinemann, 1921.

Bacon, Sir Francis. *The Advancement of Learning* (1605). Ed. G. W. Kitchin. Totowa, NJ: Rowman and Littlefield, 1974.

———. *The Philosophical Works of Francis Bacon*. Ed. John M. Robertson. Freeport, NY: Books for Libraries, 1970.

Beale, Walter. "Decorum." *Encyclopedia of Rhetoric and Composition: Communication from Ancient Times to the Information Age*. Ed. Theresa Enos, 168–69. New York: Garland, 1996.

Bush, Douglas. *Classical Influences in Renaissance Literature*. Cambridge, MA: Harvard University Press, 1952.

———. "English Poetry: Time and Man." *Prefaces to Renaissance Literature*, 65–90. Cambridge, MA: Harvard University Press, 1966.

Castiglione, Baldesar. *The Book of the Courtier*. Trans. Charles S. Singleton. Garden City, NY: Anchor Books, 1959.

Chew, Samuel. "Time and Fortune." *ELH* 6 (1939): 83–113.

Cicero. *Brutus; Orator*. Trans. G. L. Hendrickson and H. M. Hubbell. Loeb Classical Library. Cambridge, MA: Harvard University Press, 1954.

———. *De Inventione; De Optimo Genere Oratorum; Topica*. Trans. H. M. Hubbell. Loeb Classical Library. Cambridge, MA: Harvard University Press, 1949.

———. *De Officiis*. Trans. Walter Miller. Loeb Classical Library. Cambridge, MA: Harvard University Press, 1961.

———. *De Oratore*. Trans. E. W. Sutton. Loeb Classical Library. 2 Vols. Cambridge, MA: Harvard University Press, 1929.

Clements, Robert J. *Pictura Poesis: Literary and Humanistic Theory in Renaissance Emblem Books*. Rome: Edizioni di Storia e Letteratura, 1960.

Donne, John. *The Complete Poetry of John Donne*. Ed. John T. Shawcross. Garden City, NY: Archon, 1967.

Elyot, Sir Thomas. *The Booke Named the Governor* (1531). Ed. S. E. Lehmberg. London: Everyman, 1962.

Frye, Roland Mushat. *The Renaissance Hamlet: Issues and Responses in 1600*. Princeton: Princeton University Press, 1984.

Green, Henry. *Shakespeare and the Emblem Writers: An Exposition of Their Similarities of Thought and Expression*. London, 1869. Reprint, New York: Burt Franklin, n.d.

Greenblatt, Stephen. *Renaissance Self-Fashioning*. Chicago: University of Chicago Press, 1980.

Hillman, David. "Puttenham, Shakespeare, and the Abuse of Rhetoric." *Studies in English Literature* 36 (1996): 73–90.

Howell, Wilbur Samuel. *Logic and Rhetoric in England, 1500–1700*. Princeton: Princeton University Press, 1956.

Javitch, Daniel. *Poetry and Courtliness in Renaissance England*. Princeton: Princeton University Press, 1978.

Kahn, Victoria. *Rhetoric, Prudence, and Skepticism in the Renaissance*. Ithaca: Cornell University Press, 1985.

Kennedy, George A. *Classical Rhetoric and Its Christian and Secular Tradition from Ancient to Modern Times*. Chapel Hill: University of North Carolina Press, 1980.

Kiefer, Frederick. *Fortune and Elizabethan Tragedy.* Huntington, CA: Huntington Library, 1983.

————. "Fortune and the Renaissance Stage: An Iconographic Reconstruction." In "All is but Fortune." Edited by L. Thomson, 68–89. Washington, DC: Folger, 2000.

Kinneavy, James L. "*Kairos*: A Neglected Concept in Classical Rhetoric." *Rhetoric and Praxis: The Contribution of Classical Rhetoric to Practical Reasoning.* Ed. Jean Dietz Moss, 79–105. Washington, DC: The Catholic University of America Press, 1986.

Kranidas, Thomas. *The Fierce Equation: A Study of Milton's Decorum.* The Hague: Mouton, 1965.

Major, John M. *Sir Thomas Elyot and Renaissance Humanism.* Lincoln, NE: University of Nebraska Press, 1964.

Marvell, Andrew. *Andrew Marvell: The Complete English Poems.* Edited by E. Elizabeth Story Donno. New York: St. Martin's, 1972.

McAlindon, T. *Shakespeare and Decorum.* London: Macmillan, 1973.

Panofsky, Erwin. *Studies in Iconology: Humanistic Themes in the Art of the Renaissance.* New York: Harper, 1962.

Pecheux, Mother M. Christopher. "Milton and Kairos." *Milton Studies* 12 (1978): 197–211.

Peterson, Douglas L. *Time, Tide, and Tempest: A Study of Shakespeare's Romances.* San Marino, CA: Huntington Library, 1973.

Poulakos, John. "Toward a Sophistic Definition of Rhetoric." *Philosophy and Rhetoric* 16 (1983): 35–48.

Puttenham, George. *The Arte of English Poesie* (1589). Ed. Baxter Hathaway. Kent, OH: Kent State University Press, 1970.

Quinones, Ricardo J. *The Renaissance Discovery of Time.* Cambridge, MA: Harvard University Press, 1972.

Shakespeare, William. *The Complete Works of Shakespeare.* Ed. David Bevington. 4th ed. New York: HarperCollins, 1992.

Simonds, Peggy Muñoz. *Iconographic Research in English Renaissance Literature.* New York: Garland, 1995.

Sloane, Thomas O. *On the Contrary: The Protocol of Traditional Rhetoric.* Washington, DC: The Catholic University of America Press, 1997.

Smith, G. Gregory. *Elizabethan Critical Essays.* 2 Vols. Oxford: Clarendon, 1904.

Struever, Nancy S. *The Language of History in the Renaissance: Rhetoric and Historical Consciousness in Florentine Humanism.* Princeton: Princeton University Press, 1970.

Tayler, Edward W. *Milton's Poetry: Its Development in Time.* Pittsburgh: Duquesne University Press, 1979.

Taverner, Richard. *Proverbs or Adages Gathered Out of the Chiliades of Erasmus* (1569). Introd. DeWitt T. Starnes. Delmar, NY: Scholar's Facsimiles, 1977.

Thomson, Leslie, ed. *Fortune: "All is but Fortune."* Washington, DC: Folger, 2000.

Untersteiner, Mario. *The Sophists.* Trans. Kathleen Freeman. New York: Philosophical Library, 1954.

Von Martin, Alfred. *Sociology of the Renaissance.* London: Routledge and Kegan Paul, 1944.

Watson, Elizabeth See. *Achille Bocchi and the Emblem Book as Symbolic Form.* Cambridge, UK: Cambridge University Press, 1993.

Whigham, Frank. *Ambition and Privilege: The Social Tropes of Elizabethan Courtesy Theory.* Berkeley: University of California Press, 1984.

White, Eric Charles. *Kaironomia: On the Will-to-Invent.* Ithaca: Cornell University Press, 1987.

Whitney, Geffrey. *A Choice of Emblemes* (1586). Ed. Henry Green. New York: Benjamin Blom, 1967.

Wilson, Thomas. *The Art of Rhetoric* (1560). Ed. Peter Medine. University Park, PA: The Pennsylvania State University Press, 1994.

Wind, Edgar. *Pagan Mysteries in the Renaissance*. New Haven: Yale University Press, 1958.

Wisse, Jakob. *Ethos and Pathos: From Aristotle to Cicero*. Amsterdam: Adolf M. Hakkert, 1989.

Wither, George. *A Collection of Emblemes, Ancient and Moderne* (1635). Introd. Rosemary Freeman. Columbia, SC: University of South Carolina Press, 1975.

Wittkower, Rudolf. "Chance, Time, and Virtue." *Journal of the Warburg Institute* 1 (1937): 313–21.

Chronos, Kairos, Aion

Failures of Decorum, Right-Timing,

and Revenge in Shakespeare's Hamlet

JAMES S. BAUMLIN

TITA FRENCH BAUMLIN

The time is out of joint. O cursèd spite
That ever I was born to set it right!
—Hamlet (1.5.197–98)

As G. R. Elliott observes, "the predominant theme in sixteenth-century literature, whereof *Hamlet* is the consummation, was the so-called Complete Gentleman" (ix), the sort that Baldassare Castiglione, Sir Thomas Elyot, George Puttenham, and other Renaissance Humanists fashion from their readings of the Ciceronian canon. Indeed, Hamlet is "most like a gentleman" (3.1.11),[1] as Rosencrantz observes, his education as a scholar-prince having assured his thorough training in the *studia humanitatis*—which, as we saw in the previous essay, stressed *prudentia* and the vital necessity of mastering decorum or "discretion" (3.1.17), as Hamlet terms it.[2] In most respects, however, Shakespeare's Hamlet presents a study in the *failure* of *prudentia* and, thus, stands as a critical test of Humanist educational, ethical, political, rhetorical theory. The fact that Hamlet, Denmark's "chiefest courtier" (1.2.117) and the greatest Humanist in English Renaissance literature, *fails the test* reveals a crisis lying at the play's thematic center, a crisis concerning the age's optimism toward the powers of human reason (and action) and the Humanist aspiration to master worldly fortune. Applying arguments from the previous essay, the following paragraphs explore Shakespeare's complex interweaving of three broad themes: first, the nature of Hamlet's Humanist decorum; second, the Prince's bungled attempts at blood revenge; and, third, the play's philosophical exploration of competing temporalities and notions of "right-timing," particularly as reflected in the iconographic symbolisms surrounding Prudence and Fortune, Time and Eternity.

As anthropologist Clifford Geertz argues, the cultural origins and expressions of human character are marked not simply by "complexes of concrete behavior patterns—customs, usages, traditions, habit clusters," but also, and perhaps more significantly, by "a set of control mechanisms—plans, recipes, rules, instructions" (51). Clearly, the "courtesy" books of Renaissance Humanism prescribe sets of such "rules" and "recipes," in each case aimed at regulating courtly behavior. Geertz gives us an insight, then, into the "control mechanisms" operant within Ciceronian decorum. For Hamlet's great anxiety throughout is to assert control over his life and circumstances, an anxiety initially symbolized by his rage for decorum: that is, by his scrupulous observance of the social rituals intended to govern (and lend predictability to) life at court. "A true Sidneyan in his insistence upon decorum" (144), as Maurice Hunt observes, Hamlet turns such observance into a sort of security blanket, though its reliability rests upon others' willingness to follow the same rules, thereby affirming (and remaining within the bounds of) acceptable courtly behavior.

Time and again Hamlet decries others' indiscretions. "Has this fellow no feeling of his business," he asks of the grave digger, who "sings in grave-making?" (5.1.65). For such fellows, Hamlet opines, "should be consistently grave, especially when they are about their mystery. Hornpipes and funerals should not be mixed" (Hunt, 144). Yet the court, too, keeps its share of fools who violate decorum in various ways, whether by the timing, substance, or style of their importunities. Of these, Polonius proves the most egregious, coming off as a mere parody of the Humanist scholar-statesman:

> My liege, and madam, to expostulate
> What majesty should be, what duty is,
> Why day is day, night night, and time is time,
> Were nothing but to waste night, day, and time.
> Therefore, since brevity is the soul of wit,
> And tediousness the limbs and outward flourishes,
> I will be brief. Your noble son is mad. . . .
>
> (2.2.86–92)

Gertrude's response, "more matter, with less art" (2.2.95) immediately deflates such empty verbiage. Echoing Castiglione's *Il Cortegiano* (Javitch, 54), George Puttenham advises the courtier to accommodate his speech to different social classes: there is a decency in respect of the persons with whom we do negotiate, as with the great personages his egals to be solemne and surly, with meaner men pleasant and popular, stoute with the sturdie and milde with the meek, which is a most decent conuersation and not reprochfull or vnseemely" (299). Not surprisingly, one must be most careful when "negotiating with Princes," whose favor "we ought to seeke . . . by humilitie and not sternnesse" (298). Puttenham continues:

> In speaking to a Prince the voyce ought to be lowe and not lowde nor shrill, for th'one is a signe of humilitie th'other of too much audacitie and presumption. . . . Nor in speaches with them to be too long, or too much affected, for th'one is tedious th'other is irksome. (300–301)[3]

But, if not from Puttenham, perhaps Polonius could have learned better "discretion" from Hamlet himself. In "the most famous piece of literary or dramatic criticism in English" (281), as Roland Mushat Frye terms it, Hamlet's advice to the Players affirms Ciceronian-Humanist decorum:

> Suit the action to the word, the word to the action, with this special observance, that you o'erstep not the modesty of nature. For anything so o'erdone is from the purpose of playing, whose end, both at the first and now, was and is to hold as 't were the mirror up to nature, to show virtue her feature, scorn her own image, and the very age and body of the time his form and pressure. (3.1.17–24)

And the violation of such "observance," though "it makes the unskillful laugh, cannot but make the judicious grieve, the censure of the which one must in your allowance o'erweigh a whole theater of others" (3.1.25–28). Thus, Polonius' (and, later, Osric's) overblown, overly officious behavior and language earn Hamlet's mockery, however cruel.

Against the Danish court's nightly carousing Hamlet avers that, "though I am native here / And to the manner born, it is a custom / More honored in the breach than in the observance" (1.4.14–16); while we must guess who (besides Hamlet himself) might honor such "breach" of "observance," the point here, as elsewhere, is that Hamlet comes into conflict with the King and court over matters of "custom" and decorous behavior. Gertrude assumes that Hamlet's initial melancholy stems from "His father's death," followed by her "o'erhasty marriage" (2.2.57) to Claudius, the latter in violation of the prescribed time of ritual mourning. When Gertrude urges him to "cast" his "nighted color off" (1.2.68), Hamlet defends his "customary suits of solemn black" (1.2.78), suggesting a habit of dress and thus, implicitly, a generally melancholy disposition; more likely, though, the Prince intends his "solemn black" to be "customary" *to the occasion* of his father's death, Hamlet remaining (as he believes he should) in ritual mourning. For "it is decent," as Puttenham observes, "to be . . . at mournings and burials sad and sorrowfull, in feasts and bankets merry and joyfull" (298). Here, though, which shall Hamlet be? Though his "nighted color" seems incongruous, even insultingly indecorous

on the occasion of Gertrude's and Claudius' marriage, it remains fully decorous, *requisite* even, during a time of mourning. Thus, Hamlet finds himself
caught between competing *kairoi* or occasions—between "mirth in funeral,"
and "dirge in marriage" (1.2.12), as his uncle describes the moment—each of
which demands a radically different response. Claudius declares that "discretion . . . / Together with remembrance of ourselves" (1.2.5–7) has led to their
quick wedding. Given Claudius' new kingly authority, Hamlet's refusal to
join in the celebration describes an *indecorous* decorum, a failure to yield to
changed circumstances.

And a further shock awaits the Prince. For the Ghost's appearance "alters
the temporality of the moment" (122), as Barbara Everett notes, a point that
Frederick Turner affirms: "the disjointing or interruption of the ordinary flow
of time takes place with the appearance of the Ghost" (79), who is both "outside of time and also the disrupter of it" (80). Indeed, the Ghost shatters social decorum as well as durative time, destroying any security Hamlet might
once have sought from the "control mechanisms" of humane, courtly observance. Rather, responding to his terrifying new circumstances, Hamlet declares it "meet / To put an antic disposition on" (1.5.180–81), seeking thereby to
free himself from constraints that he would otherwise scrupulously obey (and
enforce upon others). As a profoundly kairotic response to changed circumstances, Hamlet's madness—feigned or otherwise—provides a means of *improvisation,* rendering his words and actions unpredictable and, thus, *uncontrollable* by others. In short, the danger that a "mad" Hamlet poses to Claudius
(and to the Danish court generally) is a capacity for action unregulated by the
"rules" and "recipes" of courtly behavior. By such means Hamlet seeks his own
self-preservation and a power over others; whether his improvisations succeed
remains, however, a matter of contention. To the rest of Denmark, Hamlet's
subsequent words and actions become imprudent, impudent, unsettling, violent, insulting—a series of indiscretions costing Ophelia, Gertrude, and others around him their happiness, security and, ultimately, their lives. As Ophelia describes him, Hamlet was once "The courtier's, soldier's, scholar's, eye,
tongue, sword, / Th' expectancy and rose of the fair state, / The glass of fashion and the mold of form, / Th' observed of all observers," though now "quite,
quite down!" (3.1.154–57). Thus, Hamlet's "antic disposition"—in effect, his
repudiation of the Humanist courtly *ethos*—costs him no less than his prior
social identity and once-precious reputation. During the graveyard scene, the
Prince reflects upon earlier outbursts and rash acts, confessing them as so
many acts of "indiscretion" (5.2.9). And yet, later in this very scene, Hamlet
commits the extreme outrage of following Laertes into Ophelia's grave, their
subsequent "ranting and wrestling match on the coffin" being, as T. McAlindon notes, "the very nadir of ritual indecorum" (74). From this moment on,

arguably, the Prince seeks to restore himself to his earlier courtly *ethos*. During the final scene (his fatal fencing match with Laertes), the Prince reasserts his former dignity and *humanitas*, behaving mannerly and humanely, expressing remorse for the madness that had become, as he now avers, "poor Hamlet's enemy" (5.2.237). In agreeing to the match, Hamlet is also, implicitly, capitulating once more to the "rules" of courtly behavior—here, specifically, to the rules of martial/athletic contest—thereby placing himself once again within the King's reach. The fact that Claudius (colluding with Laertes) takes deadly advantage proves a further failure of Humanist *prudentia*. For, though his moment of revenge finally comes, its price proves too high, costing not just Hamlet's own life, but the destruction of virtually the entire Danish blood line, leaving Elsinore to Fortinbras.

An important convention of Elizabethan revenge drama (particularly as established by Thomas Kyd's *Spanish Tragedy*) is "the justifiable hesitation of the revenger, who requires much proof, and, on the failure of legal justice, lacks a suitable opportunity for straightforward action" (Bowers, 71). Thus, planning revenge for his son's death, Kyd's Hieronimo notes that "Wise men will take their opportunitie, / Closely and safely fitting things to time" (3.8.25–260), adding that "all times fit not for reuenge" (3.8.28)—hence, the avenger's need for prevarication and prudent delay. Yet Shakespeare's ironic twist upon the typical revenge plot arises from his protagonist's *failure to act* at the "right" moment. To the Ghost's dire command that his son "Revenge his foul and most unnatural murder" (1.5.25), the Prince initially pledges a swift response. And yet, inexplicably even to himself, Hamlet delays. In the third act, having proved the King's occulted guilt by means of the Mousetrap, Hamlet comes upon Claudius alone, kneeling in prayer. With sword raised above Claudius's bent neck, Hamlet talks himself out of striking, thereby failing "to seize occasion." Though Catherine Brown Tkacz deems this the "decisive moment which makes the rest of the play inevitable and its eight deaths unavoidable" (20), it is also, ironically, a moment of failed decision and deferred action. And, within a prudential ethic grounded in *kairos*, one must emphasize that the single right moment, once passed, is apparently forever lost. Shakespeare in fact presents two scenes, back to back, either of which can be interpreted as the play's tragic climax: here in the first, spying Claudius at prayer, Hamlet *fails to act* in revenge; then in the second, visiting Gertrude in her closet, Hamlet *fails in his action*, killing Polonius in the King's place. Treated as a dramatic diptych, the two scenes depict the dire consequences of failed *kairos:* in the one the moment missed, in the other the moment misused. Thus Shakespeare tests the kairotics or problematic "right-timing" of revenge, a subject that expands into an exploration of time itself, particularly in its relation to human ethics and action.

* * *

As Barbara Everett notes, "something to do with time seems to be at the cen-
tre of *Hamlet*" (117).[4] And, to the extent that Shakespeare reflects the complexities of Renaissance attitudes towards time, we should expect *Hamlet* to
raise many of the same conflicts explored in the age's emblem tradition. Most
of the play's references to *chronos*-time reflect polite conversation, such as
Claudius' "Take thy fair hour, Laertes. Time be thine" (1.2.62), or Polonius'
"The time invests you. Go" (1.3.83); still, the word "time" recurs forty-eight
times in *Hamlet*, more than in any other Shakespearian play. "Season" in various noun and verb forms (and with a variety of meanings, including "right"
time or occasion, a specific passage or length of time, and a *process* of time—
that is, a process of maturation) is repeated eight times, again more than in
any other play. "Occasion" recurs five times. Other temporal markers—
"term," "hour," "day," "night," and "watch," among others—seem mostly dec-
orative, and yet a pattern emerges that elevates time into an explicit theme.
References to action as well, whether planned or carried out (as in both
Hamlet's and Laertes' tasks of revenge), are often judged by their temporal
circumstances and effects. Recurring twelve times (a number exceeded only
by *Romeo and Juliet*), "haste" (including "hasty" and "o'er- hasty") in one's action takes on an important (if tragic) aspect, as do "swift," "quick," "speed,"
"sweep," "untimely," "rash," and "tardy."

Of the five uses of "occasion," Laertes's alone alludes directly (and opti-
mistically) to the goddess, who "smiles upon a second leave" (1.3.54)—thereby
echoing the motto of George Wither's emblem (discussed in the previous
essay), that "Occasions-past *are sought in vaine; / But, oft, they wheele-about*
againe." In contrast, the numerous recurrences of "fortune" make continual
reference to the conventional iconography. Much as Theodore de Bry's *Em-*
blematum Liber (1593) depicts Wisdom's "freedom from Fortune" (see fig. 10),
Hamlet praises Horatio's Stoic sufferance, which takes "Fortune's buffets and
rewards . . . with equal thanks" (3.2.66 – 67), adding,

> . . . and blest are those
> Whose blood and judgment are so commeddled
> That they are not a pipe for Fortune's finger
> To sound what stop she please. Give me that man
> That is not passion's slave, and I will wear him
> In my heart's core, ay, in my heart of heart,
> As I do thee.
>
> (3.2.67 – 73)

Here, Hamlet's "pipe for Fortune's finger" recalls emblems from Guillaume de
la Perrière's *Morosophie* (1553), as Roland Mushat Frye (120) notes (fig. 11). Still,
true to Humanist ethical theory, Hamlet finds in Horatio's right "judgment"

LI.

EXPERS FORTVNÆ EST SAPIENTIA.

Le sage n'a besoin de venteuse richesse,
Ny d'autres vanitez, qui paissent l'homme bas:
L'inconstante Fortune aussi ne porte pas,
Dans son douteus esquif, la prudente sagesse:
Ainçous l'experience est sa fidelle hostesse,
Qui la loge à l'escart du sejour otieus:
Et qui veut l'acquerir, faut qu'il soit studieus,
Actif, & vigilant ennemy de paresse.

Fig. 10. Jean Jacques Boissard, *Emblemes* (1595).

and self-control a Stoic antidote to "Fortune's buffets." Other characters, however, prove less adamant. Guildenstern banters, "On Fortune's cap we are not the very button" (2.2.229), and Hamlet picks up the jest:

> Ham. Nor the soles of her shoe?
> Ros. Neither, my lord.
> Ham. Then you live about her waist, or in the middle of her favors?
> Guil. Faith, her privates we.
> Ham. In the secret parts of Fortune? O, most true, she is a strumpet.
>
> $\qquad$ (2.2.230–36)

Echoing these sentiments, the First Player rages against old Priam's murder: "Out, out thou strumpet Fortune! All you gods / In general synod take away her power! / Break all the spokes and fellies from her wheel . . ." (2.2.493–95). Such a passage recalls Georgette de Montenay's emblem, wherein God's hand smashes Fortune's wheel, thereby asserting divine Providence over worldly chance (figure 12); still, it remains a question whether in Aeneas's world—or in Hamlet's—any god would so intervene. So grievous a spectacle proves the death of Priam's wife, Hecuba, that "Who this had seen, with tongue in venom steeped, / 'Gainst Fortune's state would treason have pronounced" (2.2.510–11). Later the Player King observes, aphoristically, that

> $\qquad$ . . . 'tis not strange
> That even our loves should with our fortunes change;
> For 'tis a question left us yet to prove,
> Whether love lead fortune, or else fortune love.
>
> $\qquad$ (3.2.198–201)

As Frye notes (124–5), emblems depicting Fortune in concert with Love are commonplace, appearing, for example, in Jean Cousin's *Book of Fortune* (1568). Finally, in perhaps the most famous allusion of all, a suicidal Hamlet muses "whether 'tis nobler in the mind to suffer / The slings and arrows of outrageous fortune . . ." (3.1.58–59).

With reason, then, Frederick Kiefer observes that "hostile Fortune, rather than responsive Occasion, dominates Hamlet's mental world" (252), the play's references to fortune "convey[ing], collectively,"

> Hamlet's sense of victimization. To him circumstance seems always to favor predatory figures. It is the innocent—Hamlet's father, Priam, the Player King—who fall prey to their adversaries. It is inevitable, then, that Hamlet . . . should find it difficult to act decisively. (258)

Still, it would be wrong to assume that the play records Fortune's inevitable triumph, incidentally torturing the Prince upon her wrack. For Hamlet's failed *kairos* stands between at least two radically contrasting "ethics of time,"

Fig. 11. Guillaume de la Perrière, *Morosophie* (1553).

Fig. 12. Georgette de Montenay, *Liure d'armoires en signe* (1619).

to borrow a phrase from Wylie Sypher: "strumpet Fortune" (2.2.493) on the one hand, and Heaven's "special Providence" (5.2.218) on the other. The latter's inscrutable workings are revealed during "Hamlet's voyage to England, one of the most mysterious journeys in Shakespeare" (Kiefer, 259). Hitherto Hamlet "has been tormented by Fortune, her slings and arrows, her pipe, her wheel" (Kiefer, 260). But on the voyage, as Kiefer argues, "chance begins to work in his favor. He finds himself guided rather than manipulated" and, "believing god to be the author" of such events, Hamlet "supplants Fortune with Providence in his cosmology" (260). Kiefer continues:

> It is appropriate that this should be owing to his experience on the voyage, for in the renaissance Occasion was usually depicted on the sea, sometimes riding in a vessel. . . . And Hamlet, on his voyage, seizes an opportunity that presents itself quite literally on the sea. It is perhaps not too much of an exaggeration to say that Hamlet reenacts the shift from Fortune to Occasion that was taking place in so much Renaissance thought and iconography. That is, he moves from a world dominated by an antagonistic fortune, to one inhabited by a more responsive Occasion. (260–61)

Whereas the Humanist remaining within each of us might wish keenly to accede to Kiefer's argument, the play itself rather stridently refuses to declare *Occasio* victor over *Fortuna*. For "there's a divinity that shapes our ends, / Rough-hew them how we will" (5.2.9–10): thus Hamlet reinterprets his failures of action—of decorum, of *kairos*—as the higher workings of immutable Providence. While Humanists proffered *prudentia* as an antidote to blind fortune, Reformation theologians offered a radically different interpretation, proceeding from a conviction that "nothing could happen in this world without God's permission" (79), as historian Keith Thomas observes:

> If there was a common theme which ran through their writings it was the denial of the very possibility of chance or accident. "That which we call fortune," wrote the Elizabethan bishop, Thomas Cooper, "is nothing but the hand of God, working by causes and for causes that we know not. Chance or fortune are gods devised by men and made by our ignorance of the true, almighty and everlasting God." "Fortune and adventure," declared John Knox, "are the words of Paynims, the signification whereof ought in no wise to enter into the heart of the faithful. . . . That which ye scoffingly call Destiny and Stoical necessity . . . we call God's eternal election and purpose immutable." (79)

After his sea journey, Hamlet himself "never again . . . mention[s] fortune" (Kiefer, 260). Has Providence, then, smashed Fortune's wheel (as in Montenay's emblem), banishing the goddess from Denmark?

By no means. As Fortinbras declares, some mere dozen lines before the play's ending, "with sorrow I embrace my fortune. / I have some rights of memory in this kingdom, / Which now to claim advantage doth invite me" (5.2.390–92). As he rises to claim the Danish throne, the play ends by reaffirming medieval *de casibus* tradition, with Hamlet fallen and Fortinbras, for the moment, mounted high on Fortune's wheel.[5] As Hamlet's body is borne away by Fortinbras's soldiers, surely we are invited to ask which "ethics of time" ultimately triumphs: that of inhuman, blind Fortune, that of watchful human prudence, or that of divine Providence? Different readers have offered different answers, though Shakespeare leaves the issue deliberately unsettled. Any reading of the play that affirms a final victory of *Occasio* over *Fortuna,* or of *Fortuna* over *Providentia,* or of *Providentia* over *Occasio,* loses sight of the dialectic Shakespeare establishes among these competing temporal categories and ethical imperatives, categories that emblem tradition (as explored in the previous essay) maintains in tense suspension. But if emblem tradition offers the Danish Prince any consolation, it is the possibility that Occasion *does* often "smile upon a second leave," that one *may* find, *deo volente,* a second time within the incessant cycle of human affairs, when time and means meet once again together, allowing frail, erring humanity the opportunity, as St. Paul puts it, to "redeem the time" (*Ephesians* 5.16)—though the advent of this second, "redeeming" time, in Hamlet's case, entails his death.

Hamlet's meditations upon death point to a further complexity in the Renaissance philosophy of time: specifically, the relation between human temporality and heavenly eternity. As D. J. Bourke notes, the Hebraic understanding of time is "radically conditioned by the overriding idea of God implementing a preconceived plan from and through history" (3533). This same eschatological understanding sustains Christian notions of Providence, which view time as linear and *aion*-eternity as the fulfillment or completion of time (Cullman, 45–50). Treated in this way, time and eternity differ merely in degree (or in "fullness"), for "the eternality of God," writes Lawrence W. Fagg, "is generally expressed as everlasting time or the encompassing of all time" (184): though God's "time" differs from humankind's—"one day with the Lord is as a thousand years, and a thousand years as one day" (2 Peter 3:8)—nonetheless "Christian theology sees eternity as accessed in the fullness of time" (Fagg, 184–85), the divine manifesting itself within time and using time providentially. There is also, however, a competing Hellenic conceptualization, which views *aion* as timelessness and worldly transcendence, the Godhead existing outside of even as it enfolds time. In this alternative "mythic," "cultic," or "rhythmic" vision (Bourke, 3533), *aion* encircles earthly temporality, thereby emphasizing the cyclical nature of the seasons and their recurrence or "endless return to the origins" (Bourke, 3533).[6] In addition to the workings of Providence, Renaissance iconography records this alternative, Hellenic perspective. The previous essay cited George Wither's emblem of an uroboros encircling a flower, bearing the motto, "Time *is a* Fading-Flowre, *that's found / Within* Eternities *wide* Round," thus situating worldly time within the "*wide* Round" of an enfolding timelessness. Similar in spirit is his emblem of an uroboros encircling an infant, who reclines upon a death's head (see figure 13): bearing the motto, "*As soone, as wee to bee, begunne, / We did beginne, to bee* Vndonne," such an image conceives of life as an endless natural cycle of (re-)generation, growth, decline, death, decay.

At this point, we might ask whether Hamlet envisions death (and not just death generally or in the abstract, but *his own*) as a *fulfillment of* or as an *escape from* time? Is it an eschatology—a divine *fiat*—or a naturally-recurring cycle? Is it "fatal" or accidental—the failure of human improvisation or an affirmation of divine Providence? Is it Christian or Hellenic in spirit? It does not surprise that *Hamlet* poses us with such either-or questions. But are such issues even decidable? Must we (can we) choose? Of this, at least, we can be certain: unlike his predecessors in revenge tragedy, Hamlet alone is the *revenger who knows,* who recognizes from the onset that his own death sentence hangs upon him, that the Ghost has commanded him, in effect, to serve as his own executioner. G. Wilson Knight has argued famously that "The theme of *Hamlet* is . . . [l]ife that is bound for the disintegration of the grave.

As ſoone, as wee to bee, begunne;
We did beginne, to be Vndone.

45

FINIS AB ORIGINE PEDET

ILLVSTR. XLV.   Book. 1ᵉ

Fig. 13. George Wither, *A Collection of Emblemes, Ancient and Moderne* (1635).

... He is the ambassador of death walking amid life" (31–32).[7] But more than mortality and the disintegrations of relentless *chronos*, Shakespeare's play explores the dilemma of living in full awareness of one's own immanent death—which, in Hamlet's case, must come by the very kairotic action he is bound to execute. Ironically, Kyd's Hieronimo can blindly seek his own destruction, because he has not read *Hamlet,* can argue blithely that "all times fit not for revenge" (3.2.28), thereby excusing his prevarications. Laertes, too, allows no complicating moral or temporal vision to impede his revenge, once he has learned of his father's murder: "Let come what comes," he says, "only I'll be revenged / Most throughly for my father" (4.5.138–39), vowing even to cut Hamlet's "throat i' the church" (4.7.127). The Prince, on the other hand, enjoys no such illusions. The play, then, offers more than an exploration of failed *prudentia* (the subject with which our essay began); even as its protagonist broods over the "right-timing" of his revenge, Hamlet is left to mourn not just his father's recent but his own impending death, thus turning the play into an elaborate, emblematic *memento mori*.

"Jolted out of the coherence that durative time can give [to] life" (Sypher, 67), Hamlet vows quickly, rashly, to "wipe away all trivial fond records" (1.5.100) "from the table" of his memory (1.5.99), thus transforming his life into "a succession of agonizing instants, each a commencement deprived of the wonted context of the past" (Sypher, 67). While Wylie Sypher relates this experience to the invention of clocks and to a "new consciousness of discontinuous time" (67), Hamlet's encounter with the Ghost—that messenger from the realm of timelessness—may well have wounded his own sense of *chronos*-time, as well: ruptured from his own, remembered experience, Hamlet is thrust into a state in which the only action existing for him mentally has yet to be accomplished, though its fulfillment will end worldly life and time as he knows it. How does one reach a state of "readiness" to complete such an act? Eventually, Hamlet comes to realize that "The readiness is all" (5.2.220), a sentiment *not* to be compared but, rather, sharply contrasted with Edgar's famous pronouncement in *King Lear* that "Ripeness is all" (5.2.11), or with Touchstone's bittersweet remark in *As You Like It* that "from hour to hour we ripe and ripe, / And then from hour to hour we rot and rot" (2.7.26–27)—either of which speaks of ordinary if relentless *chronos*-time. Even Gertrude's platitude that "all that lives must die, / Passing through nature to eternity" (1.2.72-73) would offer comfort to one who believes that he will, in fact, pass "*through* nature" before passing *into* eternity. Hamlet's problem is not that he cannot appreciate the paradox of rotting while ripening; rather, he divines that he will not enjoy the luxury of decay, but must pursue a course of action causing him to die "betimes" (5.2.222)—that is, "early"—and that he will fall into the oblivion of *aion* at the very moment that he finds and embraces his *kairos*. It is no wonder, therefore, that Hamlet obsesses over the verb "to be" (or "*not* to be"), for his own sense of time and action has come thoroughly "out of joint."

"Doomed for a certain term to walk the night / And for the day confined to fast in fires" (1.5.11–12), the Ghost remains, in some mysterious manner, bound to worldly time; yet his sudden appearance before Hamlet marks an invasion of the natural world by the supernatural, pitting worldly time against eternity, *chronos* against *aion*. Confronting *aion*'s messenger, Hamlet moves from an initial state of readiness—"Haste me to know't, that I, with wings as swift / As meditation or the thoughts of love, / May sweep to my revenge" (1.5.30–32)—to a state of restless agitation, perhaps even of madness, as some critics have argued, noting his self-described "distracted globe"

(1.5.98). Counterpoised against Hamlet's initial "haste" (in pursuing a dire act of revenge) and the Ghost's timeless presence, the father's commandment, "Remember me" (1.5.92), imposes the past as a powerful, continuing claim upon the son's already terrifying present and equally dire, dreaded future. Thus, Hamlet plunges into a crisis of conflicting temporalities; indeed, as he declares upon the Ghost's departure, "The time is out of joint. O cursèd spite / That ever I was born to set it right!" (1.5.197–98). Although David Bevington glosses "time," here, as "state of affairs" (1077), has not worldly time in some sense suffered a wound? Being "out of joint," like a displaced or broken bone, time itself must be healed or "set." Of course, to "set" time suggests the winding and "setting" or correcting of a clock; but the bone setting imagery also casts Hamlet in the role of spiritual-physician, who must now remedy this wound to worldly time's natural workings.

In special need of healing is the gap or wound suddenly opened between time and eternity, that dividing line separating the living from the dead. Unlike in *King Lear*, where death means "thou'lt come no more" (5.3.313), in the world of *Hamlet* graves open both to receive human beings *and to cast them back up*. Horatio, for example, describes that portentous night when Roman "Graves stood tenantless" (1.1.118); Hamlet likewise, immediately after the play-within, observes "the very witching time of night, / When churchyards yawn" (3.2.387–88), as if such "yawn[ing]" of graves were a common, nightly occurrence. Indeed, throughout the play, graves are seen continually to "yawn," casting the dead back up as well as receiving them. Before our eyes, Ophelia's body is lowered into the grave, and Polonius's body is described as laying "barefaced on the bier," while "in his grave rained many a tear" (4.5.170–72).[8] Nowhere is this dual movement more powerfully expressed than in Hamlet's first confrontation with his father's spirit:

> . . . tell
> Why thy canonized bones, hearsèd in death,
> Have burst their cerements; why the sepulcher
> Wherein we saw thee quietly inurned
> Hath oped his ponderous and marble jaws
> To cast thee up again.
>   (1.4.46–51)

Though "quietly inurned," Old Hamlet's bones have suddenly "burst their cerements," his grave opening its "ponderous and marble jaws." The violence of such "cast[ing] . . . up" attests to the power with which *aion*'s messenger invades ordinary *chronos*-time and life—though, indeed, Hamlet himself goes twice to the grave, first with Ophelia, when he grapples with Laertes, and then in deadly earnest, when the potent poison overcomes him.

But the play's most poignant example of a churchyard's "cast[ing] . . . up" occurs in the graveyard scene, when the skull of Yorick, Old Hamlet's jester, is literally tossed up out of the grave. As the *physical* remnant of a departed spirit, Yorick's mute skull presents Hamlet with the inverse image of his father's speaking Ghost—that is, the *spiritual* remnant of a departed body. And, holding in his hand the man's skull, Hamlet's act of *remembering* Yorick seems to reverse his earlier vow to "wipe away all trivial fond records" (1.5.100) from memory. Here, too, Hamlet questions the gravedigger in a curiously personal way, asking not "How long will a corpse lie in the earth ere it rot?" but "How long will a *man* lie i' th' earth ere *he* rot?" (5.1.163), as if the grave annihilates a man's reputation and memory, as well as his body. And when the skull's former possessor is named, Hamlet recalls Yorick's "infinite jest" (184) and "excellent fancy" (185), his "songs" and "flashes of merriment that were wont to set the table on a roar" (189–90). Indeed, Hamlet's act of memory seems less an aspect of *memento mori* than a lesson in *memento vitam,* a conscious celebration of life. Here, traditionally, critics have argued that Hamlet learns to "humble himself before time," as Sypher puts it, thus submitting "to the present occasion" (84). But if Hamlet's submission, rather, is to *aion*-eternity, his recollection may more accurately record his spiritual (re-)awakening, a transformation that Neoplatonists conceived as "a homecoming, a coming into one-self rather than a journey to another self or state of existence" (Manchester, 169).[9]

Hamlet's transformation-via-memory constitutes a dramatic (as well as spiritual) turning point: not only can he declare, finally, that "we defy augury" (5.2.217), but he also admits that time—and particularly the timing of one's death—cannot, nor should it, be subject to human intervention: "If it be now, 'tis not to come; if it be not to come, it will be now; if it be not now; yet it will come. The readiness is all. Since no man of aught he leaves, knows, what is 't to leave betimes? Let be" (5.2.217–22). Whereas Sypher argues that Hamlet's "Let be" marks "his new resignation to the time" (88), we would suggest that the words mark his final transcendence of deliberative action in worldly time.[10] Here, indeed, Hamlet's earlier wrestling with "to be, or not to be" (3.1.57) resolves into "be" and "is"—into an eternal present tense. "Readiness" is a state of being, not an action in time, and it is "all" there is. And death alone, as Hamlet experiences it, proves curative to the "slings and arrows of outrageous fortune" (3.1.59); indeed, the play affirms death as the ultimate *pharmakon,* in its final merging of *kairos, chronos,* and *aion* together in a single, fatal moment of transcendence. Poisoned and dying, Hamlet makes a final emblematic reference: "Had I but time—as this fell sergeant, Death, / Is strict in his arrest—oh, I could tell you—/ But let it be—Horatio, I am dead" (5.2.323–25). Thus, the Prince merely hints at what he "*could* tell," though death too quickly "arrests" him. Might he tell of that "undiscovered country" (3.1.80), through whose "bourn" he now travels, though "No traveler returns" (3.1.80 – 81)? What is it that the dying "*could* tell" the living, as they stand in death's shadow? Unlike Kyd's Hieronimo, who ends defiantly by biting out his tongue (thereby refusing to speak and to explain his violences), Shakespeare's Hamlet *tries* to speak, though the "rest" of his instructions to Horatio dissolve into that "rest," or *quietus,* which is "silence" (5.2.360).

Or is it that he interrupts his own instructions to Horatio, to report that the "rest" or repose of eternity is itself a state of "silence"? Read in this way, Hamlet's final words return us to his third soliloquy, whose meditation upon death speaks of making a "quietus" with "a bare bodkin" (3.1.76 – 77). Modern editors tend to follow Steevens, who points out that "quietus," in Shakespeare's day, was "the technical term for the acquittance which every sheriff [or accountant] receives on settling his accounts at the Exchequer" (Furness, 212). Thus, G. Blakemore Evans (1160) glosses "quietus" as "write paid to his account," David Bevington (1087) as "acquittance," and Cyrus Hoy (45) as "settlement." True enough: writing *quietus est*—"he is quit"—becomes the medieval equivalent of stamping "paid" on a modern invoice. In its radical sense, however, the Latin phrase means *enjoying rest, keeping quiet,* and expands to include *calmness, tranquility, freedom from ambition, sleep,* and *death* (Lewis and Short, 1512). The verb *requiesco* carries this same sense of resting, repose and, hence, of death or resting *in the grave.* Thus, Hamlet's suicidal meditation, equating the dagger with a pen and writing "paid" to a debt (thereby discharging one's earthly duties and anxieties) dissolves, by the play's end, into the *quietus* or calm quietude of silent, timeless eternity, where no words can describe death's mystery—where, in fact, no words are needed (or meaningful), for the human soul has transcended time. The "noble heart" that "cracks" (5.2.361) is Horatio's own who, for his own comfort, envisions "flights of angels" singing Hamlet to his "rest" (5.2.362): for Hamlet himself has "quit" his body, transcending the niceties of princely decorum, human language, and worldly time to enter the higher, purer, timeless silence of "be" (in which state, questions of Providence are rendered moot, *kairos* meaningless, and *prudentia* irrelevant).

Notes

1. Quotations from *Hamlet* are taken from Bevington, *Complete Works of Shakespeare.*

2. In Elizabethan usage, "discretion," "decency," and "decorum" are interchangeable. As Sir Francis Bacon writes in his essay, "Of Discourse," "discretion of speech is more than eloquence" (776). George Puttenham, too, finds "a learned and experienced discretion" underlying all judgments "whether this or that action or speech be decent or

indecent" (1970, 270); indeed, the "fittest iudge" of such matters is the "discreetest man," a man necessarily "of much observation and greatest experience" (270). For further discussions of decorum in Puttenham's *Arte,* see Baumlin, "Decorum, Kairos," Hillman, "Puttenham, Shakespeare," and Javitch, *Poetry and Courtliness,* 50 –75.

3. To Puttenham, we might compare Bacon's "reproof of unreasonable and unprofitable liberty in giving advice" (825): those who "will not submit to learn . . . how to observe time and measure in affairs, flats and sharps (so to speak) in discourse, the difference between the learned and the vulgar ear, and the times when to speak and when to be silent . . . with all their efforts to persuade they scarcely can do any good" (825).

4. In addition to Barbara Everett, distinguished critics have written on the subjects of time (Buland, 119 –21, Sypher, 65 –89, Quinones, 387 –98, Turner, 69 –98, Waller), Fortune (Colley, Frye, Kiefer, Tkacz), and Providence (Colley, Kiefer, Sinfield, Matheson). Obviously, our essay benefits from and records previous Shakespearean scholarship.

5. Gary V. Monitto (6) points out the significance of this final reference to Fortune's wheel. But if emblematic tradition offers the Danish Prince any consolation, it is the possibility that Occasion *does* often "smile upon a second leave," that one *may* find, *deo volente,* a second time within the incessant cycle of human affairs, when time and means may meet once again together, allowing frail, erring humanity the chance, as St. Paul puts it, to "redeem the time" (*Ephesians* 5.16)—though, for Hamlet, this second, "redeeming" time entails his death.

6. The Greek conceptualization of *aion* finds its origins in Parmenides' poem, "The Way of Truth," which describes the One or divine Whole as existing beyond time: "It neither was at any time nor will be, since it is now all at once a single whole" (Kneale, 64). As William C. Kneale argues, "Parmenides accepted the religious teachings of Xenophanes, that the Whole is an everlasting god, and tried to defend it against Heraclitus' doctrine of universal flux by maintaining that the Whole is *spherical* in all respects—that is, temporally as well as spatially" (64). Alternatively, the cyclical nature of *aion* may have come through Pythagoras, for "there is evidence to show that a conception of cyclical time order was current in the Pythagorean school with which Parmenides is said to have been connected in his youth" (Kneale, 64). From Parmenides the concept passed to Plato, whose *Timaeus* contrasts "the created world with the eternal living being, its timeless archetype" (Kneale, 64). As Plato's Socrates declares, the creator "sought to make the universe eternal, as far as might be," though "bestow[ing] this attribute in its fullness upon a creature was impossible" (*Timaeus,* 37d):

> Wherefor he resolved to have a moving image of eternity, and when he set order in the heaven, he made this image eternal but moving according to number, while eternity rests in unity, and this image we call time. . . . The sun and moon and five other stars, which are called the planets, were created by him in order to distinguish and preserve the numbers of time, and when he made their several bodies, he placed them in the orbits in which the circle of the other was revolving—in seven orbits seven stars. (*Timaeus,* 37e-38d)

We might also note that the confusion of *aion* (meaning "life, span of life, lifetime, epoch, or eon") with *aei on* (or "always being") apparently derives from a false etymology originating in the *Timaeus* (Manchester, 169).

Though Aristotle (*Physics,* 218a-24a) and Plotinus (Third Ennead, Seventh Tractate sections 7 –13) offer variations upon the Platonic *mythos,* the *Timaeus* presents the central elements of Hellenic theory: specifically, the identification of time with solar and planetary motion (thereby causing the cyclical earthly seasons) and the creating divinity's own transcendence, who remains eternally whole and at rest. In the New Testament, instances of *aion* typically refer, apocalyptically and eschatologically, to the future *aevum* or "eon" yet to come; however, as Manchester points out, several Pauline and deutero-Pauline uses of the term reflect Eastern (specifically Persian and Zoroastrian) symbolisms, thereby "contribut[ing] to the emergence of the novel Neoplatonic sense of *aion*" (170) in Christian thought. In his *Confessions* (11.10–31), Augustine follows Plato in affirming God's "ever-present eternity," for whom "all years stand at once." And, citing Boethius, St. Aquinas asserts that eternity "has neither beginning nor end and that eternity contains no succession, being all at once *(tota simul existens)*" (Kneale, 65). Through these and other late classical and medieval conduits, the Renaissance inherited Hellenic conceptualizations of time-encircled-by-eternity, whose most famous literary depiction (in the English Renaissance, surely) occurs in Henry Vaughan's mystic lyric, "The World":

> I saw eternity the other night
> Like a great ring of pure and endless light,
>   All calm as it was bright;
> And round beneath it, Time, in hours, days, years,
>   Driven by the spheres,
> Like a vast shadow moved, in which the world
>   And all her train were hurled. . . .
>
> (1–7)

7. "The theme of *Hamlet*," G. Wilson Knight argues, "is death. Life that is bound for the disintegration of the grave, love that does not survive the loved one's death— both, in their insistence on death as the primary fact of nature, are branded on the mind of Hamlet, burned into it, searing it with agony. . . . The bereavement of Hamlet and his consequent mental agony bordering on madness is mirrored in the bereavement of Ophelia and her madness. The death of the Queen's love is reflected in the swift passing of the love of the Player-Queen, in the "Murder of Gonzago." Death is over the whole play. . . . And yet, "except for the original murder of Hamlet's father, the *Hamlet* universe is one of healthy and robust life, good-nature, humour, romantic strength, and welfare: against this background is the figure of Hamlet pale with the consciousness of death. He is the ambassador of death walking amid life" (Knight, 32).

8. Indeed, Hamlet's gruesome pun over Polonius' dead body—"This counselor / Is now most still, most secret, and most grave, / Who was in life a foolish prating knave" (3.4.220–22)—shoves aside any mockery of Polonius' *gravitas*, to emphasize that *the body and grave are already one.*

9. The earlier Platonic notion of *anamnesis*, the soul's "unforgetting" or recollection of its prelife, heavenly existence and innate knowledge (*Meno*, 85d-86b), became in Plotinus a conversion experience or, as Manchester describes it, "an interior conversion of the soul completed in contemplative immediacy—conversion both in the sense of a turning, from distracting cares to tranquil insight, and of a transformation" (1987, 169). Arguably, this same notion influences Augustine's understanding of Christian conversion (Manchester, 169). Might it offer an analogue to Hamlet's own spiritual transformation here, in the graveyard?

Much has been written about the play's exploration of memory and, though the subject is too vast to be encompassed in a note, still we might recount the ways that death and forgetfulness, life and memory, are fused symbolically throughout. Initially, memory describes a form of mental torment—as when Hamlet, in his first soililoquy, seeks to escape thoughts of his mother's earlier love for Old Hamlet: "Heaven and earth, / Must I remember? . . . Let me not think on it" (1.2.142–46). Later, in whetting Hamlet's initial thirst for revenge, the Ghost says, "I find thee apt; / And duller shouldst thou be than the fat weed / That roots itself in ease on Lethe wharf, / Wouldst thou not stir in this" (1.5.32–35), Lethe's "fat weed" symbolizing nothing less than that drug or *pharmakon* of forgetfulness-which-is-death. Traditionally, death is described as a forgetfulness or obliteration of personal memory; here, the Ghost reverses the figure, describing forgetfulness as a form of death. Indeed, in a play exploring *prudentia* and *kairos*, it is not surprising that failures of memory (as well as deliberate attempts to forget) are implicated as obstacles to action. As the Player King observes, "Purpose is but the slave to memory, / Of violent birth, but poor validity. . . . What to ourselves in passion we propose, / The passion ending, doth the purpose lose" (3.2. 186–93).

Hamlet's meditation upon Yorick's skull offers him more than a recovered "readiness" to act in the midst of death; it becomes, literally, an act of re-membering, of restoring the physical remains to its once lively personality and merry actions and, thus, serves as an inversion of *memento mori*, that medieval, ascetic injunction to "remember death." It is life, life in the midst of the grave, *life as part of the grave*, that Hamlet comes to affirm through this act of remembrance. Doubtless, more needs to be said on this complex subject.

10.   Critics have interpreted Hamlet's "readiness" speech (5.2.218–20) variously, ranging from resignation to fatalism to hopeful acceptance of Christian Providence. Martin Dodsworth claims that Hamlet's assertion, "we defy augury" (5.2.217), introduces classical "rather than Christian associations" (278), whereas Douglas L. Peterson argues that Hamlet, while "resigned to his own mortality," nonetheless "views the future hopefully" and embraces "with equanimity both the destructive and renewing aspects of time" (Peterson, 23). In contrast, G. F. Waller rejects the idea of "a providential force transcending and directing" the Prince's actions; rather, "Hamlet's restless search for the metaphysical has been replaced by a self-justifying fatalism" (129). Commenting on the lines, "Our indiscretion sometimes serves us well, / When our deep plots do pall; and that should learn us / There's a divinity that serves our ends, / Rough-hew them how we will" (5.2.8–11), Frederick Turner writes that "Hamlet is in the dark, acting rashly and without discretion; . . . Hamlet's timeless vision and timeless pain cannot be prolonged in time as action. Therefore he finds a different basis for action—acting with, not against, the current of Time" (93). As evidence, Turner cites Hamlet's "If it be not now, 'tis not to come; if it be not to come, it will be now; if it be not now, yet it will come—the readiness is all" (5.2.218–20). Here, according to Turner, Hamlet "ceases to attempt to compel himself and his world into the situation of the perfect revenge: he is content to wait, to let the whirligig of time bring in his revenges. And oddly enough, Hamlet finds that, though when he had bent mind and passion to the fulfillment of his revenge, it fled away from him, now when he waits patiently, his revenge comes to him swiftly" (94).

But "in the end," writes Gideon Rappaport, "all other readiness is included in the readiness to die, death being the final surrender of the will. What we know about death is akin to what we know about life—it is limited yet tempting knowledge. What we know about death is summed up in the 'To be or not to be' soliloquy and in the graveyard scene. Those are the limits of our knowledge. Beyond this, death is 'nothing either good or bad, but thinking makes it so,' for depending on who is speaking and when, death is 'damnation' and 'most horrible,' or it is 'felicity,' or it is 'silence.' The readiness to die when death is what is willed by Providence is all because it is the source of all other readiness to act in consonance with the divine will" (92).

Works Cited

Bacon, Sir Francis. *The Philosophical Works of Francis Bacon.* Ed. John M. Robertson. Freeport, NY: Books for Libraries, 1970.

Baumlin, James S. "Decorum, *Kairos,* and the 'New' Rhetoric." *Pre/Text* 5 (1985): 171–83.

Bevington, David, ed. *The Complete Works of Shakespeare.* 4th ed. New York: HarperCollins, 1992.

Bourke, D. J. "Time (in the Bible)." *Encyclopedic Dictionary of Religion.* Ed. Paul Kevin Meager, 3533. Washington, DC: Corpus, 1979.

Bowers, Fredson. *Elizabethan Revenge Tragedy, 1587–1642.* Princeton: Princeton University Press, 1940.

Buland, Mable. *The Presentation of Time in The Elizabethan Drama.* New York: Haskell, 1966.

Colley, John Scott. "Drama, Fortune, and Providence in *Hamlet.*" *College Literature* 5 (1978): 48–56.

Cullmann, Oscar. *Christ and Time: The Primitive Christian Conception of Time and History.* Trans. Floyd V. Filson. Philadelphia: Westminster, 1950.

Dodworth, Martin. *Hamlet Closely Observed.* London: Athlone, 1985.

Elliott, G. R. *Scourge and Minister: A Study of Hamlet.* New York: AMS, 1965.

Evans, G. Blakemore, ed. *The Riverside Shakespeare.* Boston: Houghton Mifflin, 1974.

Everett, Barbara. "*Hamlet:* A Time To Die." *Shakespeare Survey* 30 (1977): 117–23.

Fagg, Lawrence W. *The Becoming of Time: Integrating Physical and Religious Time.* Atlanta, GA: Scholar's, 1995.

Fisher, Alan. "Shakespeare's Last Humanist." *Renaissance and Reformation* 26 (1990): 37–47.

Frye, Roland Mushat. *The Renaissance Hamlet: Issues and Responses in 1600.* Princeton: Princeton University Press, 1984.

Furness, Horace Howard, ed. *Hamlet: A New Variorum Edition.* 2 Vols. Reprint, New York: American Scholar, 1965.

Geertz, Clifford. *The Interpretation of Cultures.* New York: Basic Books, 1973.

Green, Henry. *Shakespeare and the Emblem Writers: An Exposition of Their Similarities of Thought and Expression.* London, 1869. Reprint, New York: Burt Franklin, n.d.

Hillman, David. "Puttenham, Shakespeare, and the Abuse of Rhetoric." *Studies in English Literature* 36 (1996): 73–90.

Hoy, Cyrus, ed. *William Shakespeare: Hamlet.* A Norton Critical Edition. 2d ed. New York: Norton, 1992.

Hunt, Maurice. "Hamlet, the Gravedigger, and Indecorous Decorum." *College Literature* 11.2 (1984): 141–50.

Javitch, Daniel. *Poetry and Courtliness in Renaissance England.* Princeton: Princeton University Press, 1978.

Johnson, Barbara A. "The Fabric of the Universe Rent: *Hamlet* as an Inversion of *The Courtier.*" *Hamlet Studies* 9 (1987): 34–52.

Kettle, Arnold. *Shakespeare in a Changing World*. London: Lawrence and Wishart, 1964.

Kiefer, Frederick. *Fortune and Elizabethan Tragedy*. Huntington, CA: Huntington Library, 1983.

Kneale, William C. "Eternity." *The Encyclopedia of Philosophy*. Ed. Paul Edwards.Vol. 3: 63–66. New York: Macmillan, 1967.

Knight, J. Wilson. "The Embassy of Death: An Essay on *Hamlet*." *The Wheel of Fire: Interpretations of Shakespearean Tragedy*, 17–46. London, 1949.

Kyd, Thomas. *The Spanish Tragedy* (1592). London: Ernest Benn, 1970.

Lewis, Charlton T. and Charles Short. *A Latin Dictionary*. 1879. Oxford: Clarendon, 1975.

Manchester, Peter. "Eternity." *The Encyclopedia of Religion*. Ed. Mircea Eliade. Vol 5: 167–71. New York: Macmillan, 1987.

Matheson, Mark. "*Hamlet* and a Matter Tender and Dangerous." *Shakespeare Quarterly* 46 (1995): 383–97.

McAlindon, T. *Shakespeare and Decorum*. London: Macmillan, 1973.

Monitto, Gary V. "Shakespeare's *Hamlet*." *Explicator* 46 (1988): 6.

Peterson, Douglas L. *Time, Tide, and Tempest: A Study of Shakespeare's Romances*. San Marino, CA: Huntington Library, 1973.

Plato. *The Collected Dialogues*. Ed. Edith Hamilton and Huntington Cairns. Princeton: Princeton University Press, 1963.

Puttenham, George. *The Arte of English Poesie* (1589). Ed. Baxter Hathaway. Kent, OH: Kent State University Press, 1970.

Quinones, Ricardo J. *The Renaissance Discovery of Time*. Cambridge, MA: Harvard University Press, 1972.

Rappaport, Gideon. "Hamlet: Revenge and Readiness." *The Upstart Crow* 7 (1987): 80–95.

Sinfield, Alan. "Hamlet's Special Providence." *Shakespeare Survey* 33 (1980): 89–98.

Sypher, Wiley. *The Ethic of Time: Structures of Experience in Shakespeare*. New York: Seabury, 1976.

Thomas, Keith. *Religion and the Decline of Magic*. New York: Scribner's, 1971.

Tkacz, Catherine Brown. "The Wheel of Fortune, the Wheel of State, and Moral Choice in *Hamlet*." *South Atlantic Review* 57 (1992): 21–38.

Turner, Frederick. *Shakespeare and the Nature of Time: Moral and Philosophical Themes in Some Plays and Poems of William Shakespeare*. Oxford: Clarendon, 1971.

Vaughan, Henry. "The World." *The Norton Anthology of English Literature*. 5th ed. Ed. M. H. Abrams, 1375–76. New York: Norton, 1986.

Waller, G. F. *The Strong Necessity of Time: The Philosophy of Time in Shakespeare and Elizabethan Literature*. Mouton: the Hague, 1976.

Wither, George. *A Collection of Emblemes, Ancient and Moderne* (1635). Introd. Rosemary Freeman. Columbia, SC: University of South Carolina Press, 1975.

Ralph Waldo Emerson and the American Kairos

ROGER THOMPSON

In the literature and rhetoric of nineteenth-century America, the term *kairos* has little or no currency, but the idea of spiritual timing and due measure undergirds a broad range of texts. Works by authors such as Ralph Waldo Emerson, Nathaniel Hawthorne, Harriet Beecher Stowe, Margaret Fuller, and Washington Irving reflect a need to generate an American literature within a culture that was demanding that America, as a divinely rooted nation, claim a new literature as a moral right of its own. This feeling of the right time and moral entitlement for a new literature is the American *kairos*, and the purpose of this study is to demonstrate the fluency and the frequency with which nineteenth-century literary and rhetorical texts invoke the concept of *kairos* in making their claims for a new literature and a new American state. In particular, I use the writings of Ralph Waldo Emerson as a central example of a broader cultural current that consistently relies on *kairos*, and I argue that his writings invoke a concept of *kairos* in order to enact social change.

Emerson is particularly well-suited for an exploration of *kairos* because he bridges the traditional disciplinary gaps among literature, rhetoric, and theology. As a prominent preacher, writer and orator of his time, his theories shaped the course of American letters. His influence, I argue, can be understood as articulating the need for *kairos*, a moment of spiritual insight and propriety, in the rhetorical and literary arts. In terms of Emerson's cultural mission, *kairos* involves the invocation of the eternal during a specific moment in history in order to enact change. For Emerson, America itself was a *kairos*, a nation uniquely positioned in the history of the world to fulfill the destiny of God. When Emerson makes his claims for a spiritualized literature, rhetoric, or even education, therefore, he calls upon America's sense of *kairos*, its cultural mission to be the new spiritual leader of the world. Equally important, Emerson argues for a divinely appointed *rhetor* or poet to lead the new American age, a representative man who embodies the *kairos* of America.

I use *kairos* throughout this study as an integration of two understandings of the term. The first, James L. Kinneavy's, defines the term broadly as "right timing and due measure" and stresses its rhetorical functioning: how timing and propriety generate or impact a rhetorical act. Kinneavy argues for the ethical, epistemological, rhetorical, aesthetic, and civic educational dimensions of a dual notion of *kairos* as right timing and due measure, and he identifies the term primarily as situational context ("Neglected Concept," 237; "Aristotle," 134). According to Kinneavy, Plato and Aristotle "both distinguish the general rules of the art of rhetoric from their situational application" (134) and, in Aristotle especially, *kairos* unites the civic virtues that govern a society. Ultimately, *kairos* deals with "the appropriateness of the discourse to the particular circumstances of the time, place, speaker, and audience involved" ("Neglected," 224).

Kinneavy's stress on the situational context marks a significant divergence from another theoretical conceptualization of *kairos*, specifically, Paul Tillich's Judeo-Christian conception of the term.[1] Tillich argues for a spiritual interpretation of the term based on the Christ event and defines *kairos* as "the eternal breaking into the temporal" (*MW* 4: 337). Tillich stresses the transcendental nature of the term within a religious framework, describing it as "a turning point in the fact that something eternal breaks into time and history" (Ashbrook, 115). The Christ event is for Tillich *the Kairos*, "the moment at which history, in terms of a concrete situation, had matured to the point of being able to receive the breakthrough of the central manifestation of the Kingdom of God. The New Testament has called this moment the 'fulfillment of time,' in Greek, *kairos*" (*Systematic* 3: 369). From the prime *Kairos*, the Christ event, any number of *kairoi* may follow, and these *kairoi* achieve their status as special moments in the history of humanity through their association with the Christ event:[2]

> *Kairos* in its *unique* and universal sense is, for Christian faith, the appearing of Jesus as the Christ. *Kairos* in its *general* and special sense for the philosopher of history is every turning-point in history in which the eternal judges and transforms the temporal. *Kairos* in its *special* sense, as decisive for our present situation, is the coming of a new theonomy on the soil of a secularized and emptied autonomous culture. (*MW* 4: 338)

Tillich's special moments of divinity in history often center on significant crises that give rise to a "fulfillment of time" (*Systematic* 3: 370), a position remarkably similar to Emerson's, as will be discussed. These crises require a providential moment in which the Spirit enacts change in the world. The moment of spiritual change, then, is the center of Tillich's theory.

Tillich's and Kinneavy's theories derive from classical sources and, when synthesized, they offer a sensitive heuristic to explain how timing, propriety, and appeals to spiritual power become inextricably intermixed in nineteenth-century American literary culture.[3] Furthermore, they explain how those texts function rhetorically; that is, how they demand social action through their appeals to spiritual timing and propriety. For the early American orator or writer, to demand social action was to invoke a sense of providential timing. For example, in his Independence Day oration of 1815, Joshua Slack praises America: because "her reign is the last, so shall it be the most illustrious of time! . . . The foundation and the progress of our empire has been marked by circumstances, that authorize the most exalted anticipations" (190). *Kairos,* for nineteenth-century American rhetoric and literature, invokes a Tillichian frame for spiritual power: the flowing of the eternal into the temporal, the manifestation of Spirit in the world. Simultaneously, it focuses on a specific time and place, what Kinneavy has argued as a specific time event in which it is appropriate to make a claim or argument. In terms of American literature, *kairos* involves a sense of fulfillment of divine promise and the mission to enact that prophesied promise.

Sacvan Bercovitch has described this sense of American mission and divine right as the American "errand," and he has discussed at length the sense that the Puritans had of America and New England as "the apex of history" (*Ends,* 179). Bercovitch's analysis of Puritan rhetoric rests essentially on a discussion of *kairos,* though he never uses the term. The phrase "the apex of history," however, recalls a Tillichian vision of *kairos* and, as Bercovitch points out, it invokes a sense of "end-time" and Providence inextricable from a transcendental view of *kairos.* The difference between *kairos* and the "errand," however, is the involvement of timing and the propriety implicit in *kairos.* The errand suggests the mission, but *kairos* suggests the timing and moral right to perform the errand. The errand might be said, then, to generate the cultural power of the *kairos* of nineteenth-century America; in other words, the sense of divine mission underlies the sense of timing and propriety that emerges in the literature of the time. *Kairos,* however, becomes the trope, the "ritual mode of our literary tradition" (189). Indeed, even the opening lines of the Declaration of Independence call upon this ritualistic kairotic tradition:

> When, in the course of human events, it becomes necessary for one people to dissolve the political bands which have connected them with another, and to assume, among the powers of the earth, the separate and equal station to which the laws of nature and nature's God entitle them, a decent respect to the opinions of mankind requires that they should declare the causes which impel them to the separation.

The power for change within the Declaration derives in part from its invocation of a divine *kairos:* the proper time and moral propriety of the act of separation is judged by its relation to "nature's God." It appeals for change within a transcendental framework, one in which God enjoins the time and rightness of the break for an American nation.

As part of a literary culture that views America as a providential nation, Emerson envisions literature as grounded in a transcendental *kairos.* Emerson's desire to move American literature from mechanical imitation of European models to the creation of a new, enlightened literature is what Lawrence Buell has described as a movement from "revolution to renaissance" in the birth of New England literary culture. In a meticulous study on the rise of literary craft in America, Buell traces the "Puritan's habit of seeing history in typological terms as fulfillment of biblical prophecy" (201) throughout early American literature. The habit of typologically interpreting history translates into debates as to the timing and appropriateness of a distinctly American literature: what should it be and when is the time for it?

Washington Irving suggests in his *Sketch Book* (1820) that America as yet needs to keep European models because it has not matured in its literary endeavors (63–4), but Emerson begins his "American Scholar" (1837) with a declaration that America's time as imitators has come to an end and that a new spiritual literature needs to be born on American soil. He opens his lecture with a call for a new American literature based in *kairos:* "Perhaps the time is already come, when it ought to be, and will be, something else; when the sluggard intellect of this continent will look from under its iron lids, and fill the postponed expectation of the world with something better than the exertions of mechanical skill" (*Essays,* 53). The *kairos* for American letters has arrived, Emerson asserts, and the world is waiting for America to lead the world with a new literature. His dismissal of the "sluggard intellect," the "iron lids," and the mere "mechanical skill" is powerful, because it assumes that America is the location and time for a new spiritual awakening. The time for a spiritually enlightened nation of writers has arrived: "Who can doubt, that poetry will revive and lead in a new age, as the star in the constellation Harp, which now flames in our zenith, astronomers announce, shall one day be the pole-star for a thousand years?" (53). The "new age" announced by the symbolic "pole-star," by which time and direction is told and which recalls the star announcing Christ's birth, leads to a proclamation for a new spiritual literature. The proclamation is mirrored in the final paragraph of the oration, which makes a similar appeal to *kairos.* In it, Emerson laments the tragedy of American scholars not realizing the divine goal of a new nation and pleads, "Not so, brothers and friends,—please God, ours shall not be so" (71). He invokes an American *kairos,* the sense that the time for America to seize upon its divine promise has come:

> The study of letters shall be no longer a name for pity, for doubt, and for sensual indulgence. The dread of man and the love of man shall be a wall of defence and a wreath of joy around all. A nation of men will for the first time exist, because each believes himself inspired by the Divine Soul which also inspires all men. (71)

Emerson calls the new American scholar to seize this special historical moment and to change the course of American literature, indeed of world literature. The scholar "must be able to take up into himself all the ability of the time, all the contributions of the past, all the hopes of the future" (70). He is, in fact, himself a *kairos,* the leader in a new American age of spiritualized letters. As Emerson writes about the poet, "the experience of each new age requires a new confession, and the world seems always waiting for its poet" (*Essays,* 450). He enacts change on a broad social scale by seizing upon the special divine moment that America embodies, and he uses it to advance the spirit within himself. The new American scholar is the harbinger, literally the first teller of news, of a new literature.

Emerson's invocation of *kairos* for a new American literature, to be founded by the American scholar, also appears in his call for a new type of education. Just as literature needed a spiritual purpose, so too education needed reform. Driving Emerson's argument for reformation of a spiritually bankrupt educational system in essays such as "Education" (1860), then, is an underlying belief in America's destiny to become a great nation: he praises New England, "because it is the country in the world where is the freest expenditure for education. We have already taken, at the planting of the Colonies (for aught I know for the first time in the world), the initial step, which for its importance might have been resisted as the most radical of revolutions, thus deciding at the start the destiny of this country" (*Works* 10, 125). Here, Emerson explicitly grounds his argument in American *kairos;* he asks his readers to seize upon the moment of educational revolution, a revolution that extended beyond Emerson himself. Indeed, writers like William Tyler also appeal to America as the chosen nation for educational change: "The commencement of the new era of benevolence—the era of missionary and Bible and tract and education societies—was marked by the establishment of the unusual number, we might almost say, a new kind of colleges" (345). Both Tyler and Emerson insist that the opportunity, the right moment in history, has arrived for a spiritualized literacy and educational system.

Emerson's concern to fashion a new literature, and a new educational system to support and encourage it, underlies his desire for a new rhetoric as well. Indeed, rhetorical education was a significant part of early American educational systems, and as Nan Johnson and Warren Guthrie have discussed, rhetorics and rhetorical theories of the time were concerned with how to define themselves in relation to European models and how to distinguish themselves as appropriate to the democratic spirit. For the rhetorical culture, like the literary culture, a sense of America as a uniquely ordained nation drove the revision of the rhetorical crafts. The divine American mission thus inspires rhetorical theories grounded in a transcendental *kairos,* a sense of divine urgency and right.

Emerson's influence in rhetorical culture was no less significant than his work in literary circles, and like his vision of a new spiritually charged literature, his vision of a new rhetoric rested on *kairos.* Emerson describes his theory of rhetoric in several essays, but the most important are his two "Eloquence" essays. The first "Eloquence" essay (1847), dubbed by William Charvat as "perhaps the most popular of all Emerson's lectures" (24), argues for a rhetoric that is more than a political art unconnected to a sense of the divine. Though he argues that "every man is an orator" (*Works* 7.61), he insists that a true eloquence is rare and requires a spiritually charged moment in order to be effective: "in transcendent eloquence, there was ever some crisis in affairs, such as could deeply engage the man to the cause he pleads, and draw all this wide power to a point" (92). This "crisis in affairs" is a hallmark of Emerson's rhetorical theory because he makes it prerequisite to true eloquence. He calls it "the new opportunity for painting in fire human thought" (63) and argues that "there is no calamity which right words will not begin to redress" (64). The true *rhetor* invokes the "new opportunity," is himself ultimately greater than the occasion because he wields the "right words" for change: "the occasion always yields to the eminence of the speaker; for a great man is the greatest of occasions" (84). The great orator possesses "the power of Nature running without impediment from the brain and will into the hands" (79), so that "it is not powers of speech that we primarily consider under this word *eloquence,* but the power that being present, gives them their perfection, and being absent, leaves them merely superficial value" (81). Emerson's *rhetor* gains his power from something greater than himself; not unlike Plato's and Augustine's view of the *rhetor,* the speaker's persuasive power here is divinely rooted.[4]

The *rhetor*'s yielding to a greater power in a special moment when the spiritual charges the temporal is the foundation of Emerson's theory of rhetoric. Frequently in his writings, Emerson depicts a great man seizing and being possessed by a great moment. For example, in "The Divinity School Address" (1838) he distinguishes between a good and a bad preacher based on his transcendence of time (85), and in "Lecture on the Times" (1836) he argues that an eloquent man is perfectly at home in all times (155). The great orator surrenders his identity to the "Oversoul" in a special moment of spiritual insight. Roberta K. Ray recognizes that Emerson's conception of the orator includes a relinquishing of the will to divine power (221), and John Sloan relates this surrender to the orator's "'miraculous uplifting'" of an audience by focusing on truth (13).[5] Emerson's conception of rhetoric as an expression of divinity, then, is grounded in the rhetor's ability to be momentarily possessed by truth, and thus to lose himself in divinity. In short, he seizes upon an exigency when the Spirit brings timing and propriety into itself.

In discussing Emerson's central appeal to the "rhetorical exigency," James Berlin mistakenly identifies Emerson's intention as primarily political, divorced from the spiritual sphere. Berlin argues that, for Emerson, rhetorical exigencies give rise to eloquence: "But the desire and willingness of a person to speak are not enough. What is required is inspiration, but not the inspiration that emanates from the absolute. Instead, the impulse to speak comes from the occasions that continually arise in a democracy" (53). Berlin misunderstands Emerson's view of time, history, and language, by suggesting a schism between the occasion to speak and inspiration from the "absolute."[6] For Emerson, the occasion to speak, "the crisis in affairs," is at its root transcendental, a metaphorical representation in the material world of a spiritual crisis.

In the second essay on "Eloquence" (1867), Emerson continues to identify rhetoric as a spiritual act and as requiring a spiritual moment for expression. He argues that rhetoric ascends to the transcendent realm, and he appeals to the American *kairos:* "It [eloquence] is eminently the art which only flourishes in free countries" (112), and "if there ever was a country where eloquence was a power, it is the United States" (132). Furthermore, as in the first "Eloquence" essay, rhetoric's power derives from something greater than the orator himself. Emerson insists "that a greater spirit speaks from you than is spoken to in him" (131) and that a "great sentiment" (132) is necessary for true eloquence. This great sentiment generates the opportunity for eloquence; when it "makes itself deeply felt in any age or country, then great orators appear . . . so the great ideas that suddenly expand at some moment the mind of mankind, indicate themselves by orators" (132). The moment of great ideas and sentiment is the *kairos* for eloquence.

Emerson's lecture on "The Emancipation Proclamation" (*Works* 11. 1862) exemplifies his view that rhetoric derives from a great spiritual sentiment. The lecture, delivered on October 12, 1862 in Boston, shortly after Lincoln issued the Proclamation on September 22, begins with an overt appeal to *kairos:* "In so many arid forms which States incrust themselves with, once in a century, if so often, a poetic act and record occur" (*Works* 11. 293). Lincoln's poetic acts are "jets of thought into affairs" that occur when "roused by danger or inspired by genius" and "break the else insurmountable routine of class and local legislation, and take a step forward in the directions of catholic and universal interests" (*Works* 11. 293). Lincoln's act embodies proper timing and propriety and moves the American state toward transcendental principles. Indeed, for Emerson, Lincoln's proclamation is a fulfillment of divine promise: "It [Liberty] comes, like religion, for short periods, and in rare conditions, as if awaiting a culture of the race which shall make it organic and permanent" (293). The vision of liberty here is Tillichian in its assumption of a divine *kairos* and is distinctly American in its implication that the Emancipation Proclamation has fulfilled a new "theonomy." As Alan Hodder argues about the rhetoric of *Nature*, Emerson's rhetoric in the lecture on the "Emancipation Proclamation" suggests that the time for apocalyptic change has arrived (133–135).

Just as Emerson couches the timing of the Proclamation in spiritual terms, he also attributes the propriety of Lincoln and his words to "Divine Providence" (295). He seemingly criticizes Lincoln early in the lecture, describing the President as moving with "extreme moderation" and being "so reticent that his decision has taken all parties by surprise" (294–5), but he goes on to link the President's words and action to spiritual power:

> The firm tone in which he announces it, without inflation or surplusage,—all these have bespoken such favor to the act, that, great as the popularity of the President has been, we are beginning to think that we have underestimated the capacity and virtue which the Divine Providence has made an instrument of benefit so vast. He has been permitted to do more for America than any other American man. (295)

The power of Lincoln's words, actions, and judgment is ascribed to divine providence. The passive construction, "he has been permitted," reinforces Emerson's appeal to a *kairos,* propriety in particular, that is spiritually charged: Lincoln is a vessel for God's intervention. Indeed the "dazzling success" (295) of the Proclamation is its power to enact spiritual goodness in the American state through a great man's willing surrender to a providential moment.

Emerson writes that "we have pointed out the opportuneness of the Proclamation," but goes on to insists that "the President had no choice" (300). He has no choice because the opportunity is spiritually empowered: "The measure he has adopted was imperative" (300), not only because of the outbreak of the Civil War, but more broadly because of "the piratic feature in [Southern society] which makes it our enemy only as it is the enemy of the human race" (300, 302). America's manifestation of spirit contrasts America as a slave nation. Slavery, Emerson asserts, violates "moral sentiment" (297) and he compares America as a slave nation to a "more moral age" in which slavery is abandoned and the slaves can "defend their independence" (303). The opportunity for change, specifically the Civil War, highlights the South's break in moral law and propriety, but it potentially ushers in a new spiritually enlightened state for the entire nation.

Emerson couches Lincoln's "Proclamation" in a cultural tradition of the American *kairos,* the time and place for a new spiritual nation. Emerson's own lecture, therefore, draws upon the tradition that empowers the Declaration of Independence and that is unique because it constitutes a reenactment of a broad cultural mission to, in Bercovitch's terms, make real the errand of God. Emerson desires to make America the spiritual nation that will live up to the expectations of a waiting God, and his literary and rhetorical theory centers upon the moment during which God's presence is made real in the individual. That moment could be enacted by the great man; he could call the Divine to himself. The American *kairos* is a moment not just when the eternal breaks into the temporal, then, but when the temporal individual invokes the eternal in order to transcend his realm.

The power of the individual to invoke spiritual power and the resulting moment of spiritual transformation that Emerson describes undergird a broad range of nineteenth-century literary texts. For example, like Emerson, Harriet Beecher Stowe and Margaret Fuller ground their arguments for social change within an American *kairos,* and their literary works function rhetorically because they demand social action through invoking a moment of spiritual crises. Indeed, Stowe wrote her novel *Uncle Tom's Cabin* in a moment in which she felt America had severed itself from its spiritual foundations. Her novel, therefore, ends with several appeals to *kairos:* "This is an age of the world when nations are trembling and convulsed. A mighty influence is abroad, surging and heaving the world, as with an earthquake. And is America safe?"; "O, Church of Christ, read the signs of the times"; "But who may abide the day of his appearing?"; "A day of grace is yet held out to us" (629). Stowe's final words in the novel overtly appeal for America to fulfill its spiritual destiny. Emerson's "crisis in events" drives the action of Stowe's novel, and her final exhortations make explicit the implicit argument for nationwide spiritual change.

Margaret Fuller similarly argues that "this country is as surely destined to elucidate a great moral law, as Europe was to promote the mental culture of man" (236). She relies on *kairos* not simply as a significant moment for change, but as a significant moment for spiritual and spiritually guided change. *Woman in the Nineteenth Century* demands equality for women by suggesting that America, as a spiritually guided nation, has arrived at an appropriate moment in history to empower women. It asks that America's citizens be vessels of God's actions, but requires that the individual acts in her own right in order to make the temporal something worthy of the spiritual promise. Like Emerson, she desires that great individuals cede to divine intervention and begin a new era for America.

In a very real sense, then, nineteenth-century American rhetoric as a whole is grounded in *kairos;* that is to say that a cultural mission involving the invocation of *kairos* dominates nineteenth-century American writing. When Emerson asserts in "Power" (1860) that "in history, the great moment is, when the savage is just ceasing to be savage, with all his hairy Pelasgic strength directed on his opening sense of beauty. . . . Everything good in nature and the world is in that moment of transition" (980), he calls upon a kairotic tradition that sees America on the cusp of a fulfillment of divine promise. The nineteenth-century for Emerson was a unique time of transition, when God's divine plan might be realized. His writing, as well as a range of American texts, invoke the American *kairos* in order to actualize a new nation and a new sense of individual being and spirituality.

Notes

1. As Professor Kinneavy described in an interview, he first encountered the term *kairos* while reading Paul Tillich and was intrigued by the possibilities of interpretation that the term might offer a rhetorician (Thompson). Actually, Tillich's introduction of *kairos* into the field of theology has met with considerable confusion, particularly given the term's complexity and Tillich's refusal to offer a simplistic definition. Leonard Wheat drives at the heart of this in a rather disdainful review of Tillich's theology, declaring that "the reader who attempts to understand Tillich's highly abstract description of ethical progress in terms of actual history is wasting his time. Like Georg Hegel, Tillich is ready to read thesis, antithesis, and synthesis into almost anything; like Marx, he has little inclination to be specific" (229). James Ashbrook indicates that the theological community needed a clarification of Tillich's stance on *kairos,* in order to understand his view of history and philosophy of time. In fact, Tillich seems to integrate a philosophical exploration of the problem of time with Christology and with a revisionist perspective on the concept of history, in order to associate *kairos* with the appearance of Christ.

2. As Tillich writes, "the relation of the one *kairos* to the *kairoi* is the relation of the criterion to that which stands under the criterion and the relation of the source of power to that which is nourished by the source of power" (*Systematic* 3.370). In other words, if a special moment in history exhibits the same divine principles and values and judgments that empower the Christ event, it is a *kairos* in its own right.

3. Tillich, for instance, addresses the Greek roots of the term as "the right moment to do something" and acknowledges "the situation which makes it possible to do something" (Ashbrook, 112), both central features of Kinneavy's theory. Tillich's additional assignation of transcendental value to *kairos,* however, helps to articulate a difficult position in the history of rhetoric, namely, certain transcendental thinkers' positions regarding the search for a "true" rhetoric. Understanding *kairos* as a rhetorical term that

includes a theological perspective helps to explain how, in the works of Plato and Augustine, discussions of rhetoric's role in society are inevitably joined to discussions of spirituality.

4. For Augustine and Plato alike, the purpose of rhetoric is to communicate universal and transcendental truth, not to find the available means of persuasion in order to adjudicate situational truths. This transcendental nature of their rhetorics is especially apparent in their conceptions of *kairos,* Augustine's no less so than Plato's. Indeed, Augustine's conceptualization of *kairos* is more specifically and explicitly transcendental than Plato's; like Plato, a sense of divine *kairos* undergirds the purpose of his rhetoric as a whole; but unlike Plato, he explicitly invokes deity as the empowering force of rhetoric. For example, in his *De Doctrina Christiana,* Augustine quotes from Matthew 10: 19–20: "'Take no thought how or what to speak: for it shall be given you in that hour what to speak. For it is not you that speak, but the Spirit of your Father that speaketh in you'" (140). Augustine's choice of biblical quotation here even addresses the timing of oratory, suggesting that human agency is not sufficient to carry the power of the word, that in fact God must bring the correct time and message to change the heart of a parishioner.

5. Recent scholarship has focused on this sense of submission throughout Emerson's writing. For example, Christopher Newfield's *The Emerson Effect: Individualism and Submission in America,* ties Emerson's sense of submission to an American cultural trend of submission to the corporate. See also Richard Poirier's *Poetry and Pragmatism,* which notes that in Emerson's writings, especially in relation to capitalism, "loss and sacrifice are the condition of gain" (52).

6. At this point in his argument James A. Berlin shifts from the word "ideal" and "spiritual" to "absolute," a rhetorical maneuver that conflates idealism and spirituality with absolutism.

Works Cited

Ashbrook, James B, ed. *Paul Tillich in Conversation.* Bristol, IN: Wyndham, 1988.

St. Augustine. *On Christian Doctrine.* Trans. D. W. Robertson, Jr. New York: Macmillan, 1958.

Bercovitch, Sacvan. *The American Jeremiad.* Madison, WI: Wisconsin University Press, 1978.

———. "The Ends of American Puritan Rhetoric." In *The Ends of Rhetoric: History, Theory, Practice.* Ed. John Bender and David E. Wellbery, 171–190. Stanford, CA: Stanford University Press, 1990.

Berlin, James A. *Writing Instruction in Nineteenth-Century American Colleges.* Carbondale, IL: Southern Illinois University Press, 1984.

Buell, Lawrence. *New England Literary Culture: From Revolution Through Renaissance.* Cambridge, England: Cambridge University Press, 1986.

Charvat, William. *Emerson's American Lecture Engagements: A Chronological List.* New York: The New York Public Library, 1961.

The Declaration of Independence and the Constitution of the United States of America. Washington, DC: National Defense University Press, 1995.

Emerson, Ralph Waldo. *Complete Works of Ralph Waldo Emerson.* Ed. Edward W. Emerson. 12 Vols. Boston: Houghton, Mifflin, 1903–1904.

————. *Essays and Lectures*. Ed. Joel Porte. New York: Literary Classics of the United States, 1983.

Fuller, Margaret. "Woman in the Nineteenth Century." *The Portable Margaret Fuller*. Ed. Mary Kelley. New York: Penguin, 1994.

Guthrie, Warren. "The Development of Rhetorical Theory in America, 1636–1850." *Speech Monographs* 13 (1946): 14–22; 15 (1948): 61–71.

Hodder, Alan. *Emerson's Rhetoric of Revelation: Nature, the Reader, and the Apocalypse Within*. University Park, PA: The Pennsylvania State University Press, 1989.

Irving, Washington. *The Sketch Book of Geoffrey Crayon*. New York: Penguin, 1981.

Johnson, Nan. *Nineteenth-Century Rhetoric in North America*. Carbondale, IL: Southern Illinois University Press, 1991.

Kinneavy, James L. "*Kairos:* A Neglected Concept in Classical Rhetoric." *Landmark Essays on Rhetorical Invention in Writing*. Ed. Richard E. Young and Yameng Liu, 221–239. Davis, CA: Hermagoras, 1994.

Kinneavy, James L. and Catherine R. Eskin. "*Kairos* in Aristotle's *Rhetoric*." *Written Communication* 11 (1994): 131–142.

Newfield, Christopher. *The Emerson Effect: Individualism and Submission in America*. Chicago: University of Chicago Press, 1996.

Plato. *The Phaedrus and Letters VII and VIII*. Trans. Walter Hamilton. New York: Penguin, 1973.

Poirier, Richard. *Poetry and Pragmatism*. Cambridge, MA: Harvard University Press, 1992.

Ray, Roberta K. "The Role of the Orator in the Philosophy of Ralph Waldo Emerson." *Speech Monographs* 41 (1974): 215–225.

Slack, Joshua P. "An Oration, Delivered in the Presbyterian Meeting House at Trenton, New Jersey, July 4th." *The American Orator: Comprising an Extensive Collection of Extracts, Principally from American Authors, Adapted to Public Recitation, or for the Use of Schools, as a Reading Class Book*. Ed. Slack. Trenton, NJ: D. and E. Fenton, 1817.

Sloan, John H. "The Miraculous Uplifting': Emerson's Relationship with His Audience." *Quarterly Journal of Speech* 52 (1966): 10–15.

Stowe, Harriet Beecher. *Uncle Tom's Cabin Or, Life Among the Lowly*. New York: Penguin, 1981.

Tillich, Paul. *Writings in the Philosophy of Religion*. Ed. John Clayton. New York: Walter de Gruyten, 1987.

————. *Systematic Theology Vol. 3: Life and the Spirit; History and the Kingdom of God*. Chicago: University of Chicago Press, 1963.

Thompson, Roger. "*Kairos* Revisited: An Interview with James L. Kinneavy." *Rhetoric Review* 19 (2000):

Tyler, William S. "The College and the Church." Reprint in *Annals of America*. Vol. 8. Chicago: Encyclopaedia Britannica, 1968.

Wheat, Leonard. *Paul Tillich's Dialectical Humanism: Unmasking the God Above God*. Baltimore: Johns Hopkins University Press, 1970.

In Praise of Kairos in the Arts

Critical Time, East and West

GREGORY MASON

He said, "What's time? Leave Now for dogs and apes! Man has forever."
—Robert Browning, *A Grammarian's Funeral*

In our received notions of value in general and of art in particular, we continue today to devalue or belittle the time-bound. Like Robert Browning's nineteenth-century grammarian, we scoff at the rich and varied qualities of passing, present experience. Instead, we amass material objects as hedges against our own transience. In our estimation of art, we give pride of place to enduring artifacts. Residual Platonists, we endow the greatest art, the classics, with the special status of timelessness.

The arts need fresh perspectives to describe and discriminate within the time-bound in a positive way. It is remarkable that we persevere with such a meager aesthetic vocabulary to help us think about time and our actions within it. The Sophists of ancient Greece recognized the qualitative dimension of time by the term *kairos:* "the right, the favorable, the critical or the opportune time." We moderns, by contrast, tend to think of time only in terms of quantity, as a commodity to be used with maximum efficiency. We struggle to negotiate an incessant flow of uniform time with no thought for qualitative differentiation. The experiential issue at the heart of *kairos* sets quantitative against qualitative time. Are we willing to live *within* time, to be sensitive to its inherently dramatic and changing character, to recognize and to seize the critical moments—the *kairoi*—as they present themselves; or do we wish to try to define or refine the time dimension out of truly significant experience? The more we attempt to transcend time, the more we encounter it not as the critical element within which all experience unfolds, but as a compromising, contaminating factor in the search for life's true value. An understanding and appreciation of qualitative time, of *kairos,* has disappeared from our imaginative vocabulary; our understanding of art (and of life) would surely be enhanced by reclaiming it. As a first modest step in such a project, this essay will first reflect briefly on the demise of *kairos* in Western aesthetic discourse, and then suggest how it might be rehabilitated, with help and inspiration from aesthetics and practices from Tibet and Japan.

A major premise of my argument is that a recognition and affirmation of qualitative time, *kairos,* is linked to a broader affirmation of transience in life. Plato, by contrast, stressed the value of a timeless world of ideal forms, and claimed that "those who pursue philosophy aright study nothing but dying and being dead" (5: 223). Western aesthetic theories developed largely under the influence of Plato, and their continuing neglect of the kairotic dimension has left us with a significantly diminished definition of art. As an alternative, I shall build on the writings of John Dewey and others, and propose a view of art which incorporates *kairos* and the interrelated notions of timeliness and transience. This view stresses the practice and experience of the aesthetic activity, rather than the value of the artifact as a commodity.

Paul Kristeller has shown how our modern system of fine arts classification has radically narrowed the meaning of the term "art" since antiquity. The ancient Greeks did not have a term for the fine arts, but instead thought of art as accomplishment, *techne,* skill in mastering a range of activities, including those that we now call "sciences" and "crafts." This general concept of art persisted throughout the Middle Ages; Aquinas even included shoemaking, cooking, and juggling in his list. A decisive change came in the Renaissance with the renewed influence of Plato. Gradually a recognizably modern system evolved in which the fine arts were considered discrete activities whose special province was the pursuit and expression of beauty.

In the eighteenth century, Immanuel Kant completed the process by dividing human activity into three categories: the cognitive, the moral, and the aesthetic. As an expression of aesthetic activity, art for Kant represented a "purposiveness without purpose," excluded by definition from the realm of practical utility. The fine arts became rigidly delimited to specific pursuits—painting, sculpture, architecture, music, and literature—and prescribed within set boundaries. No accommodation was made for a broader range of activities, or for new, temporal arts like photography and film. This categorical separation of the aesthetic from the practical had far-reaching social consequences. Citing Kant, Benjamin Constant in 1804 first coined the term "art for art's sake" and drove a wedge which still persists to some extent today. Albeit unwittingly, Kant ushered in a radically redefined conception of art, as subsequent theorists pursued his line of thinking much further than he was prepared to himself. As René Wellek observes, "autonomy of art becomes something Kant would never have dreamed of, an assertion of the superiority of the artist to the Philistine, a proclamation of his hostility to the society in which he lives and which he has long ago given up hope of changing or conforming in his own image" (136). Complementing this is Arthur Schopenhauer's ideal of the receiver of art, the spectator suspended in a will-less, timeless stasis, above the vagaries and flux of everyday life. These are the extreme though logical consequences of the removal of art to a privileged, timeless realm.

By contrast, a prophet of the new democratic art of the twentieth century, film director Jean Renoir proposes a much more inclusive definition of art. Dismissing the caviling arguments about the status of film as an art or a non-art, Renoir prefers to collapse conventional aesthetic boundaries:

> To the question "Is the cinema an art?" I answer "What does it matter?" You can make films or you can cultivate a garden. Both have as much claim to be called art as a poem by Verlaine or a painting by Delacroix. If your film or your garden is a good one it means that as a practitioner of cinema or gardening you are entitled to consider yourself an artist. The ploughman with an old-fashioned plough creates a work of art when he ploughs a furrow. Art is not a calling in itself, but the way in which one exercises a calling, and also the way in which one performs any human activity. I will give you my definition of art: art is "making." The art of poetry is the art of making poetry. The art of love is the art of making love. (97)

Likewise for John Dewey, "Art is a quality of doing and of what is done" (214). For Dewey, art belongs to concrete experience: "A work of art, no matter how old and classic, is actually, not just potentially, a work of art only when it lives in some individual experience" (108). Dewey laments that "the elevation of the ideal above and beyond immediate sense experience has operated . . . to impoverish and degrade all things of direct experience" (31). Everything we know is a function of our experience, which takes place in time. At the same time, this does not reduce experience to a meaningless chain of atomized and disconnected moments. We also experience moments of *kairos* when a pattern of events presents itself with startling clarity:

> When a flash of lightning illumines a dark landscape, there is a momentary recognition of objects. But the recognition is not itself a mere point in time. It is the focal culmination of long, slow processes of maturation. It is the manifestation of the continuity of an ordered temporal experience in a sudden discrete instant of climax. (Dewey, 23–24)

Art fastens onto and fashions these *kairoi:* "Art celebrates with peculiar intensity the moments in which the past reinforces the present and in which the future is a quickening of what is now" (Dewey, 18).

Dewey goes far beyond attempting to rehabilitate discredited arts or crafts. The greater task is to endow as much of life as possible with the richness of aesthetic experience: purposive, ordering, pleasurable, and harmonious. Why for instance, he asks, are our contemporary buildings and daily artifacts so ugly? Dewey's theories of art expand ultimately into a social manifesto: "The values that lead to the production and intelligent enjoyment of art have to be incorporated into the system of social relationships" (344). With this broader call, Dewey rejects any notion of art merely as "the beauty parlor of civilization" (344).

John Berger has also argued that our inherited sense of time has diminished the quality of our lives. Berger sees each person as living in two time frames. He contrasts "the event of the biological organism," the span of a person's life as physically determined, with "the event of consciousness," the awareness that each person has of a relationship between the past, present, and the future. He sees modern Europeans as victims of their own positivism, since they work only with "a uniform, abstract, unilinear law of time which applies to everything that exists, including consciousness" ("Go," 202). For Berger the artist must capture a significant tension between the transient and the transcendent. If everything is presented and evaluated simply in terms of the here and now, the outcome is mere banality: "The ephemeral, no longer appealing to the timeless, becomes as trivial and instant as the fashionable. . . . Without an acknowledged coexistence of the ephemeral and the timeless, there is nothing of consequence for pictorial art to do" ("Painting," 210). Great artists recognize kairotic moments in life and seize them as occasions and subjects for their art.

How might a reader benefit from a sharpened awareness of *kairos* in approaching a work of literature? As an interpretive strategy, attending to *kairos* shows readers how characters create meanings out of critical moments in their lives. Not all *kairoi* are necessarily self-evident or unavoidably recognizable. The occasion always demands that it be recognized and appropriated by the person whom it confronts. As Frank Kermode notes, the reader of fiction engages throughout in such making of meaning, as he progressively interprets an entire plot. For his purposes, Kermode defines *kairos* as "a point in time filled with significance, charged with a meaning derived from its relation to the end" (47). He emphasizes the subjective dimension of individual choice in *kairos* whereby the reader draws significance from the flux of events and orders them into a meaningful pattern. He sees first the author's and then the reader's task in making sense of narrative as "the establishment of a significant relation between the moment and a remote origin and end, a concord of past, present and future" (50). In art as in life, we employ fictions to negotiate the chaotic world around us: "It is not that we are connoisseurs of chaos, but that we are surrounded by it, and equipped for co-existence with it only by our fictive powers" (64). Thus, for Kermode, *kairoi* are coherent patterns of experience, intuited and observed and then applied to order the random sequentiality of passing events.

Once we achieve this sharpened awareness, we shall find *kairos* inscribed in all major genres of Western literature. For example, *kairos* is vividly dramatized in the earliest recorded literature we possess, the Mesopotamian *Epic of Gilgamesh.* The oppressive King Gilgamesh is made sensitive and caring through his friendship with Enkidu. Created by the goddess Aruru as a companion for Gilgamesh, the long-haired, loving warrior Enkidu represents "a male embodiment of certain parts of the feminine" (Absher, 21). When Enkidu dies, Gilgamesh is devastated with sorrow. Now viscerally aware of his own mortality, Gilgamesh embarks on an urgent quest for eternal life. On his quest, Gilgamesh encounters Siduri, a woman who counsels him to enjoy the pleasures of the mortal moment: "Let your clothes be fresh, bathe yourself in water, cherish the little child that holds your hand, and make yourself happy in her embrace; for this too is the lot of man" (102). But Gilgamesh, fixated with grief at the death of Enkidu, ignores Siduri's advice and will settle for nothing less than eternal life.

Tom Absher points out the inherent futility in such a quest. If Gilgamesh is so future-oriented that he is unable to live within any single present moment, what benefit would an infinite number of such moments be to him?

> Immortal life would just be a longer series of moments, and if we don't know how to value a finite series of breaths and waking days, having an infinite series at our disposal would only prolong our ignorance and our abuse of time. Immortal life would be wasted on us. (27–28)

Gilgamesh gains the flower of immortal life, but then loses it, tellingly, through a momentary lapse of attention while attempting to carry it back to his people. He feels that his life has been a failure. He is dejected at the loss of his trophy, and in no way consoled by the fact that he had for a time possessed it, or by the wisdom that he had gained in the search. Absher suggests that, in his quest for immortality, Gilgamesh exhibits "a male or patriarchal approach to time. Gilgamesh wants to master, to dominate time and thereby live forever" (27). By contrast, Ann Belford Ulanov maintains that "the feminine sense of time is always of the moment; it is not *chronos* but *kairos*" (304). Ironically, Gilgamesh dismisses his own very real achievements and inner growth, and simply laments the failure of his impossible attempt to transcend his mortal state. Were he to have lived *within* time, he might have savored his triumphs, those significant moments of crystallization, insight and fulfillment, the *kairoi* that revealed to him his life's meaning and value.

Plots in fiction are all more or less kairotic, although they vary, depending on the sharpness of the crisis points. The short story tends to be pointedly kairotic. A prime example in modern literature occurs in James Joyce's "Araby," where the narrator experiences an epiphany that shows him how his life will unfold: "Gazing up into the darkness I saw myself as a creature driven and derided by vanity; and my eyes burned with anguish and anger"

(35). Most novels assume a flatter overall profile, conforming more closely to the rhythms of everyday time. Jane Austen's heroine Emma confronts a moment of *kairos* in the domestic sphere when "it darted through her with the speed of an arrow, that Mr. Knightley must marry no one but herself" (32). The grander scale of Leo Tolstoy's *War and Peace* ties the personal to the metaphysical and the cosmic:

> From the day when Pierre, after leaving the Rostovs' with Natasha's grateful look fresh in his mind, had gazed at the comet that seemed to be fixed in the sky and felt that something new was appearing on his own horizon—from that day the problem of the vanity and uselessness of all earthly things, that had incessantly tormented him, no longer presented itself. (736)

Drama presents the clearest examples of kairotic moments of heightened time, although their subsequent meaning often invests them with comic or tragic irony. These moments coincide frequently with what Aristotle called *"anagnorisis"* or "recognition." Often there are also smaller *kairoi,* as when Shakespeare's Othello lands on Cyprus and joyfully embraces his young bride. A brief *kairos* of "expanded time" of fulfillment occurs before tragedy closes in: "If it were now to die, T'were now to be most happy" (*Othello* 2.1.188 – 89). The major *kairos* in a drama comes at the hinge point where time hangs suspended and the characters recognize the nature of their destinies which their perception of a constellation of circumstances has revealed to them. Such a moment occurs in Arthur Miller's *Death of a Salesman* when the deluded hero, Willy Loman, experiences the joy of realization that his errant son Biff still loves him, even though Biff will not become the business success his father had hoped he would be:

> BIFF *(at the peak of his fury):* Pop, I'm nothing! I'm nothing, Pop. Can't you understand that? There's no spite left in me any more. I'm just what I am, that's all.
> (BIFF's fury has spent itself, and he breaks down, sobbing, holding on to WILLY, who dumbly fumbles for BIFF's face.)
> WILLY *(Astonished):* What're you doing? What're you doing? *(to* LINDA*)* Why is he crying?. . . *(after a long pause, astonished, elevated)* Isn't that–isn't that remarkable? Biff–he likes me! . . . Oh, Biff! *(Staring wildly.)* He cried! Cried to me. *(He is choking with his love and now cries out his promise.)* That boy–that boy is going to be magnificent! (374)

Tragically, Willy is not healthy or wise enough to capitalize on this kairotic moment to build a reconciliation with his son Biff; instead he interprets the occasion as a signal to commit suicide to enable his son to inherit his life insurance settlement. Nevertheless, the moment of *kairos* stands as a critical moment of recognition for Biff and for the audience. Willy, too, sees some positive new truths that partially offset his tragic delusion.

Kairoi in the lyric often lead the poet from experience to meditation, as in Wordsworth's "The Solitary Reaper." Here the poet is struck by the seemingly timeless beauty of the lone girl's singing, and by a sense that his intense experience of it has attenuated its transience:

> Whate'er the theme, the Maiden sang
> As if her song could have no ending;
> I saw her singing at her work,
> And o'er the sickle bending;
> I listened till I had my fill
> And as I mounted up the hill,
> The music in my heart I bore,
> Long after it was heard no more.

(3: 77)

The mid-twentieth-century Welsh poet Dylan Thomas' "Fern Hill" is more reflexive. The poet contrasts the carefree unconscious days of his boyhood on a farm with his adult self as he revisits the same scene. In his childhood, he had lived "once below a time." Looking back, it seemed to him then as if time had allowed him to exist in a blessed stasis: "Time let me play and be / Golden in the mercy of his means" (178). Now he realizes that his timeless sleep of innocence was only apparent: "And nightly under the simple stars / As I rode to sleep the owls were bearing the farm away." With the maturity of adulthood, the poet looks back on the *kairos* of what felt like an endless childhood dispensation. The poet projects a wistful and even melancholy mood in reflecting on transience and on the loss of his own innocence (and ignorance!), but he strongly affirms the *kairos* of his childhood experiences, for all its limitations in perspective: "Oh as I was young and easy in the mercy of his means, / Time held me green and dying / Though I sang in my chains like the sea" (180).

Some strikingly differing perceptions of qualitative time emerge in the cultures of Tibet and Japan. The *kalachakra* ("the wheel of time") is one of Tibetan Buddhism's most complex tantras, or esoteric teachings. As part of the *kalachakra* initiations given to large groups of people, the Namgyal monks of Tibet have traveled to various Western countries and constructed sand sculptures to depict and convey the meaning of the tantra in graphic form. Using fourteen different colors of sand applied by small funnels, groups of monks have constructed these breathtakingly beautiful and intricate, circular sculptures called "sand mandalas," some eight feet in diameter. Their work has resulted not in permanent monuments or artifacts since, shortly after they are completed, the sculptures are dismantled. When the *kalachakra* rite has been performed, the ceremony is over and the gods who had been invoked to inhabit the sculpture are sent back to their customary places. The sand making up the sculpture is removed by the monks, collected in an urn, and ceremonially poured into a nearby river, lake, or ocean.

This attitude toward the artifact is unfamiliar in the West, since it places no value on the work of art as a product or as a commodity. It values the sculpture instead for its function in the ritual which is not complete until the sculpture itself has been undone. According to Barry Bryant,

> [T]he dismantling of the sand mandala may be interpreted as a lesson in nonattach-ment, a letting go of the "self-mind." The ceremony reflects the Buddhists' recogni-tion of the impermanence and transitory nature of all aspects of life. . . . [Since] the things we cling to are impermanent, and none is more insubstantial than the "I" which does the clinging . . . the idea of possessing and holding on to either their form or the accomplishment derived from them, defeats the purpose. (230, 250)

Similar to the ideas proposed by John Dewey, this Tibetan approach is un-concerned with the work of art as a product, but focuses instead on the pro-cess, in this case "perfecting the mind of the practitioner," through the *kala-chakra* initiation ceremony in which the sculpture plays a part (Bryant, 250). Attention and value reside ultimately in the experience, in the kairotic mo-ment of initiation for which the mandala was constructed. This whole pro-cess has been witnessed with fascination, awe, and sometimes with near alarm by observers in the West. Kay Larson reported for *New York* magazine: "A sand mandala is an extraordinary thing, collaborative, ephemeral, un-signed, ahistorical—contrary in every way to 'art' as we mean it in the [West-ern] world" (Bryant, 34).

Japan is also a country rich in aesthetic and spiritual practices that drama-tize and model alternative ways to live more richly within passing time. The art of drinking tea, which originated in China, has been developed and re-fined in Japan over the course of centuries. Central to the notion of *cha no yu*, the Japanese tea ceremony, is the idea of a quiet, structured gathering of guests to enjoy taking tea in a particular manner in a tranquil setting. This setting should be aesthetically pleasing yet sparse (*wabi*), and conducive to quiet fellowship and contemplation, attuned to the ambiance of the time and season. The similarities to the ideas and practice of Zen Buddhism have often been noted, expressed in the saying *chazen-ichimi*, "tea and Zen are one and the same way" (Hammitzsch, 63). Just as Zen Buddhism recognizes the importance of a direct, unmediated experiencing of a sense of unity and "oneness" in all creation, so, too, the *cha no yu* attempts to reenact a sense of harmony and centeredness for the participants in the simple ritual of the tea ceremony.

An important dimension of the disposition and behavior of the partici-pants at a tea ceremony flows from their awareness of their own ephemeral condition and of the necessarily singular quality of any given human occasion or encounter. The tea master Naosuke captured this sentiment with the phrase *ichigo ichie* ("one time, one meeting"), a formulation that has become central to the ethos of the tea ceremony. He wrote:

> Great attention should be given to a tea gathering, which we can speak of as "one time, one meeting" (*ichigo ichie*). Even though the host and the guests may see each other often socially, one day's gathering can never be repeated exactly. Viewed this way, the meeting is indeed a once-in-a-lifetime occasion. The host, accordingly, must in true sincerity take the greatest care with every aspect of the gathering and devote himself entirely to ensuring that nothing is rough. The guests, for their part, must understand that the gathering cannot occur again, and, appreciating how the host has flawlessly planned it, must also participate with true sincerity. This is what is meant by "one time, one meeting." (Varley, 187)

The most distinctive Japanese form of poetry, the haiku, likewise has much in common with the spirit of Zen Buddhism, and shows an equally keen awareness of *kairos*. Indeed each haiku poem could be said to build upon its own particular *kairos*, its "haiku moment." This "haiku moment" denotes a kind of *kairos* when a seemingly commonplace event becomes the inspiration for a poem (Yasuda, 31). The event presents an intersection of the transient with the enduring, and the concrete image embodying it resonates with associations and connotations. The haiku form is radically kairotic, urging a sensitivity to experience that enhances the quality of each passing moment. In haiku poetry, the haiku moment is seldom clearly described but only implied. A haiku of Basho (1644–1694) will illustrate the point:

> On a withered bough
> A crow alone is perching;
> Autumn evening now.
> (Yasuda, 41)

Only an outline is given. The event has to be completed by the reader who infers the context, brings his or her own experience to the poem, and completes its meaning. The reader is required to reflect on the poem and to bring to it some deeper significance behind the bare images. Each reader cocreates a somewhat different poem.

Another example from Japanese art, the motion picture *Ikiru* (*Living*, 1953), illustrates how the film medium is particularly appropriate for the portrayal of *kairos*, since it can embed dramatic situations within a fluid portrayal of time. Enhanced moments of time and experiences of sychronicity can be expressed in film through technical means such as slow motion, split screen, and flashback. *Kairos* is richly expressed and explored in Akira Kurosawa's *Ikiru*. The hero Kanji Watanabe's life as Chief of the Citizen's Section at

City Hall is transformed when he discovers that he is suffering from terminal stomach cancer. Somehow this jaded bureaucrat seizes the *kairos*, and takes his summary death sentence as a summons to action. He resolves to devote his remaining days to supervising a project to build a children's park on waste ground in the city. His sudden manic energy startles his somnolent colleagues, who have long since given upon bold actions of any kind. His actions are unwelcome, both with his family who suspect senility or debauchery, and with the local crime syndicate whose attempts at intimidation the relentless Watanabe brushes aside.

Our hero builds the park and duly dies, but the film is only half over. The second part unfolds at his wake where the meaning of Watanabe's actions are interpreted. At first, his jealous colleagues claim equal credit for Watanabe's achievements, but as they drink more *saké*, they reproach themselves, become maudlin, and finally resolve to turn over a new leaf and dedicate the rest of their lives to living in the spirit of their late boss. Next day at the office, however, business has returned to normal and the timid clerks are again deferentially shuffling mountains of papers. This film offers a wonderful illustration of the intrusion of a *kairos*, a time of crisis, into the life of an individual. It shows the energizing, disruptive and sometimes terrifying character of heightened experience. At the same time, it casts the hero's coworkers as a surrogate audience and forces us to evaluate not only whether we could respond to the *kairos* in the heroic way that Watanabe did, but also whether we could bear any better witness than did his colleagues.

This essay has argued that the neglect of *kairos*, the dimension of qualitative time, has diminished our culture and distorted our appreciation of the arts. A process of neglect has occurred over a long period of time for a cluster of interrelated reasons. It has involved us, in Dewey's words, in "contempt for the body, fear of the senses, and the opposition of flesh to spirit" (20). To recognize and seize a *kairos* is not to follow the line of least resistance. Involving heightened awareness, it requires an act of perception of the circumstances by the individual whom it confronts and a sometimes uncomfortable act of choice. In a time-bound world, bereft of the comforting backdrop of timeless ideal certainties, the individual has to trust his own experience and to participate in the making of meaning.

This experience of a sense of impermanence is by no means a recent dilemma. The sixteenth-century Michel de Montaigne, the first of our contemporaries, recognized his own temporality in his essay "Of Repentance":

> I do not portray being. I portray passing. Not the passing from one age to another, or, as the people say, from seven years to seven years, but from day, from minute. My history needs to be adapted to the moment. . . . The soundness of any plan depends on the time; circumstances and things roll about and change incessantly. (611, 618)

Montaigne, alert, alive, and aware of the quality of the passing moment, contrasts sharply with Browning's Grammarian, "famous, calm and dead."

In the opening lines of his poem, "The Morning Train," W. S. Merwin (1989) presents the metaphor of a journey, with its shifting horizons and fleeting epiphanies that we are not always ready to seize:

> In the same way that the sea
> becomes something else the moment we
> are on it with its horizon all around
> us and its weight
> bearing us up so a journey seems not
> to be one as long as we are
> traveling
>
> (1–7)

If we affirm that we live in a moving, changing universe, this need not mean that our life is valueless because of its transience. To the contrary, Sigmund Freud maintained that "transience value is scarcity value in time. . . . The beauty of the human form and face vanish for ever in the course of our own lives, but their evanescence only lends them a fresh charm" (288).

The attempt in our culture to deny the spirit of *kairos,* to deny acknowledging our own movement in time through various postures of evasion and repression, has been indeed pathological. The bold imaginative syntheses of twentieth-century Western physics and astronomy—which have shown us that the story of time is not an even and endless unfolding, but a dramatic scenario with significant moments of revelation and crisis—have been lost on us. Ours is a deep-seated condition, reflecting an alienation from our own fuller natures, and an intense anxiety about our own mortality. It also entails a corrosive view of who we are, and of what we make and do as simply commodities, strangely divorced from a full awareness of our own natures. Some possible ways out of this sad fixation have been suggested by the socially committed aesthetics of John Dewey, John Berger, and others, and by some striking and largely unfamiliar perspectives from the East. Recognizing that we are subject *to* time, that each occasion in life is indeed *ichigo, ichie* ("one time, one meeting"), liberates us to accept and affirm our own transience. Recognizing that we are subjects *in* time empowers us to see *kairos,* its varied, qualitative character, and to seize our opportunities to act within it.

Works Cited

Absher, Tom. "Gilgamesh and the Feminine." *Anima* 15 (1988): 20–27.
Austen, Jane. *Emma (*1816). Boston: Houghton Mifflin, 1957.

Berger, John. "Go Ask The Time." *Granta* 15: 197–212. New York: Viking, 1985.

———. "Painting and Time." *The White Bird.* 205–211. London: Chatto and Windus, 1985.

Browning, Robert. "A Grammarian's Funeral." *The Complete Poetical Works of Robert Browning.* 366–368. New York: Macmillan, 1933.

Bryant, Barry. *The Wheel of Time Sand Mandala.* New York: HarperCollins, 1992.

Burnham, Jack. *The Structure of Art.* 2d ed. New York: Braziller, 1973.

Dewey, John. *Art As Experience.* 1934. Reprint, New York: Putnam's Sons, 1980.

The Epic of Gilgamesh. Trans. N. K. Sandars. New York: Penguin, 1981.

Freud, Sigmund. "On Transience." *Art And Literature.* Pelican Freud Library 14: 283–290. New York: Viking-Penguin, 1987.

Hammitzsch, Horst. *Zen in the Art of the Tea Ceremony.* Trans. Peter Lemesurier. New York; Dutton, 1988.

Ikiru. Dir. Akira Kurosawa. With Takashi Shimura. Toho, 1952.

Joyce, James. *Dubliners.* 1914. Reprint, New York: Viking, 1969.

Kant, Immanuel. *The Critique of Judgment.* 1793. Trans. James Creed Meredith. Reprint, Oxford: Clarendon, 1957.

Kermode, Frank. *The Sense of An Ending.* New York: Oxford University Press, 1967.

Kristeller, Paul Oskar. "The Modern System of the Arts." *Journal of the History of Ideas* 12 (1951): 465–527; 12 (1952): 117–46.

Miller, Arthur. *Death of Salesman.* In *Modern and Contemporary Drama.* Ed. Miriam Gilbert, Karl H. Klaus, and Bradford S. Field. New York: Saint Martin's, 1994.

Merwin, W. S. "The Morning Train." *The New Yorker* 29 (Aug. 1989): 32.

Montaigne, Michel de. *The Complete Essays of Montaigne.* Trans. Donald M. Frame. Palo Alto, CA: Stanford University Press, 1965.

Plato. *Plato.* Ed. W. R. M. Lamb. 7 Vols. Loeb Classical Library. Cambridge, MA: Harvard University Press, 1914–1926.

Renoir, Jean. *My Life and My Films.* London: Collins, 1974.

Schopenhauer, Arthur. *The World as Will and Representation.* 1819. Trans. E. F. J. Payne. Reprint, New York: Dover, 1969.

Tanaka, Sen'o. *The Tea Ceremony.* New York: Harmony, 1977.

Thomas, Dylan. *The Collected Poems of Dylan Thomas.* New York: New Directions, 1957.

Tolstoy, Leo. *War and Peace.* 1869. Trans. Louise and Aylmer Maude. Reprint, New York: Norton, 1966.

Ulanov, Ann Belford. *The Feminine In Jungian Psychology and Christian Theology.* Evanston, IL: Northwestern University Press, 1971.

Varley, Paul, and Kumakura, Isao, eds. *Tea in Japan.* Honolulu: University of Hawaii Press, 1989.

Wellek, René. "Immanuel Kant's Aesthetics and Criticism." In *Discriminations.* 122–142. New Haven: Yale University Press, 1971.

Wiener, Philip, ed. *Dictionary of the History of Ideas.* 4 Vols. New York: Scribner's, 1973.

Wordsworth, William. *The Poetical Works of William Wordsworth.* Ed. E. de Sélincourt. 5 Vols. Oxford: Clarendon, 1940–49.

Yasuda, Kenneth. *The Japanese Haiku.* Rutland, VT: Tuttle, 1957.

Changing Times in Composition Classes

Kairos, *Resonance, and the Pythagorean Connection*

CAROLYN ERIKSEN HILL

> Resonance . . . determines what we see, and what's reflected; what goes
> right through, what gets stuck, and what sinks in.
> —K.C. Cole, *Sympathetic Vibrations*

> The music of the spheres . . . provides the perfect pattern for art in any
> medium. . . . It encompasses the full range of Pythagorean reality, from
> the highest celestial abstraction to the most affective of human
> experiences. Whenever that sweet harmony touches our lives we are
> changed, improved, brought closer to divinity.
> —S. K. Heninger Jr., *Touches of Sweet Harmony*

In the culturally tumultuous world of fifth-century B.C. Greece, signs of discord were in the air everywhere: clashing political factions along with opposing ideas and values, all pitting community against community. But in Athens a budding democracy looked for ways to heal its own breaches, and into the divisive climate came Sophists, those traveling teachers who wove theories and discursive practices together as they taught argumentative skills for public life. Protagoras, for instance, urged that both sides of any question be given respect in deliberations, Gorgias, that rhetors must recognize the insoluble "contradictory nature of things" (Untersteiner, 186) and depend not on logical truth of one side over another, but on *psychagogia,* or rhetorical enchantment, to lead listeners to the desired side. No wonder sophistic rhetoric has gained such appeal in our own contemporary field of rhetoric, itself immersed in institutions echoing ancient social problems: our cultural "wars," our fading trust in "facts" and single truths, and our resulting sense that centers of values and knowledge are not holding.

Still, though as teachers we might find that sophistic rhetoric gives us a lens through which to recognize our students' (and our own) immersion in worlds of competing values, we might also find that sophistic concepts are difficult to use pedagogically. How does one enchant readers, for instance, and why should one want to? How, moreover, does this almost magical practice of enchantment or *psychagogia* (de Romilly, 15) connect with our insistence (following Aristotle) that writing reflect fairness and logical structure in its argumentative taking of sides? Or, when Werner Jaeger tells us that "what was common to . . . all [the Sophists] was that they all taught political arete" (293), how are we to bring it into our classrooms, this arete that F. E. Peters translates as excellence or virtue (25) but that Robert Pirsig labels, simply, "Quality" (377) in writing and in life itself? And most intriguingly of all, when James L. Kinneavy claims that *kairos*—which he defines as "situational context" and "the right or opportune time to do something" (80)—is "the dominating concept in sophistic . . . rhetoric" (83), does he not complicate beyond repair our practical understanding of sophistic rhetoric and its ability to engage value-challenged students more fully and competently in their writing tasks?

Kinneavy himself hints at an answer in his tracing (through the work of Augusto Rostagni) the *kairos* principle back to the crucial influence of the Pythagorean school (82–83) on Gorgias (himself reputedly a student of Pythagoras' disciple Empedocles). Rostagni claims that Gorgias's teachings "explicitly reveal their indebtedness to Pythagoras and the issues he raises," and that "Gorgias is nothing but an intermediary, a translator of a doctrine prior to him which was widespread in Sicily and the greater part of Greece" ([12 in manuscript]). Perhaps Pythagoras can help us understand how these important concepts might once have been functionally connected to each other.

What is valuable in the Pythagorean idea of *kairos*, I will claim, is that it grounds our notion of sophistic (in this case Gorgian) rhetoric in its more coherent and more pedagogically useful historical roots. Drawing quality, enchantment, and oppositional thinking into a graceful, and I believe teachable, whole, it opens a door into an ancient, but still dimly recognizable habit of mind, one that expresses itself in a kind of time that is living and creative.

With the assumption that when we teach writing we are teaching the interactive and socially situated habits of mind involved in discourse, I look first at ways we might translate Pythagorean habits of mind into our own. I examine them as a cosmos in which *kairos*, embedded as its moving, time-oriented, and transformative principle, functions for Pythagoras as a kind of resonance: esthetically, interactively, and analogically; in the elements and the stars, in music, minds, bodies, and discourse. It moves from patterns of discord to concord, with what Shakespeare more than a millennium after

Pythagoras's time, would echo as "touches of sweet harmony" in the music of the spheres (*Midsummer Night's Dream* V.i.57).

I look finally at ways I've sought to teach writing by awakening students to an experience of the energies actively expressed in thinking and writing, energies which, to be sure, have been described by many who have experienced them throughout the ages, but which Pythagoras connects so elegantly to the *kairos* that moved into our own rhetorical history. What we—our students and we—today tend to experience as binary oppositions, the static, intractable polarized thinking that shows up in our lives and in our discourse, was for Pythagoras a matter of those forces expressing themselves kairotically and energetically, shaping and changing our experience of time, and themselves being transformed by it. Rather than our speaking in static terms about such matters as unity and coherence, for instance, the discursive structures of student writing, I argue, can as easily be described through the language of *kairos*, resonance, and energy, in fact, a very perceivable energy whose expression (as George Kennedy [1998] notes [3]) lies at the very heart of rhetoric. Thinking through Pythagoras, I can more easily bring my students' structural or rhetorical problems into the language of the motions and emotions of actual thinking, feeling, breathing people, connected intrinsically and analogically to their subjects and their readers. So it is to that language and those ideas (with their twentieth-century analogs) that I now turn.

The Pythagorean Cosmos: Number and Analog

The Pythagorean cosmos, much to the annoyance of Aristotle and many others who have written about it, is a matter of numbers. "If certain things happened to have the same number," says Aristotle, "on the Pythagorean view they would be the same as one another, because they would have the same form of number, *e.g.*, sun and moon would be the same" (*Metaphysics*, 1093a). With just as much disdain for the Pythagorean system of numbers, W. K.C. Guthrie praises Aristotle for wasting "little time over what was to him a manifest absurdity" (1962, 303), noting in passing that Pythagoras's "opportunity"—which Guthrie does acknowledge to be an inadequate translation of *kairos* (301)—"was 7."

Are we then, with some embarrassment for Pythagoras, to sweep that numerical equation under the carpet as we investigate more plausible and seemingly more useful qualities of *kairos* and its cosmic connection? A more interesting possibility would be to turn toward cultural and historical contexts for sources of what we know to be, in its own time and through the Renaissance, an enormously influential way of thinking.

Granted it is not our preferred academic way of thinking, and certainly not Aristotle's. Pythagoras, after all, lived a full two centuries before Aristotle, in a social climate "not far removed from those magical fraternities, characteristic of . . . tribal society" (Thomson, 255). He is reputed to have been, at least loosely speaking, a kind of shaman (Dodds, 143), with a shaman's characteristic straddling of two worlds (an ordinary reality and a hidden non-ordinary one), as well as a magician, healer, spiritual leader, philosopher, musician, and of course, mathematician. It is on the fringes of sixth-century Greek culture in Croton, Italy, that this many-faceted man heard the music of the spheres permeating every other phenomenon in the cosmos.

Believing with some cultural psychologists and philosophers (Varela et al.) that worlds are mutually enacted with their inhabitants (rather than being pre-given and simply represented), and finding precedence in the work of anthropologists and historians who are studying the many ways this enacting can happen (e.g., Howes; Golden and Toohey), I read Pythagoras's work and world—his music of the spheres with its septenary *kairos*—as one of those ways we have been neglecting, to our pedagogical loss.

Pythagoras, for instance, could not have thought of numbers in the mechanistic ways we think of them, since he lived in an ancient Mediterranean climate of traditions about numbers very different from our own, traditions relating to their quality just as much as their quantity, and to their relationship to time as well as to energy. Pythagorean number was, as David Fideler puts it, "a living qualitative reality which must be approached in an experiential manner" (21). Whereas "we use numbers as tokens to represent things,"

> for Pythagoreans Number is a universal principle, as real as light (electromagnetism) or sound. As modern physics has demonstrated, it is precisely the numeric, vibrational frequency of electromagnetic energy—the "wavelength"—which determines its particular manifestation. Pythagoras, of course, has already determined this in the case of sound. (Fideler, 21)

Marie-Louise von Franz finds a "convincing argument" in an 1891 German source (V. Preyer) "that the conception of number may well have arisen out of a sense either of tone or of rhythm and frequencies" (Franz, 32). It is such a connection that can lead us into the Pythagorean world of music out of which *kairos* arose. Though numbers in this world were related to arithmetic and to geometry, it was music, with its *rithmos* of *arithmos* (rhythm of number), its movement through time, its tones, harmonies, felt energies and resonances, in which Pythagoras lived and from which he drew his ideas about every phenomenon in the cosmos, with words themselves considered full of musical qualities. Because the cosmos was a system, a patterned, coherent, music-like whole, its phenomena became capable of resonance, of being attuned to each other through lived worlds of analogies. Resonance is a responding, a being drawn to another, being, in the ancient vocabulary, entranced into harmony through *psychagogia* at all levels, human or nonhuman.

Moreover music from ancient times has been known to have a curative effect. It was thought then to enchant dissonant parts of the soul (and society) into harmony with each other. Nowadays we are coming back to similar ideas, hearing, for instance, about such effects on mind, body, and emotions as those Don Campbell calls (in his book of the same name) "The Mozart Effect." In our own field of rhetoric, Steven Katz has elaborated on the also ancient idea that "dissonance and disequilibrium, that harmony and resolution in reading and writing [could well be] musical in nature" (176). Here is a twentieth-century Pythagorean mind set, healing breaches, creating a microcosm as a "reconciliation of opposites" which "function coordinately or harmoniously in a stable system" (Heninger, 147).

My own path into the *kairos* principle as the essence of this kind of healing is to understand the connection between hearing the many analogs of music and bringing other senses into play. "It is possible to 'feel' the rhythm of the waltz," says Desmond Varley, "without mentally humming a particular tune and, by analogy, it is possible to visualize the order and pattern of number without attaching number to particular objects" (4). The sensation seems not different from the kinesthetic, even synesthetic, absorption we can feel in performing or listening to music we love. There is no need, says Varley, to mentally attach numbers to objects or concepts in order to sense the order or pattern involved. Moreover, when we experience such differences as those between 3:4 time and 4:4, we are already touching the grouping of threes and fours Pythagoras may have sensed in the seven of *kairos*.

Varley says that the oldest traditions of the ancient world were founded on patterns of creative forces embodied in septenary patterns, in which three forces of creation are "represented as a pair of opposites plus an interacting factor" (31). The opposing pair is usually thought to be full of primordial tension or conflict, having split in two opposing directions—positive and negative—from an original undifferentiated oneness. To release the tension, a third, relational force of resonance or reconciliation is needed between them (often pictured as the third line of a triangle and called love or desire). The three angles or three points then embed themselves into a cross or square of four forces, a trinity of energies entering the material world as four elemental substances, continually transforming themselves into as many combinations as there are phenomena in the created world. This is the creative, septenary process of *kairos*. Today we have workers such as Luce Irigaray in the vineyard of elemental psychology, exploring the fluidity of our lives and thoughts, their solidity, fieriness, or airy qualities. Water, earth, fire, and air: for Pythagoras long ago and Irigaray now (nodding implicitly toward her ancient sources), these elements are adjectival and even verb-like qualities as much as they are substantial nouns.

Aristotle throws special light on Pythagoras's *kairos* when he tells us that the Pythagoreans understood the number three as "beginning, middle, and end" (*On the Heavens,* 268a). If we think of seven as a three related to four, uniting threefold energy and fourfold elemental matter, Pythagoras's kairotic rhythmic/vibratory phenomena can be sensed (in stories or sentences, for instance) as a rising movement through beginnings that go on to an energetic peak in the middle, and finally to a feeling of completeness of a now-manifest creation at the end. But in order that there be an energetic peak to harmonize a possible beginning with a possible ending, the *aporia* between them has to be sensed—by the universe or by us—as need and opportunity for decisive, resonant action. Pythagoras's *kairos,* in at least this creative scenario, would be a sensed opening, then, in the middle of two opposing forces, a chance for the *psychagogia* that draws a reconciling force into action. Only if it can relate these two forces, bring together a discordant beginning force with its now concordant Other, can the three now-coherent forces land in an elemental creation, in other words, in an incarnation, which by nature is, in this ancient numerological system, a sevenfold whole or harmony of opposing elements. (When John Dewey describes the human time involved in a full and therefore esthetic experience [23], he is surely describing such a kairotic event.)

If we find that Pythagoras explains more satisfyingly than Gorgias the ancient idea of *kairos,* would *kairos* be then that middle "point" (as Alan Smithson calls it), a single moment that opens an opportunity for harmonizing and healing breaches? Or is it the field-like, full episodic time of beginnings, middles and ends (or past, present, and future) that Elliott Jaques contrasts with *chronos* (14–16), the wave phenomenon as opposed to the atomistic one it oscillates with in our varied experiences?

It is both. In a Pythagorean cosmos, a kairotic event is an instantaneous now that embeds the whole episode. Every circumstance has its own continually transforming moments that resonate with others, so kairotic openings are indeed points of present time tied to all other moments, past and present, which have unfolded qualitatively in the time of this situation, this set of circumstances. Kairotic happenings are single events containing multiple ones: cycles of old forest growth, rising and falling of civilizations, political campaigns, writing of essays: both the one and the many as holographic, Pythagorean, musical phenomena.

For human action they involve intent and sensitivity to situation. More than one scholar has looked at the transformational capacities of *kairos* in terms of its directionality or goal-directedness. Jaques Elliott sees these capacities as the "interpenetrating present, past, and future" of "living memory, living perception, and living desire and intent" (125). Eric Charles White understands *kairos* to establish "the living present as a point of departure or inspiration for a purely circumstantial activity of invention" (13), much like the Chinese concept of *wuwei* as unforced or spontaneous action (or, I would add, like the *I Ching* or *Book of Change*'s sixty-four ways to sense right timings amidst changing circumstances). When action rides the wave of a full esthetic experience, no forcing is necessary. At the university where I taught last year, a poster hanging on the wall above the copy machine had a wonderfully Pythagorean sentiment (joined, I concede, by a Buddhist one): "Zen cat rides a rainbow over the rough edges of the world." And there he was, jagged peaks below, looking fiercely pleased with his easy move across that vibrant pathway.

Pythagorean Pedagogy

For our writing classes, *kairos* can certainly be thought of as a rhetorical situation or the circumstances that open moments of opportunity. But if we are to use it fully and efficaciously, we will want to think of it as so much more, in the sense that it involves a whole-person sensitivity—physical, intellectual, emotional, even spiritual—to all the social and psychological nuances and resonances in one's environment, almost what we would call nowadays "reading the vibes." For us this sensitivity to kairotic moments is closer to unconsciousness than it may have been over two millennia ago in Croton, and certainly nearer the non-ordinary reality that the old shamans knew. But I believe that students can become sensitized to it if we work from several angles, and sensitized especially to how this very different kind of vibrational time can draw them into (even enchant them into, with different degrees) their reading of situations. My own object is that they feel the resonance that defines an esthetic experience, and write with what Robert M. Pirsig described as a greater "awareness of Quality" (247).

I first used contemporary variants of Pythagorean principles in a freshman writing class several years ago, knowing that this was an apt place to nurture thoughts about the energies of writing. Because the freshman composition program at my university is based on readings from natural and social sciences, fine arts, and humanities, I had an opportunity to create a late twentieth-century analogy of a Pythagorean cosmos, one meant to connect all known areas of knowledge. Teachers in this program choose their own selections from three of the four disciplinary divisions, and choose at the same time how they would like to address thematically the varied ways of thinking embedded in the readings. My thematic choice was to capture the spirit of *kairos* in a word used in the physical sciences—resonance—and then find plenty of apt cross-disciplinary readings for this theme, at least slightly imitating, I hoped, the Pythagorean spirit of cosmos as a harmony of everything.

I was not concerned about finding opportune moments to use the word *kairos* with my students, but felt implicitly its unfolding nature as the semester progressed. I was finding Pythagoras a stunning stimulus to my own understanding of how systems of thought can move across time, be echoed in later ideas, and open new windows on both old ways of thinking and new. Early on, my interest was in students' thinking process: how can a teacher stimulate a pattern-making frame of mind that will allow students to hold in mind, handle, see through and give graceful order to quantities of what might seem to them unrelated information? I was not yet addressing the feeling or sensing level that would later be necessary, I believed, to their understanding the core of *kairos* in the quality of rhetorical timing.

We started with chapter 12, "Sympathetic Vibrations," from K. C. Cole's book of the same name, a readable translation of scientific concepts for a lay audience. In describing a resonating universe in terms students can understand, she creates a fine analogy for the idea of *kairos* I had in mind. The reading is broader in its import than what we might think of as *kairos,* but then, that would be fitting for a Pythagorean sense of cosmic parallels. Here is a sample from this rich chapter:

> Resonance is the physics lesson all children learn the first time they try to pump themselves on playground swings. The trick, they soon learn, is timing. Pushing forward or leaning backward at the wrong place or time gets them nowhere. The thrust of the pump has to coincide with the natural rhythm of the swing. The key to resonance is pushing or pulling in time with the way the swing (or anything else) naturally wants to go. It is the synchrony of many small periodic pushes that work in unison to add up to a much larger one....
>
> Little did I know that resonance was behind the very nature of matter—not to mention the sound of music, the color of autumn leaves, the rings of Saturn, the spectral lines that write the signature of the stars, and according to one source perhaps even the evolution of life. It accounts for everything from the low whistle of the wind over the Grand Canyon to the sound of a lover's voice....
>
> When people talk about resonance, they are usually referring to the confluence of more than one action: two partners in a business feeding each other ideas and energy at just the right times and place to get big results....
>
> The power of resonance comes literally from being in the right place at the right time.... Adding energy without timing gets you nowhere. (263–267)

The next reading was "Waves and Splashes," chapter 13 of Cole's book, whose first sentence reveals my purpose: "A vibration is a wiggle in time; a wave, a wiggle in space" (277). We spent the first two weeks of the semester talking about as many variations of vibratory and wavelike phenomena as we could find, and I tried to put everything we discussed in terms of resonance, especially their experience of the subjects they were writing about. If students were writing about the quality of their own rooms at home, for instance, I urged them to find patterns and resonances between the rooms and their lives, their whole houses (a Western *feng shui* of sorts), their neighborhoods. Then we tried to find ways to make parts of their essays resonate with each other: I was looking for a logic embedded in a whole-person resonance rather than in intellect-only skills.

Wanting to strengthen pattern-thinking from many angles, I often made analogies, extending the meaning of resonance from sound and time into vision and space. In the midst of students bringing in tapes of their favorite music, I played on the tape recorder a few bars of a Chopin etude, an etude Douglas Hofstadter discusses and visually diagrams in one of our readings. I asked students to diagram a bar/section of their music as we talked about Hofstadter's point that "phenomena perceived to be magical are always the outcome of complex patterns of *non*magical activities taking place at a level below perception. More succinctly: The magic behind magic is pattern" (174). We discussed the op art in our packet that had a moire pattern, an illusion of wavelike motion created by patterns of geometric shapes; students could see the vibratory phenomena as they changed the position of the pages ever so slightly. Or they might notice them sometimes too in their everyday lives, in patterns made by overlapping of picket fences, for instance, or in some Japanese silk fabrics.

When we read a second article on resonance by Ralph Metzner, I asked students to sense the rhythm of the whole piece in relation to that of Cole's. The Metzner article is ostensibly written for laypersons, yet it is harder to read than Cole's. Why? The style is scholarly, academic. I worked with students on movement of their eyes and minds: could they sweep through and around both pieces, let their minds sense the whole in the parts and the parts in the whole in order to feel the differences? This sensing of differences in generic patterns was hard for them. We practiced a little; their reading habits were so rigidly unrhythmic at that time. My hope was that gradually they would become aware of pattern and structure as forces or energies in both reading and writing.

My hope, too, was that in this semester-long kairotic journey, students might be experiencing some phenomena in their daily lives more kinesthetically, and feeling some resonance between their intellectual engagement in reading and their perceptive lives as well. I found that when they could sense more clearly the rising and falling of the ideas that ran through their sentences, paragraphs, and even whole essays, their writing tended to resonate more with readers.

Participating in Phenomena

I am still, several years later, exploring ways to help students reach that point. I've paid careful attention to what W. K. C. Guthrie says about the early Pythagoreans. They had far different ways of experiencing the world than we, he claims (and here he uses a quote from Philip Sherrard's *The Marble Threshing Floor*):

> For these people, the natural world was not an object suitable for experiment, analysis, and exploitation. It was not an object at all. It was alive with certain mysterious and powerful forces, and man's life still possessed a richness and a dignity which came from his sense of participation in the movement of these forces. (Guthrie, 212)

The notion of "participation" in phenomena has a long and interesting history in both philosophy and anthropology, but basically it might be described, in Owen Barfield's words, as stemming "from a time before that exclusive disjunction between outer and inner" (119) that characterizes modern consciousness. Anthropologist Bradd Shore, in discussing Lucien Levy-Bruhl's "law of participation," notes that participation is a psychic activity whose "concepts are sensuous, colored by feeling and by bodily activity" (27). It would resemble what W. K. C. Guthrie describes as Pythagorean *mimesis* that "meant acting as much as imitation" (230), he says, like an actor's "getting inside" his role, "or rather," he says, the role "gets inside him and shows forth through his words and gestures" (230). Moreover, "we cannot understand Pythagorean thought if we allow ourselves to forget that it . . . was primarily religious . . . [with *mimesis* involving] assimilation to god as the end of human life" (231).

But Barfield claims that participation as that sensed link between self and world has not disappeared from mental experience today (34). It can enter people's lives at different times, but is found often in states of reverie or on the edge of dreaming. Students usually recognize such states of mind when described, and can often cultivate a similar state of relaxed "entrainment" with words they read (especially poetry) or people they talk to. "Fairness" in the arguments they make, I tell them, is closely tied to their sensing a resonance with, or participation in, others' values or ideas. So difficult, of course. But when they reduce tension, slow down from their busy daily pace, notice their breathing rhythms, they can sometimes better note how much more open they become to the rhythms of situational dynamics.

Though I may never be able to fully empathize with a cosmos in which proportions, angles, and directions were resonating everywhere and embedding kairotic moments, I—and I'm sure others—can easily understand descriptions of similar habits of mind. For my writing classes, I look especially at talk involving linguistic resonance. Philosopher and ecologist David Abram, for instance, claims (drawing on the work of Merleau-Ponty) that when we repress the "physically and sensorially resonant" (80) qualities of language, we close off our ability to perceive and experience the relationships in the "whole of the system" (83) that includes both our language and the world we live in.

Readers and Writers in Systems of Analogs

The more poetic kinds of thinking I can bring into my writing classes, I've found, the more apt students are to sense connections between the meanings of words on a page and their inner and outer worlds. Thus, I often call attention to metaphors in readings and urge that they be used in writing as much as possible, trusting the Pythagorean point that "like is known by like, that is, the better one knows something the more one is assimilated to it" (W. K. C. Guthrie, 206).

For years I tackled problems with conceptual connections and structural ones by concentrating on different traits of the writers themselves, thinking, for instance that if only students could establish, say, a strong voice in relation to the writing situation, the rest would fall in place. I do not disbelieve that now, but I have come to believe that the energies needed for writing (and its close relation, reading) must come first from a much stronger sense of one's own resonance with the many kairotic situational rhythms within which one writes or reads. Problems with these rhythms abound: the difficulties in changing tempos from reading to writing, the shrinking or contracting in the face of the Reading Other (or wilting "on stage," losing voice), the inability to move out of "content" thinking into structure, or out of product into process or vice versa. Direction of thought is not smoothly analogic, in other words, not able to turn or double back, to gather parts into a whole, to move beyond a chronological (speaking) line without faltering and digitalizing itself, flying off into fragments.

So in every writing class I teach nowadays, I stress the resonance issue from as many different angles, times, and sensory relations as I can find appropriate. Granting the importance of the cutting edge between things ("cut" following the Greek root of "critic," as in *krinein*), I stress the idea that critical thinking needs both the cuts and the connections, the contrasts and the comparisons.

I made a start with this dual focus in that freshman composition class I described earlier. Students brought in pieces of their favorite writing for the whole class to read; we looked at the structure of the sentences (noticing how

nearly always the writing they liked was narrative), imitated parts of its structure in our own writing (I did it too), and, finally, noticed the reasons (detail,
chronology) for the appeal of narrative as opposed to other ways of structur-
ing writing. We noticed three-part structures beyond stories: beginning,
middle, and end of a sentence, for instance, that might flow forward (transi-
tive verb) or forward and backward (linking verb) through the threeness of
subject, verb, and complement. I urged students to think of structure as force
or energy (rather than as a soporific, abstract overlay on content), and to notice how and where it moved. For noticing the energy dynamics embedded in
sentences, I found (and still do find) Ernest Fenollosa useful, who writes that
"transferences of force from agent to object which constitute natural phenomena, occupy time" (139), and that transferences are reproduced, in the
imagination when we use the English language. Further Pythagorean connections came from other readings. Two of my favorites came from architect
Christopher Alexander's *Timeless Way of Building* and his *Pattern Language*.
In *The Timeless Way,* he discusses the "quality without a name" (19–40) of
buildings and towns that make people who live in them or move through
them feel more alive. He thinks such places have a pattern language of some
sort that relates to their episodic rhythms.

But some of the most productive analogy-creating work in that same early
class occurred when education professor Wendy Atwell-Vasey worked with
my students twice during the semester, helping them explore how they might
create patterns of meaning by bridging the gap between mental and physical
lives. Deeply committed to what she has more recently written about as
"theatrical enactment" (77), she drew students and their thinking about current pieces of writing into a space-time theater world, asking them in pairs to
mirror each other's gestures, to notice how reading an other must always be
done with a difference in the sameness, how "getting in sync" is a doubling
with a difference. She drew them into making analogies between gestures,
each transforming the other's gestures into their own, asking for return imitation, noticing how the rhythms varied, and how comfort increased when
they could change the tempo of their partner's movement into their own version of it (a hint, I told them, about their discomfort in giving other sides of
arguments). On another day, she had students "score" the rhetorical situations they were writing about at that time, direct other students in a playing-
out of sides, change the directions when they could see some dissonance with
their original intentions, then reflect on the outcome. Writing is a similar
kind of learning, I told them, a matter of going outside oneself into a world
that feels different (unknown order or boundaries, lacking limits). When
they were able to find points of resonance, they could reshape their thinking.

That semester I had accidentally omitted from the packet the last pages of an article (which I did supply later); I turned the omission into a pedagogical opportunity, wanting students to sense the frustration of no resolution. "It's like leaving a movie before it's finished," they were quick to remind me. I reminded them in turn how sentence fragments can affect my sense of emotional well-being.

Not all those freshmen "got it," of course. Many did. Some were able to emerge from the semester better readers, better analyzers, and better synthesizers in their writing, though their sentence structure didn't improve much; others improved on both fronts. I had designed the course to work with students who had trouble noticing, giving attention to, and writing about what felt foreign to them, opposite in at least some ways to what felt comfortable to them, culturally, personally, syntactically, perhaps. I wanted them to contrast the states of dissonance and consonance, to work toward—of course—resonance with what felt "other" to them. I had simplistically supposed that the most proficient writers were probably the most flexible in their thinking. But one of my severest critics that semester was an A student whose evaluation form complained that I was trying to get her to write on a non-college level (her high school English teacher had had strong opinions about academic prose and had a very formative effect on her). Her major complaint? My telling her that some of her sentences heavy with multisyllabic words didn't flow well for me as a reader. My valuing flow over convention felt foreign to her. Though part of me wanted to call her back in to defensively explain my position, the other part told me not to forget that if I was, after all, a Pythagorean at heart, I should respect the fact that she was playing out her own kind of harmony with her high school teacher. There would be plenty of other opportunities for me to play out mine.

Works Cited

Abram, David. *The Spell of the Sensuous: Perception and Language in a More-Than-Human World.* New York: Pantheon Books, 1996.

Alexander, Christopher. *A Pattern Language.* New York: Oxford University Press, 1977.

———. *The Timeless Way of Building.* New York: Oxford University Press, 1979.

Aristotle. *On the Heavens.* Trans. W. K. C. Guthrie. Loeb Classical Library. Cambridge, MA: Harvard University Press, 1960.

———. *Metaphysics.* Trans. Hugh Tredennick. Loeb Classical Library. Cambridge, MA: Harvard University Press, 1977.

Atwell-Vasey, Wendy. *Nourishing Words: Bridging Private Reading and Public Teaching.* Albany: State University of New York Press, 1998.

Barfield, Owen. *Saving the Appearances: A Study in Idolatry.* New York: Harcourt, Brace and World, Inc., 1965.

Campbell, Don G. *The Mozart Effect.* New York: Avon, 1997.

Cole, K. C. *Sympathetic Vibrations: Reflections on Physics as a Way of Life*. New York: Bantam Books, 1985.

De Romilly, Jacqueline. *Magic and Rhetoric in Ancient Greece*. Cambridge, MA: Harvard University Press, 1975.

Dewey, John. *Art as Experience*. 1934. Reprint, New York: Capricorn-Putnam's, 1958.

Dodds, E. R. *The Greeks and the Irrational*. Berkeley: University of California Press, 1968.

Fenollosa, Ernest. "The Chinese Written Character as a Medium for Poetry." In *Prose Keys to Modern Poetry*. Ed. Karl Shapiro, 136 –155. New York: Harper, 1962.

Fideler, David R. "Introduction." *The Pythagorean Sourcebook and Library*. Comp. and trans. Kenneth Sylvan Guthrie. Grand Rapids, MI: Phanes, 1987.

Golden, Mark, and Peter Toohey, eds. *Inventing Ancient Culture: Historicism, Periodization, and the Ancient World*. London and New York: Routledge and Kegan Paul, 1997.

Guthrie, W. K. C. *A History of Greek Philosophy*. 6 Vols. Cambridge: Cambridge University Press, 1962.

Heninger, S. K., Jr. *Touches of Sweet Harmony: Pythagorean Cosmology and Renaissance Poetics*. San Marine, CA: Henry Huntington Library, 1974.

Hofstadter, Douglas R. "Pattern, Poetry, and Power in the Music of Frederic Chopin." In *Metamagical Themas: Questing for the Essence of Mind and Pattern*. 173 –189. New York: Bantam, 1985.

Howes, David, ed. *The Varieties of Sensory Experience: A Sourcebook in the Anthropology of the Senses*. Toronto: University of Toronto Press, 1991.

Irigaray, Luce. *Marine Lover of Friedrich Nietzsche*. Trans. Gillian C. Gill. New York: Columbia University Press, 1991.

Jaeger, Werner. *Paideia: The Ideals of Greek Culture*. Trans. Gilbert Highet. 2d ed. Vol. 1. New York: Oxford University Press, 1945.

Jaques, Elliott. *The Form of Time*. New York: Crane, Russak, 1982.

Katz, Steven B. *The Epistemic Music of Rhetoric: Toward the Temporal Dimension of Affect in Reader Response and Writing*. Carbondale: Southern Illinois University Press, 1996.

Kennedy, George A. *Comparative Rhetoric: An Historical and Cross-Cultural Introduction*. New York: Oxford University Press, 1998.

Kinneavy, James L. "*Kairos:* A Neglected Concept in Classical Rhetoric." In *Rhetoric and Praxis*. Ed. Jean Dietz Moss. Washington, DC: The Catholic University of America Press, 1986.

Metzner, Ralph. "Resonance as Metaphor and Metaphor as Resonance." *Revision* 10 (1987): 37 –44.

Peters, F. E. *Greek Philosophical Terms: A Historical Lexicon*. New York: New York University Press, 1967.

Pirsig, Robert M. *Zen and the Art of Motorcycle Maintenance: An Inquiry into Values*. New York: William Morrow, 1974.

Rostagni, Augusto. "Un nuovo capitolo nella storia della retorica e della sofistica." *Studi italiani de filologica classica*, n.s. 2 (1922): 148 –201.

Shore, Bradd. *Culture in Mind: Cognition, Culture, and the Problem of Meaning*. New York: Oxford University Press, 1996.

Smithson, Alan. *The Kairos Point: The Marriage of Mind and Matter*. Rockport, MA: Element, 1997.

Thomson, George. *The First Philosophers: Studies in Ancient Greek Society*. London: Lawrence and Wishart, 1955.

Untersteiner, Mario. *The Sophists.* Trans. Kathleen Freeman. New York: Philosophical Library, 1954.

Varela, Francisco J., Evan Thompson, and Eleanor Rosch. *The Embodied Mind: Cognitive Science and Human Experience.* Cambridge: MIT Press, 1991.

Varley, Desmond. *Seven: The Number of Creation.* London: G. Bell and Sons, 1976.

Von Franz, Marie-Louise. *Number and Time: Reflections Leading toward a Unification of Depth Psychology and Physics.* Evanston, IL: Northwestern University Press, 1974.

White, Eric Charles. *Kaironomia: On the Will-to-Invent.* Ithaca and London: Cornell University Press, 1987.

On Doing the Right Thing at the Right Time

Toward an Ethics of Kairos

AMÉLIE FROST BENEDIKT

In two thought-provoking essays, "Time, Times, and the 'Right Time'" (1969) and "Time and Qualitative Time" (1986), John E. Smith describes *kairos* in ontological terms. I will try to show how his ontological reading of kairic time can be brought together with elements from Gorgias' view, to create an account of *kairos* capable of informing a system of ethics. I will argue that *kairos* is not just about subjective time, as distinct from objective, clock-measured time. *Kairos* has important objective qualities, in addition to the "psychological" dimensions that Gorgias stressed.

Let us begin, as Smith and others do, by contrasting *kairos* to *chronos*. Let us agree that *chronos* is the kind of time measurable by clocks and dependent upon "asymmetrical serial order," "cardinality," and universal standards for its measurement. From this it follows that *chronos* is "objective" and "ontological" (Smith, "Qualitative Time," 4). *Kairos,* by contrast, is "qualitative and experiential" time operating according to the principle of "ordinality" and naming a relative moment in a series of events. More specifically, *kairos* refers to the moment within an event that is judged to have "a critical ordinal position set apart from its predecessors and successors" (Smith, "Qualitative Time," 11). Kairic time is made up of discontinuous and unprecedented occasions, instead of identical moments within "a causally related sequence of events" (White, 14). Kairic time, therefore, marks opportunities that might not recur, moments of decision. Whereas *chronos*-time is absolute, universal, and objective, *kairos* is interpretive, situational and, thus, "subjective."

This objective-subjective distinction is standard in the literature devoted to our subject, but using it uncritically can cause us to miss the ontological and objective dimensions of *kairos*. On this point I am in agreement with

Smith: we should not focus so exclusively on the interpretive, rhetorical, and "anthropological" nature of *kairos*, for *kairos* depends on temporal frames that are independent of human action. In short, *kairos* has an ontological, "physical and metaphysical" dimension of its own (Smith, "Qualitative Time," 5). Although *kairos* seems to refer only to individual action and subjective judgment, such judgment "does not *create* the 'when' out of itself" (Smith, "Qualitative Time," 13; emphasis added). Opportunities really do come and go, whether anyone sees them or not, seizes them or not.

Through the following essay, then, I will argue that concern for *kairos* begins with an effort to recognize opportunity, making one sensitive to the critical character of moments that require decision. The decision concerning the right moment signifies understanding concerning *this* moment as distinct from others, concerning *this* moment as the culmination of a series of events. A concern for *kairos* signals an interest in being "on time" chronologically speaking, which leads to being "on time" ethically speaking. What this means is that the right action at the wrong time is not kairic. Neither is the wrong action at the right time kairic. An action that is morally right at the present moment may not be so in the next. This way of thinking about time results in greater attention to the idea of favorable and unfavorable opportunities that must be seized before they are lost—or avoided before they occur, as the case may be. Judgments of "too late" or "too soon" or "now" or "never" are qualitative decisions about the ordinality of historical events in the temporal order, decisions about moments that seem discontinuous, or "set apart," from the succession of moments before and after.

This view of *kairos* draws on the "realist" philosophical belief that human history is "not only an order of interpretation" but, also, "an order of actual happenings" (Smith, "Qualitative Time,"10).[1] In order to understand how the "order of interpretation" can be grounded in the "order of actual happenings," consider an example. The pearl industry depends on knowing when to harvest and when to allow pearls to continue to grow in size. Leaving pearls in their oysters too long exposes them to the dangers of extreme weather conditions, which can destroy whole oyster crops. A pearl farmer must decide how long to age pearls, much as a vintner must decide how long to age wine; each must act in the "ripeness of time" (Smith, "Qualitative Time," 9). Although the decision to harvest a crop ultimately rests on subjective judgment, it also depends on a body of skills and knowledge that are independent of interpretation. The decision is made based on information about weather conditions, seasonality and growth rates, nutrition levels, maturation rates, and other characteristics of the specific crop. Given all of these "objective" data, a judgment must then be made about their ultimate significance to realizing a specific goal. Further, a determination must be made concerning which moment in time is right for achieving a result whose desirability is also established, in part, by variables outside the realm of subjective interpretation.

Assessing the positive or negative significance of events belongs to the "order of interpretation." Nonetheless, the events themselves belong to the "order of actual happenings." Consider the way people speak about important events such as a death or a birth. A person approaching death may say, "My time has come." A pregnant woman who feels the onset of labor might say, "It is time," but her meaning is kairic as well as chronological. A platoon leader scans the horizon and yells, "Time to go!" At such moments, time changes from *chronos*-centric to *kairos*-centric. Although people say that things happen at the right or wrong time, what they mean, in fact, is that things happen at a right or wrong *kairos*. As Smith points out, calling events auspicious or inauspicious makes use of a *kairos*-centric view of time, and such discursive practice is as vital for historians as it is for anyone making quotidian, after the fact assessments of opportunities that were recognized and seized, as well as of those opportunities that were not (Smith, "Right Time," 13).

Gorgias, too, considered this kind of assessment, and thought of it as a fundamentally creative act. As Mario Untersteiner describes it, Gorgianic rhetoric stressed the pure subjectivity, spontaneity, and creativity of *kairos* that invites one to "seize the time." For Gorgias, *kairos* names moments of "willful imposition of choice on conflicting opportunities." Drawing upon the Pythagorean doctrine of opposites, Gorgias was committed to the view that the world's underlying ordering principle, or *logos,* is unapproachable rationally. Given the concurrence of "special circumstances" (Untersteiner, 141), interpretations perpetually split into opposing viewpoints; indeed, all circumstances are potentially "special" in this way. This commitment resulted in Gorgias's denial of rational explanations of experience—the philosophical doctrine known as "irrationalism"—since every decision is an imposition of one of the opposing viewpoints or alternatives upon an otherwise irreducible antithesis. All interpretive judgment, therefore, is fundamentally irrational, a matter of seizing the *kairos* (Untersteiner, 137, 262).[2]

In the face of the gap between what is and what can be known, Gorgias responded with kairic spontaneity, indeed with courage.[3] Only the gods, Gorgias believed, could have an absolute measure of time. In contrast, human time is kairic: worthless from the point of view of the divine *logos,* but capable of informing human action nonetheless. Untersteiner calls Gorgias' view "tragic," because—despite all efforts to capture the ordering principle— human beings only see the conflicts and opposite poles within propositions. By contrast, White characterizes Gorgias' view of *kairos* as anything but tragic, calling it "inventive, even playful" (Miller, 314). Whether tragic or playful, Gorgias seems committed to taking action in the face of uncertainty by calling on *kairos* to create something new and irrational, in place of the inescapable and endless clash of antitheses (Untersteiner, 159). Instead of merely "repeating the ready made categories of tradition" (White, 18), Gorgias insisted that we remain "open to the irrational novelty of the moment" (White, 14). Through kairic spontaneity and radical openness to chance, one regains creative control over the world.

The control that we win back through spontaneity is not, however, a principle or rule-based control. For Gorgias, *kairos* never becomes a principle or a doctrine for organizing human history. As White explains, Gorgias recognized the inherent impossibility of treating *kairos* as a formal principle, since "any science of 'kaironomy' would find itself incoherently promising foreknowledge of chance" (White, 20). Gorgias' view of history and *kairos* is "social-constructivist," then, insofar as he held that the historical record is due entirely to kairic interpretation of events which are arbitrarily privileged and maintained by an "order of interpretation." Tradition and human record are unreliable, and they prevent spontaneous invention and sensitivity to the newness of the moment. Instead of the certainty of tradition and appeal to history, Gorgias cultivated spontaneity and radical openness to chance.

It is time to consider the ethical dimension of these ideas. Not all of the ancient Greek Sophists preferred the spontaneity of the moment over the guidance provided by tradition, memories, and historical record. As W. K. C. Guthrie notes, Protagoras differed from Gorgias by subordinating "the appearance of the moment" to "a higher standard, the end or purpose of human nature and society" (White, 21). In other words, Protagoras would join us in asking Gorgias to ground the "order of interpretation" in the "order of actual happenings." Plato and Aristotle, too, expressed concern that a world view founded on *kairos* might give too much attention to the qualities of invention, novelty, and openness to chance. In the *Laws*, Plato distinguishes *kairos* from chance and argued that, by developing the kairic skill for recognizing one opportunity as more significant than another, people become less subject to chance alone.[4] Judging the right *kairos* depends on reflecting on the objective qualities of a situation that lie outside of one's character and preferences. To judge whether an action has the kairic qualities of timeliness, appropriateness, fitness, or opportuneness, one must "take stock" of the situation as well as of one's response—take stock, that is, of the entire situational context (Kinneavy and Eskin, 132).[5]

When judging the *right* moment for an action, a sense of *kairos* gives us creative control over the world by introducing a sense of possibility, of opportunity. But there are limits to how much is subject to interpretive change. Although I can change my action to fit a situation, the only part of the situation itself that I can change unilaterally is that part of the moment that consists of myself; and the most significant change I can make to the moment often occurs, simply, by increasing or decreasing how much of the situation I am aware of. This is what it means to ground the "order of interpretation" in the "order of actual happenings." And this is also part of what it means for *chronos* to be altered by sensitivity to the kairic context (as I explain later, our kairic actions can also affect the *kairos* of others).

Another way of speaking about this is to say that a sense of *kairos* depends on a sufficient degree of *self-knowledge* to be able to assess the situational context in the first place. And this requirement of self-knowledge introduces another question: If self-knowledge is essential for a sense of timeliness, should we call "timeliness" a *skill* or a *virtue*? Both have ethical implications ("virtue" by definition, and "skill" because being skilled is considered "better" than being unskilled). But how can a sense of *kairos* ever really become a *virtue*? If timeliness is, say, knowing how to calculate the right time to deliver a speech so as to achieve a desired effect, then a sense of *kairos* describes a skill which may develop into a virtue—assuming that it is asked to meet the further ethical requirement that the effects of one's good timing produce morally good results. For *kairos* begins to achieve morally good results only as a result of reflection upon the "goodness" or "badness" of one's "timing."

"But surely," one might object at this point, "people may only be praised or blamed for good or bad timing if timeliness is a quality of actions over which they have some *control*. And do they have such control?" In answer, let me make some basic observations regarding ethical agency and responsibility. It is always tempting to blame or credit "luck" instead of one's skill (or lack thereof) in seizing opportunity. But sometimes "bad timing" really is due to "bad luck." Can we avoid assigning credit (or blame) to people for good (or bad) timing that occurs due to events outside of their control? And can we do so without giving up our commitment to a sense of kairic time? Indeed we can, by re-conceiving *kairos* as a unity of factors that are both ontological and psychological.

One cannot claim responsibility for instances of good and bad timing when something "lucky" or "unlucky" happens that was not under one's control. Bad timing is not always a sign of our failure to reflect adequately on a course of action. It may be the result of coincidence, random chance, or even unavoidable ignorance: features of the situation of which we could not possibly have known. As Aristotelian-inspired virtue ethicists point out, one's moral goodness sometimes rests on "moral luck"—which is to say that it rests on events entirely outside of one's control, events for which one is in no way responsible, but which determine whether or not one preserves moral goodness. Credit for timeliness due to "moral luck" strikes us as undeserved.

If timeliness—that is, "good timing"—were a moral issue only, then blame might be assessed in cases where intuition tells us it should not. For there simply are circumstances lying outside of our control; and this is where the objective, ontological nature of *kairos* enters. Overemphasizing the idea of "moral luck" ignores our need to cultivate a sense of *kairos*, whereas underemphasizing such luck ignores the chronological aspect of the situational context.

Any adequate account of *kairos* must also explain how, and how long, to deliberate when immediate circumstances are changing. This requires understanding as much of the situational context as one can without becoming constrained by too great a respect for the norms of the present. Situational contexts necessarily change. Located in the present time, a sense of *kairos* leads one to look beyond the factuality of the present to counterfactual worlds that are not, or not yet, as well as to look beyond tradition and the historical record, when these are unduly limiting. For conventions, as Gorgias taught us, can be otherwise than they now are. This is one way to understand why it is sometimes more appropriate to ignore the "apparently appropriate." Consider another master of inappropriate and troublesome discourse, Socrates, whose "mantic sign" opposed him when he "was about to do something wrong . . . often [holding him] back in the middle of speaking" (*Republic* 40a-b; see also *Euthydemus* 272e, *Apology* 31d, and *Phaedrus* 242b). A keen sense of "when-ness" thus helped him avoid doing the "right thing" at the "wrong time," and vice versa. For example, Socrates decided that the occasion of his trial was an appropriate one for philosophizing, even though it seemed the "wrong time" to his opponents as well as to many of his friends and students. He seized the moment. And when Crito tried to persuade Socrates to flee Athens before his impending execution, Socrates reminded him that leaving the city was once, but is no longer, the right thing to do. The moment had passed, kairically speaking, so that the self-exile that would have been appropriate before, or even during, the trial became no longer so after his sentence was delivered. Leaving the city by stealth after rejecting the offer to flee it freely would have been a case of "bad timing."

Evaluations of timing also require evaluating the kairic sense of the readiness of others who form part of the situational context. As Gorgias explained, one cannot evaluate the kairic fit of an action to a particular moment without considering the response of others. Taking others into consideration can lead to the conclusion that one is taking action at a "bad time." The other person might be preoccupied or unreceptive. But saying that one has come "at a bad time" often allows a means of conciliation. Thus, the other might respond by saying, "You could not have known (that this would be a bad time for me)," indicating that one's kairic miscalculation is due not to culpable but, rather, to unavoidable ignorance. If, on the other hand, the other person too eagerly agrees that the present moment is a "good time" when it is not, it may happen that only one party has given sufficient thought to the matter at hand—creating a situation that will require too high a degree of spontaneity from the unprepared party, preventing one from developing a fully considered, reflective response. By asking, "Have I come at a bad time?" the speaker allows the addressee the same opportunity to engage in kairic assessment of the opportunities now presented. It allows the addressee a chance to balance reflection with action—which is the essence of wisdom. If the addressee answers that the speaker has come at a good time, one signifies that one has taken the time to reflect on the unfolding situation. Those who are sensitive to the right moment will not hesitate to inquire as to preparedness when necessary, without using it as a strategy for evading evaluations concerning time, place, agency, or act. For timing is everything.[6]

Recall that Socrates, master of appropriate inappropriateness, was not shy in expressing his unpreparedness for the judgment at hand. By remaining unwilling to offer conclusive views even on the subjects that most interested him, Socrates was in effect saying, to those who pushed him for his views, "Because I have not spent enough time in thought on this topic, this is a bad time for me (to talk about virtue or justice or temperance)." This unwillingness to rush to judgment in order to stay in step with the timing of others is something Socrates credits to his "mantic sign," which restrains him by saying, in effect, "It is a bad time for you to decide on this matter, Socrates, because you are not ready."

The right thing done at the right time must also be done by the "right person." This means that one must judge whether one is the right person to seize an opportunity. In this light, consider the famous dictum of Rabbi Hillel: "If not now, when? If not me, who?" Hillel might initially be taken to be teaching a kairic lesson: "now" is always the right time and the "I" who asks the question is always the right person for the job at hand. But this reading of Hillel does not acknowledge the *kairos*-driven insight that the right time is *not* always "now," and the right person to undertake an action is *not* always the person asking, "who?" "Me, now" may not be the right answer in every case, even though it may seem preferable to inaction or indecision. Whether or not Hillel's dictum shows an understanding of *kairos* depends on the situational context in which the dictum itself is called to mind. As with all advice, one has to know how, whether, and when to seize it. Read this way, Hillel's dictum presumes a level of kairic wisdom.

And one's mental health, much like one's moral soundness, often rests upon another's timely interventions. Thus, *kairos* has recently gained the attention of psychoanalysts, for much the same reason that Hippocrates gave it attention. Just as a physician must judge the right moment for treatment, so too a psychoanalyst; both are in search of the "auspicious moment" for a cure. Indeed, defining *kairos* as "psychological moment," *The Oxford Classical Dictionary* reflects the close tie between *kairos* and psychological judgment. As psychoanalyst Harold Kelman explains it, *kairos* is a moment of crisis brought on by burdensome cares. Thus, the term, as Kelman uses it, describes a major life change, a breakthrough or turning point in analysis—a single important moment.[7] Considered a prerequisite for psychological breakthrough and healing, such a crisis can be brought about either by reflecting on an insoluble personal dilemma, by dream work, or by an encounter with another person (such as the psychoanalyst, who consciously tries to bring about a confrontation). The analyst helps bring about an analysand's sense of crisis by acting at the auspicious moment for intervention in a specific context. A kairic moment in the psychoanalytic tradition, then, depends on some measure of control over the timing of a psychological crisis that forces one to make a choice about whether or not to hold to a belief, a memory, or an idea that has led to trauma.

Thus, the infelicities resulting from insensitivity to *kairos* go beyond scheduling incompatibilities and missed opportunities to far weightier consequences; for the vintner, the pearl farmer, the teacher, the philosopher, the diplomat, and the psychoanalyst, failure to grasp how the objective qualities of a moment shape interpretive judgment can lead to ethically bad results. An account of *kairos* that does draw on ontological and psychological themes can help us discover what it means to "do the right thing at the right time." Perhaps, too, a rich account of *kairos* can move us beyond the suggestions made here, leading us toward an even larger ideal for ethical action: the right person doing the right thing at the right time *and for the right reasons*.

Notes

1. Another way of putting this difference is captured by Scott Consigny, who discusses the role of both the "creative rhetor" and the "concrete situation" (or opportunity) "as discerned" and "as defined." A more historical way of describing the difference is to contrast the Socratic "Know thyself" with the pre-Socratic "Know the opportunity." Doro Levi originally pointed out this contrast, to which James L. Kinneavy (81) later refers.

2. Given Gorgias' irrationalism, we oversimplify when we speak about his view of the subjectivity of experience and judgment, since he does not believe in the possibility of either experience or of judgment. It is an oversimplification that I will not be able to correct in this brief essay, but one that does deserve attention.

3. As Eric Charles White notes, *kairos* records "Gorgias' attempt to make the best of the unresolvable dilemma that ensues from the lack of coincidence between Being and knowledge, the inability of knowledge to give definitive expression to the essence of

Being. A decision made on the spur of the moment, on the basis, that is, of *kairos*, would resolve the epistemological dilemma by pure force of will, trusting to the force of the moment to produce an utterance that truly answers to its occasion" (White, 16).

4. In the *Laws*, Plato writes, "the all controlling agent in human affairs is God, assisted by the secondary influences of 'chance' and 'opportunity.' A less uncompromising way of putting it is to acknowledge that there must be a third factor, namely, 'skill,' to back up the other two. For instance, in a storm the steersman may or may not use his skill to seize any favorable opportunity that may offer. . . . [A professional] could hardly go wrong if he prayed for conditions in which the workings of chance needed only to be supplemented by his own skill" (*Laws*, 709b). As the example shows, the steersman does not seize just any moment, but only the most favorable one. Instead of depending on his spontaneity and creativity, the steersman must have something against which to judge and evaluate the appropriateness of one moment against the next. Where the risk is high, as in a storm, a good steersman uses skill to supplement chance.

5. Cynthia Sheard also writes about sensitivity to "situational context," though she is aware of the abbreviations and amendments she makes to *kairos*. This is clear when she writes, "the complexities of the ancient notion of *kairos* have been diminished by those who see it simply as a summary term for 'situation' or 'context'" (292). Sheard would want to say, with Smith, that treating situational context as the *sole* meaning of *kairos* loses sight of its ontological and metaphysical qualities, which are not subject to interpretation.

6. To take an example from theology, Paul Tillich has described the perfect sense of *kairos* possessed by the Holy Spirit, who always comes "at the right time" and in the "fullness of time." In Scripture, *kairos* is the "fulfilled time" for the appearance of Christ, marking the rebirth of the faithful into a state of grace. Christ's future appearance will mark the great or central *kairos*, which will be preceded by many smaller *kairoi*, each prophetic of the final *kairos* event (Kinneavy, 89). In large part due to the influence of Tillich, *Kairos* is the name given to a contemporary Christian Liberation Movement working for political and racial justice in South Africa, Namibia, and several Central American countries. The *Kairos* Group believes that the present time is the opportune moment for great spiritual and political changes. Thus, *kairos* comes to mark the moment of social, religious, and political transition. It signifies the right time for liberatory political action aimed at creating greater racial equality and social justice.

7. As early as 1956, A. Kielholz appropriated the term for psychoanalysis, specifically in describing his case work with a schizophrenic. Kielholz explains that his advice was not different from that of other specialists consulted by the patient previously, but that it was received by the patient at the right time: as he wrote, "the *kairos* came to my aid" (Kelman, 294). Drawing on Kielholz, Kelman's use of *kairos* compares to a passage from Kenneth Burke, in which he describes the moment before one makes a decision. Burke calls that moment "the state of intolerable indecision just preceding conversion . . . [which is] uncomfortably like suspended animation" (294).

Works Cited

Consigny, Scott. "Rhetoric and its Situations." *Philosophy and Rhetoric* 7 (1974): 175–186.
De Romilly, Jacqueline. *The Great Sophists in Periclean Athens*. Trans. Janet Lloyd. Oxford: Clarendon, 1982.

Guthrie, W. K. C. *The Sophists.* Cambridge: Cambridge University Press, 1969.

Kelman, Harold. "*Kairos:* The Auspicious Moment." *The American Journal of Psycho-analysis* 29 (1969): 59–93.

Kinneavy, James L. "*Kairos:* A Neglected Concept in Classical Rhetoric." In *Rhetoric and Praxis: The Contributions of Classical Rhetoric to Practical Reasoning.* Ed. Jean Dietz Moss, 79–105. Washington, DC: The Catholic University of America Press, 1986.

Kinneavy, James L., and Catherine R. Eskin. "*Kairos* in Aristotle's Rhetoric." *Written Communication* 11 (1994): 131–142.

Miller, Carolyn R. "*Kairos* in the Rhetoric of Science." In *A Rhetoric of Doing: Essays in Written Discourse in Honor of James L. Kinneavy.* Ed. Stephen P. Witte, Neil Nakadate, and Roger D. Cherry, 310–327. Carbondale: Southern Illinois University Press, 1992.

Murphy, James, ed. *A Synoptic History of Classical Rhetoric.* New York: Random, 1972.

Plato. *Laws.* Trans. T. J. Saunders. New York: Penguin, 1970.

Sheard, Cynthia Miecznikowski. "*Kairos* and Kenneth Burke's Psychology of Political and Social Communication." *College English* 55 (1993): 291–309.

Smith, John E. "Time and Qualitative Time." *Review of Metaphysics* 1986 (40): 3–16.

———. "Time, Times and the 'Right Time.'" *The Monist* 53 (1969): 1–13.

Untersteiner, Mario. *The Sophists.* Trans. Kathleen Freeman. New York: Philosophical Library, 1954.

White, Eric Charles. *Kaironomia: On the Will-to-Invent.* Ithaca, NY: Cornell University Press, 1987.

A Bibliography on Kairos and Related Concepts

TANYA ZHELEZCHEVA AND JAMES S. BAUMLIN

While not exhaustive, the following bibliography gathers together major twentieth-century publications, in various languages, on *kairos* and related subjects A perusal of titles reveals the concept's relevance to contemporary discussions in theology, ethics, classical philology, psychology, the visual arts, and literary criticism, as well as in philosophy, composition theory, and the history of rhetoric.

Ardenne, Paul. "L'Oeuvre du peintre Tonnerre dans la revocation se l'edit de Nantes de Pierre Klossowski: Le motif pictural du kairos comme matrice de l'ecriture." La Licorne 35 (1995): 77–86.

Armstrong, Betty Anne. "Kairos: An Out-Patient Progress Report." *School Guidance Worker* 39 (1983): 41–47.

Asselin, Mark Laurent. "'A Significant Season': Literature in Time of Endings." Ph.D. diss. (cmi5.271) University of Washington, 1997. *DAI* 58 (1997): 2215A-16.

Bannerth, Ernst. *Islamische Wallfahrtsstatten Kairos*. Schriften des Osterreichischen Kulturinstituts Kairo. Wiesbaden: Harrassowitz, 1973.

Barr, James. *Biblical Words for Time*. London: S. C. M. Press, 1969.

Barrera, Pablo. "The Indigenous Kairos and the Pagan Faith in Saint Matthew." *International Review of Mission* 82 (1993): 39–49.

Baumlin, James S. "Decorum, *Kairos,* and the 'New' Rhetoric." *PRE/TEXT* 5 (1987): 171–83.

Bazerman, Charles. "Whose Moment? The Kairotics of Intersubjectivity." *Constructing Experience*. 171–93. Carbondale: Southern Illinois University Press, 1994.

Berciano, Modesto. *Kairos: Tiempo humano e histórico-salvífico en Clemente de Alejandria*. Burgos: Ediciones Aldecoa, 1976.

Bijlsma, Roelof. *Chronos en kairos: het tijdsprobleem in het Nieuwe Testament*. Assen: Van Gorcum, 1952.

Bini, Daniela. "'Kairos' and 'Chronos' in Svevo's *Confessions* of Zeno." *Canadian Journal of Italian Studies* 3 (1980): 102–107.

Bitzer, Lloyd F. "The Rhetorical Situation." *Philosophy and Rhetoric* 1 (1968): 1–14.

———. "Functional Communication: A Situational Perspective." In *Rhetoric in Transi-*

tion: Studies in the Nature and Uses of Rhetoric. Ed. Eugene E. White, 21–38. University Park, PA: Pennsylvania State University Press, 1980.

Blauhut, Robert. "Heimito von Doderer, der Dichter des Kairos: Analyse seiner Novellen." *Wort in der Zeit* 10 (1964): 69–77.

Boeckl, Matthias. *Kairos: Die Sammlung Otto Mauer im Wiener Dommuseum: Erzbischöfliches Dom und Diözesanmuseum, Wien, Museum Moderner Kunst- Stiftung Wörlen, Passau.* Wien: VBK Wien, 1993.

Booth, Gotthard. "The Auspicious Moment in Somatic Medicine." *The American Journal of Psychoanalysis* 29 (1969): 84–88.

Booth, Wayne. "Metaphor as Rhetoric: The Problem of Evaluation." In *On Metaphor.* Ed. Sheldon Sacks, 47–70. Chicago: University of Chicago Press, 1978.

Brown, Robert McAfee, ed. *Kairos: Three Prophetic Challenges to the Church.* Grand Rapids, MI: Eerdmans, 1990.

Bruce, Gregory C. "Capturing Kairos: The Challenge of Visual Culture." *Religious Studies News* 11 (1996): 11–26.

Buland, Mable. *The Presentation of Time in The Elizabethan Drama.* New York: Haskell, 1966.

Bye, Lilian. "Kairos." *Samtiden* 86 (1977): 73–81.

Cadorette, Curt. "The Deconstruction of Peru: Social Chaos as Ecclesial Kairos." *Missiology* 22 (1994): 177–186.

Calvert, N. G. "The *Mono-Kairos* Windmills of Lasithi." *The Annual of the British School at Athens* 70 (1975): 51–57.

Campbell, Joseph. *Man and Time: Papers from the Eranos Yearbooks.* Vol 3. New York: Pantheon, 1957.

Carey, John, ed. *Kairos and Logos: Studies in the Roots and Implications of Tillich's Theology.* Cambridge, MA: North American Paul Tillich Society, 1978.

———. *Theonomy and Autonomy: Studies in Paul Tillich's Engagement with Modern Culture.* Macon, GA: Mercer University Press, 1984.

Carinci, Filipo. "Eros e Anteros: Alcune osservazioni a proposito di un rilievo della Galleria Colonna." *Rivista dell'Istituto nazionale d'archeologia e storia dell'arte* 3 (1985–86): 63–109.

Carter, Michael. "*Stasis* and *Kairos:* Principles of Social Construction in Classical Rhetoric." *Rhetoric Review* 7 (1988): 97–112.

Chesnut, Glenn F. "Kairos and Cosmic Sympathy in the Church Historian Socrates Scholasticus." *Church History* 44 (1975): 161–166.

Chew, Samuel. "Time and Fortune." *ELH* 6 (1939): 83–113.

Cook, Arthur Bernard. "Appendix A: Kairos." *Zeus: A Study in Ancient Religion.* Vol. 1, pt. 2: 859–68. Cambridge: Cambridge University Press, 1925.

Cope, Jackson I. "The Rhetoric of Kairos in Dryden's *Absalom and Architophel.*" In *Rhetorics of Order/Ordering Rhetorics in English Neoclassical Literature.* Eds. Douglas J. Canfield and J. Paul Hunter, 89–97. Newark, DE: University of Delaware Press, 1989.

Cullman, Oscar. *Christ and Time: The Primitive Conception of Time and History.* Trans. Floyd V. Filson. Philadelphia: Westminster, 1950.

Danièlou, Jean. "Le *kairos* de la messe d'après les Homélies sur l'incompréhensible de St. Jean Chrysostome." *Die Messe in der Glaubensverkündigung: Kerygmatische Fragen.* Ed. Franz Xaver Arnold and Balthasar Fischer, 71–78. Freiburg: Herder, 1953.

Delling, G. "Kairos." *Theological Dictionary of the New Testament.* Ed. Gerhard Kittel. Trans. Geoffrey W. Bramley. Vol. 3: 833–39. Grand Rapids, MI: Eerdman, 1986.

Delucchi, A. D. "La teoria del kairos nella poetica pre-Platonica." *Revista de Filosofia* 23 (1973): 27-33.

Dickson, Keith M. "Kairos and the Anatomy of Praxis in Pindar." Ph.D. diss. State University of New York at Buffalo, 1981. *DAI* 43 (1986): 1532.

Doheny-Farina, Stephen. "The Individual, the Organization, and Kairos: Making Transitions from College to Careers." In *A Rhetoric of Doing: Essays on Written Discourse in Honor of James L. Kinneavy*. Ed. Stephen P. Witte, Neil Nakadate, and Roger D. Cherry, 293-309. Carbondale: Southern Illinois University Press, 1992.

Doro, Levi. "Il *kairos* attraverso la letteratura greca." *Reconditi della Reale Accademia Nazionale dei Lincei classe di scienzia morali,* RV 32 (1923): 260-81.

Eckardt, A. Roy. "An American Looks at 'Kairos.'" *Theology Today* 43 (1986): 217-228.

Ehrenwald, Jan. "'Hippocrates' 'Kairos' and the Existential Shift." *The American Journal of Psychoanalysis* 29 (1969): 89-93.

Eichrodt, Joan Beecher. "Anarchy and Culture: Dmitri Merezhkovsky and the Kairos." Ph.D. diss. Columbia University, 1975. *DAI* 38 (1975): 4313.

Enos, Richard Leo. *The Literate Mode of Cicero's Legal Rhetoric.* Carbondale: Southern Illinois University Press, 1988.

———. *Roman Rhetoric: Revolution and the Greek Influence.* Prospect Heights, IL: Waveland, 1995.

Erikson, Keith. *Plato: True and Sophistic Rhetoric.* Amsterdam: Rodopi, 1979.

Fascia, Livia. "I quattro tempi di *Antony and Cleopatra.*" *Annali Istituto Universitario Orientali: Anglistica* 33 (1990): 31-62.

Filochowski, J. "A Kairos Moment." *The Month* 30 (1997): 254-254.

Fraser, J. T. *The Voices of Time: A Comparative Survey of Man's Views of Time as Expressed by the Sciences and by the Humanities* 2d ed. Amherst: University of Massachusetts Press, 1981.

Fuhrman, Rainer. *Kairos: Roman.* München: W. Heyne, 1996.

Funkenstein, Amos. "Gershom Scholem: Christina, Kairos, and the Messianic Dialectic." *History and Memory: Studies in Representations of the Past* 4 (1992): 123-40.

Furlani, Andre. "'In Place': Kairos in *Samson Agonistes.*" *Seventeenth Century* 10 (1995): 219-35.

Gagé, Jean. "La balance de Kairos et l'épée de Brennus a propos de la rançon de 'l'aurum gallicum' et de sa pesée." *Revue archéologique* 43 (1954): 141-76.

Gale, Richard M. *The Philosophy of Time: A Collection of Essays.* Totowa, NJ: Humanities, 1978.

Gallet, Bernard. *Recherches sur kairos et l'ambiguïté dans la poésie de Pindare.* Bordeaux Talence: Presses Universitaires de Bordeaux, 1990.

Gates, Rosemary L. "Understanding Writing as an Art: Classical Rhetoric and the Corporate Context." *Technical Writing Teacher* 17 (1990): 50-60.

Gily Reda, Clementia. *Temporalità e Comunicazione: Chronos, Kairós, Ritmo.* Napoli: Parresía, 1996.

Glover, Carl Wesley. "Kairos and Composition: Modern Perspectives on an Ancient Idea." Ph.D. diss. University of Louisville, 1990. *DAI* 52 (1990): 895A.

Glowka, Arthur Wayne. "Rhyme and Rhythm in Layamon's Brut: A Study in Prosodic Decorum." Ph.D. diss. University of Delaware, 1980. *DAI* 41 (1990): 1064A.

Goldwert, Marvin. "Kairos and Eriksonian Psychology." *Perceptual and Motor Skills* 72 (1991): 553-554.

Guillamaud, P. "L'essence du kairos." *Revue des études anciennes* 90 (1988): 359-371.

Hainline, R. "*Kairos:* A Jungian View of Time." *The American Journal of Psychoanalysis* 40 (1980): 325–33.

Halton, Thomas. "The *Kairos* of the Mass and the Deacon on John Chrystosom." In *Diakonia: Studies in Honor of Robert Meyer.* Eds. Halton Thomas and Joseph P. William, 53–59. Washington, DC.: The Catholic University of America Press, 1986.

Haynes, Stephen. "*Krisis* and *Kairos:* An International Case Study Perspective on Teaching Issues of Church and State." Ed. Menanchem Mor. *International Perspectives on Church and State,* 201–208. Omaha, NE: Creighton University Press, 1993.

Hecht, F. "Der 'Kairos' des Ritus in der Beurteilung der vorexilischen Propheten des Alten Testaments." *Man: Anthropological Essays Presented to O. B. Raum.* Ed. E. J. De Jager, 104–120. Cape Town: C. Struik, 1971.

Heisel, Dorelle. *The Kairos Dimension.* New York, Gordon and Breach, 1973.

Higdon, David Leon. *Time and English Fiction.* Totowa, NJ: Rowman and Littlefield, 1977.

Hunsberger, George R "The Hidden Element of Kairos." *International Review of Missions* 86 (1997): 57–59.

Hunt, Maurice. "Kairos and the Ripeness of Time in *As You Like It.*" *Modern Language Quarterly* 52 (1991): 113–35.

Jauss, Hans Robert. *Toward an Aesthetic of Reception.* Trans. Timothy Bahti. Minneapolis: University of Minnesota Press, 1982.

Jeffrey, Paul. "Cuba, Crisis, Kairos." *Christianity and Crisis* 52 (1992): 333–36.

Jenkins, Carl. *The Kairos Effect: A Biological Approach to Social Problems.* Springfield, OH: Medical Place, 1997.

Kairos: Three Prophetic Challenges to the Church. Grand Rapids, MI: Eerdmans, 1990.

Kairos Theologians. *Challenge to the Church: A Theological Comment on the Political Crisis in South Africa: The Kairos Document.* New York: Theology in Global Context, 1987.

Keiser, Elizabeth B. "The Festive Decorum of Cleanness." *Studies in Medieval Culture* 14 (1980): 63–75.

Kellerman, Bill Wylie. *Seasons of Faith and Conscience: Kairos, Confession, Liturgy.* Maryknoll, NY: Orbis, 1991.

Kelman, Harold. "'Kairos' and the Therapeutic Process." *Journal of Existential Psychiatry* 1 (1960): 233–69.

———. "'Kairos': The Auspicious Moment." *The American Journal of Psychoanalysis* 29 (1969): 59–83.

Kennedy, George. *The Art of Persuasion in Greece.* Princeton: Princeton University Press, 1963.

Kerkhoff, Manfred. *Kairos: Exploraciones ocasionales en torno a tiempo y destiempo.* San Juan: Editorial de la Universidad de Puerto Rico, 1997.

———. "Zum antiken Begriff des Kairos." *Zeitschrift für philosophische Forschung* 27 (1973): 256–74.

Kermode, Frank. *The Sense of an Ending: Studies in the Theory of Fiction.* New York: Oxford University Press, 1976.

Kiefer, Frederick. *Fortune and Elizabethan Tragedy.* Huntington, CA: Huntington Library, 1983.

Kinneavy, James L. *Greek Rhetorical Origins of Christian Faith: An Inquiry.* New York: Oxford University Press, 1987.

———. "*Kairos:* A Neglected Concept in Classical Rhetoric." *Rhetoric and Praxis: The Contribution of Classical Rhetoric to Practical Reasoning.* Ed. Jean Dietz Moss, 79–105. Washington, DC: The Catholic University of America Press, 1986.

———. "The Relationship of the Whole to the Part in the Composing Process." *Linguistics, Stylistics, and the Teaching of Composition.* Ed. Donald McQuade, 292–312. Carbondale: Southern Illinois University Press, 1986.

Kinneavy, James L. and Catherine R. Eskin. "*Kairos* in Aristotle's Rhetoric." *Written Communication* 11 (1994): 131–42.

Kitteridge, G. L. "To Take Time by the Forelock." *Modern Language Notes* 8 (1893): 459–69.

Koether, Jutta. *Kairos: Texte zu Kunst und Musik.* Berlin: Edition ID-Archiv, 1996.

Kolin, Philip G. "'Night, Mistuh Charlie': The Porter in Tennessee Williams's 'The Last of My Solid Gold Watches' and the *Kairos* of Negritude." *The Mississippi Quarterly* 47 (1994): 215–20.

Kort, Wesley A. *Modern Fiction and Human Time.* Gainesville, FL: University of South Florida Press, 1985.

Kubler, George. *The Shape of Time.* New Haven: Yale University Press, 1962.

Kucharski, Paul. "Sur la notion pythagoricienne du kairos." *Revue philosophique* 153 (1963): 141–169.

Le Poidevin, Robin and Murray MacBeath, ed. *The Philosophy of Time.* Oxford: Oxford University Press, 1993.

Leroy, Robert and Pastor, Eckart. "Zu Gottfried Benns 'Welle der Nacht.'" *Colloquia Germanica* 11 (1978): 53–63.

Levi, Doro. "Il kairos attraverso la letterature greca." *Rendiconti della Reale Academia Nazionale dei Lincei classe di scienzia morali* RV 32 (1923): 260–281.

———. "La psicologia dei personaggi Sofoclei e l'opportunita." *Atene e Roma* 4 (1923): 18–46.

———. "Il concetto di kairos e la filosofia di Platone." *Rendiconti della Reale Academia Nazionale dei Lincei classe di scienzia morali* RV 33 (1924): 93–118.

Lieshout, R. G. A. Van. "A Dream on a 'Kairos' of History. An Analysis of Herodotos 'Hist.' VII 12–19; 47." *Mnemosyne* 4 (1970): 225–49. 4th s. 23.

Ley, Klaus. "Kunst und Kairos: Zur Konstitution der wirkungsasthetischen Kategorie von Gegenwartigkeit in der literatur." *Poetica: Zeitschrift für Sprach und Literaturwissenschaft* 17 (1985): 46–82.

Madrigal, Jose A. "Cronos y kairos: Un ensanyo sobre la media y los comienzos." *Selected Proceedings of the Mid-America Conference on Hispanic Literature.* Ed. del Valle Luis T. Gonzalez and Catherine Nickel, 53–61. Lincoln, NE: Society of Spanish and Spanish-American Studies, 1986.

Mason, Gregory. "*Kairos:* A Neglected Concept in Time Criticism." *The Journal of Intercultural Studies* 25 (1998): 202–17.

Massey, Lance. "On the Origin of Citizenship in Education: Isocrates, Rhetoric, and *Kairos.*" *SMSU Journal of Public Affairs* 1 (1997): 57–66.

May, Hilda R. "El tiempo como kairos en la poetica de Gonzalo Rojas." *Chasqui* 22 (1993): 37–41.

McComiskey, Bruce. "Disassembling Plato's critique of Rhetoric in the *Gorgias* (447a-466a)." *Rhetoric review* 11 (1992): 79–90.

Menk, Peter D. *Kairos and Courage: Using an Ethical Method to Resolve the Army Rift.* Carlisle Barracks, PA: U.S. Army War College, 1998.

Meyerhoff, Hans. *Time and Literature.* Berkeley: University of California Press, 1955.

Miller, Bernard Allan. "Heidegger and the Gorgian Kairos." Ph.D. diss. Purdue University, 1987. *DAI* 49 (1987): 1152.

Miller, Carolyn R. "*Kairos* in the Rhetoric of Science." In *A Rhetoric of Doing: Essays on*

Written Discourse in Honor of James L. Kinneavy. Ed. Stephen P. Witte, Neil Naka-date and Roger D. Cherry, 310 – 27. Carbondale: Southern Illinois University Press, 1992.

Montesano, Mark. "Kairos and Kerygma: The Rhetoric of Christian Proclamation." *Rhetoric Society Quarterly* 25 (1995): 164 – 78.

Moser von Filseck, Karin. *Kairos und Eros: Zwei Wege zu einem Neuverständnis griechischer Bildwerke.* Bonn: R. Habelt, 1990.

Mouroux, J. *The Mystery of Time.* Trans. John Drury. New York: Desclee, 1964.

Moutsopoulos, Evanghélos. *Chronos et kairos: entretiens d'Athenes: Institut international de philosophie, 1986.* Publications de la Societe hellenique d'etudes philosophiques. Paris: Librairie philosophique J. Vrin, 1988.

———. *Kairos: la mise et l'enjeu.* Paris: Librairie philosophique J. Vrin, 1991.

———. "Kairos and Kairic Activity in the Works of Plotinus." *Etudios Classicos* 26 (1984): 443 – 47.

———. "Éros 'kairos.'" *Revue philosophique de la France et de l'étranger* 179 (1989): 15 – 19.

———. "La fonction du kairos selon Aristote." *Revue philosophique de la France et de l'étranger* 175 (1985): 223 – 26.

Müller, Harro. *Geschichte zwischen Kairos und Katastrophe: Historische Romane im 20. Jahrhundert.* Frankfurt am Main: Athenäum, 1988.

Mussner, Franz. *Der nicht erkannte Kairos: (Mt 11,16–19=Lk 7,31–35).* Roma: Pontificio Istituto Biblico, 1959.

———. "Der nicht erkannte Kairos (Mt 11, 16 – 19 = Lk 7, 31 – 35)." *Biblica* 40 (1959): 599 – 612.

Neki, J. S. "Ausar ('Kairos') and Its Place in Creative Psychotherapy." *The Psychoanalytic Review* 68 (1981): 425 – 449.

Oestereicher, Emil. *Thinking, Feeling, and Doing: Critical Essays.* Hartsdale, NY: Hermes, 1992.

O'Keefe, Frances St. Anne, Sister. "Caliban's Dream: 'Kainos' and 'Kairos' in *The Tempest.*" *American Benedictine Review* 19 (1968): 370 – 85.

Onians, Richard Broxton. "Kairos." *The Origins of European Thought: About the Body, the Mind, the Soul, the World, Time, and Fate.* 2nd ed. 343 – 49. Cambridge: Cambridge University Press, 1954.

Ordnung, Carl. *Nachfolge Christi in Parteinahme für die Armen: "Der Weg nach Damaskus," ein "Kairos," Dokument aus der Dritten Welt.* Berlin: Sekretariat des Hauptvorstandes der Christlich-Demokratischen Union Deutschlands, 1989.

Otten, Robert Theodore. "Metron, Mesos, and Kairos: A Semasiological Study." Ph.D. diss. University of Michigan, 1957. *DAI* 18 (1957): 1419.

Panofsky, Erwin. *Studies in Iconology: Humanistic Themes in the Art of the Renaissance.* Boulder, CO: Westview, 1972.

Parke, David B. *Kairos the Right Time: The Best of Kairos.* Boston: Skinner House, 1982.

Pecheux, Mother M. Christopher. "Milton and 'Kairos.'" *Milton Studies* 12 (1979): 197 – 211.

Périgord, M. "Vladimir Jankélévitch ou improvisation et 'kairos'." *Revue de métaphysique et de morale* 79 (1974): 223 – 52.

Petersen, Robin M. "Time, Resistance and Reconstruction: Rethinking Kairos Theology." Ph.D. diss. University of Chicago Divinity School, 1995. *DAI* 56 (1995): 1851.

Peterson, Douglas L. *Time, Tide, and Tempest: A Study of Shakespeare's Romances.* San Marino, CA: Huntington Library, 1973.

Pfister, Friedrich. "Kairos und Symmetrie." *Wurzburger Studien zur Alterumswissenschaft* 13 (1938): 131–150.

Philippson, P. "Il concetto greco di tempo nelle parole Aion, Chronos, Kairos, Eniautos." *Rivista di storia della filosofia* 4 (1949): 81–97.

Piltz, Elisabeth, ed. *Kairos: Studies in Art History and Literature in Honour of Professor Gunilla Akerstrom-Hougen.* Studies in Mediterranean Archaeology and Literature. Jonesered, Sweden: P. Aströms, 1998.

Pohlenz, Max. "*To Prepon:* Ein Beitrag zur Geschichte des griechischen Geistes," *Nachrichten von der Gesellschaft der Wissenschafien zu Goettingen, Philologisch-historische Klasse, Heft* 1 (1933): 53–92. Reprint *Kleine Schrifen.* Ed. Heinrich Dorrie, 2:100–39. Hildesheim: G. Olms, 1965.

Pouillon, Jean. "Time and Destiny in Faulkner." *Faulkner: A Collection of Critical Essays.* Ed. Robert Penn Warren, 79–86. Englewood Cliffs, NJ: Prentice, 1966.

Poulakos, John. "Rhetoric, Sophists, and the Possible." *Communication Monographs* 51 (1984): 215–26.

———. *Sophistical Rhetoric in Classical Greece.* Columbia, SC: University of South Carolina Press, 1995.

———. "Terms for Sophistical Rhetoric." *Rethinking the History of Rhetoric.* Ed. Takis Poulakos, 53–74. Boulder, CO: Westview, 1993.

———. "Toward a Sophistic Definition of Rhetoric." *Philosophy and Rhetoric* 16 (1983): 35–48.

Priestley, John Boynton. *Man and Time.* London: Aldus, 1964.

Quinones, Ricardo J. *The Renaissance Discovery of Time.* Cambridge, MA: Harvard University Press, 1972.

Race, William H. "The Word *Kairos* in Greek Drama." *Transactions of American Philological Association* 111 (1981): 197–213.

Raleigh, John Henry. *Time, Place, and Idea: Essays on the Novel.* Carbondale: Southern Illinois University Press, 1968.

Raymond, Bernard. "Paul Tillich et le socialisme national (nazisme) allemand." *Studies in Religion/Sciences Religieuses* 13 (1984): 353–361.

Redford, Bruce B. "'I Believe Again': Auden's 'Kairos and Logos' in the Context of Christianity Regained." *Thought: A Review of Culture and Idea* 55 (1980): 393–411.

Reimer, A. James. "Theological Method and Political Ethics: The Paul Tillich–Emanuel Hirsch Debate." *Journal of the American Academy of Religion* 47 (1979): 171–192.

Reither, James A. "Some Ideas of Michael Polanyi and Some Implications for Teaching Writing." *Pre/Text* 2 (1981): 33–43.

Rieff, Philip. "The Meaning of History and Religion in Freud's Thought." *The Journal of Religion* 31 (1951): 114–131.

Rostagni, Augusto. "Un nuovo capitolo nella storia della retorica e della sofistica." *Studi italiani di filologica classica,* n.s. 2 (1922): 148–201.

Salonia, Giovanni. *Kairòs: direzione spirituale e animazione comunitaria.* Bologna: EDB, 1994.

Sartre, John-Paul. "On *The Sound and the Fury:* Time in the Work of William Faulkner." *Faulkner: A Collection of Critical Essays.* Ed. Robert Penn Warren, 87–93. Englewood Cliffs, NJ: Prentice, 1966.

Schwarz-Graz, Gerda. "Der lysippische Kairos." *Grazer Beiträge* 4 (1975) 243–266.

Sheard, Cynthia Miecznikowski. "*Kairos* and Kenneth Burke's Psychology of Political and Social Communication." *College English* 55 (1993): 291–310.

Short, Bryan C. "The Temporality of Rhetoric." *Rhetoric Review* 7 (1989): 367–79.

Sikes, Walter W. "Crisis and Kairos." *Encounter* 33 (1972): 46–55.

Sipiora, Phillip. "*Kairos* in the Discourse of Isocrates." In *Realms of Rhetoric: Phonic, Graphic, Electronic.* Ed. Victor J. Vitanza and Michelle Ballif, 119–35. Arlington, TX: Rhetoric Society of America, 1991.

Slater, George Richard. "Regression of Cancer as an Instance of Gotthard Booth's Concept of Kairos." Ph.D. diss. Boston University, 1982. *DAI* 43 (1982): 1183.

Smith, John E. "Time and Qualitative Time." *The Review of Metaphysics* 40 (1986): 3–16.

———. "Time, Times and the 'Right Time': *Chronos* and *Kairos*." *The Monist* 53 (1969): 1–13.

Smithson, Thomas Alan. *The Kairos Point: The Marriage of Mind and Matter.* Rockport, MA: Element, 1997.

Stewart, A. F. "Lypsippan Studies, I: The Only Creator of Beauty." *American Journal of Archeology* 82 (1978): 163–171.

Sullivan, Dale L. "*Kairos* and the Rhetoric of Belief." *The Quarterly Journal of Speech* 78 (1992): 317–32.

Sypher, Wiley. *The Ethic of Time: Structures of Experience in Shakespeare.* New York: Seabury, 1976.

Tayler, Edward. *Milton's Poetry: Its Development in Time.* Pittsburgh: DuQuesne University Press, 1979.

The Kairos Document: Challenge to the Church. Foreward by John W. de Gruchy. Grand Rapids, MI: Eerdmans, 1986.

The Road to Damascus: Kairos and Conversion. 2d ed. London: Catholic Institute for International Relations, 1990.

Tillich, Paul. "Kairos." *Die Tat* 15 (1922): 330–350.

———. ed. *Buch des Kairos-Kreises.* Darmstadt: O. Reichl, 1926–1929.

———. *Ein Brief zu Eduard Heimanns siebzigstem Geburtstag: Kairos, Theomomie, das Dämonische.* Tübingen: J. C. B. Mohr, 1959.

———. *Kairos* (I). *Zur Geisteslage und Geisteswendung.* Darmstadt: Reichl, 1926.

———. *Kairos* (II). *Protestantismus als Kritik und Gestaltung.* Darmstadt: Reichl, 1929.

———. "Die Theologie des Kairos und die gegenwärtige geistige Lage: Offener Brief an Emanuel Hirsch." *Theologische Blätter* 11 (1934): 306–28.

———. *Kairos.* Jena: E. Diederichs, 1922.

———. "Kairos." *The Protestant Era.* Trans. James Luther Adams. Chicago: University of Chicago Press, 1948. 32–51.

———. "Kairos and Kairoi." *Systematic Theology Vol. 3: Life and the Spirit; History and the Kingdom of God*, 369–72. Chicago: University of Chicago Press, 1963.

———. *Kairos und Utopie.* Gütersloh: Gütersloher Verlagshaus Gerd Mohn, 1959.

———. *Protestantismus als Kritik und Gestaltung.* Ed. Adolph Allwohn. Darmstadt: Otto Reichl, 1929.

———. *Lo spirito borghese e il kairos.* Roma: Doxa, 1929.

———. *Writings in the Philosophy of Religion.* Ed. John Clayton. New York: Walter de Gruyten, 1987.

Tobin, Patricia Drechsel. *Time and the Novel: The Genealogical Imperative.* Princeton: Princeton University Press, 1978.

Toit, Braian M. Du. "Theology, Kairos, and the Church in South Africa." *Missiology* 16 (1988): 57–71.

Tortora, Giuseppe. "Il senso del kairos in Gorgia." Siculorum Gymnasium 38 (1985): 537–64.

Trédé, Monique. Kairos: L'à-propos et l'occasion: Le mot et la notion, d'Homère à la fin du IVe siècle avant J.-C. Paris: Editions Klincsieck, 1992.

———. "Kairos: L'à-propos et l'occasion, le mot et la notion." Information littérair 41 (1989): 4–7.

———. "'Kairós': 'problème d'étymologie'." Revue des études grecques 97 (1984): xi–xviii.

Turner, Frederick. *Shakespeare and the Nature of Time: Moral and Philosophical Themes in Some Plays and Poems of William Shakespeare.* Oxford: Clarendon, 1971.

Untersteiner, Mario. "Kairos come fonte del fatto 'poetico'." In *La Formazione Poetica di Pindaro*, 65–102. Messina, Firenze: Casa Editrice G. D'Anna, 1951.

———. "La Poesia come Armonia al di Sopra di ogni dissidio e come unità di *kairoi*." In *La Formazione Poetica di Pindaro*, 35–45. Messina, Firenze: Casa Editrice G. D'Anna, 1951.

———. *The Sophists.* Trans. Kathleen Freeman. New York: Philosophical Library, 1954.

Vallozza, Maddalena. "Kairos nella retorica di Alcidamante e di Isocrate." *Quaderni urbinati di cultura classica* 50 (1985): 119–23.

Vardman, Jerry, ed. *Chronos, Kairos, Christos II: Chronological, Nativity, and Religious Studies in Memory of Ray Summers.* Macon, GA: Mercer University Press, 1998.

Vardman, Jerry, and Edwin M. Yamauchi, ed. *Chronos, Kairos, Christos: Nativity and Chronological Studies Presented to Jack Finegan.* Winona Lake, IN: Eisenbrauns, 1989.

Waller, G. F. *The Strong Necessity of Time: The Philosophy of Time in Shakespeare and Elizabethan Literature.* The Hague: Mouton, 1976.

Warren, Robert Penn. "Faulkner: The South, the Negro, and Time." In *Faulkner: A Collection of Critical Essays.* Ed. Robert Penn Warren, 1–22. Englewood Cliffs, NJ: Prentice, 1966.

Warren, William Henry, III. "Kairos and Liberation a Critical Comparison of the Theologies of History of Paul Tillich and Selected Latin American Liberation Theologians." Ph.D. diss. Emory University, 1989. *DAI* 50 (1990): 2120.

White, Eric Charles. *Kaironomia: On the Will-to-Invent.* Ithaca: Cornell University Press, 1987.

Williams, Delores S. "Kairos Time: Challenge of the Centrisms." *Christianity and Crisis* 52 (1992): 16–18.

Wilson, J. B. "Kairos as 'Due Measure.'" Glotta 58 (1980): 177–204.

Wilson, John R. "Kairos As 'Profit.'" Classical Quarterly 31 (1981): 418–420.

Wittkower, Rudolf. "Chance, Time, and Virtue." Journal of the Warburg Institute 1 (1937): 313–21.

Wittkowski, Wolfgang. "Propitious Moments with Greek Ladies: Goethe's Orester and Iphigenia, Faust and Helen." *Phenomenological Inquiry: A Review of Philological Ideas and Trends* 17 (1993): 62–73.

Woudenberg, Adriaan Stephan Laurens. *Kairos en het eeuwige nu: een onderzoek naar de verhouding tussen het presentische en het futurische in Tillichs theologie van de geschiedenis.* Bolsward: Het Witte Boekhuis, 1993.

Zwicky, Laurie. "*Kairos* in 'Paradise Regained': The Divine Plan." ELH 31 (1964): 271–277.

Contributors

James S. Baumlin is Professor of English at Southwest Missouri State University, where he teaches English Renaissance literature and the history of rhetoric. His publications include *John Donne and the Rhetorics of Renaissance Discourse* (Columbia, MO: University of Missouri Press, 1991) and *Ethos: New Essays in Rhetorical and Critical Theory*, coedited with Tita French Baumlin (Dallas: Southern Methodist University Press, 1994).

Tita French Baumlin is Professor of English at Southwest Missouri State University. A specialist in Shakespeare and early modern drama, she is editor of the scholarly journal, *Explorations in Renaissance Culture*, and coeditor (with James S. Baumlin) of *Ethos: New Essays in Rhetorical and Critical Theory* (Dallas: Southern Methodist University Press, 1994).

Amélie Frost Benedikt is Adjunct Professor of Philosophy at St. Edward's University New College in Austin, Texas. Her research centers on the role of wisdom for contemporary students and teachers of philosophy. As an APPA certified Philosopher Practitioner, she puts ideas about *kairos* and *sophia* to the test.

Richard Leo Enos is Radford Professor of Rhetoric at Texas Christian University. His many publications in the history of rhetoric include *The Literate Mode of Cicero's Legal Rhetoric* (Carbondale: Southern Illinois University Press, 1988), *Oral and Written Communication: Historical Approaches* (Newbury Park, CA: Sage, 1990), and *Roman Rhetoric: Revolution and the Greek Influence* (Prospect Heights, IL: Waveland, 1995).

Catherine R. Eskin is Assistant Professor of English at Florida Southern College in Lakeland, Florida, having previously taught at Drexel University in Philadelphia, the University of Trondheim, Norway, and the University of Texas at Austin. Her research interests include sixteenth-century English prose, women's rhetoric, Renaissance English rhetorical and educational treatises, and the history of early modern printing.

Carolyn Eriksen Hill is Associate Professor of English and Cultural Studies at Towson University in Baltimore and has been Visiting Associate Professor at the University of Washington in Seattle. Her publications include *Writing from the Margins: Power and Pedagogy for Teachers of Composition* (New York: Oxford University Press, 1990). Her latest work is tentatively titled *Bicycles in Beijing: Chinese Pathways toward Global Learning*.

Joseph J. Hughes is Professor of Classics at Southwest Missouri State University. He is the author of numerous articles and book chapters treating the relationships between comedy and rhetoric in Republican Rome. He has also published scholarly articles on ancient epic, Kurt Vonnegut, and the Internet.

James L. Kinneavy was Blumberg Professor Emeritus of English at the University of Texas at Austin. His numerous distinguished publications in rhetorical theory include *A Theory of Discourse* (Englewood Cliffs, NJ: Prentice-Hall, 1971), *Writing in the Liberal Arts Tradition* (New York: Harper, 1985), and *Greek Rhetorical Origins of Christian Faith: An Inquiry* (New York: Oxford University Press, 1988). Professor Kinneavy passed away August 10, 1999.

Gregory Mason is Professor of English and Director of Peace Studies at Gustavus Adolphus College in Saint Peter, Minnesota. He has published widely in the fields of world literature, film history and aesthetics, and peace studies. He is editor of *Arrows of Longing: The Correspondence Between Anais Nin and Felix Pollak, 1952–1976* (Athens, OH: University of Ohio Press, 1998), and is particularly interested in interdisciplinary approaches to the arts.

John Poulakos is Professor of Communication at the University of Pittsburgh. His publications in the history of rhetoric include *Sophistical Rhetoric in Classical Greece* (Columbia, SC: University of South Carolina Press, 1995), and *Classical Rhetorical Theory* (Boston: Houghton Mifflin, 1999).

Phillip Sipiora is Professor and Associate Chair of English at the University of South Florida, where he teaches American literature, film, and the history of rhetoric. His recent work in rhetoric includes *Ethical Issues in the Teaching of Writing*, coedited with Fredric G. Gale and James L. Kinneavy (New York: Peter Lang, 1999).

John E. Smith is Clark Professor Emeritus of Philosophy at Yale University. A past president of the American Philosophical Association, his numerous publications include *Purpose and Thought: The Meaning of Pragmatism* (Chicago: University of Chicago Press, 1984), *Quasi-Religions: Humanism, Marxism, Nationalism* (Hampshire, UK: Macmillan, 1994), and *Experience and God* (New York: Fordham University Press, 1995).

Roger Thompson is Assistant Professor of English at Virginia Military Institute, where he teaches American literature and composition/rhetoric. A graduate of Texas Christian University, his dissertation explores *kairos* in nineteenth-century American literary and rhetorical theory.

Tanya Zhelezcheva is completing an M. A. in English at Southwest Missouri State University. Her research interests include Shakespeare, the history of rhetoric, and modern critical theory.

Index

Names of gods capitalized but not italicized, e.g., *kairos* and Kairos, *chronos* and Chronos.

The root word is used to reference all forms of a Greek word used in text. For example, *topos* is indexed, though the page number may reference *topoi*; *kairos* is indexed, though the page number may reference *kairon*.

Neoclassicizing, 146–47
Humanist rhetoric, *see* rhetoric: Humanist
humor, 134
  through impersonation, 135–36
  see also comedy
hupogrammateus, 77–78, 85

I Ching, 217
Iamblichus
  Life of Pythagoras, 34–35, 37–38, 41, 65
IBYCUS, 98, 109–10
ichigo ichie, 207, 209
Iliad, see Homer: *Iliad*
immediate time
  concept of, in Greek rhetoric, 79–80
  constraints of, 78–79
immortality, 203
improvisation, 168
Irigaray, Luce, 215–16
Irving, Washington
  Sketch Book, 190
Isocrates, 1, 7, 19 *n. 14,* 28, 33, 62, 82, 117
  Against the Sophists, 9–11, 117
  Antidosis, 7, 8–11, 13, 117
  Archidamus, 12
  Helen, 10
  Nicocles, 12
  On the Peace, 13–14
  paideia in, *see paideia:* rhetorical
  Panathenaicus, 11, 14
  Panegyricus, 28
  To Nicocles, 11–12
Italy, Croton, 214

Jaeger, Werner, 5, 7, 212
  Early Christianity and Greek Paideia, 114
James, William, 53, 57
Janus-Figure, 141, 150
Japanese art, 205
  film, *Ikiru,* 207–8
  haiku, 16, 207
  tea drinking ceremony, 206–7
Jaques, Elliott, 216
Javitch, Daniel, 139, 143–44
Johnson, Nan, 192
Joyce, James
  "Araby," 203–4
Judaism, 55
Judeo-Christian
  conception of *kairos,* 188
  rhetoric, 68

judgment, *see* crisis
justice, 56, 61
  see also dikaion

Kahn, Victoria, 141, 160 *n. 1*
kairos, 42, 79, 87, 89, 140, 145, 180, 203
  as advantage, 120
  as aesthetic, 16, 64–65, 201–2
  American, 188–96
  anthropological, 227
  civil education and, 37–38, 65
  creating a kairic moment, 91–92
  and *decorum,* 128–37
  defined, 2–7, 58, 61–71, 115, 116, 188–89,
    199, 212
  doctors' bedside manner and, 104–8
  due measure, 2, 10, 89–90
  in eloquence, 29–31, 43
  and emotions, 69–71
  energies, 213, 215–16, 222
  epistemological dimensions of, 62–64
  ethical dimensions of, 61–62, 71
  experience and, 99
  extraordinary circumstances, 91–92
  history of the word, 58–60
  the mean as kairic, 105–6
  ontological structure of, 47–48, 226–27,
    231, 234 *n. 5*
  opinion and, 33–34
  propriety of time, 53
  proper measure, 60–62
  and reason, 71–72
  as reflection, 205
  rhetorical dimensions of, 46, 64
  style of, 72–73
  teachability, 89–90
  transcendental, 190, 194, 196 *n. 3*
  transformational capacities, 216–17
  trope of, 189–90
  see also akairos; chronos; eukairos; decorum;
    prepon; opportunity; rhetoric; time
Kairos, the Greek god, xii *fig. 1,* 65
Kairos, representing a force of time, 79–80
kairos-time, 140, 149
  compared to *chronos*-time, 46–50, 226
  see also chronos-time
Kairos Document, The, 125–26 *n. 4*
Kairos Group, The, 234 *n. 6*
kairotic moment, *see* opportune moment
kakakairos, 2, 4, 116
kalachakra, 205–6